The Clinton Riddle

The Clinton Riddle

Perspectives on the Forty-second President

Edited by
TODD G. SHIELDS
JEANNIE M. WHAYNE
DONALD R. KELLEY

Foreword by
David H. Pryor

The University of Arkansas Press
Fayetteville
2004

Designed by Ellen Beeler

⊗ The paper used in this publication meets the minimum requirements
of the American National Standard for Permanence of Paper for Printed
Library Materials Z39.48-1984.

Library of Congress Cataloging-in-Publication Data

The Clinton riddle : perspectives on the forty-second president / edited
by Todd G. Shields, Jeannie M. Whayne, Donald R. Kelley.
      p. cm.
Includes bibliographical references and index.
ISBN 1-55728-780-5 (pbk. : alk. paper)
      1. United States—Politics and government—1993–2001. 2. United
States—Foreign relations—1993–2001. 3. Clinton, Bill, 1946– Political
and social views. 4. Clinton, Bill, 1946– 5. Presidents—United States—
Biography. I. Shields, Todd G., 1968– II. Whayne, Jeannie M. III. Kelley,
Donald R., 1943–
E885.C554 2004
973.929'092—dc22
                                                                    2004012844

*This project is supported in part by The Blair Center of Southern Politics and
Society and the Fulbright Institute of International Relations.*

To Diane,

in memory of
the minds and lives she has touched . . .

Contents

Foreword

DAVID H. PRYOR

Three years since leaving the White House, when most former presidents begin the habitual "public fading" process, William Jefferson Clinton continues to provoke an intensity of interest accorded to only a very short list of world leaders. Some might say his persistent magnetism borders on the phenomenal. Normally the rush and weight of world events tends to overshadow individuals and their contributions as their actual holding of public office fades from view.

Our constitution obliged Bill Clinton to exit the front and center portion of the public stage, but the sheer power of his personality and unique leadership skills have reached almost mystical proportions in the public mind-set. Who is this man? What makes him tick? And why is he still everywhere?

America is now only beginning the search for the defining legacy of Bill Clinton and his extraordinary eight-year occupancy of the White House. To search his early boyhood might provide some clues as to his intense aspirations to seek and achieve acceptability. A voracious appetite to learn and dispense knowledge serves to further enhance his unique-ness and explain the public thirst and curiosity associated with our forty-second president.

To be sure, Bill Clinton brought excitement to the White House. He and first lady Hillary Rodham Clinton gave Washington and the country an electrical charge not seen or experienced since the Kennedys.

It was only fitting that in June of 2002, on the very terrain he knew so well, the University of Arkansas campus, the initial public dissection of his presidency took place. Here, in Old Main, the venerable symbol of the Fulbright College of Arts and Sciences, historians, scholars, journal-ists, friends and adversaries gathered to reflect upon the Clinton years.

Some observers wondered if it were premature to expound upon the Clinton years, as history would provide the more objective assessment of his stewardship. But the panelists could not resist the plunge. They graded, embellished, lauded and criticized. Controversy did not take a back seat, and the audience packed in Giffels auditorium hung on every word and nuance. Many of us in the auditorium wished for the guid-ance of Diane Blair, the late eminent political scientist who knew Bill Clinton better than all of us. She would have added a level of insight that could come only from her.

Possibly this was the first such in-depth journey through the Clinton years by such an array of panelists—but certainly it will not be the last. Like the Roosevelts, Churchill or DeGaulle, Bill Clinton's legend only looms larger and more ominous as the passage of time seeks to define its dimensions.

For those of us who are observers, the pursuit to properly define Bill Clinton's aura and the momentous role he played in his era will be chal-lenging—and certainly endless.

David H. Pryor

Introduction

TODD G. SHIELDS,

JEANNIE M. WHAYNE

AND DONALD R. KELLEY

Who We Are and What We Do

In the spring of 2000, a group of faculty submitted a proposal to the dean of the J. William Fulbright College of Arts and Sciences at the University of Arkansas for the creation of a research center that would facilitate and focus attention on the importance of politics in Arkansas and the other southern states. The center would be created in order to honor the work of Diane Divers Blair, both a longtime member of the department of political science at the University of Arkansas and an active participant in state, regional, and national politics. The original idea was expanded to include not only faculty in the political science department but also distinguished scholars in the departments of history and English whose research involved the southern region. In the fall of 2000 a final proposal to establish the Diane D. Blair Center of Southern Politics and Society received enormous support from the across the college

xi

and the university and ultimately bipartisan endorsement from the entire Arkansas congressional delegation with whose assistance, a congressionally appropriated endowment was granted in the fall of 2001. The endowment helped create the Diane D. Blair Center of Southern Politics and Society, one of the few research centers across the nation established by congressional appropriation and one of the only centers established to honor an individual who was not a former member of Congress. The Blair Center continues to support scholarship, study, and outreach relevant to Arkansas and the southern states, and many interdisciplinary groups and organizations across the campus participate in Blair Center activities. Participating groups and affiliated organizations include the Arkansas Center for Oral and Visual History, the Center for Arkansas and Regional Studies, and the Southern Literature Group. Some of our current activities include an annual survey of the residents of Arkansas that helps to identify trends and patterns in public opinion relevant to politics and business across the state; fellowships for students who are studying southern politics, history, and literature; and inviting speakers who present current research in southern studies. In addition, the Blair Center sponsors conferences on various topics pertinent to southern politics and society and works closely with the University of Arkansas Press in order to publish the works that result from the colloquia.

For the inaugural Blair Center conference, held during the spring of 2002, we chose to bring together an eclectic and interdisciplinary group of scholars to present their ideas and evaluations of the Clinton administration. The spring of 2002 represented a full decade since Gov. Bill Clinton successfully challenged twelve years of Republican control of the executive branch and was approximately six years after Bill Clinton became the only Democratic president since FDR to win two consecutive presidential terms. Consequently, it was not only a timely and important topic but one we knew Diane would appreciate.

During the inaugural conference, the Blair Center collaborated with the J. William Fulbright Institute of International Relations, also located at the University of Arkansas. The Fulbright Institute is dedicated to the scholarly examination of important international issues and was created to honor the memory of Senator J. William Fulbright, who served both as the president of the University of Arkansas and later, with greater national and global impact, as the chairman of the Senate Foreign Relations Committee. The Fulbright Institute attempts to mirror the senator's dual commitment to serious and unbiased scholarship and to timely examination of important issues that define America's place in a tumultuous world. We were convinced that through cooperation between the

Fulbright Institute and the Blair Center we would be able to bring internationally known scholars, those with expertise in both domestic and foreign policy, to the university campus in order to conduct an insightful analysis of the forty-second presidency. Even more importantly we would begin a series of colloquia that would substantially help the Blair Center live up to the rigorous standards set by its remarkable namesake.

Professor Diane D. Blair

Diane Divers Blair, the daughter of William Keeveny Divers and Minna Rosenbaum Divers, was born October 25, 1938, and raised in Washington, D.C. She received her BA from Cornell University in 1959, cum laude and Phi Beta Kappa. She worked in Washington, D.C., in the early sixties as a contract analyst for the President's Committee on Government Contracts, as a research assistant for a Senate Special Committee on Unemployment, and as legislative secretary and speechwriter for Senator Stuart Symington of Missouri. She moved to Arkansas in 1963 and was active in numerous civic and political organizations, including the Modern Literature Club. She received her master's degree in political science from the University of Arkansas in 1967. She is listed in *America's Who's Who in Government and Politics* and in the *World's Who's Who of Women*. She debated Phyllis Schlafly before the Arkansas Legislature on Valentine's Day 1975 on behalf of the Equal Rights Amendment, and in 1992 she was selected to cast one of Arkansas's ballots in the Electoral College.

Diane taught at the University of Arkansas for thirty years, establishing a record of accomplishment simply unparalleled in its combination of serious scholarship and practical involvement in both local and national politics. In May 2000, Diane was awarded an honorary doctor of laws by the University of Arkansas, and she was twice nominated to the board of the U.S. Corporation for Public Broadcasting by President William Jefferson Clinton and twice confirmed to that position by the United States Senate. She served two terms as chair of the Corporation for Public Broadcasting, and the corporation has now named its governing board after her. She was appointed by Gov. Dale Bumpers in 1971 to serve as chair of the Governor's Commission on the Status of Women; by Gov. David Pryor in 1976 to chair the Commission on Public Employee Rights; and by Gov. Bill Clinton in 1980 to serve as a member of the Arkansas Educational Television Network commission, on which she served until 1993 and which she chaired from 1986–87. In 1992, she took leave from the University of Arkansas to serve as senior researcher for the Clinton presidential campaign and again took leave in 1996 when she served as senior advisor to the Clinton-Gore reelection campaign.

In addition to establishing a breakneck record of service to her state and nation, Diane was also an accomplished scholar, teacher, and mentor. She published two books, the first an analysis of Senator Hattie Caraway, the first woman elected to the United States Senate, entitled *Silent Hattie Speaks; The Personal Journal of Senator Hattie Caraway* (Greenwood Press, 1979). Her second book was titled *Arkansas Politics and Government: Do the People Rule?* (University of Nebraska Press, 1988), which continues to be a primary text used in Arkansas high schools, colleges, and universities. In addition, she authored fourteen chapters in edited volumes and authored or co-authored over ninety articles in various publications. Her research interests focused primarily on women and politics, state and local government, and the politics of Arkansas and the South. In 1993, she served as a guest scholar at the Brookings Institution in Washington, D.C.

Diane was three times named Outstanding Faculty Member by University of Arkansas students, and in 1982, she was one of the first recipients of the Fulbright College Master Teacher Award. In 1995, she was honored by the Midwest Political Science Association for her body of work in political science, and the Southern Political Science Association now has a competitive annual award in her name given to a scholar, chosen by committee, who successfully combines rigorous analyses of contemporary politics with a commitment to political activism.

Future activities of the Blair Center will continue to honor Diane through a commitment to excellence in research and teaching about the importance of southern politics and society, as well as through a commitment to service in the state and region. Future conferences will likely examine the changing influences of race and ethnicity in the contemporary South, the importance of the South in American presidential elections, and the importance of the South in contemporary jurisprudence (and the singular role of the South in death-penalty litigation). This current volume attempts to evaluate the Clinton presidency from the same interdisciplinary and eclectic approach that characterized much of Diane's own research.

Purpose of the Book

In the fall of 2001, we began to identify and invite scholars across several disciplines to a conference that we would host in the spring of 2002. We focused our efforts on internationally known scholars who were conducting investigations into topics relevant to the forty-second president of the United States—or to politics and society during the 1990s more generally. In addition to our commitment to scholarly excellence, we wanted to include a wide range of area expertise. Too often in contemporary academic life, the explosion of research, even in clearly defined subfields, causes scholars to focus narrowly on specific topics. Even with a narrow focus it is often difficult to keep pace with current research, and as a result there is a decided lack of interdisciplinary dialogue. Consequently, we purposely invited scholars with widely divergent research expertise and interests. We selected individuals from political science, foreign policy and international relations, comparative politics, history, journalism, and popular culture. We discussed lists of scholars who were widely recognized as leaders in their respective areas, and we ultimately chose individuals from several disciplines who had established impeccable credentials.

We realized that some of the participants might be concerned about their ability to speak freely about President Clinton—particularly given that President Bill Clinton and Senator Hillary Rodham Clinton both taught at the University of Arkansas Law School and were both close friends of Diane Blair. We made it a point to consistently assure all our participants that we were intensely committed, as was Diane, to unflinching scholarship and that we had no expectations about what conclusions the participants would reach or, for that matter, any hidden ideological or partisan agenda. We simply wanted their expert reflections on the Clinton presidency, whatever they may be. Overall, we assembled a group of scholars representing a variety of disciplines, all of whom possessed impressive international reputations and academic credentials; also, by sheer luck, we forged a decidedly mixed ideological group of scholars who have provided not only one of the first evaluations of the eight years of the Clinton-Gore administration, but certainly one of the most interdisciplinary evaluations of the forty-second president of the United States.

Benefits and Problems with an Interdisciplinary Conference

While the benefits of an eclectic evaluation of the Clinton presidency were promising, we were (and are) aware of the difficulties associated with such an endeavor. First, while there has been ample time to allow the media frenzy over the scandalous aspects of the Clinton administration to all but disappear, many governmental documents and personal papers of the president and the executive branch remain unavailable. In fact, given the necessary time for most presidential libraries to organize and present information, some of the most revealing information regarding the politics of the 1990s and the Clinton presidency will remain unavailable for several years. Consequently, we approach our task with a healthy appreciation that the process of evaluating presidential performance is an iterative, fluid, and on-going dialogue, and our contribution to this process is based on preliminary and incomplete information.

Another potential caveat for our volume is the extremely divergent perspectives of the contributors. While we believe that this is ultimately one of the strongest, and certainly most unique, qualities of this volume, we readily admit that coming to grips with such divergent methodologies, units of analyses, and areas of interest and specialization is a complex task. The risk we face is missing common themes and conclusions due to the widely diverse foci and methods. We have attempted, however, to approach this responsibility carefully, but we encourage readers to identify areas of commonality that we have missed.

Another potential problem for our task is the complexity of the 1990s, which represents an incredibly unique period in contemporary American history. Even a casual glance suggests that the decade preceding the new millennium was decidedly different. For example, consider the following: the explosion of new technologies, the aging of the baby-boom generation, a singular form of divided government, eight years of Democratic control of the White House, the dominance of women voters (and the growing importance of minority voters), an impeached president, the most partisan and ideologically distinct politics in decades, an explosion of media outlets (including cable networks and Internet sites), the globalization of the world economy, the end of the Cold War, rising ethnic and religious hatred throughout the world accompanied by international terrorism and new forms of security threats—all of which suggest that the 1990s was a unique decade full of change. In fact, the unprecedented pace of change during the 1990s renders comparisons of the Clinton presidency to prior administrations difficult. Of course, we do not suggest that previous decades were bereft of change or difficulties. Far from it—the civil-rights movements, violent political riots, the Vietnam War, the Cuban Missile Crisis, stag-flation, hostages, space travel, third-world poverty, and the persistent threat of nuclear war provided dramatically difficult environments for effective leadership. Nonetheless, we submit that the decade of the 1990s presented such a unique environment—in both domestic and international contexts—that a good deal of caution must be exercised when making comparisons to prior decades and administrations.

A final caveat is the sheer difficulty of evaluating presidential performance. Of course, there is no lack of scholars (and pundits) who jump at the chance to evaluate a president and his performance. In reality, such a task is simply daunting. Internationally renowned historian Arthur Schlesinger Sr. attempted to rate presidential greatness, first in 1948 and then again in 1962. His method was simple enough—he asked fifty-five "authorities" in American history to rate presidents across five categories: great, near great, average, below average, and failure. While he provided no definition of "greatness," and each evaluator was allowed to interpret both the definition of greatness and the subtle differences between "great" and "near great," the six most generally agreed upon great presidents were (in order) Lincoln, Washington, FDR, Wilson, Jefferson, and Jackson. They were followed by four "near great" presidents: Theodore Roosevelt, Cleveland, John Adams, and Polk. At the bottom of the ranking, labeled "failures," were Grant and Harding. Schlesinger conducted other "surveys" throughout the 1960s, often with different measures, directions, and "experts," but with some minor variations. Jackson fell from "great" to "near great," and Truman entered the list as "near great."[1] Many historians and political scientists disagreed strenuously with both the methodology and conclusions of Schlesinger's studies.[2] In fact, Dean Keith Simonton, who reviewed dozens of studies investigating "presidential greatness," correctly notes that not only do "experts" disagree on what qualities a president must possess (while some scholars argue that one of the most important qualities a president must have is the ability to adapt and remain flexible, others have upheld the quality of doggedly remaining true to ideological positions and campaign promises) the "best" qualities are most certainly dependent on the changing crises and political contexts during each administration.[3] As a result, judging "presidential greatness" seems to be more art than science and contains many more subjective evaluations than objective measures. Consequently, we approach the entire process of evaluating presidential performance and accomplishments with an appropriate appreciation for the difficulty and ambiguity central to such an endeavor. Nevertheless, it is important to realize that while many may disagree on what makes a president "great," or why some presidents are considered better than others or even what qualities "great" presidents must possess, there continues to be remarkable regularity, even consensus, on which presidents rank highly and which rate as failures. Our goal in this volume is not so grand, or presumptuous, as to render an initial "ranking" of President Clinton and his administrative performance; rather in this unique volume, we provide an eclectic view of the Clinton administration by scholars from widely divergent backgrounds that will provide a solid (and interdisciplinary) foundation for future work that may, after years or even decades of academic and scholarly dialogue, arrive at a placement and ranking of the "greatness" of the Clinton administration.

1 Bill Clinton

The Character Issue Revisited

BETTY GLAD

In this essay, Professor Glad examines various perspectives and traditions for defining and identifying presidential character. She begins with a discussion of how the theoretical concepts of "integrity" and "moral character" are complicated, controversial, and difficult not only to define but also to evaluate. She discusses some of the morally questionable actions of presidents throughout American history and then focuses specifically on President Clinton. She is careful to focus the discussion of presidential character centrally in the political circumstances of the time, for that is certainly how character is revealed, and in this respect, she introduces one of the central themes of this volume: the neo-liberal doctrine espoused by President Bill Clinton left him in the ideological middle where he was potentially able to capture swing voters during election years but found himself without "interest group structure in the middle in which Clinton could rely" during his governing years. This may well be most easily viewed in the case of Clinton's economic policies, his support for NAFTA, and the difficulties of forging foreign-policy coalitions after the end of the Cold War. Professor

Glad reviews President Clinton's actions and motivations across several policy areas and concludes with her evaluation of President Clinton's character.

A Historical Perspective

There are basically two options in evaluating presidential character. The Yale jurist Stephen Carter has provided a definition of character that seems to undergird most of the contemporary critiques of William Jefferson Clinton. Carter's chief assumption is that a moral person is one who has integrated various aspects of his life. This integration is manifest in one's ability to examine one's basic values, to publicly articulate those values, and to act consistently on them. Moral virtue is seen as a seamless web in which promises to cherish and be faithful to one's mate are but a manifestation of the ability to make public commitments that have been considered and will be honored.[1]

Reinhold Niebuhr offers us an alternative perspective, arguing that the relevant virtues of an individual differ in accord with the realm in which he or she is acting. Love and self-sacrifice are the most important virtues for the private realm, where intimate knowledge of the people one is dealing with is possible and the interests involved are one's own. But the statesman acts in another context in which he cannot ignore group self-interests and power. Prudence and a commitment to justice are the relevant virtues in such circumstances.[2]

The Stephen Carter perspective provides an ideal that not very many humans reach. When it comes to character, most people are apt to be uneven in their development. There are many virtues, and a human being may excel in some but not others. Nor is sexual purity the only standard in traditional Christian doctrine. The seven deadly sins, for example, include not only lust but also pride, covetousness, envy, sloth, anger, and gluttony. Even Benjamin Franklin recognized this in his journal. Listing thirteen virtues, he decided to try to master one virtue each week rather than address them all at once.[3]

Most important for our discussion, a person's strengths may vary in accord with the contexts in which he or she acts. Rectitude in one's private life is not always a clear indicator that one will also follow the straight and narrow in business or public life. Many Americans recognized this fact when they chose Grover Cleveland over James G. Blaine as president in 1884. A majority of Americans evidently saw the acts of a man who had possibly fathered a child out of wedlock as less ignominious than the acts of possibly receiving bribes from various railroad interests while in Congress.[4]

The political leader, moreover, cannot simply be judged as a clergyman might on the basis of his articulating all his values and sticking to them. The American political system, with its many subcultures and complex value systems, is one in which it may not be smart for the leader to clearly define and publicly articulate all his or her values. To be successful politicians must adapt to circumstances as they find them and appeal to a broader congeries of people and values than those in many other professions. Grand lies about where one stands politically and where one wants to lead the country, of course, raise accountability issues central to the political process. But hedging on some issues and adapting policy commitments to the political facts encountered once in office are essential components of the successful politician's trade. Politicians, in short, need a flexibility that is not always attractive for one in a smaller or private capacity. And if they are statesmen, they should have some deeper and abiding concern with providing for a broader justice, however difficult that may be to define.[5]

These points are borne out in U.S. history. Many of the founders—George Washington, Thomas Jefferson, Alexander Hamilton, Benjamin Franklin—in their private lives were led into morally ambiguous waters by their passions.[6] But even in their public lives most of them made compromises with their earlier stated principles. At Philadelphia, Washington, Franklin, and Hamilton went beyond the instructions given by the Continental Congress to reform the confederation. Going into a highly secret meeting, they aimed at a higher good: the establishment of a completely new American republic. A few years later, Jefferson, a strict constructionist of the Constitution, became a liberal constructionist when he had the chance to essentially double the size of the United States for a mere $15 million via the purchase of the Louisiana Territory from France. During the U.S. Civil War, Abraham Lincoln opted for the Emancipation Proclamation months after many governors and civic leaders had urged it upon him. Even then, the proclamation did not apply to the border states in the union. Lincoln did not want to take a step that would drive them into secession.[7] The political necessities of fighting the war led the president even to suspend the writ of habeas corpus throughout the entire nation and authorize the arrest of any person guilty of any "disloyal practice, affording aid and comfort to the Rebels against the authority of the United States."[8]

Recent presidents offer similarly complex moral examples. Sometimes they transcended what might be seen as their personal shortcomings. John Fitzgerald Kennedy's complicated sex life did not stop him from showing extraordinary commitment to preventing a possible war with the USSR during the Cuban Missile Crisis.[9] Lyndon Johnson, profligate in many ways, committed himself to the passage of the Civil Rights Act of 1964 and the Voting Rights Act of 1965—knowing full well that these would have long-run costs for the Democratic Party. At other times, basic principles would be sacrificed to overall political expediencies. To secure friendlier relations with the People's Republic of China, Jimmy Carter compromised his commitment to human rights by supporting the continued sitting of the murderous Pol Pot regime in the United Nations even after the Vietnamese had thrown that regime out of office in Cambodia.[10]

Presidents, in short, have been politically flexible from the very beginning of the Republic. Thomas Paine described George Washington's character as a sort of "[c]hameleon-colored thing, called prudence. It is, in many cases, a substitute for principle, and is so nearly allied to hypocrisy, that it easily slides into it."[11] Jefferson, as Elizabeth Marvick has pointed out, became known as "Jeff the Trimmer."[12] Lincoln explicitly reserved for himself the ability to adapt to circumstances. "My policy is to have no policy," he used to say. Concerning Reconstruction policies, he once compared himself to riverboat pilots who "steer from point to point as . . . setting the course of the boat no farther than they can see."[13] In the twentieth century Jimmy Carter, who Stephen Carter suggests was too moral a man to be a politician, was a master at hedging on his messages in the 1976 campaign. As Carter told a group of network executives and correspondents on one occasion, "the only presidents he knew of who had emphasized the issues were Dewey, Goldwater, and McGovern."[14] Eisenhower has even been praised for his political astuteness because of his ability to avoid responsibility for some of his more controversial policies, placing responsibility for such measures on his subordinates.[15]

Clinton: Working from a Neo-Liberal Base

In evaluating Bill Clinton's character from this political perspective, it seems he has been truthful about the most fundamental facts of both what he is and what he wants to do. He has been very upfront about being a politician and clear about the major lines of policies he would follow. As a "New Democrat" he chaired, shortly before running for president in 1992, the neo-liberal Democratic Leadership Council (DLC). His commitments in his campaign in 1992 were to decrease the national deficit, provide universal healthcare for U.S. citizens, end welfare "as we know it," and promote free trade. But he wanted to accomplish these objectives in ways that would neither increase public spending in any major way nor challenge corporate America in any significant ways.

The bottom line for Bill Clinton was not that he believed in big government, but that unlike his opponents on the right, he believed in some government.[16] In this he was in tune with his times. The American people had not elected a New Deal Democrat since Johnson's reelection in 1964 and by the early nineties were clearly in a conservative mood. As a Democrat, Clinton went just as far in a liberal direction as he could while winning the office of the presidency. As William Leuchtenburg has noted, "he is one of the great politicians in all of American history. He has an extraordinary sense of where to position himself."[17]

The problem for Clinton as president was that he had no stable coalition on which he could rely for the success of his programs. The neo-liberal doctrine was one calculated to win over swing voters. Democratic candidates would have to move to the ideological middle of the road to win the presidency. But whatever successes in campaigning there might be, it would be more difficult to govern from that position. Both the Democratic and Republican political parties had become increasingly ideological, and legislative proposals in the middle would stir up partisan juices. Moreover, there was no alternative interest-group structure in the middle on which Clinton could rely.[18]

Clinton's economic plan of 1993—an experiment in "principled centrism"—is one example of the difficulties he faced in his attempt at finding a middle ground. His goal was reducing the deficit but doing so in a way that would moderate program cuts and limit tax breaks for the very wealthy.[19] Ironically, this first attempt at finding a middle ground did not bring him bipartisan support. The stimulus part of the package involved a few relatively low-cost new spending projects—for example, summer-job programs, construction and environmental cleanup projects, "most of which would go toward public-works and community-development projects designed to create jobs."[20] To reduce the deficit, new taxes would be required, taxes that would affect middle-class taxpayers as well as wealthier individuals. But with this kind of package, the Republicans were able to attack Clinton as a "tax and spend Democrat." A budget resolution supporting the plan passed the House in March 1993 with no Republican support.

The problem Clinton had in securing a legislative majority even when working from a Democratic base was made clear in the final vote for the conference version of his budget in the summer of 1993. Securing no Republican votes and with several Democratic defections, he had to rely on two Democratic women from conservative districts—Rep. Marjorie Margolies-Mezvinsky of Pennsylvania and Rep. Pat Williams of Montana. They placed their own careers on the line by putting the Clinton budget over the top in the House. The vote was 218–216.[21]

The final vote in the Senate was fifty to fifty, with Vice President Albert Gore voting to break the tie. Even to secure that final vote, the president and his advisors spent an inordinate amount of effort and time wooing two conservative Democrats—Senator Robert Kerrey of Nebraska and Senator John Breaux of Louisiana. Kerrey, who held out "on principle" for a long time, may have been persuaded to move when Warren Buffet of Omaha, one of the wealthiest men in the United States, suggested that a vote for the measure was a move in the right direction.[22] Democratic senator David Boren of Oklahoma resisted all White House efforts at a compromise, voting against the plan and taking several members of the Oklahoma delegation in the House with him.[23]

Clinton's plan for a comprehensive healthcare system for all Americans was based on a neo-liberal compromise for which he had no solid support. Rejecting a direct-service medical system that some liberals urged, his advisors constructed a complicated system based on private enterprise and government supervision. The whole effort came to an ignominious end on September 22, 1994, when the bipartisan supporters of a much watered-down compromise plan—Republican senator John Chaffee and George M. Mitchell, the Democratic leader of the Senate—agreed that they did not have the votes to salvage even a comprehensive effort.

The supporters of the plan had been out-financed and out-finessed by their opponents, and the public, which first favored the plan, ultimately found it to be too complex.[24] In February 1994, members of the Business Roundtable, the CEOs of the one hundred largest corporations in the United States, met in a ballroom at the Willard Hotel and voted sixty to twenty to support a much smaller Cooper plan then in the works. Subsequently the National Association of Manufacturers and the U.S. Chamber of Commerce came out against the Clinton plan. In the end, the Health Insurance Association of American mounted a fifteen million dollar campaign against the plan. Most effective were the associa-tion's ads featuring Harry and Louise sitting at their kitchen table, wor-ried about the complexity of the system and fearful (inaccurately) that under it they could not choose their own doctors.[25]

As Gary Wills pointed out, the basic fault of the Clinton health plan was that "its complexity, its clumsy attempt to combine private insur-ance and doctors and hospitals' own organizations with government supervision—was due to the effort to find something that is not a 'big government solution.'" The result was a plan that was "hard to sell, easy to misrepresent and impossible to imagine" as functioning smoothly.[26]

The president did have one major legislative accomplishment during his first two years in office. In the fall of 1993 NAFTA passed the U.S. Congress with a bipartisan vote. Clinton had pledged his support for NAFTA in the 1992 campaign, a measure he supported on ideological grounds. As he said at the time of the vote for NAFTA, "this is really a vote about whether we're going to try to hold on to yesterday's economy or embrace tomorrow's economy."[27]

Politically, his problem on NAFTA was within his own party. The Republican leaders, including Newt Gingrich, were early proponents of NAFTA. Fearing the supporters of Ross Perot in their own camp, they and many other Republicans wanted Clinton to take the lead on this issue. As Republican Doug Bereuter said, "Republicans fear being out front and 'alone' in support of NAFTA if the president is not going to lead the way and bring Democrats with him."[28] But many Democrats, as the vote in the House suggested, objected to NAFTA on the basis that it would cost jobs. Richard Gephardt, the House Democratic majority leader, claimed that NAFTA "would open Mexican markets to U.S. investors in search of cheap labor and exert downward pressure on American wage scales."[29] Ron Carey, leader of the Teamsters, saw NAFTA as protecting corporate interests at the expense of public interests and laborers. To win Demo-crats' support, Clinton proposed "tri-national commissions to deal with issues relating to the environmental protection and labor laws affected by the trade with Mexico and Canada." He also proposed a one hundred million dollar job retraining program to help those people who lost their jobs due to NAFTA."[30]

Certainly support for NAFTA was a risky move for both political par-ties. A *Washington Post* survey found that 46 percent of the public opposed NAFTA, while 36 percent supported it.[31] "With every House seat up for reelection next year, lawmakers worried about how their votes would affect their careers. The opposition of organized labor put Democrats at risk of political retribution, while Republicans were threatened more by Texas billionaire Ross Perot's GOP-leaning followers."[32]

As it turned out, the Democrats paid the price. Labor leaders and other Democratic activists did not rally their troops in the 1994 midterm elections. Voter turnout was low and a disciplined Republican right was able to sweep the polls, winning control of both houses of Congress.[33]

After the 1994 elections, with conservative Republicans in charge of the House and the Senate, Clinton found his veto power as another way of exercising power. Yielding for a time the initiative to the Republicans, he vetoed for the most part deep cuts into popular programs such as education, job training, environmental protection, and medical care. Clinton's strategy was to score political points by portraying the Republicans as extremists, while positioning himself as a moderate.

For the budget, the end result was a game of chicken, in which Clinton risked government shutdowns to exact concessions from the Republicans. On November 13, 1995, for example, Clinton refused to sign a stopgap spending measure that would have provided funding for government activities for the next two weeks, thereby forcing a partial shutdown of the federal government. A few days later, Clinton vetoed the House and Senate Republican-backed reconciliation bill that would have sharply cut spending for Medicare and Medicaid and turned over many programs including Medicaid to the states. By the spring of 1996 the Republican Congress had to restore much of what he wanted in the budget. The agreement, as one news headline suggested, "reflected the end of the failed GOP strategy of using the fiscal 1996 budget as leverage against Clinton."[34] And the public generally held the Congress, not the president, responsible for the shutdowns. Opinion polls showed that most Americans disapproved of the Republicans' tactics of using government funding as a bargaining chip to get the president to accede to their demands regarding the federal budget.

Before the opening of the 1996 general-election campaign, Clinton carried out another one of his neo-liberal campaign promises. On August 22, 1996, Clinton signed the Republican-sponsored welfare-reform bill: "Today we are taking a historic chance to make welfare what it was meant to be: a second chance, not a way of life."[35] Building primarily on the Republican base that pushed the program, Clinton made his approval conditional on a certain measure that would soften the original Republican bill and bring some Democrats along with him.[36] Even then Clinton saw the measure as "far from perfect," reiterating his earlier criticisms of the new law's treatment of immigrants and its reductions in spending on nutrition-assistance programs. But he claimed some of these matters could change in the future: "We can change what is wrong," he said.[37]

This decision was very unpopular with many liberal Democrats. They argued that the changes would cause harsh treatment of poor families. But for Clinton, it neutralized the advantages the Republicans might have had in the fall presidential election. Without his support for the bill, they could have claimed that Bill Clinton had reneged on his earlier campaign promise for welfare reform and that only the Republicans could be counted upon to do something about that matter. As it turned out, Clinton won reelection by winning thirty-one states and the District of Columbia for 379 electoral votes, while Robert Dole won nineteen states and 159 electoral votes.[38]

In early February 1995, shortly after the first midterm election, Clinton made another bold move. Bypassing the U.S. Congress he provided $20 billion in a short-term loan for Mexico. The goal was to stabilize the peso and prevent Mexico from suffering an economic collapse. The administration officials had found the money for this loan in the Exchange Stabilization Fund to back it up further. Clinton officials manned the phones to persuade the IMF to put up $17.4 billion. The Swiss–based Bank of Intel settlement pledged another $2 billion. The immediate result was a rally in the bond market on Wall Street.

In January Clinton had sought with the support of the leaders of both parties in both houses of Congress to deal with the problem with a legislative bailout. But when members began to discuss conditions they might attach to the bill, he found an alternative course of action. A legislative delay could have caused Mexico to default on its short-term bonds, with very negative consequences for the entire international capital market. As House Banking and Financial Service chair Jim Leach, a Republican from Iowa, noted, "the tenor of these times, the lack of comity, partisanship and suspicion made it difficult to get an agreement."[39]

This time Clinton's move won the plaudits of the congressional leadership. Robert Dole, Richard Gephardt, Newton Gingrich, and Thomas Daschle had issued a joint statement saying that the plan was necessary under these conditions.[40] Vice President Gore noted that people had been saying that "something ought to be done, and somebody else ought to do it. Well, the president said I'll do it. And he did."[41] The measure, as Jim Hoagland emphasized, should have been called "Operation Peso Shield." Clinton had placed his presidency on the line in this crisis, much as George Bush had done back in the summer of 1990 when he decided to send troops to Saudi Arabia.

Defining a Post–Cold War Foreign Policy

On foreign-policy matters, generally, Clinton had to find his way in a new world order where the national interests were not obvious, the enemy unclearly defined, and the public ambivalent about most overseas ventures.[42]

In particular, his endeavors to involve U.S. troops in peacekeeping operations abroad were met with resistance. In 1993, when Clinton decided to reinforce U.S. troops in Somalia, he went against a bipartisan call for the withdrawal of the U.S. troops already there. U.S. troops, he decided, would stay there for another six months. What had started out as a humanitarian expedition had led to a military skirmish with warlord Gen. Mohammed Farah Aidid in Mogadishu. This skirmish resulted in the death of twelve American soldiers.[43] Not understanding U.S. interests in the area, many Americans just wanted out. The opposition in Congress included Senator Robert Byrd, chair of the Senate Appropriations Committee, who had threatened to cut off funding for the mission if U.S. troops were not withdrawn.[44]

Shortly before the congressional election in the fall of 1994, President Clinton conducted an especially high-risk operation that could have failed and subjected him to serious political fallout.[45] On September 15, 1994, he gave a public ultimatum to the Haitian military regime—ordering them to either relinquish their power over Haiti to the democratically elected Jean-Bertrand Aristide or face U.S. military intervention. Four days later, on September 19, U.S. troops landed in Haiti. There was no military opposition: The Haitian generals at the last moment had agreed to abdicate their power and vacate their positions on October 15. The Haitian military police were allowed to retain some control and were permitted to temporarily handle any street conflicts among the Haitian people.

The whole operation was a masterful example of coercive diplomacy. Former president Jimmy Carter, Chairman of the Joint Chiefs Gen. Colin Powell, and Senator Sam Nunn had been successful in brokering an agreement that provided Raul Cedras with a face-saving out, thereby avoiding a military confrontation for the U.S. troops.[46] While Carter tried to find some common human ground with Cedras, Powell and Nunn kept reminding him that U.S. military power was far superior to Haiti's and that Congress "would set aside whatever misgivings it had and back

Clinton once an invasion was initiated." All three members of the Carter team stressed to the military officials that they would save lives and project "the very essence of military honor" if they would relinquish their power in Haiti.[47]

Central to their bargaining power, however, were two facts: first, President Clinton told General Powell on the phone that the generals had to agree on a date for their departure; second, Clinton ordered the Eighty-second Airborne Division to take off for Haiti even as the negotiations continued.[48]

Very few people expected such a peaceful outcome to the whole confrontation. Clinton's political advisor Richard Morris had counseled him against the operation, suggesting instead a massive demonstration of force several miles outside of Haiti.[49] Senators William Cohen (Republican), Robert Dole (Republican), and Robert Torricelli (Democrat) expressed reservations about the invasion. Rep. John Conyers (Democrat) was one of the few supportive voices in public: "I support President Clinton's call for troops to support democracy in Haiti because all other alternatives have failed, while the repression, torture, and anti-democratic activities have continued."[50] The night before his announcement, Clinton had told his old journalist friend Taylor Branch that he had practically no support for the enterprise and that he saw his whole presidency as being on the line.[51]

But when the intervention was met with no armed opposition, there was almost a collective sigh of relief in the United States. On September 19, 1994, Congress passed a resolution praising the diplomatic end to the crisis in Haiti and promising support for the American troops. But it also urged an expedient withdrawal. The vote on this resolution was 94 to 5.[52] Democratic political advisor Robert Squier noted that Clinton's success on this issue "had addressed his 'character problem'" by showing "that when he needs to be strong for the whole country he can be."[53]

The operation, albeit with a few bumps along the way, not only got rid of a murderous regime in Haiti, it also resolved a domestic political problem for Clinton. With the end of the junta, Haitians could no longer come in massive numbers to the United States claiming political asylum. Richard Morris and others had warned him that should the Haitian refugees continue coming to the United States in such threatening numbers it would hurt him and the Democratic Party in the upcoming midterm elections.[54]

In August 1995, when Clinton reluctantly waded into the very complex Bosnian issue, he again received little support at home. Vetoing a bill that would have ended the U.S. embargoes against the Bosnian government, he explained that such a move would frustrate U.S. peacekeeping efforts.[55] When the United States secured in the following December the reluctant assent of the major warring parties to redraw the map in Bosnia, the U.S. Congress gave the administration only a grudging sort of support. The House resolution supporting the deployment of the U.S. troops in Bosnia also noted the opposition to Clinton's decision to send them there. Senator Dole publicly endorsed Clinton's prerogative as the president's right to send troops into the area. But he did not support Clinton's peace plan. Still, in late December 1997, Clinton extended the troops' stay in the area beyond the original deadlines.

In addition to these measures, the Clinton administration took several steps that would foreshadow later U.S. antiterrorist policies. As early as 1995 Clinton issued an executive order that targeted possible U.S. funding sources of groups and individuals with alleged links to terrorist activities in the Middle East. Banks and other financial institutions were ordered to freeze the accounts of any of these groups or individuals they found in their records.[56]

Then, on August 20, 1998, Clinton ordered the firing of U.S. missiles at bases in Afghanistan and Sudan thought to have links with terrorist activities. The target in Afghanistan was a base camp that housed training facilities and large weapons and ammunition stockpiles. In Sudan, the target was a pharmaceutical factory believed to be a chemical-weapon factory. The actions, a response to the bombing of the American embassies in Kenya and Tanzania on August 7, were timed to coincide with what intelligence agencies believed was a gathering of suspected terrorist groups at the camp. The suspicions that they were operations of the bin Laden Al Qaeda group had been affirmed on August 19, when a "coalition of militant Islamic groups assembled by bin Laden" claimed responsibility for these acts, saying that they had been carried out by the Islamic Army for the Liberation of the Holy Land. More terrorists' attacks, they threatened, were on the way.[57]

Most of the measures noted above were taken without broad public support. At the time Clinton was pushing for NAFTA, a *Washington Post* survey found that only 36 percent supported it, while 46 percent opposed it.[58] When Clinton extended the army's commitment in Somalia, only 21 percent supported Clinton; 51 percent did not understand why the United States was there at all.[59] A *New York Times*/CBS News poll in 1995 showed that 58 percent of the Americans polled opposed the placing of U.S. troops in Bosnia Herzegovina.

Even the success of the Haitian intervention did not end all criticism of Clinton's policies. The wording of the Senate resolution of commendation was strategically devised so that members of the Senate could still oppose the president's Haiti policy. Many Senate leaders from both parties—John McCain (Republican), Paul Wellstone (Democrat), and Tom Harkin (Democrat)—suggested that the junta had been let off too gently.[60] Rep. Dave McCurdy (Democrat) said, "A large-scale, long-term peacekeeping mission still poses substantial risks."[61] As Senate Democrat leader George Mitchell noted "to hear the speeches, there's almost a regret that things have turned out so well."[62]

Clinton's bombing strike against Al Qaeda bases in Afghanistan and Sudan also created problems for him. The bombings received bipartisan support in Congress, and the public was 66 percent positive. But his moves were also the object of a lot of second-guessing. Some congressmen questioned whether this decision was based on military considerations or was an attempt divert attention away from Clinton's recent admission to a sexual relationship with Monica Lewinsky.[63] For example, Republican senators Dan Coats and Arlen Specter accused Clinton of using "diversionary" tactics. In this case Clinton's reckless private life had made him vulnerable to these kinds of charges.

These steps had been taken in the face of great uncertainty in the Washington foreign-policy community about who the terrorists were and what should be done about them. According to news accounts, the FBI had yet to find enough evidence to blame Osama bin Laden or any other individual. The information that pinned bin Laden came from the intelligence agencies.[64] Military leaders, according to a report in the *Washington Post,* were warning that a military strike against him in Afghanistan could be "a nightmare."[65] It would more than likely also result in a significant loss of American lives. Other experts suggested that Osama's role in terrorist networks might be more financial than operational.[66] Moreover, the target in Sudan, as Secretary of Defense William Cohen admitted on September 2, was a plant that made medicines. He said bin Laden played an indirect role in the plant, but he still supported the decision to strike the plant.

Relevance for Judging Character

What the above shows is that many of Clinton's apparent flip-flops were due to the fact that he was attempting to govern from the middle, as he saw it, in a period when that was particularly difficult, given the increasing polarization in the political parties. Coalitions had to be built on an ad hoc basis for almost every major legislative plan, a task that someone like Franklin Roosevelt never had to face, at least for the success of his early domestic New Deal programs. Moreover, Clinton's major legislative efforts—healthcare reform, NAFTA, a balanced budget, welfare reform— were in accord with the neo-liberal promises he had made on the campaign trail. With the Republican control of both houses of Congress after 1994, his compromises on welfare and other items were of necessity further to the right than he would have liked. Relying on the veto, he salvaged as many liberal programs as he could.

In the foreign-policy arena, where he had more discretionary power, he began the task of defining and implementing, often against the wishes of a reluctant Congress and public, the role of the United States in the post–Cold War world. In some of these operations, such as the intervention in Haiti, he undertook a risky operation, the failure of which could have mortally damaged his presidency. Throughout Clinton was never a slavish follower of his pollster Richard Morris or of public opinion more generally. He used the polls, as Morris himself has suggested, figuring out the best way to present those policies he favored.[67]

One could argue that Democrats should have a longer-term perspective—focusing on party building and the shaping of public opinion—as the conservatives have done since Barry Goldwater's disastrous defeat in 1964. But that was never how Bill Clinton defined his task, and from that perspective, he cannot really be faulted for something he never promised to do.

Bill Clinton, in short, has shown over the years a kind of self-discipline on major *public* matters that confounds his critics. Indeed, even Joe Klein, in light of Clinton's recent performance in the presidency, has backpedaled on his earlier assessment of the president. In an interview with freelance journalist James D. Retter, he said, "I thought it might be a case where Clinton's private lack of discipline was reflected in his public lack of discipline. Turns out I was wrong. Turns out he's become one of the most disciplined public figures that we've seen."[68]

Clinton also has other politically relevant virtues. He is charming and he likes people. Robert Reich has noted he has a "capacity for sheer, exuberant joy."[69] At his White House reception after the first inauguration, he looked into the eyes of the people whose hands he shook and seemed to genuinely like them. He spent six hours chatting with many of the over two thousand visitors.[70] After the Oklahoma City bombing and Yitzhak Rabin's assassination in 1995, Clinton showed the nation real emotion and a "take charge determination."[71]

Moreover, he is an extremely hard worker and has an unreal ability to absorb and master quickly a large volume and variety of material relating to his work. He put in extremely long days in the Oval Office and in meetings handled a great variety of problems, and sought many diverse opinions.[72] As Secretary of Treasury Lloyd Bentsen noted, he is highly intelligent and has a "superior inquisitive mind."[73]

Still, he has several vulnerabilities as a leader. As it became clear in his first few months in office, he is not a good manager.[74] His selections for major governmental posts were slowly made, and the backgrounding of some nominees (Zoe Baird, Lani Guinier) was not well done. The fiascoes in his staff's handling of the replacement of the travel-office employees, the blanket request for FBI files, and the handling of documents in Vince Foster's office after his suicide created the appearance of possible wrongdoings that would later provide grist for the independent prosecutor's mill.[75] The result of his attempt to distance himself from the national press was that he was practically nibbled to death for a while with stories such as how he held up traffic at an airport while receiving a two-hundred-dollar haircut from Christophe. Indeed, as it turned out, Clinton had no real honeymoon with the press.[76] A study by the Center for Media and Public Affairs shows that only one third of the network-news coverage (plus CNN) about Clinton was positive, compared to 55 percent for George W. Bush.[77]

Partly these early problems were corrected when Clinton brought in a chief of staff with greater experience in Washington. But these problems were also due to Clinton's proclivities to try to do too much himself, to think out loud about his alternatives, to reverse positions in public, to admit mistakes he made. Maybe he attempted too much to win over "enemies," compromised too much with his opponents. At base his problem was that he had the ability to see almost every side of a problem and had difficulty in dealing with the tradeoffs. As his advisor for the 1996 election campaign, Richard Morris, noted, Clinton had an extraordinary appetite for receiving information. But his ability to categorize and prioritize was not that strong. Morris suggested he was like a pelican trying to eat all the fish in his beak, poor at fully digesting it all.[78] The result was endless meetings, exhaustion, and a growing reputation with the Washington influential for being undisciplined and indecisive.

Hillary Clinton, too, compounded his early management problems. True, she provided a kind of discipline on the campaign trail that served to keep him on track. But her inexperience in Washington affairs and desire to control events may have contributed to the political mistakes the White House made the first two years in office. On healthcare, Richard Morris suggests Hillary was extremely rigid about what type of plan she would accept and was not willing to compromise at any point in the process.[79] She and her close associates also seemed to have been major players in the Zoe Baird nomination. They may have played a role in handling the travel-office affair and the documents in Vince Foster's office after his death.[80] And as Secretary of Labor Robert Reich suggests, her reluctance to admit that the public might think she is guilty of any wrongdoing may have been the source of her first impulse not to talk about her participation in Whitewater land deals.[81] Her naiveté was also manifestly evident in her underestimation of the cynicism with which interviewers could treat her. Dressed in an all white outfit, she made it easy for Michael Kelly in a *New York Times* article on her moral and religious views to caricature her as Saint Hillary.[82]

Relationships

We do not yet have the memoir materials, the letters, and working papers that would enable us to make more than some preliminary hypotheses about Clinton's relationships to political intimates in the White House and colleagues on Capitol Hill. Robert Reich's book *Locked in the Cabinet,* the most positive of the memoir materials published at this date, focuses primarily on Reich's work and his relationship to the relevant officials in the White House. George Stephanopoulos's memoir is very useful for describing the relationship of various aides to one another, as well as his own interactions with the president. But Stephanopoulos was in the White House for only four years, and the title of his memoir, *All Too Human: A Political Education,* fits himself as well as the president. His version of events, as he makes clear, is that of a disappointed liberal. Richard Morris's *Behind Closed Doors,* as we have seen, sheds some light on the Clinton modus operandi, but it overplays Morris's role. Clinton's proclivities for "triangulation" were built into his political agenda before Morris was brought back to the White House to advise, and Clinton certainly did not mindlessly follow the polls that Morris and his associates provided him with.

We do have, however, considerable data on Clinton's relationship to the media and the public. What we can see, as Taylor Branch suggests after reviewing the early Clinton literature, is that the major media has been very hard on Bill Clinton. "Only a spineless Clinton runs free on the pages," Branch writes.[83] Indeed, in 1996 two of the most widely reviewed critiques of the Clinton presidency were published. James Stewart's *Blood Sport* and Roger Morris's *Partners in Power* recirculated the corruption and other charges against him made by the same dozen or so Clinton antagonists in Arkansas that David Brock used, plus a plethora of anonymous sources.[84]

Some journalists announced their beliefs in the charges against Clinton that the scandal machine ground out, even before there was substantial proof that he had done what his antagonists claimed he had done. Indeed, the smoke it created made it difficult for even honest observers to see clearly. A. M. Rosenthal of the *New York Times,* for example, uncritically noted in 1996 that the "allegations are that Mr. Clinton and his wife are *guilty of something,* that cover-up was going on in the White House, and even that the death of Vincent Foster . . . was connected (emphasis added)."[85] In another column, Maureen Dowd stated, "We pretty much know that the Clintons did *something wrong* in Whitewater, wrong (emphasis added)" without documenting exactly what it was they did.[86] Stuart Taylor decided that he believed Paula Jones despite his knowledge that she had reserved movie rights on her story. Indeed, to doubt her was to be guilty of applying a class-based double standard. Why should the Yale-educated Anita Hill be believed and the words of working-class woman from a small Southern town rejected?[87] Later as Press Secretary Mike McCurry noted, much of the press never cut Clinton any slack after the Monica Lewinsky story broke in early 1998. They blew it "way out of proportion? Too early, way too quickly. And then never figured out how to climb back from the precipice."[88]

This suspicion, as we have seen, certainly had its roots in the early attempts of both of the Clintons to cut themselves off from the representatives of the major media. And it was fed by the early blunders on the part of an amateurish staff.

Still, there is something about Clinton that contributes to his difficulties with many others in elite circles. Clearly many members of the press have mixed feelings toward him. There is something about him they cannot explain. He is an awesome force—with his energy, his capacity for work, for meeting with and enjoying people. Yet, as Joe Klein notes in his recent book, there was "strangeness" to his long late-night conversations: "There was an odd, vacant, needy quality to it: it was the conversational equivalent of someone standing too close to you (although there was never any real intimacy to it)."[89]

Earlier, certain journalists from Arkansas, those who followed him for a long time, tried to explain why they felt uncomfortable around him. Meredith Oakley suggests that he goes too far, trying to please too many people.[90] Others have seen him as too boyish, "unfinished." Whatever it is, something about him compels some to strike out against him. As John Brummett notes: "Over the years in Arkansas, I had criticized Bill Clinton with a frequency and fervor that I did not apply to older Democratic politicians in the state. . . ." Brummett suggests that this Clinton vulnerability "served to make critics feel powerful. A self-assured politician who never responded to journalistic criticism was much less fun to pick on than one who had a translucent need for approval and would let you get under his skin."[91]

One can make some preliminary hypotheses as to the reasons for these interactions. As for Clinton's own contribution, it is clear that his apparent "openness" with so many people has undermined his authority relative to them. As any politically savvy head of state knows, keeping a certain distance from others is a requisite for maintaining the "awe" that those others are inclined to offer those in office. Why did Bill Clinton not appreciate this fact? Perhaps unmet needs for intimacy in the private realm may have been projected onto a larger, public stage. Seeking satisfaction from a broader stage, he could avoid the risk of relying too much on any one person. Certainly what we know about Clinton's early life suggests that this is a real possibility. His mother, Virginia Blythe Clinton, provided him with a love suggesting that he was special but that he could be abandoned. Moreover, she set before him a model of how to deal with pain that was at once functional while limiting her capacity to share the vagaries of life with him or any other vulnerable human being. As she stated in her memoir: "I trained myself not to worry about what ifs, either, because nine times out of ten they don't happen. And when bad things do happen, I brainwash myself to put them out of my mind. . . . Inside my head I construct an airtight box. I keep inside it what I want to think about and everything else stays behind the walls." That Clinton may have adopted this same coping mechanism is evident in his capacity for taking chances and dealing with reverses while in the presidency.[92]

But whatever Clinton's vulnerabilities are, why do they put others who deal with him on edge? Perhaps those who are most ambivalent about him see something in him that they have given up, or a fear in themselves. Can a strong man really take pleasure in relating to ordinary people as he seems to do? Does a show of vulnerability indicate that one is fundamentally weak? Maybe Clinton's success shows that the world is not fair. How could such a man—one with ordinary roots, one who is not very disciplined in his personal life—make it to the top of the political ladder as he has done? He didn't pay the price![93] Or perhaps, seeing his extraordinary political and intellectual abilities, they expected too much of him. The cynicism of younger journalists, Mike McCurry suggests, may have been due to his failure to measure up to what many of them thought he was going to be like. Or, as McCurry continues, they are possibly following new standards of journalism. No longer does the profession reward the "practice of elegant, fruitful reporting that helps people understand things."[94]

What is most interesting is that those further removed from the president—the American public—never turned on Clinton the way certain members of the establishment did. Most ordinary people were able to see and to sustain a distinction between the public and private character of the president. Most focused on his job-performance ratings. In a January 25–26, 1998, Gallup poll, 70 percent of those polled thought that Clinton was tough enough for the job; 62 percent said he was a strong leader. His performance in the State of the Union address shortly after Lewinsky's purported affair with him was made public reinforced this view. The address itself was rated as excellent by 75 percent of the individuals interviewed in a January 29–31 *Los Angeles Times* poll. In a Gallup poll of March 20–22, 1998, 77 percent of the respondents thought the words "Can Get Things Done" applied to Bill Clinton. This was an 11 percent rise since January 23–24, 1998.

Indeed, Clinton's job-performance ratings in the polls remained high throughout 1998. On February 1, a *Washington Post* poll showed Clinton's approval rating at 67 percent, the highest it had ever been. As late as July 14, a *Washington Post* poll found Clinton's approval rating at 63 percent.[95]

Some in the public even saw his other virtues despite his apparent lying about sex. In an April 2–4 *Washington Post* poll, 56 percent of the respondents said he understood the problems of "people like them." Women, who were Clinton's strongest supporters, were clearly influenced by what many of them saw as his positive record on women's issues.[96] Voter satisfaction with the way he handled the economy also worked to his advantage. According to a January 21, 1998, *Washington Post* poll, Clinton's job-approval rating stood at 68 percent among those who thought the economy was doing well.[97]

While Clinton sustained a high job-performance rating, many Americans were viewing with suspicions the motives of Clinton's accusers. An early April 1998 *Washington Post* poll suggested that a majority of Americans saw Starr's inquiry as politically motivated (56 percent), and one in three thought he should quickly wind up his investigation. By this time, Clinton was being ranked higher on some morality scales than Paula Jones, Monica Lewinsky, or Kathleen Willey.[98]

Conclusions

What the above suggests is that for contemporaries, at least, there are many advantages in evaluating a president's character in terms of the most directly relevant political behavior. Data regarding his political commitments, his decision-making style, and his skills as a manager are subject to direct scrutiny by the press and are clearly politically relevant. Moreover, with this kind of focus outside observers are somewhat less likely to hold him up to standards that no successful political leader could ever employ and be successful. A politician has some goals and a craft and most often operates in an environment that requires a certain amount of flexibility. Others should judge him on what he wants to accomplish, the impediments he faces in his political environment, and his skills in getting there.[99]

In these respects Clinton was a good president. He undertook a neoliberal, New Democratic approach to domestic issues at a time when the increasing polarization of the political parties would make it difficult to govern from that position. With considerable skill he put together a series of ad hoc coalitions and resorted to vetoes and executive agreements to secure his goals. In foreign policy, he undertook the difficult task of redefining American goals in a new epoch where there was no longer a clearly defined enemy, and the major problems revolved around the makeup of the new global economy and the need to deal with some areas of political and military instability in various parts of the world. Not only was he flexible and sometimes tough, he was extremely intelligent and worked very hard. He even liked campaigning—whether it was for the vote of a senator on a bill he backed or the vote of citizen in an election in which he had something at stake.

As John Brummett suggests, Clinton is a "special politician, the best of his generation . . . a decent person committed to the idea that he could do good work in public office . . . and a man whose glaring foibles, while exasperating and making him not at all likable, were neither dark nor malignant."[100] Journalist Taylor Branch has noted that his reacquaintance with Bill Clinton had long since restored his belief "in his human decency and his devotion to the world and meaning of his office."[101] Recently, Mike McCurry noted that, "he's got a strong personality and you sense that he's fundamentally a good person, a guy who's capable of enormous things in his personal life. We now know more than we need to know about that. But in his heart he really does care about the American people and about this country, and he probably expected a lot better of himself."[102]

Clinton's chief vulnerability as a politician was that he allowed too many people to see how he made his decisions. He thought out loud, weighed and reweighed various alternatives, and asked too many people for their advice and possibly their approval. For some reason only guessed at in this study, Clinton never seemed to really understand that the American president can only preserve his dignity if he first keeps a zone of privacy around himself.

The Clinton presidency, more generally, should also alert us to the downside of the collapse of the walls between the public and private in a politician's life. Biographers, removed from the partisan controversies of the moment, with access to private letters and diaries, may want to construct an image of the whole man or woman, including his or her sex life. However, probes into the private lives of sitting presidents almost inevitably are used by foes of that president as a form of political warfare. The juicier the details, the more the man can be stripped in public, the greater his loss of authority and influence.[103]

The focus on the sex life of a major political actor also opens the door to the corruption of our political discourse in other ways. If President Clinton is to be questioned as to his sex life, then in all fairness the private lives of other presidential possibles can be examined too.[104] Moreover, the president as an ordinary human being has a right to defend himself. What this means is that the credibility of his accusers can also be addressed. Some observers of the Clinton scandals forgot this elementary fact when they simply chose to believe Paula Jones or Kathleen Willey, or Juanita Broaderick, labeling any attempt to verify or question the credibility of their stories as a misuse of presidential power.[105]

Certainly this kind of inquiry does not provide us with a balanced account of what the man's politically relevant character is. As David Brock, whose charges in the *American Spectator* initially set off the sexual inquiry, stated in an open letter to the president, the whole inquiry did not help us to understand Bill Clinton the president: "Regardless of how the drama plays out, as the first reporter who leered into your sex life, I do know that I didn't learn a damn thing worth knowing about your character. I also know that if we continue down this path, if sexual witch-hunts become the way to win in politics, if they become our politics altogether, we will destroy everyone in public life."[106]

2 Clinton and the Press

KEN BODE

In this essay, Professor Bode examines his early investigative reporting on then-governor Bill Clinton and recounts his experiences with the changing media environments in both local (Arkansas) politics and the national media. He recounts how, particularly in the 1960s and 1970s, the media was not entirely certain how to present press coverage of candidates' personal lives and how this uncertainty changed through the 1980s and 1990s into a "feeding frenzy" of tabloid journalism—often obsessively focused on the sex lives of elected officials. He then examines how the media focused on (and how, in his opinion, the Clinton administration mistakenly encouraged) continual scandals. Ultimately, Professor Bode depicts an environment in which the adversarial, yet dependent, relationship between the president and the press reached a peak of bitter conflict. The substantial changes in technological infrastructure resulting in wide access to cable channels and Internet news sources represents an information age with which no prior presidential administration has been forced to contend. In fact, the Kennedy administration's efforts to conceal the president's ill health and sexual forays, while successful at the time, appear almost juvenile by contemporary stand-ards. The "new media environment" has certainly changed the way the American public learns about its chief executive, and as we find throughout this volume, President Clinton was the first executive to face such a dramatic change in the relationships between the press, the executive office, and the public.

I covered Bill Clinton for all nine years of his presidential campaign and his presidency, first as a senior correspondent and analyst for Cable News Network, later as moderator of *Washington Week in Review* on PBS, a roundtable of working reporters who gather weekly to empty their notebooks. I prepared this chapter partly as a personal memoir, partly as an analysis of what Hollywood once called *A Walk on the Wild Side.*

In late spring 1991, accompanied by three CNN producers, I flew to Little Rock to begin reporting for the network on Bill Clinton's presidential campaign. We had appointments all over Arkansas—no cameras yet, just paper and pencil, shoe-leather reporting—and visits to local television stations to begin assembling biographical footage and coverage of his lengthy governorship. Clinton clearly was going to run, but no announcement was yet scheduled. Our job was to gather information for a number of magazine-length reports for the CNN program *Inside Politics* covering his terms as governor and the preparations for his presidential candidacy. All this reporting would be rolled into an hour-long, preelection documentary should Clinton become the party's nominee.

This is the period often called "The Invisible Primary," those months when the candidates raise money, hone their messages, hire consultants, and watch the polls. It is the time when potential contributors, party professionals, and pundits size up the candidates, measure their bankbooks, watch the polls, and rate their chances.

For full-time political reporters, it is also the "profile period," when we take the time to pull back the covers and find out what makes each potential president tick. Our job, as we saw it, was to answer the question, "Who is this guy and what is his story?" For each potential candidate in 1992, we began by looking for a core, central question: What does the voter need to know to truly understand this man?

For Paul Tsongas, a defining attribute was the fact that he was a cancer survivor. When he was diagnosed with an incurable lymphoma and it seemed clear he was going to die, Tsongas had resigned from the U.S. Senate to spend his remaining days back in Massachusetts with his family. Later, he took a successful gamble on a risky, experimental treatment that had saved his life. Tsongas spoke of "the obligation of my survival."

For Bob Kerrey, we focused on his experience in Vietnam as a combat Navy Seal, a tour of duty that won him a Congressional Medal of Honor but sent him home an amputee, without the lower part of one leg.

For Tom Harkin, our job was to convey the roots of his agrarian populism, his commitment to the poor and the handicapped, along with his uncompromising faith that government had a positive role to play in people's lives.

For Bill Clinton, we began to follow two paths. First, we looked at his relationship to Arkansas as reflected in the story of his life. Born after his natural father had died, Clinton was raised by his working mother and grandparents in a poor town in a poor state. As he was growing up, he watched Arkansas struggle with civil rights, then, filled with promise and ambition, set his course on securing the best education he could get, Georgetown, Oxford, Yale Law.

Clinton had never made a secret of his political ambitions, and with a world of lucrative possibilities before him in the field of corporate law, he was drawn to public service, drawn back to Arkansas, and spent his entire adult life either in elective office or running for it. Hillary Rodham Clinton, also a Yale-educated lawyer and a professional woman, was active and deeply involved in his commitment to public life and a major part of his story. And so was his 1980 loss of the governor's job, a transforming event in Clinton's life.

So, the second question we set out to address in rough form was this: How much better off is Arkansas after ten years with Bill (and Hillary) Clinton in the governor's mansion?

Two months before, as the research phase of this campaign-coverage plan began, CNN's political director Tom Hannon gathered a small group together for a brainstorming session. I was in the room along with syndicated columnist Jack Germond and the *Washington Post's* lead political reporter, David Broder. Never one to bury the lead, Germond asked the very first question: "What are we going to do about Clinton's women?"

Some context is in order. Following his strong second-place showing in the 1984 campaign, Gary Hart was a prohibitive favorite to win the 1988 Democratic nomination, polling over 60 percent against the field in some surveys. However, among the Washington and Colorado political cognoscenti, among his own staff, and among many political reporters, Gary Hart had earned the reputation as a man who seemed to enjoy the company of women who did not share his last name.

"He'll be OK if he can keep his pants on," one of his top political advisors was quoted as saying.[1] Hart dismissed all this with a glancing disdain. "Follow me," he told E. J. Dionne who was preparing a profile for the *New York Times Magazine*. "Follow me. You'll be bored." When *Miami Herald* reporters took up that challenge (on an inside tip) and found Hart had been sharing dinners, weekends, and pleasure cruises to Bimini with a Miami model, the candidate's days were numbered. One week of a media feeding frenzy devoted to Hart's extracurricular sexual adventures and he returned, with wife Lee, to lick his wounds at home in Colorado.[2]

But media critics and the public had not enjoyed the experience of watching Hart "forced out" of the campaign, and the political press had something of a hangover from it as well. Hart had accused the *Miami Herald* reporters of hiding in the bushes, invading his privacy. What if you had held John F. Kennedy to the same standard, we in the press were often asked, do you think he ever would have been president?

As political reporters we were asking ourselves, when it comes to sex and people in public life, what are the boundaries of privacy? Specifically, when is a private, consensual sexual act, albeit extramarital, a newsworthy, reportable event? When is it relevant to the biography of the candidate, how is it relevant to his story, and is there some statute of limitations?

History now records that John F. Kennedy ran a randy White House. The press who covered him—if they knew—did not report it to the public. While his brother, the attorney general, was running the first serious campaign against organized crime at the Justice Department, JFK was in the sheets, sharing a mistress with a Chicago mobster, Sam Giancanna, a notable killer who was himself killed gangland style. And none of this was reported? Go figure. If Kennedy had been president after Watergate, his behavior would have been sensational news.

Still, during the frenzied 1987 Gary Hart episode, many reporters faced ethical dilemmas about privacy and relevance, and they did so on the road, on the run, against deadlines, and against competition. There was no real appetite to tackle the private life of another presidential candidate in 1992. Also there was still no real consensus on what kinds of sexual shenanigans it was proper to report.

Shortly after Hart dropped out in May 1987, rumors circulated that the governor of Arkansas would get into the race. Bill Clinton never made a secret of his ambition to be president one day. It was all a question of timing. With Hart out, there seemed to be a spot in the 1988 field for a young, outside-Washington, progressive-thinking Southerner. Clinton called his friends and advisors to Little Rock for consultation, a gathering that was expected to result in the news that he would soon announce for president. Instead, he took himself out of the race for 1988. The timing was wrong, he said, for his family and especially for his daughter Chelsea.

When his disappointed Washington friends returned home, they shared with reporters a second reason for the decision. Clinton's long-time political aide, a feisty Texan named Betsey Wright, had presented the governor with a list of women who he had bedded as governor, or it was rumored that he had. How do you expect to deal with this, Wright demanded?[3] Unprepared for the eventuality that the list would become the grist of a journalistic feeding frenzy that might destroy the possibility of his ever becoming president, Clinton was convinced to back away. But the fact of the list was indelible political gossip, still around when he flirted more seriously with running in 1992, still fresh in Jack Germond's mind when CNN convened its planning meeting.

No names, just the reputation of a young, handsome governor, ambitious for national office, with an attractive family and a zipper problem. A predicate condition, as they say, something to watch for.

Times have changed since JFK's day. Party leaders no longer quietly and privately vet the candidates for president, determining if they have good minds, salable personalities, acceptable character, winning possibilities. Now, in the era of multiple primaries and heavy media, when voters essentially bypass party leaders and make up their own minds about candidates, the press has the first cut at the plate. We have the responsibility to tell the voters what they need to know about the candidates seeking their party's nominations. Who are these guys and what are their stories? We sort through the details and decide what is important, what the voters need to know.

On our early trips to Arkansas, Jack Germond's question was really not on our agenda. Over the next few weeks, we had appointments all over Arkansas, with party leaders, labor leaders, environmentalists, educators, reporters, columnists, editors, economic development leaders, legislators, lawyers, judges, lobbyists, bankers, Clinton's family, his boyhood friends, his political friends and enemies, those who worked for him and those who worked against him.

We needed to learn how Arkansas worked and who pulled the strings. We found it a densely textured fabric, its politics a series of intricate relationships among politicians and business interests, bankers and regulators, legislators and manipulators.

So far as we knew, however, there was no public record of Clinton having a zipper problem, only rumors. We were there to report on his governorship and his ideas about being president, not his private life and extramarital appetites.

Over the next four months, we assembled reports for CNN's daily *Inside Politics* program on Arkansas under Clinton—civil rights, tax policy, economic development, jobs, wages, working conditions, education reform, the environment. All of this was before Jeff Gerth of the *New York Times* uncovered Jim and Susan McDougal and the infamous Whitewater investment, and none of it involved anything resembling a financial, political, or sexual scandal.

There was one other aspect of Clinton's life that was not touched in the early biographical profiles, that being the dysfunctional nature of his early family life. There was nothing in the archives of Arkansas press coverage about stepfather Roger Clinton's violent drunkenness, nothing about Clinton's teenage confrontation with his stepfather, telling Roger that he would never again lay a hand on his wife, Bill's mother. Clinton's handlers had a hard time getting Clinton to delve into these unpleasant memories, even though they believed it would have a humanizing effect on his image. For Bill, "Going through all that meant trying to pull things back out of the old locked box, and it was exceedingly painful," according to Betsey Wright.[4]

Overall, Clinton's political record was impressive. He was defeated after his first two-year term as governor when the voters and reporters who covered the capitol found him, his aides, and his wife a little too arrogant and indifferent, too impatient and confrontational.

The unexpected loss in 1980 became our fulcrum for understanding Clinton, both as politician and governor. Our theory was that to understand how he would govern should he win the presidency we needed to look at how he had governed over the years in Arkansas. What did he stand for? What would he fight for? How big a gap was there between promises made and goods delivered? Those were the questions of Clinton's leadership.

Bill Clinton sat out two years, and when he came back, most Arkansans agreed, the liberal-populism that characterized his two years as attorney general and first term as governor was gone, both in rhetoric and policy. After the loss in 1980, he took on winnable causes and built bridges to his enemies. The trucking, timber, and poultry industries along with the electric utilities, which were his reformist targets in the first term, soon numbered among his most important contributors and boosters. Clinton could learn, that was clear, his tone was softer, his agenda more narrow. His strongest instinct was for survival.

In the end, his supporters and friends, along with the reporters who covered Bill Clinton's governorship, were generally united in their over-all assessments. They pointed not to what he had accomplished, but what he failed to do, not what he achieved, but to the retreats from his agenda. He never lived up to his potential, they said. On tax policy, eco-nomic development, and the environment, he took the route of least resistance. He was so talented, we were told, he could have accomplished so much more.

On a trip back to Washington, CNN senior producer Richard Cohen and I had lunch with Ron Brown, then chairman of the Democratic Party. Together we ran through the strengths and weaknesses of the prospective Democratic candidates. Friendly to all and neutral, as a chair-man must be, Brown was also candid in his assessments.

Clinton he saved for last. The Arkansas governor, Brown said, had fabulous possibilities. He was a governor with demonstrable executive experience, which carried the added advantage of being from outside Washington. His life story, a kind of bootstrap rise from modest begin-nings, made compelling biography. He had a strong family, counting Hillary and Chelsea as important assets, and was handsome, articulate, and charismatic, with the best political instincts Brown had seen since Robert F. Kennedy.

Also, Clinton had lived through the civil-rights movement in Arkan-sas, had years of experience of campaigning in black churches and a natural resonance with African American voters. He had once been a populist-liberal but was no more. Now, said Brown, Clinton is a southern moderate, with ideas tuned closely to the centrist Democratic Leadership Council. And because he was from the South, Clinton offered the Democrats their best hope of picking up electoral votes in that region along with the border states.

Brown, however, had one reservation. If we nominate Clinton, he said, I'm afraid the Republicans will drop a dozen women on us in October. "They'll take him down and the whole party with him," the chairman cautioned. Ron Brown offered no specifics, but it was an unforgettable assessment.

Returning to Little Rock, we found a similar buzz. Legal papers surfaced from a lawsuit filed a year before by a disgruntled former state employee, Larry Nichols. Nichols named five women who, he claimed, were Clinton's sexual partners and charged that the governor had in some way used the resources of state government to facilitate the affairs or to cover them up.

Court documents are strong protection against libel, but Arkansas journalists assured us out-of-state reporters that every woman on the list had denied the allegation, and some (including Gennifer Flowers, who had a job in Arkansas state government) even produced notarized affidavits. As much out of privacy considerations for the women as for Clinton, the Nichols story remained on ice for many weeks.

Clinton's deputy campaign chair, Betsey Wright, remembers this period as a time when there was an enormous amount of "money on the street." Tabloid newspapers and television programs were looking for a Clinton mistress ready to tell all, and they were ready to pay for the story. It had a "profound impact on the kind of defense mechanisms" put together by the campaign to counter that possibility, said Wright, including, as we later learned, the hiring of private detectives to gather dirt on the ladies. The campaign's policy was to create the equivalent of a nuclear standoff, mutually assured destruction on both sides.[5]

In matters of scandal and gossip, especially about sex, politicians normally are given a general presumption of innocence. In a celebrity culture, the famous and powerful are often the targets of malicious innuendo. Betsey Wright famously described part of her job in the Clinton campaign as managing "bimbo eruptions."

But the rumors were legion in Little Rock, and the sources tended to be not Republicans or Clinton's enemies, but Democrats, often friends, close to Clinton, and worried. "Reporters did not have to ask politicians about Clinton's extramarital activities," *Los Angeles Times* reporter Robert Shogan wrote, "politicians asked *them*."[6]

Finally, I queried a longtime associate of both Bill and Hillary: tell me, I said, how important is this part of the story? Very important, she replied. How many women are we talking about? She rolled her eyes, shook her head and answered, "Oh, maybe two hundred." In conversations like these, which were repeated all over Arkansas, Bill Clinton began to forfeit the presumption of innocence.

In 1991, our reporting included interviews with all the potential Democratic First Ladies. Hillary Rodham Clinton seemed no more attractive, intelligent, or articulate than Niki Tsongas or Ruth Harkin, for example, but she was far more involved, it seemed, than any of the others in her husband's public life.

The local playbook on Hillary included her insistence on retaining her own last name, Rodham, a break with Arkansas tradition that carried unacceptable political baggage and proved costly at the polls in the 1980 defeat. She was a partner in one of the state's most prominent, politically well-connected law firms, and known to be aggressively supportive of her husband's political ambitions. Arkansans told the story of Hillary bursting into a news conference called by one of Bill's gubernatorial opponents and commandeering the event, as a one-woman truth squad.

But the most important story about Hillary was her leadership of Clinton's educational reform program in Arkansas, campaigning county-by-county to put education firmly on the state's policy agenda. There was ample videotape of this crusade, and it was featured prominently in our documentary, *Bill Clinton of Arkansas*. No journalist who studied Hillary's role in that cause doubted her political talent or her effectiveness, nor could be surprised when Clinton later handed over responsibility for healthcare reform to the First Lady.

Our interviews with Bill and Hillary were scheduled for a morning in late December 1991. At the mansion, Christmas decorations were still up, and the family's gifts were laid out on public display. The interview with the governor lasted nearly ninety minutes, all about his five terms as governor, his ideas about the presidency, foreign policy, and the themes he had begun to develop on the campaign trail.

Clinton was at ease and impressive. He defended his record in every specific and parried blame back on the critics who claimed he had accomplished too little during his years as governor. He talked passionately about growing up in segregated Arkansas and had a much fuller grasp of foreign-policy issues than one might have expected. He had not forgotten what he learned at Georgetown and Oxford, along with his days working on Capitol Hill for Arkansas senator J. William Fulbright. No question, Bill Clinton had prepared himself well to run for president.

For the last subject in the interview, I took Ron Brown's concerns and formulated a question. Are you certain, I asked, that there is nothing in your personal life that might prove detrimental to your candidacy and your party if the Republicans used it against you in the fall campaign? Clinton recognized it as a question about his reputation for infidelity and finessed the matter by saying that he and Hillary were committed to each other and there was nothing to worry about. What he was worried about, he said, was that the press would take unsubstantiated allegations and blow them out of proportion.

After the interview, the governor steered me aside for a private word. Obviously concerned, he pointed out that Republicans in Arkansas had offered one woman money to claim she was a Clinton mistress. Then he said, "I thought the Gary Hart rule was in effect." "What is that?" I asked. "If there is nothing going on contemporaneously, it won't be reported," he replied.

There is, as I said, an ongoing debate among reporters and editors about what constitutes an appropriate statute of limitations in reporting the extracurricular liaisons of a presidential candidate. These certainly include some who believe that the line on adultery should be drawn entirely on current conduct. However, I had never heard it called the Gary Hart rule, and in any case the questions about Clinton seem to center on a reckless number of incidents, not only *when* they happened.

"The Gary Hart rule? I don't think you can count on that, Governor," I told him. And our interview was over.

Later that day I received a call from an editor at *Playboy* magazine, Jim Petersen, who wanted my opinion on something: "We have a woman who has done a photo layout for the magazine, and she claims to have had an affair with Bill Clinton. Her name is Elizabeth Ward and she is a former Miss America. You know a lot more about Clinton than I do, could she be telling the truth?"

I don't know, I told Petersen, but you could certainly find a few people in Arkansas who would tell you it's possible.[7]

In this period the polls, financial statements, endorsements, and press coverage seemed to sort the field of Democratic hopefuls into two tiers, with Tom Harkin, Bob Kerrey, and Clinton on the top rung, and Paul Tsongas, Douglas Wilder, and Jerry Brown in the second level. As the date approached for the first primary in New Hampshire, there was a general consensus that the governor of Arkansas was emerging as a strong frontrunner.

Then came the memorable six-week period in which Clinton was bombarded with a trifecta of scandals: sex, drugs, and the draft. This occurred at about exactly the moment that the general public really began to pay attention to the 1992 presidential campaign.

It began with sex. Gennifer Flowers, a former television reporter, lounge singer, teenage beauty queen, and employee of the state government in Arkansas, sold her story of a twelve-year affair with Bill Clinton to the supermarket tabloid, the *Star.* At about the same time, Jerry Nachman, the aggressive editor of the *New York Post,* decided that the decision *not* to publish the Larry Nichols lawsuit amounted to a national press conspiracy to cover up the story, so his paper carried the full details on page one with the headline blaring, *"Wild Bill!"* Clinton characterized the report as "an absolute, total lie" and reminded reporters that Flowers had previously produced an affidavit denying any sexual relations with him.

The *Star* story detailed Gennifer's account of the affair in gaudy detail. In what was to become standard operating procedure in dealing with unwelcome press coverage, Clinton's rapid response team attacked back, calling it "trash for cash" and typical supermarket-tabloid junk reporting. But it was sex, it was lurid, it fit the predicate notions of Clinton's past behavior, and it set off a fierce feeding frenzy in the mainstream media.

Desperate to respond, the campaign sorted through several offers from the television networks to confront the allegations, Bill and Hillary together, if they chose. They picked *60 Minutes,* the most highly rated news show in the country, and that is how many Americans were introduced to Arkansas's first couple.

Following the Super Bowl broadcast on CBS, just three weeks before the New Hampshire primary, Bill and Hillary Clinton appeared on a special edition of *60 Minutes* with an audience of some forty million viewers. Clinton once again denied Flowers's charges, admitted his marriage had not been perfect, and said he and Hillary were committed to each other for the long run. He made no specific reference to infidelity but said, "I think that most Americans who are watching this tonight, they'll know what we're saying, they'll get it." Hillary added, "If that's not enough for people, then, heck, don't vote for him."

The *60 Minutes* appearance was a classic "defining moment" in American politics, destined to take its place with the George Bush–Dan Rather contretemps over Iran-Contra and Lloyd Bentsen's barb to Dan Quayle that, "You're no John F. Kennedy." It was unforgettable television. Watching that night, I thought that what Americans "got" from the Clintons, Bill in particular, was that there had been some infidelity in the past, but that Hillary had clearly forgiven him. Also, it was in the past and *would not be happening again.* That was the deal Bill Clinton was offering the country.

The next day, Gennifer Flowers held her famous rebuttal press conference at the Waldorf-Astoria ballroom in Manhattan. Flanked by huge blow-ups of the *Star* cover, she played tapes, which, she said, were recordings of conversations with Governor Clinton. CNN carried the event live but did not play the unauthenticated tapes. Clinton refused comment, saying he had not heard the tapes.

That night, Gennifer topped every network evening-news broadcast.

Most Americans never have heard the Flowers tapes because the only place they ever were broadcast in their entirety was on C-SPAN at midnight. For those who did hear the tapes, however, in newsrooms all over America, the voice was unmistakably Bill Clinton's. And they heard him coaching Gennifer on how to handle the coverup of their affair: "If they ever hit you with it, just say no and go on . . . if everybody is on record denying it, no problem."

What fueled the adultery issue, even after *60 Minutes*, was the fact that Gennifer Flowers had a job with the state government in Arkansas, as Larry Nichols originally had attested. Betsey Wright and other Clinton loyalists believed that this was nothing more than a convenient wedge to keep the story alive,[8] but most reporters believe that if an elected official has a mistress tucked away on the state payroll, it's legitimate to let the public know.[9] Moreover, we soon had copies of Gennifer's resume and test scores from the Arkansas Employment Security Administration, which showed she ranked below several other applicants for the job she held. Notwithstanding Clinton's denials, the pieces of the story were pretty damning.

What got Clinton out of the mess over sex was the mess over the draft. This time it was reported by the *Wall Street Journal*'s Jeffrey Birnbaum, and thus it was more difficult to impugn the source. Clinton had squiggled out of serving in the military (and possibly Vietnam) through a convoluted series of moves that involved intentionally misleading his draft board and Col. Eugene Holmes, who headed the National Guard unit in Arkansas. This was a generational test, and Clinton's insistence that he was ready to serve, if called, did not stack up well against the actual record of his dipping and dodging on induction.

While most of his presidential competitors stayed clear of commenting on Gennifer Flowers, the draft evasion was a different matter. Bob Kerrey, the bona fide Vietnam hero in the field, predicted (on the draft) that if Clinton were the nominee, the Republicans "would open him like a soft peanut in November."

Clinton's dissembling on tough questions, one of the things that earned him the appellation "Slick Willie" in Arkansas, entered his cosmos as a character trait in this period. For much of the final weeks leading up to the February 18 New Hampshire primary his campaign was enveloped in a frenzy of largely negative, mostly tabloid coverage.

In this period, Clinton's handlers hit upon a tactic in dealing with the media that they followed throughout the balance of the campaign and on into the White House. Convinced that the political press would be unrelenting on the matters of sex, drugs, and the draft, the campaign team took a leaf from the playbook of John F. Kennedy. "I always said that when we don't have to go through you bastards, we can really get our story out to the American people," JFK once told his friend Ben Bradlee.[10] So Clinton was booked at events that involved only New Hampshire voters, who, the campaign believed, would be less interested in the pestering questions of the national press.

This may have been the period in which James Carville hit upon the slogan, "It's the Economy, Stupid." In January 1992, New Hampshire was mired in one of the worst recessions in recent memory. Five of the state's seven major banks had failed, and home values had decreased 30 percent in the previous two years. Factories had closed, and white-collar unemployment was so severe that empty storefronts in Manchester were being used as places for laid-off workers to network and build their resumes. Facing dire economic circumstances, voters were less interested in Gennifer Flowers than they were in what Clinton had to say about the economy, jobs, and his middle-class tax cut.

The campaign bought a half-hour of television time, surrounded the candidate with New Hampshire Democrats, and let them fire questions at Clinton. Only one voter asked about the scandals, and she was booed.

Our current front-loaded nomination system was designed by America's political parties to produce an early nominee. Each succeeding Tuesday following New Hampshire, the primaries come in a swarm. In 1992, coverage of the Clinton scandals soon gave way to coverage of primary winners and losers. With his second-place finish in the Granite State, Clinton had proved he could take a punch, that he was no quitter. Then, debates between the remaining candidates began to generate interest. There were stories about money drying up in some campaigns and candidates dropping out. The exit polls provided grist for analysis of which issues were finding traction, what the voters really cared about. In other words, there was real news to cover, and the scandals took a back seat.

By early April, when the campaigns moved to New York, Clinton was reinstalled as the clear frontrunner in terms of delegates and primaries won. However, the bruising early coverage left voters with deep misgivings. New York exit polls showed that over 60 percent of the voters thought that the Arkansas governor did not have the honesty and integrity to be president. That too was a story. Following his victories in New York, Kansas, and

Wisconsin, *Time* magazine put Clinton on the cover. The cover photo was a glaring reverse negative, a close-up of Clinton's face, with the accompanying caption "Why Voters Don't Trust Clinton."

Watching the Democrats Tsongas, Clinton, and Brown pound on through the primary schedule, operatives in the Bush campaign decided, in the words of Mary Matalin, that Clinton probably was the guy, but he was pretty much damaged goods.[11]

The Clinton strategists also recognized that they had to reframe their candidate, restart a conversation with the American people, and their solution to this problem had two tracks. First, they needed to shift the public's attention away from Clinton's foibles and back to his biography. Voters, they learned from their own polling, knew very little about Clinton's poor-boy-makes-good life in Arkansas before the elite institutions of Georgetown, Oxford, and Yale. They also knew so little about Clinton's current family circumstances that a significant proportion did not even know Chelsea existed.

The second track was to choose their method of communicating this message. They decided to continue to avoid traditional venues of established news, choosing instead what they called the "popular culture shows." They did the Don Imus radio show, the Arsenio Hall late night television show, *Larry King Live,* and a ninety-minute *Rock the Vote* program on MTV.

Clinton's pollster Stan Greenberg said, "On the popular culture talk shows, you go directly to people, but more importantly it was a format in which you could talk about biography, you could talk about your life, which you didn't get the opportunity to do on *Face the Nation.*"[12]

The epitome of this effort came in a movie, a Hollywood-quality biopic, *The Man From Hope,* produced for prime-time viewing at the Democratic National Convention by Clinton's Hollywood friends Harry and Linda Bloodworth-Thomason.[13] Horatio Alger was never handled with kinder kid gloves.

The campaign strategists were right: biography is very important to Americans, especially in their choice for president. Bill and Hillary Clinton finally figured out how to get the story out in their own terms.

From the convention to the bus trip to the televised candidate debates, the Clinton-Gore team enjoyed generally positive coverage throughout the fall campaign, and, as election day neared and independent candidate Ross Perot slipped, they were buoyed as the major beneficiaries of a public that genuinely believed that the country was on the wrong track.

Honeymoons begin on election night. Everyone steps back, takes a breath, examines the consequences of the voters' decisions, and prepares to cover the assembling of a new administration. Again, it is a period of real news, as the press prepares to introduce to America the cabinet officials who are going to govern the country for the next four years.

But as the transition team gathered in Little Rock, there was a sense in the press of a residual resentment among the Clintonites, including Bill and Hillary, for the rough treatment they had received during the early primaries. The Bloodworth-Thomason, Arkansas-Hollywood pals edited a get-even video for viewing at the inaugural parties that showed a series of famous commentators and pundits spouting their opinions on talk shows during the darkest days of the primary campaign. A sampling:

"Clinton is not electable."

"Clinton will have to get out of the race."

"Bill Clinton is a loser."

"He's dead meat."

"Bush will clobber him."

After about four minutes of this, Bill and Hillary appear laughing and holding hands, with strains of Frank Sinatra singing, "Who's Got the Last Laugh Now?" It is actually a very funny, well-produced video, but rolled out when it was, there was an underlying sense of a thumb in the eye of the press. Jeffrey Birnbaum, White House reporter for the *Wall Street Journal*, wrote, "Probably not since Richard Nixon has a president come into office with so much antagonism toward the media."[14]

For the pre-inaugural period, the Clintons stayed camped in Arkansas while potential cabinet appointees trekked to meetings at the governor's mansion in Little Rock. And there quickly began a series of missteps that made the honeymoon period nasty, brutish, and short. Clinton did not get a honeymoon, he got an autopsy, opined the *Washington Post*.[15]

Little daily news was generated from Little Rock, and that which was involved a series of missteps. First, Clinton promised to honor an obscure campaign pledge to get gays into the military, an event which put the draft-dodging president-elect at odds with the top brass of the armed forces and which he later said was the biggest mistake of his first term. Then came the Nannygate contretemps, leading to the withdrawal of his first two choices for attorney general.

Clinton's old friend Lani Guinier was appointed to head the civil rights division of the Justice Department, a certain sign that the indifference to voting-rights enforcement of the Reagan-Bush years was over, but when her published legal theories were criticized, Guinier was quickly jettisoned.

By the time the Clintons actually moved to Washington, where the new president promised in his inaugural address to run the most ethical administration in history, relations with the White House press corps were already in a state of mutual acrimony. Whitewater, a scandal that should have been shut down during the primary period, followed them to Washington. Hillary and Bill made it clear they felt they were being mistreated by the press assigned to cover them. George Stephanopoulos, the new communications director, closed the door to his office, and there was talk of moving the entire press corps out of the White House across the street to the Old Executive Office Building.

In the very early days, Ann Devroy, the veteran White House reporter for the *Washington Post,* called the administration the "most operationally dysfunctional" that she had ever covered.[16] A few months later, her colleague, Ruth Marcus, published an extraordinary Sunday news analysis entitled "The White House Isn't Telling Us the Truth."[17]

Looking back on the opening days of the administration, it is hard to avoid the judgment that the Washington press corps was very hard on Clinton. On the second Sunday of the new administration, Sam Donaldson was on ABC's *This Week With David Brinkley* saying, "This week we can talk about, 'is the presidency over?'" The *Los Angeles Times* media critic David Shaw, who writes perceptively about the culture of news coverage, blamed it on an increasingly confrontational, increasingly competitive news media. Shaw concluded: "The media battered Lyndon B. Johnson over Vietnam and savaged Richard Nixon over Watergate, but perhaps never in the nation's history has a president so early in his term been subjected to a greater barrage of negative media coverage than Bill Clinton endured in his first months in office."[18]

The administration's response tended to exacerbate the problem. Jeff Eller, a media-savvy Hoosier, was deputized to institutionalize the old campaign strategy of going around the bastards. Eller found ways to favor local reporters from outside Washington, television and print, who flew in for favored interviews with the president and vice president. He arranged for Clinton appearances on radio talk shows by telephone from the Oval Office. Eller brought dozens of these talk-show hosts to the White House lawn and made administration officials available for interviews, many of whom were notoriously unavailable to regular White House reporters. *Larry King Live,* the home of softball questions, became a favored venue.

Then, from the podium of a black-tie White House correspondent's dinner, the president himself announced the new strategy, saying, in effect, I really don't need you, "I have Larry King." Sitting at King's table that night, a CNN producer remarked, "Larry was preening so hard I thought he would peck his head off."

Lyndon Johnson once complained, "The press will chase you like a bitch dog in heat and if you ever stop running, they'll slip it to you."

No, Bill Clinton was not the first chief executive who complained about his treatment by the press. Calvin Coolidge once suggested that every president ought to have the right to shoot two reporters each year, without cause.

But Clinton did complain. Dick Morris, his longtime friend and aide from his days as governor in Arkansas, said Clinton simply hates the press: "He is contemptuous of reporters. He feels they're a sleazy group of people who lie a lot, who pursue their own agendas, who have a pack mentality. He feels they are a necessary evil."[19]

And if Bill detested reporters, any time he seemed to be going soft, Hillary could be counted on the buck up his resolve. His aides often related how the First Lady complicated their efforts to get Whitewater information out, for example, because her general view was that it was no one's business but her own; thus her preference was to stonewall.

As press secretary, Mike McCurry ran an entirely professional communications operation. Occasionally McCurry got rough with reporters who, he felt, had been needlessly harsh on the president, but reporters who covered the White House as a permanent beat, as well as those who worked the Sunday morning and other serious talk shows, were always well briefed in instances of foreign crises or new policy initiatives. Occasionally, McCurry could persuade Clinton to call in selected reporters for iced tea, cookies, and informal conversation. However, the administration was so often engaged in damage control that these discussions could not be held to the presidential agenda, and so they happened only infrequently.

For the entire course of his administration, President Clinton considered his new hometown newspaper, the *Washington Post,* to be dedicated to his undoing. The *Wall Street Journal,* he knew, was ground zero of the enemy camp, especially its unrelentingly negative editorial page. And, finally, following his usual tendency to personalize his differences with the press, he felt similarly estranged from the *New York Times* editorial-page editor, Howell Raines, a fellow southerner, who, he felt, resented Clinton's success.

Imagine waking each morning with the certain knowledge (true or not) that the three newspapers with the largest following in the nation's capitol were arrayed against you. In fact, all three editorialized in favor of Clinton's resignation during the height of the Lewinsky scandal, though the *Post* and *Times* did not favor impeachment. At one point, both the President and Mrs. Clinton claimed they gave up reading the daily press, though the president always seemed to keep track of reporters who, he believed, were treating him unfairly.[20]

In retrospect it's possible to conclude that the tenor of Bill and Hillary Clinton's relations with the press was set in the worst days of the primary period. Neither side ever reestablished the trust and confidence necessary to carry on business in a truly healthy atmosphere in a twenty-four-hour-a-day news cycle lasting eight full years.

There are two books devoted to analyzing Clinton and the press during the White House period. In *Spin Cycle: Inside the Clinton Propaganda Machine,* Howard Kurtz, the media critic for the *Washington Post,* exhibiting exceptional access both to White House reporters and to the main players inside the White House press operation, describes the relationship from both points of view.

The second book, written by Lanny Davis, special counsel to the president, *Truth to Tell: Notes from My White House Education,* is an insider view of the administration's news-management tactics during the scandal period. Davis, a lawyer who knew both Clintons since their law-school days together at Yale, was deputized to handle damage control, leaving Mike McCurry free to keep the public focus on the president's agenda. Though Davis left the White House shortly after the mega-scandal (Monica Lewinsky) broke, *Truth to Tell* relates how the Clinton team added new dimensions of throw-weights to the tactics of leaking, spinning, rapid response, and damage control.

Despite the president's inaugural promise to run an ethical administration, in Clinton's entire tenure in the White House, no day in the eight years was ever free of scandal. Whitewater followed him into the White House, morphed into Troopergate, then Paula Jones and finally Monica Lewinsky. In between came Travelgate, the president's haircut, Hillary's commodity trades, the case of the missing documents (called Filegate), the Vince Foster suicide, the Lincoln bedroom, the White House coffees, and the efforts of both Clinton and Gore to raise campaign money from foreign sources. Following Clinton out of the White House were the 177 midnight pardons, including one for the noted fugitive Marc Rich, who remained on the FBI's most wanted list even as the president issued his reprieve. Some of these matters were trivial and transitory; others metastasized into impeachment.

Larry Speakes, press secretary in the Reagan White House, kept a sign on his desk, which read, "You don't tell us how to stage the news and we won't tell you how to cover it." Clinton's last press secretary, Joe Lockhart, put it another way: "The press has its agenda and we have ours and every day it's war."[21]

It has been estimated that Clinton's top aides, many not in the communications division, spent as much as half their time on any given day dealing with the press. Most of this was finding ways to get positive coverage for presidential initiatives, but plenty of hours were devoted to knocking down scandal stories, spinning, and leaking, using every possible tactic to put a positive spin on administration policy and control damage from the other side.

Throughout the scandal coverage, the press was criticized for using leaks and unnamed sources, and Ken Starr's office was lambasted for leaking confidential information. The charges were certainly true, but a couple of caveats are necessary: First, the administration leaked back on the same terms, background, off-the-record, don't use my name. In fact, the Clinton White House leaked so profusely that the president made a rule never to say anything sensitive in a room with more than one aide. He thought he might as well just give it to the AP. In other words, the White House aides denouncing the unnamed sources were often themselves the designated leakers for the home team.

It also should be noted that in the newsrooms of all but the most tabloid publications, a reporter's unnamed sources are scrutinized and verified before the information is used. Editors and executive producers in major newspapers and networks insist that reporters taking information with the promise of anonymity share the names of those confidential sources, how they are in a position to know the information they proffer, and what political stakes they have in the game. Confidential sources remain confidential in the newsroom, but they are checked. In other words, when Jackie Judd of ABC News (correctly) reported the existence of Monica's stained blue dress, *World News Tonight* producers surely knew how Judd came by the information.

That said, there were changes in the news culture in America commensurate with the Clinton years, which guaranteed that the scandals, especially those involving sex, would be ratcheted into the media stratosphere. And Clinton himself had something to do with it.

The '90s dawned the era of celebrity, a period so sodden with the value of being famous that it seemed perfectly natural to the president of the United States to go on MTV and talk with a teenage girl about his choice of underwear. By using Oprah, Donahue, Larry King, and Don Imus to get around the working reporters in the White House pressroom, by advertising his affinity for friends from Hollywood, Bill Clinton made himself America's First Celebrity. It was no accident that his nickname was Elvis, and as Walter Kirn put it, the president himself helped to create a fusion of show business and constitutional democracy, a Hollywood-Washington nexus of the '90s.[22]

As president, Clinton was no longer personally available to wear wraparound shades and play his sax on stage, but his foibles became constant fodder for Leno, Letterman, and every other entertainment venue from *Politically Incorrect* to Comedy Central. Bill Clinton went through the entire 1996 presidential campaign without holding a single press conference. At the same time, pollsters were reporting that ever-increasing segments of new voters, those eighteen to twenty-nine, were getting their information about the presidential election from late-night comedy shows.

Then, too, the Clinton presidency coincided with an explosion of new media sources that completely transformed the culture of news and information. Lyndon Johnson and Richard Nixon may have been pilloried by the press, but the media of their day was staid by comparison. There was no CNN, MSNBC, or Fox News Channel, and the supermarket tabloids had not yet discovered the fusion of politics and sex.

Beginning in the early eighties, network news shows lost 40 percent of their viewers and newspapers a similar proportion of their readers. This lost audience seems to have found a home in the more freewheeling, round-the-clock world of cable television. Celebrity, scandal, money, sex, and death are what draw audiences to cable, as the long-running O. J. Simpson trial and the death of Princess Diana proved. But the Clinton scandals, particularly those involving sex, were like chum on the waters for cable television. They literally created a new industry.

Shows like *Geraldo, Crossfire, The McLaughlin Group,* and *Hardball* were stocked with opinionated talking heads in an atmosphere where instant judgment, pugnacious opinion, and shrill verbal combat were the stock in trade. The sharper the differences, the louder the voices, the more polarized the dialogue, the greater the audience appeal. In this sound and fury, there was an army of anti-Clinton talking heads and a counter force provided by the White House of pro-Clinton spinners. Truth and objective reality, once the goals of mainstream journalism, were lost in the heat of tendentious argument.[23]

Add to this the intervention of the Internet, which came of age during the Clinton era and rapidly became the black hole of manipulation and misinformation in all matters involving Monica. The Clinton scandals and the commensurate media explosion were an almost perfect symbiosis, and at a time when Americans seemed more inclined to be entertained than informed, they constituted a terrific challenge for mainstream journalism. Many would argue that this was a challenge that journalism lost.

> There ought to be an arch over Memorial Bridge just before the Lincoln Memorial that every politician has to pass under before being sworn in or inaugurated. On the arch would be the slogan, "The Cover-up is worse than the Crime."

So what are the lessons we might learn from the eight-year-long walk on the wild side with Bill Clinton and the press?

First, actually being *in* the White House seriously ratchets up the stakes on all sides. There is no person on earth more prominently or intensively covered on a minute-by-minute basis than the president of the United States. Every initiative becomes a headline, every misstep is magnified. Had Bill and Hillary made a clean breast of the Whitewater investment during the primaries when the *New York Times* first carried the story—documents, records, explanations, everything—they might have closed the books on that matter before arriving at the White House. The president might have avoided his first congressional investigation and special counsel, not to mention the years of intensive and skeptical press scrutiny that followed. The more you hunker down and cover up, the more certain the press becomes that you have something to hide.

Second, as Joe Louis once said, "You can run, but you can't hide." In Clinton's case, there were too many overly ambitious investigative reporters, too many political enemies, too many skeptical members of Congress, and an independent counsel all asking the same question: "Where are the Whitewater documents?" When the White House stonewalled the press about the roll call of the Lincoln bedroom visits, reporters simply got the usher's logs from a congressional-committee source. Lanny Davis, the chief Clinton White House scandal spinner, had a rule: "Tell the truth. Tell it early. Tell it all. Tell it yourself. And if it's bad, tell it sooner." It was a rule the administration unfortunately honored most often in the breach.

Also, no matter what language you use, the press will figure it out. Clinton was famous for his lawyer-like splitting of hairs. Never broke the laws of my state. Didn't inhale. Never had sex with that woman. Depends on what you think the meaning of "is" is. Over time, his habits crept into the lexicon of his official spinners. The fictional pretense for the White House coffees held that they were not fundraisers, they were "donor maintenance." The Clinton spinners took linguistic caginess to new depths of meaning and contributed to an ever-escalating atmosphere of mistrust.

Finally, there is the matter of the future privacy rights of public figures. What have we learned from the Clinton years? When will it be considered proper, relevant, and necessary to report on extramarital affairs of presidential candidates? When we look at history, it is clear there has been an evolving standard in this matter, a complete swing of the pendulum from Roosevelt through Eisenhower to Kennedy, then on to Gary Hart, Bill Clinton, and even Robert Dole.

Told briefly, the Dole story is instructive. As the 1996 Republican nominee, Bob Dole ran a campaign contrasting his own character with that of the incumbent president. During the autumn of 1996, late in the general-election campaign, several news organizations, including the *Washington Post* and CNN, had verifiable evidence that Senator Dole had had a fairly long-running affair twenty-five years before, during his first marriage. Leonard Downie, executive editor of the *Post,* once had argued, "For presidential candidates . . . the American people should know everything about a man's private life."[24]

But among the newspaper's talented, high-profile staff some expressed doubt about whether events, so long before, were "relevant," and whether dusting off the tale so close to election day would unduly affect the outcome. Others at the newspaper argued the story should be published because the facts were known and because Dole had been promoting character as a prominent point of difference between himself and Clinton.

Ultimately, the "relevance" argument prevailed. The executive editor, Downie, changed his mind and the *Post* sat on the story. A week later, a supermarket tabloid, the *National Enquirer,* published the story, got the facts right, and injected the issue into the final days of the campaign. Once published, the story was, of course, picked up in the mainstream press. However, it did not dominate the coverage, and there is no indication that it materially affected the outcome on election day. In other words, American voters reelected Clinton, but by no means based on Dole's decades-old affair.[25]

By contrast, Monica Lewinsky was both contemporaneous, and the events took place inside the White House. There was no debate about relevance or whether it should be reported. Nor was there any doubt that the story would achieve stratospheric coverage.

The networks devoted more air time to the Lewinsky soap opera in a single week than they had given to all the Clinton scandals, from Gennifer Flowers to campaign-fundraising abuses, combined.[26] At its essence, the affair with the intern confirmed the predicate assumption that the president was a reckless womanizer. Like the Paula Jones case, the Lewinsky affair found its way into the precinct of the punctilious and combative independent counsel Ken Starr, then to the impeachment process in the Congress, and the rest is history.

For once, Clinton was undeniably right: he faced the most intensive scrutiny, the most negative, judgmental press of any president, ever. And it could not be said that the public was out of sync with the coverage. As Howard Kurtz put it, "The Monica Lewinsky mess was a gripping train wreck of a story, racing down the tracks of real-time television, the seeming self-destruction of a president who only days earlier had been riding so high."[27]

It was a brutal time for journalism and for Bill Clinton. No one could argue that the public didn't know enough about what transpired in the Oval Office between the president and his intern. But, in the end, a satiated public, enjoying the longest period of post-war economic prosperity on record, clearly did not want Clinton to resign, to be impeached, to be forced from office.

Salacious as the story was, the press pursued it punishingly, and there was never an argument about relevance. In fact, the First Amendment, which protects press freedom, implies nothing about reporters and editors deciding whether the American public can handle the facts or whether they are outside the bounds of what the public needs to know. If the information is true, the objective duty of good journalism is to put it out to the public and let the readers and viewers decide. As the story of Dole's mistress indicates, in the current media environment, dithering in the mainstream press will only lead to publication in a lesser venue.

And, in the Lewinsky case, the public did decide. In the end, there seemed to be a general understanding that the American electorate knew what it was getting when it elected Bill Clinton in 1992, a man of imperfect character and morals. And, yes, he did violate a compact he had made implicitly with his wife at his side on *60 Minutes*. So, that, too, proved to be a Faustian bargain. All Clinton had really done was to honor the Eleventh Commandment: *If you can commit adultery, you can lie about it.* But where things really mattered, the booming economy in particular, the citizens wanted to take no chances. They would risk no disruption. They heard all the needed to hear, knew all they needed to know, and they wanted Bill Clinton to finish his term.

The axiom, "Tell the truth, tell it all," applies equally to the press. In all matters, including those of personal character, the truth eventually will come out. For politicians, covering it up only exacerbates the eventual consequences. For the press it carries the risk of eventually following the lead of those who practice the lowest standards of our profession. Lay out the facts, all of them that can be proved, and let the voters determine the matter of relevance. They are pretty good at it.

So, perhaps, the most enduringly simple lesson of the Clinton era is that no president better ever try what Bill Clinton did during a recession.

3 Assessing the Clinton Presidency

The Political Constraints of Legislative Policy

DAVID BRADY

D. SUNSHINE HILLYGUS

In this essay, Professors Brady and Hillygus present their intriguing theory of how presidents find success or failure for their desired policies in Congress, based on minor changes in the ideological composition of the Senate and House. Following the midterm elections of 1994, the Republican Party gained control of the Congress for the first time in decades, and President Clinton was forced to alter his legislative strategy. President Clinton faced divided government after just two years of gaining the presidency. Not only did he face a Congress controlled by the opposition party, but he also confronted a party that believed that it was elected to enact a mandate embodied in its Contract with America. In this essay, Brady and Hillygus present a theory of presidential success in Congress where the key is the ideological position of specific legislators relative to the ideological placement of the president. They argue that, depending on the ideological positions of individual senators, the president may find substantial changes in legislative success or even gridlock. They then specifically evaluate the legislative success of President Clinton across various policy areas. Ultimately, they conclude that "given the constraints—and the

Republican leadership's policy preference, Clinton's policies did very well."
This conclusion hints, again, at the recurring theme of limited success given
the singular context of political constraints that characterized the Clinton
administration.

E valuating a president is a difficult task. The difficulty stems, in part,
from the ambiguity of an American president's job description and
the complexity of presidential duties. As scholars have long noted, presidents must play a number of important roles—manager, politician, party
leader, military and foreign-affairs leader, chief executive and head of
state, just to name a few. There are also a number of different perspectives from which to evaluate a president. The answer to the question
"What makes a president great?" undoubtedly depends on whom you
ask. A psychologist might point to the importance of presidential personality, a historian might identify political accomplishments as the critical criterion, and a journalist might suggest that greatness ultimately
depends on public approval.[1] Each of these approaches provides a different, though valuable, glimpse into the presidency. What can political scientists contribute?

Political scientists typically focus on the president in his myriad roles
and assess his power vis-à-vis the bureaucracy, the military, the public,
and so on. Classic presidential research in political science has offered
systematic qualitative analyses of the various facets of the presidency,[2]
while some political-science research has focused on more quantitative
analyses of presidential policy making.[3] The research of political scientists contrasts with that of presidential biographers, who typically focus
on the person and the things that make him tick. Biographers enhance
our understanding in part because they are willing to make value judgments.[4] David McCullough's recent study of John Adams, for instance,
uses Thomas Jefferson as a counter antagonist to show Adams's superiority
—an interesting work, but one that is value laden.[5] Political scientists'
research, on the other hand, tries to be free of value judgments, which
limits to some extent the richness of the story that we can tell. Political-
science evaluations of presidents are expected to offer a set of criteria by
which any president can be judged.

Despite the differences in various approaches, there are also a number of similarities in any study of the presidency. For one, all scholars are
limited in their scope of analysis. Presidential studies typically focus on
the single person elected president, yet there are actually thousands of

people serving in the executive office of the president, each contributing to presidential actions. It is also impossible to cover the "entire presidency" in a single study. It is necessary to choose the particular aspect of the presidency on which to focus in order to make a contribution. In this paper, we focus on legislative policy successes. Recent political-science research has shown that executive orders and other unilateral actions can have significant policy consequences, but we examine only the president's interaction with the U.S. Congress.[6]

In evaluating the policy record of the Clinton presidency, we consider the institutional constraints within which he had to work. We employ a simple theoretical model in which the president and the Congress (through median and pivotal actors) strategically interact over policy outputs, and we show that the American political system in large part determined Clinton's potential policy output. By analyzing in this way, rather than focusing on personality, management style, or even political parties, we are able to estimate Clinton's likelihood of passing particular policy proposals based on objective criteria—(1) the preferences of members of Congress regarding particular policies and (2) supermajority institutions, the Senate filibuster and the presidential veto.

In this paper, we briefly explain the theoretical model and then apply the model to Clinton's first term. Specifically, we compare the budget battles in the 103rd and 104th Congresses to illustrate how institutional constraints changed and their effect on potential policy output. We then consider Clinton's overall policy record within this context.

The Model

In evaluating the policy successes of the Clinton presidency, we take into consideration the changing institutional constraints within which President Clinton had to work during his presidential term. The president is just one of several actors that determine American legislative policy. We utilize a theoretical model that allows us to predict legislative output based on the preference orderings of President Clinton, the Senate, and the House. Once we have identified the expected policy outcomes at different stages in Clinton's presidency, we are then in a position to evaluate his policy successes relative to the constraints of the American political system. We argue that the constraints caused by legislator positions and supermajority institutions largely account for both the failure of Clinton's policy proposals in the 103rd Congress and for his subsequent successes.

The theoretical model we employ has been well developed both formally and empirically in political-science literature, so herein we will outline only the basics of the model.[7] The U.S. Constitution establishes that the president, the Senate, and the House of Representatives each have a hand in American policymaking. We assume that individuals in these institutions each have preferences over policy. For any given issue (for example, welfare, environmental policy, budget spending), we assume that, based on their preferences, the institutional actors can be located along a liberal-conservative dimension (that is, a one-dimensional spatial model). We expect, for instance, that when the Senate considers a bill about gun control, the preferences of Democratic Senator Ted Kennedy (Mass.) place him on the liberal or left side of the policy preference dimension, while the preferences of Republican Senator Jesse Helms (N.C.) locate him on the conservative or right side of the dimension. Typically, the status quo policy is located somewhere near the middle of these preferences, neither as liberal as many Democrats would prefer nor as conservative as Republicans might wish.

By comparing the position of the policy status quo point with the preferences of the legislators and the president, we are able to estimate the location on the preference dimension where a proposed bill needs to be located in order to be made into law. In other words, we can identify which individual actors must support a bill for it to pass, so we can deduce how liberal or conservative a bill must be for those actors to support it. Specifically, the Senate filibuster and the presidential veto are the key institutional constraints that must be considered in the policy-making process. If a new presidential initiative is to pass, it must obtain a majority in the Congress and not be killed by a filibuster or a veto. A filibuster will successfully block legislation in the Senate unless three-fifths of Senators are able to invoke cloture. With no vacancies, this means that just forty-one Senators are able to block legislation. Similarly, a presidential veto is able to block legislation from becoming law unless Congress can override the veto with a two-thirds majority in each house—so just thirty-four senators are necessary to sustain a presidential veto. In sum, it is not enough to know the majority party in Congress—in order to predict policy outcomes, it is necessary to take into account the preferences of the individual legislators and these supermajority constraints.

Figure 1 helps to illustrate the general characteristics of the model. The range from F_L to F_R represents the central twenty members of the Senate, with M being the median member. The forty-one senators to the left of and including F_L could filibuster a bill. Likewise, F_R and the forty senators to the right could also filibuster successfully, so no policy movement will occur if the status quo (Q) on an issue is between F_L and F_R. This gridlock region shown in figure 1 is even larger when we also consider the role of the presidential veto. If the president prefers a conservative policy, then the gridlock region extends further to the right; vice-versa if the president prefers a more liberal policy. If the status quo (Q) is conservative and Congress passes a bill to move policy left, the president vetoes the legislation (because he prefers the status quo to the new policy). The president needs only thirty-four votes to sustain his veto rather than the forty-one necessary for a successful filibuster.

Figure 1: Policy Constraints Caused by Senate Filibuster

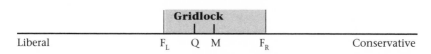

Figure 2 shows the extended gridlock region for the example given above—a conservative president facing a Congress wishing to move policy leftward. In this case, the gridlock region stretches from the forty-first senator to the sixty-seventh. With a liberal president holding veto power, this region stretches to the left, from the thirty-fourth Senator to the sixtieth. If the present policy is in this region, then it cannot be moved because movement to the left or right will be prevented by successful filibusters or vetoes as indicated by F_L and V in figure 2.

Figure 2: Full Gridlock Region

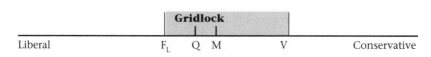

The gridlock regions shown in figures 1 and 2 are important with respect to policy action as well as inaction. Figure 3 shows the policy region for the Senate with a liberal president stretching from the filibuster pivot (F) to the veto point (V). The senator at F is the filibuster pivot. If the status quo policy (Q) is to the left, that senator pairs with forty senators to her right to block any policy change. If the policy (Q) is to the right, then policy change can occur as long as the shift is in her interest. The veto pivot (V) holds similar powers. In figure 3, the point Q represents the policy status quo that is outside the gridlock region. Here the Senate can make policy changes, but that policy change is again constrained by the threat of a filibuster. If the Senate proposes a bill to the left of Q', the bill would surely be filibustered. The senator at F and the forty senators to the right would all be disadvantaged by a bill at F because it is further from their ideal point than Q. A proposal to shift policy to Q' results in F being indifferent between the status quo and the new proposal, and such a policy could be passed. Thus the shaded region from Q to Q' is the region of possible policy change. In actuality, the region between F and Q' is the real change because all movement from Q to F is advantageous to F and only as Q shifts too far left is a filibuster considered. Exactly where between F and Q' the policy ends up is subject to agenda setting, bargaining, political context, and so on.

As with any theoretical model, it is necessarily a simplification of reality. This model assumes, for instance, that the status quo and alternative proposals are easily located on a policy dimension. In reality, we know that there is considerable uncertainty involved in policymaking. In particular, there is uncertainty over the policy results of passing a bill, and there is uncertainty over constituent reactions to voting for or against a bill. This uncertainty can contribute to inaction or action on the part of legislators. Some of these uncertainties are resolved within the legislative process, with proposed legislation changing to reduce uncertainty among key members in order to obtain a majority.[8] For instance, a legislator's uncertainty about the policy preferences of his constituents might cause him to negotiate a "safer" policy. To the extent that these uncertainties are resolved, the model fairly accurately predicts policy outputs.

In sum, if the status quo is in the gridlock region with large numbers of members on either side, policy change will be thwarted by filibusters and/or vetoes. If the status quo is outside the region, as in figure 3, policy will change but not as much as those pushing change would wish.

Figure 3: Possible Outcomes with a Filibuster Threat

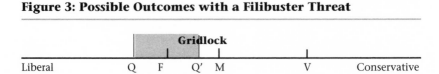

| Liberal | | Q | F | Q' | M | | V | | Conservative |

Gridlock

ELECTIONS AND EXOGENOUS SHOCKS

Diverse legislator preferences combined with an institutional structure that includes a filibuster and veto power creates a policy gridlock region that constrains legislative policy output—if a status quo policy is in the gridlock region, no changes to that policy will succeed. Status quo policies outside the gridlock region, however, can be brought just inside it. Given this model of policymaking, it would seem that over time Congress would get around to dealing with every policy area, bringing each policy outcome into the gridlock region where it is then held in place. This is not the case, however, because of exogenous shocks to the system. In the constantly changing world of politics and policy, a number of exogenous factors impact policy outcomes by changing the preference structure. These factors include the election of new politicians, the changing preferences of constituents, and the shifting of policy realizations.

The gridlock region is defined by the preferences of legislators in a given Congress, so a change in membership in Congress has the potential to shift the size and place of the gridlock region. Major electoral swings like 1932, 1946, 1964, 1980, 1986, and 1994 dramatically shift the composition of the Congress so that status quo policies may be located outside of the new region.[9] A second shock that might shift the region is a change in constituent preferences, which can occur in any number of ways—significant events, presidential appeals to the public, and so on. The events of September 11, 2001, for instance, shifted voters' views regarding military expenditures—Congress shifted its preferences appropriately, and new legislative policies were successfully passed. Finally, the gridlock region can move over time as policy reactions to different shocks move policy. One example is the shift in pre– versus post–New Deal welfare policy. Prior to the New Deal, the debate was about whether or not the government should provide any welfare or government assistance. Post New Deal, the debate is now about how much governmental assistance should be provided, typically with Republicans favoring less and Democrats favoring more.

THE PRESIDENT

Though there are a number of ways that the president can affect legislation, we consider four primary influences on policy outcomes. First, and most directly, the president can veto legislation (or threaten to veto legislation). This formal constitutional tool gives the president the power to moderate policies that he sees as too far left or too far right. Legislators are aware of and take into account the probability that the president might veto bills. The president can also influence the preference of legislators—through visiting the members' district, providing extra pork barrel, helping to fundraise for a campaign, pushing for a position that gains publicity, and so on. The third way that the president affects policy is through bargaining with key legislators to get majorities for bills he prefers. The president knows which members matter on what bills and can do individual bargaining with those legislators to gain their support. The final way the president affects policy output is through "going public."[10] Brandice Canes-Wrone[11] has recently shown how important going public can be in influencing policy.[12] Each of these presidential actions can play a role in the resulting policy output but can be somewhat difficult to measure, so we will focus primarily on formal veto power.

In sum, the model is relatively straightforward: policy is the result of the strategic interaction between legislative pivots (based on supermajority institutions) and the president. This model illustrates that new legislative policy will pass only if it moves the status quo policy from outside to inside the gridlock region. Thus, institutional constraints limit the range of policies that can be successfully made into law.

In this paper, we take into account the constraints of the political system in evaluating Clinton's policy successes during his presidential term.

Clinton's First Term

We first look in detail at Clinton's first term because the two Congresses with which Clinton had to work in his first term (the 103rd and 104th) contrast so starkly—a Democratic-controlled Senate and House in the 103rd Congress and a Republican-controlled Senate and House in the 104th. Public expectations of Clinton seemed to follow directly from the particular party controlling Congress. By contrasting Clinton's interactions with these two distinct Congresses, we are able to demonstrate the importance of the institutional constraints of the American political system. This will allow us to better evaluate Clinton's policy successes within the correct bounds. We first turn to Clinton's first two years in office, a time of unified gridlock.

CLINTON AND THE 103RD CONGRESS: UNIFIED GRIDLOCK

When Arkansas governor Bill Clinton was elected president in 1992 along with a Democratic majority in Congress, the United States had its first unified government in twelve years. Optimists saw an opportunity for the new president to make difficult decisions and to offer new policy proposals that could easily be passed through the Democratic Congress. Many politicians, commentators, and scholars believed that unified Democratic governance would bring an end to gridlock. On February 24, 1993, Brookings held a conference called Beyond Gridlock,[13] and a number of the participants professed the view that progress was forthcoming. Howard Paster, Clinton's liaison to Congress, said, "That we can now, with a Democratic majority on the Hill and a Democrat in the White House, govern successfully, I think will be borne out." Representative Thomas Downey (D, N.Y.) said, "We have a Democratic President and there is not much that we have to do now. Now that we have eliminated divided government we will have eliminated gridlock." As we all know, it did not turn out quite like that.

After Clinton's first two years as president, many believed that Clinton was destined to be a one-term president because of his inability to bring about major policy changes, most notably on healthcare. Liberals criticized him for "waffling" and moving to the right. Some scholars attributed Clinton's failures with the 103rd Congress to bad strategy. Skocpol, for instance, argues that the failure of the healthcare reforms was due to bad strategic choices such as pushing NAFTA late in 1993 instead of the president's health proposal, emphasizing cost containment instead of coverage, and poor marketing to the public.[14] We argue that the most parsimonious explanation for the failure of Clinton's healthcare proposal was that Clinton was constrained by the political system. Clinton could not have been expected to have passed liberal legislation—despite the presence of a Democratic majority—because the critical or pivotal legislators would prevent its passage. The model applied to the first two years of Clinton's presidency illustrates that many of the policies that people criticized him for not passing were simply not feasible policy outcomes given the constraints of the spatial policy model.

PREFERENCES IN THE 103RD

The first step to predicting the set of potential policy outcomes is to place the legislators in the 103rd Congress on the left-right continuum (see appendix for ordering). The details of this placement can be found in Brady and Volden.[15] The left-right placements of the legislators are not surprising to anyone familiar with the U.S. Congress—the pivots and median voters are conservative southern Democrats or moderate Republicans.[16]

Thus, though the 1992 election gave the country its first unified government in twelve years, it did not move the Congress to the left. If anything, the election yielded a slightly more conservative Congress than the 102nd. House elections yielded the lowest Democratic vote percentage since 1980—50 percent of the vote with a loss of ten seats. Thus, the median and the filibuster pivot in the House shifted slightly to the right. In the Senate, the Democrats held fifty-seven seats before the election and held fifty-seven seats after the election. The thirteen new Senators fell evenly on either side of Senator Ben Campbell, creating no real shift in the Senate.[17] More importantly, all six new Republicans were quite conservative (right of the filibuster pivot), thus creating a constraint on left-leaning policy proposals. In sum, the Congress elected in 1992 looked a little more conservative than the 102nd. However, with the election of Bill Clinton to the presidency, the veto pivot shifted from the right to the left.

POLICY OUTPUTS IN THE 103RD

With an eye toward these legislative preferences, we now turn to an analysis of policy in the first two years of the Clinton presidency. Our argument is that members' preferences in combination with Clinton's policy positions and supermajority institutions largely accounted for Clinton's policy output. Clinton's initial policy proposals were left of the congressional median and the Senate filibuster pivot; in order to capture the majority or supermajorities necessary to win passage, these policies had to be shifted to the right.

The model predicts that policies requiring a supermajority for passage must move toward the filibuster pivot (conservative Republicans in this case) or they fail; and proposals requiring a simple majority for passage must move toward the floor median (moderate Democrats/ Republicans). In other words, the bills that passed Congress in Clinton's first two years are characterized by their appeal to the preferences of institutionally placed pivotal members not by their partisan appeal. The changes to Clinton's most prominent legislative proposals are summarized in table 1. For a more detailed account of these proposals see Brady and Volden.[18] Given the constraints of space, we will focus attention on budget battles in the 103rd and 104th Congresses to illustrate the constraints of the political system within which Clinton had to work.

As described in table 1, the difference between victory and defeat on various Clinton proposals was his willingness to compromise so that the appropriate pivots would support the bill. The family-leave bill passed easily, largely because the president submitted a proposal that had been hammered out between congressional Democrats and Republicans in

Table 1: Summary of Legislative Changes in 103rd Congress

Type of Legislation	Bill	Presidential Proposal	Provisions	Changes	Pivotal Members
Majority Only					
	1993 Budget Act	Left of floor median	(1) BTU energy tax (2) Not many cuts (3) 36% top rate on individuals	(1) Eliminate BTU (2) $60 billion in cuts (3) 33.5% top tax rate	Breaux Boren Nunn
	NAFTA	Left of floor median	(1) Renegotiate (2) Trinational commission sanctions (3) Tax for worker retraining	(1) Not renegotiated (2) No real sanctions (3) Dropped	Johnston DeConcini Stenholm
Supermajority					
Proposed in earlier Congress	Family Leave	Republican filibuster point	(1) 12 weeks coverage (2) Companies >50 employees (3) Exempt 10% (4) Full-time employees	(1) None; Clinton supported package worked out in 1992	Bond
	Motor Voter	At floor median	(1) Registration required in welfare offices	(2) Dropped/modified	Durenberger
New Proposal	Job Stimulus	Left of floor median	(1) Urban spending (2) Youth summers (3) Pell grants (4) Unemployment	(1) Dropped (2) Dropped (3) Dropped (4) Dropped	Boren Breaux
	National Service	Left of floor median	(1) $650 million 1st year (2) 5-year authorization (3) $10,000 education awards	(1) $300 million (2) 3 years (3) $4,725	Chafee Kassebaum Packwood
	Health-care	Left of floor median	(1) Universal coverage (2) Employer mandates	(1) Dropped (2) Dropped	Cooper Andrews

SOURCE: Brady and Volden (1998), page 124

1990 but had been vetoed by Bush. With Clinton's election, the veto pivot had moved to the left of the bill, so it was easily passed and signed into law. The Motor Voter Act followed a similar story, though Republican senators filibustered an early version that included a provision allowing individuals to register to vote in welfare offices. Once the provision was dropped, the bill passed and was signed into law by President Clinton. The national service legislation, one of Clinton's pet programs, passed only after shifting far enough to the right to appease the moderate-conservative senators. The National Service Program was initially proposed at $650 million and was cut to $300 million before it passed. The Job Stimulus package was proposed at $16.3 billion and was reduced to a $4 billion unemployment-compensation extension. And the healthcare bill was abandoned entirely.

The 1993 budget agreement illustrates how Clinton was constrained—not by the Republican Party, but by the preferences of individual legislators, including members of his own party.

THE 1993 BUDGET AGREEMENT

In his first State of the Union address, Clinton proposed an economic plan focused on reducing the budget deficit. Through a combination of increased taxes (on the upper 1 percent of income earners) and budget cuts (mainly from defense and bureaucracy), Clinton's proposal promised to reduce the budget deficit by five hundred million dollars over five years. With the BTU energy tax, minor cuts in spending, and an increase to a 36 percent tax rate on the wealthiest individuals, Clinton's original proposal was very near the median preferences of his party. With the Democratic Party holding a majority in Congress, Clinton seemed poised for a major policy success. However, the pivotal players in Congress were not the median members of the Democratic Party but instead were the median members of Congress—the moderate and conservative Democrats. And these centrist Democrats were able to move the budget toward their preferences. In the end, the 1993 budget proposals were made more conservative than Clinton had initially intended in order to appeal to these centrist Democrats.

The median senators and representatives made a number of demands in exchange for their support. The median senators such as John Breaux (La.), David Boren (Okla.), and J. Bennett Johnston (La.) were from energy-producing states and were thus negatively affected by the BTU energy tax. Without the votes of these senators, there was not a majority of votes necessary for passage. These same senators, along with median

House members (for example, Charles Stenholm [Tex.]), also forced a drop in the proposed top tax rate from 36 percent to 33.5, and they added nearly $60 billion in cuts to current programs. Though the diluted Clinton budget was ultimately passed (with *only* the votes of Democrats), it took an incredible amount of cajoling, bargaining, and pleading within his own party, and it arguably cost the jobs of several pivotal legislators who had supported Clinton.

The rightward movements in the budget, based on the demands of Democratic legislators, illustrate the preference constraints within which Clinton had to maneuver. Given the distribution of preferences in Congress, there was little or no possibility for major policy change across a wide swath of legislative proposals.[19] Anecdotal evidence suggests both that the public did not consider these constraints when evaluating his job approval and that Clinton himself was unprepared for this reality. Liberal commentators and activists criticized Clinton's policies as too conservative. As one journalist lamented, "Like many liberals, I recall watching the 1992 Democratic National Convention with awe. As Bill Clinton outlined plans to reform the American medical system, defended reproductive and sexual rights, and spun the story of 'a place called Hope,' I felt caught up in his optimism. Yet during Clinton's presidency, these promises collapsed. After health care reform failed and military intransigence prompted the 'Don't ask, don't tell' policy towards homosexuals in uniform, the president . . . turned into a spineless, ethically vacuous centrist."[20] Clinton also seemed unprepared for the institutional constraints he would face in passing legislation. Robert Reich, former secretary of labor, remarked:

> The president was told that the stimulus package was just not going to be passed. There was too much opposition. And he was upset. This was the first big blow to his presidency. I think he was upset, not so much because the stimulus package itself was not going to go through. . . . I think he was upset that as president, given that the Congress was Democrat, he didn't have enough power, enough authority to get what he wanted done. Already opposition was forming. Already his ability to change the direction of the country was being challenged, even in his own party.[21]

After Clinton's first two years in office, with less legislative success than hoped for, the media began predicting Clinton would be a one-term president, and when the midterm elections switched control of Congress to the Republicans, they were likewise interpreted as a referendum on Clinton's poor performance. As we have explained, however, the expectations were unrealistic. Given the preferences of Congress and the institutional structure, Clinton had much less ability to change policy than he initially thought.

CLINTON AND THE 104TH CONGRESS: CURTAILING THE REPUBLICAN REVOLUTION

In 1994, Republicans gained control of the Senate and House for the first time in forty years. The 104th Congress came to Washington intent on shifting policy in a conservative direction. The new Republican majority promised to end Democratic gridlock. It was thought that the election sealed the fate of Clinton as a one-term president. The freshmen Republicans offered the Contract with America, pledging to pass new governmental reforms, to balance the budget, and to lower taxes.

The Republican majority did indeed shift congressional preferences further right to a large degree, making Congress, not the president, the agenda setter. However, the Republican majorities had to face Democratic filibuster pivots and, more importantly, the presidential veto. If the Republican proposals are too conservative for the public, the president can veto legislation and seize the middle ground. However, if the Republican proposals are considered moderate by the public, the president is inclined to sign them rather than veto and appear too liberal. In signing, the president upsets the liberal wing of his party. Ultimately, however, Clinton was able to use his weapon of the presidential veto to shift policy back toward the left, away from the preferences of the Republican Congress. Without the ability to garner the votes of two-thirds of the Senators to override a veto, the Republicans found their Contract with America largely reduced to an unfulfilled wish list. Clinton was able to moderate the policies of Speaker Newt Gingrich's House, holding their output to little more than unfunded decrees. And, in doing so, he exceeded the expectations of the American electorate, won a major public relations battle, and ultimately won reelection.

THE REPUBLICAN AGENDA

The Republicans in the 104th Congress were committed to political reform, much of which was at odds with the preferences of President Clinton. Besides a number of internal reforms, the Republicans sought (1) a balanced budget amendment; (2) a Congressional term limits amendment; (3) a line-item veto for the president on budget issues; (4) an end to unfunded mandates; and (5) campaign-finance reform. In order to achieve both lower taxes and balanced budgets, the Republicans also proposed a number of budgetary cuts in domestic programs. These policy proposals were reflective of the preference structure of the Republicans in the 104th Congress. Republicans held the majority (and median member) in the House. In other words, the House would easily be able to pass the Contract with America proposals. In the Senate, Majority Leader Bob Dole (Kans.) was also supportive of the popular Contract with America. Dole was seeking the Republican nomination for president, so if he could not deliver the necessary votes for the Contract bills, his conservative opponents (Pat Buchanan and Phil Gramm) would benefit. However, in the Senate, the Democrats could use the filibuster to move policy in their direction, and the presidential veto would provide an even greater constraint. And as the model shows, the new filibuster pivots in the Senate were quite moderate and unlikely to support the entire conservative Contract.[22] This would create a particularly large obstacle for passing the proposed amendments (balanced budget and term limits), which require two-thirds support to start the amendment process (in other words, they required Democratic support). The Republican revolution may have captured the House by storm, but the battle lines would be drawn in the Senate and fought by the presidential veto pen.

President Clinton actually was put in an easier situation because he would no longer have to initiate the agenda, but rather he just had to work at moderating the Republican agenda. Though his Democratic colleagues in Congress would not stick with him in passing legislation on healthcare, they would rally around his decisions to veto Republican policy proposals. Now he only had to oppose change by the Republicans. And by protecting the children, environment, and so forth from the Republicans, Clinton was heralded as a great leader.

POLICY OUTPUT OF 104TH

Table 2 shows the major proposals of the 104th Congress and their resolution. Again, a more detailed account of these proposals can be found in Brady and Volden.[23] The House quickly passed a number of internal reforms that did not require presidential approval. By January 5, the House passed a rules revision and a congressional accountability act. They cut staffs by one-third, rearranged committees, limited the terms of the committee chairs, ended proxy voting, and passed a bill ending legislative exemptions from federal laws. On January 11, the Senate passed the congressional accountability act, and by March 7, the Congress had

Table 2: Major Legislation in the 104th Congress

Type of Legislation	Bill	Initial House Proposal	Provisions	Changes	Pivotal Members
Constitutional Amendments					
	Balanced Budget	Right of median	(1) 3/5ths vote on tax increases (2) Balance by 2002	(1) Stripped (2) Lost in Senate	Bingaman Daschle Dorgan
	Term limits	Right of median	(1) Three 2-year terms	(1) Six 2-year terms (2) Defeated	Senior Democrats and Republicans
Supermajority Legislation					
	Line-item veto	About median	(1) Enhanced rescissions	(1) Weakened slightly (2) Dole pressure	Breaux Heflin
	Unfunded mandates	Right of median	(1) 3/5ths point-of-order override (2) $50 million on private business	(1) Stripped (2) $100 million on private business	
	Budget	Right of median	(1) Cut $894 billion in spending (2) Reduce increases in entitlements (3) Reduce taxes $245 billion (4) Balance by 2002	(1) Smaller cuts (2) Abandoned	Multiple coalitions attempted and abandoned
	Welfare	Right of median	(1) $82 billion in savings (six years) (2) AFDC to states (3) Medicaid to states (4) School lunches, food stamps, options to states	(1) $54 billion in savings (2) Retained (3) Abandoned (4) Abandoned	Moderate Democrats up for reelection

SOURCE: Brady and Volden (1998), page 148

passed a paperwork reduction act. Unfunded mandates, lobbyist registration, and a gift ban also quickly passed and became law.

But President Clinton's veto pen was able to limit the policy output of the 104th Congress to internal reforms that did not require the president's signature. By the end of the first session, only two of the Contract's ten provisions had been signed into law. Still unfinished were a major telecommunications bill, a final version of the line-item veto, an intelligence-authorization bill, a defense-authorization bill, the product-liability bill, a significant banking-reorganization act, some nonreconciliation farm matters, the Superfund toxic-cleanup act, just to name a few. What accounts for the end-of-session malaise on substantive legislation despite the House's success after one hundred days? The Senate failed to pass some House legislation (as in the case of the balanced-budget amendment); failed to pass the *same version* (as in the case of the line-item veto); or failed to act on the legislation at all.[24]

The demise of the Contract with America can be attributed to the preference constraints of the Senate and President Clinton. The Senate was more moderate than the House (the median senator was to the left of the median House member), and Senate rules allow individual senators more influence, which leads to delays in policymaking. More importantly, however, the possibility of a filibuster by the Democratic minority or of a presidential veto increased uncertainty over what would pass. In order for Senator Dole to win a majority vote, he needed the votes of party moderates: Lincoln Chaffee (R.I.), William Cohen (Maine), Arlen Specter (Pa.), Nancy Kassebaum (Kans.), Jim Jeffords (Vt.), Ben Nighthorse Campbell (Colo.), and others. In order to beat a filibuster, he had to have not only these votes, but also the votes of moderate Democrats like Howell Heflin (Ala.), Sam Nunn (Ga.), John Breaux (La.), and J. Bennett Johnston (La.). And overriding a presidential veto was completely unlikely. Thus, getting major legislative shifts passed was a much more difficult task than Republicans seemed to expect initially.

Major policy shifts downsizing government would have been difficult under any conditions, but the actions of House Republicans, especially the freshmen, exacerbated the problem. In their fervor to "keep faith with America" the freshmen—unaccustomed to the give-and-take of politics—tried to push the Senate into action by attaching riders. For example, House Republicans attached to a housing-appropriations bill a set of provisions that stripped the Environmental Protection Agency of its power to regulate and enforce major sections of the air and water pollution laws. In another bill, they attached a rider allowing exploratory drilling in the Alaska National Wildlife Refuge. Senator Chaffee (R-R.I.), chair of the Senate Environment and Public Works Committee, refused to even consider the House legislation: "The so-called clean water bill they sent over went way beyond what was acceptable to me and way beyond what was acceptable in the Senate as a whole."[25] These clashes of preferences, between chambers and with the president, came to head with the 1995 budget battle.

95–96 Budget Battle

The House Republicans believed that they had been elected to transform American politics by downsizing the role of government as regulator, provider of entitlements, and tax collector. President Clinton and the congressional Democrats believed the Republican proposal went too far, and this conflict played out with considerable drama in the 1995–96 budget battle. The newly elected Republican majorities had promised Americans that they would both reduce taxes and balance the budget by shrinking the size of the government. The vehicle for accomplishing this was the standard reconciliation budget. [26]

The reductions in federal revenue that would result from the Republican's proposed tax cut meant they would have to make large cuts in popular entitlement programs. One of the Republicans' earliest positions was to take Social Security off the table, so the largest entitlement program could not be touched. To achieve a balanced budget over seven years, the Republicans instead proposed reductions in Medicare and Medicaid, but these were the programs for which President Clinton and congressional Democrats were seeking increases, not decreases. The Republican congressional majorities thus had three possible strategies with regard to the budget package. They could (1) forge a budget deal that the president would sign, (2) attempt the unprecedented (and highly unlikely to succeed) maneuver of gaining the two-thirds necessary to override a veto of a budget bill, or (3) score some political points by proposing a major budget bill and having the president veto it despite being unable to override the veto.

Given the fundamental differences in the preferences and rules between the House and Senate, and the fact that a Democratic president could veto legislation, the reconciliation process ran behind schedule, though this is hardly unusual. In the past, continuing resolutions were easily passed before the end of the government's fiscal year to allow government spending to continue (at the previous year's level). At that same time, the government would ordinarily seek an increase in the debt limit in order to borrow money to pay off the federal deficit. In 1995, the continuing resolution questions, the extension of the debt ceiling, and the final reconciliation budget all needed to be simultaneously addressed in early November.

The reconciliation budget passed by Republicans in Congress included $894 billion in cuts to projected federal spending by 2002, producing a $4 billion surplus. The bill proposed reducing welfare funding by $82 billion, Medicare funding by $270 billion, Medicaid funding by $163 billion, and proposed paring back agricultural subsidies with the ultimate goal of eliminating them. In addition, the reconciliation bill reduced taxes by $245 billion over seven years.

Meanwhile, the president promised to veto any "bill that requires crippling cuts in Medicare, weakens the environment, reduces educational opportunity or raises taxes on working families."[27] President Clinton vetoed the stopgap and debt-limit measures, signaling his willingness to use the veto to force Republicans to compromise on their reconciliation package. Moreover, Clinton said that he would not sign any bill with cuts too large, even if it takes "90 days, 120 days, or 180 days."[28] The use of the presidential veto can be risky unless he has public support for the action. If the public generally supports the legislation being passed, the president runs the risk of looking like he is not following the will of the people if he vetoes a popular bill. Research on the presidency often concluded that "the use of the veto is usually a last resort and as much an indicator of presidential failure as success."[29]

The Republicans, knowing they would not have all thirteen appropriation bills finished on time, passed two stopgap measures. However, both bills contained poison pills—items that the president had previously threatened to veto. President Clinton was faced with going back on his word (facing another "waffling" accusation) or vetoing the measures, which would shut the government down. On November 13, 1995, President Clinton vetoed the measures. On November 14, more than 14,800,000 non-essential federal employees were sent home. Given the shutdown and the Republicans' inability to override the president's veto, both sides compromised on a continuing resolution, passed November 20, that would keep the government running until December 15.

As a compromise, Clinton agreed to a balanced budget by 2002 as scored by the Congressional Budget Office (CBO);[30] in exchange, Republicans agreed to have the CBO reestimate the effects of their budget given the stronger-than-expected growth in the U.S. economy in

1995 (thus fewer cuts would be necessary). The rough CBO estimates yielded about $130 billion more than the original estimates.[31] By December, both sides began renegotiating the tax cuts and expenditures of the budget on an "oranges-to-oranges" basis.

Normal politics, however, was not to be. President Clinton successfully rallied public opinion on his side. His strategy of criticizing the Republican budget as too harsh and thus "against our [American] values" was being reflected in the polls. President Clinton's approval ratings climbed over 50 percent for the first time in more than a year. Moreover, the president and the Democrats had a 23 percent margin over Republicans in public-opinion polls asking who could better handle the deficit —a major reversal from the early days of the 104th Congress. The December 15 deadline for a continuing resolution passed with no agreement, so parts of the government closed down once again. The president and Democratic legislators argued that it was the ideological freshman class of 1994 that was responsible for shutting down the government. Republicans insisted that the president was not to be trusted because he had not yet presented his own balanced-budget proposal.

On January 6, 1996, the ball began to roll again. The Republican Congress passed and the president signed a series of continuing resolutions to keep parts of the government operating through September and all of it through at least January 26, 1996. The president submitted a budget (using CBO scoring) that would balance the budget by 2002 with cuts in Medicare, Medicaid, and welfare that were about one-half the size of those proposed by Republicans. The Clinton budget included tax cuts in the form of a five-hundred-dollar child credit and a small capital-gains cut, while closing tax loopholes that would in effect increase taxes on corporations. And President Clinton refused to cut agricultural programs and student loans. Though Clinton's plan projected an increase of $97 billion more in savings than his December proposal, the Republicans were still proposing substantially more cuts than Clinton, including $99 billion more in Medicare, $65 billion more in Medicaid, $88 billion more in discretionary spending, $37 billion more in welfare, combined with a whopping $154 billion more in tax cuts.[32] The negotiation and bargain that would ultimately occur should by now be familiar given the model. The pivotal voter for this process was the legislator whose vote was needed to override the veto point, and was thus solidly in the liberal wing of the Democratic Party.[33]

Again, the budget battle was being played in the public-relations arena. The initial Republican reaction was to try to portray the Clinton budget as more tax-and-spend liberalism. Clinton, on the other hand, portrayed his budget as a responsible plan that put the burden of payment where it belonged, while preserving the social safety net. And, again, Clinton won the public-relations battle, undoubtedly giving him more bargaining leverage (the veto threat seemed credible if the public supported Clinton's views). Congressional Republicans made an attempt to negotiate with conservative and moderate Democrats in order to offer a bipartisan bill (still closer to their original bill) to try to force the president to move right. But, with the near impossibility of Congress overriding a veto, and the additional leverage and support received from the public-relations boost, the bills moved more dramatically toward Clinton's preferences.

On April 25, Congress passed an omnibus appropriations bill that rolled together all that remained of the thirteen appropriation bills. Though the bill covered only about 16 percent of the federal budget, these domestic appropriations represented the funding for all federal bureaucracy and nearly everything the government does other than defense and cash transfers. Republicans sought policies and budget numbers to the right of the president, who vetoed bills he did not like, believing that he could win the public-opinion battle. Thus, the policies and the numbers moved left, back toward the president. The president was able to protect education, job training, and the environment. Clinton was able to get Congress to keep his AmeriCorps National Service Program (albeit at a 30 percent reduction) and his Goals 2000 project in the budget. With regard to the environment, Clinton forced Congress to drop provisions and riders that he viewed as detrimental, such as proposals to change wetlands policy and to allow salvage logging. The original Republican proposals for cuts in Medicare, Medicaid, and other entitlement programs were left stranded because the president's veto could not be overridden. The final budget contained a 9.1 percent reduction in domestic appropriations over the 1995–96 period (a $22 billion cut in expenditures), but the programs that Clinton deemed as important were left relatively untouched.

The president seemed to have won the day that the government shutdown was blamed on the Republican Congress, especially Speaker Gingrich. Prior to the government shutdowns (early 1995), the *Wall Street Journal*/National Broadcasting Company (*WSJ*/NBC) poll put Speaker Gingrich's job-approval rating at plus 11 (46 percent approval, 35 percent disapproval). The first government shutdown occurred on November 14, 1995. On November 19, Speaker Gingrich's public-approval rating was minus 33 (27 percent approval; 60 percent disapproval). The *WSJ*/NBC poll continued to ask about the Speaker through the budget battle, and his approval ratings never rebounded. The early December *WSJ*/NBC poll put the Speaker's approval rating at minus 24; by mid-January 1996, it dropped to minus 28. In contrast, the president's approval ratings shot up. From January 1995—shortly after the Republican sweep in November —through April, the president averaged an approval rating of plus 4. For a president presiding over a relatively strong economy, these numbers were historic lows. From June through October in two *WSJ*/NBC polls, the president was plus 3 and plus 4. Five days after the first shutdown (November 19, 1995), the president increased to an approval rating of plus 7; by the first week in December, he was up to plus 11. Clinton ultimately fell back to a plus 3 approval rating by mid-January, but that was still 31 points higher than Speaker Gingrich—a reversal of over 40 points within a period of six to seven months.

In sum, an eager Republican Congress proposed significant policy changes. And the supermajority constraint of the presidential veto became real and relevant. Policy proposals that were shifted to the left passed; those that did not either died or were vetoed. Thus, the only policies to move out of the gridlock region were the ones that could be moved far enough toward President Clinton's preferences such that he was willing to sign them. In short, a liberal-moderate president willing to veto legislation that he viewed as too conservative had an excellent chance to persevere if the newly elected Republicans pushed policies too far to the right. His party may not have gone with him on healthcare, fuel taxes, campaign finance, and a series of other policies in the 103rd Congress, but they would vote to sustain his vetoes on policies that they also viewed as too conservative. The model shows that the Republican victory in the 1994 election was not a guarantee of major policy shifts to the right.

Clinton's Second Term

By vetoing legislation that he (and public polls) viewed as too conservative in the 104th Congress, Clinton boosted his own electoral fortunes and reduced the Republicans' chances to head a unified government after the 1996 elections. By Clinton's second term, it appeared that both Clinton and the Republicans had come to terms with the fact that a party majority is not a sufficient condition for major policy change. As the model demonstrates, and as we have illustrated with budget negotiations during these Congresses, policy change is limited by supermajority institutional constraints and the preferences of individual legislators. Thus, Clinton's policy successes should be evaluated from this perspective. We now turn to a brief description of the preference structure of the 105th and 106th Congresses and then look at a few of Clinton's key policy successes within this context.

PREFERENCES OF 105TH AND 106TH CONGRESSES: POLITICAL FAMILIARITY

The institutional constraints that President Clinton had to work with during his second term were fairly similar to those he faced with the 104th Congress. However, the fundamental difference was that both Clinton and the Republicans seemed to learn about the constraints that they each faced in passing new policies. In the 105th Congress, the Senate median legislators remained moderate Republicans like Olympia Snowe (Maine), Lincoln Chaffee (R.I.) and conservative Democrats like John Breaux (La.). The filibuster pivot on the left featured included Democrats like Joseph Biden (Del.), Mary Landrieu (La.), Jay Rockefeller (W.V.) and Republicans like Arlen Specter (Penn.); the filibuster on the right included Republicans such as Orrin Hatch (Utah), Kit Bond (Mo.), and Pat Roberts (Kans.).[34] In the House, the median included the usual set of characters: William Lipinski (Ill.), Charlie Stenholm (Tex.), Ike Skelton (Mo.), and so on.[35] The veto pivots in both chambers were safely in the Clinton range.

The midterm (1998) elections yielded a gain for the president's party for only the second time in the twentieth century, but still left him with a Republican-controlled Congress. The 106th Congress held preferences quite similar to the 105th with the exception that the Democratic filibuster moved even further to the left—making it almost impossible for policy to shift in a conservative direction. The new filibuster pivots were senators such as Evan Bayh (Ind.), Kent Conrad (N.Dak.) and Daniel Patrick Moynihan (N.Y.). The median senators were still legislators such as Olympia Snowe (Maine), Lincoln Chaffee (R.I.), and Peter Fitzgerald (Ill.). In the House, the median moved slightly left, but still left members like Gene Taylor (D, Miss.), Sue Kelly (D, N.Y.), and Thomas Campbell (R, Ca.) at the median.

POLICIES OF 105TH AND 106TH

Clinton's win in 1996 and the Republican loss of seats in 1998 (and the Speaker) meant that bipartisan compromise was essential for any policy changes, and this seemed to largely be recognized by both the president and legislators. After the lessons of the 104th Congress, Republican legislators realized that they did not have the support to beat the filibuster in the Senate or to override a presidential veto. The only policies that were able to be moved out of the gridlock regions in the 105th Congress were characterized by bipartisan support—policies such as tax credits (for higher education, families with children), a balanced-budget agreement, and a Clinton proposal to improve education. Likewise, the only notable policy changes in the 106th Congress were Clinton proposals—extending permanent normal trade relations to China, and a bill expanding Medicaid and Medicare so that people with disabilities continue to receive health-insurance coverage if they go to work. In general, the 105th and 106th Congresses did not produce an overwhelming number of policy outputs; they spent much of their time and energy on Clinton investigations and impeachment hearings.

Though there seemed to be general recognition about the type of compromise necessary for a bill to succeed, the Republican Congress nonetheless passed some bills that they knew would never be signed into law. As one journalist noted, Congress "seemed to be almost as much about positioning for the elections as about making law."[36] The Republican Congress was again constrained by Clinton's veto pen in the 105th—late-term abortion ban and school vouchers are notable examples. Republicans knew that these bills would not ultimately succeed, but passing the bills at least satisfied the conservative faction of the Republican Party. Similarly, in the 106th Congressional Republicans passed their proposed repeals of the "marriage penalty" and estate taxes vetoed by Clinton, and they were again unable to override his vetoes.

Once again, much of the policy wrangling was over the budget. And, as in the 104th Congress, Clinton typically came out on top. President Clinton was able to achieve his most important goals in the budget battles of his two Congresses—from eliminating several anti-environment riders to new money for schoolteachers, the International Monetary Fund, and distressed farmers. One journalist provides a telling assessment of Clinton's role in the 106th budget negotiations: "In some cases, Mr. Clinton has refused to accept legislation because it was missing something he very much wanted. . . . But most energy has been spent beating back last-minute riders he does not like. . . . The Republicans believe that they will profit from these confrontations. But Mr. Clinton has won these standoffs in the past, and there is no reason why he cannot do so now."[37]

Evaluating President Clinton

We have made the case that in the 103rd Congress, President Clinton could not have moved policy too far left due to supermajority institutions and the distribution of legislative preferences. Similarly, in the following Congress, the Republicans could not shift policy too far right for the same reasons. In the next two Congresses, both sides seemed to have adjusted their view of what was possible, and at least substantive policy proposals were more centrist. So what did this mean for Clinton's overall policy record? It is quite clear that President Clinton was able to work within the institutional constraints created by Republican-controlled Congresses and nonetheless champion his pet policies over the 104th–106th Congresses.

Many of Clinton's programs actually had budget increases under the Republican-controlled Congress. Table 3 shows the 1993 and 2000 budget outlays for several of Clinton's favorite programs. Also reported is the percentage change in budget outlays *above inflation* between the 1993 (Democratic majority) budget and the 2000 (Republican majority) budget. For instance, Head Start had budget outlays of $2,776 million in 1993 under the Democrat-controlled Congress. If Head Start's budget outlays increased only with the rate of inflation under the Republican-controlled Congress, we would predict outlays of $3,137 million in 2000. However, Head Start actually had their budget outlays increase to $5,267 million in 2000—a 36 percent increase above inflation.

Showing that Clinton's favorite programs found increased financial support is not evidence in and of itself that Clinton had a successful policy record. After all, the strong economic times during Clinton's presidency may have led the Republicans to have increased domestic spending across the board. And, in fact, the domestic budget as a whole did grow between 1993 and 2000 by roughly 14 percent. The budget outlays on all of these programs increased an average of 56 percent. Not surprisingly, this difference is statistically significant with $p < .001$. The expansion of Clinton's programs above inflation far eclipses the average increase in spending over all programs. The programs that Clinton emphasized simply had much more substantial financial support, despite the Republican-controlled Congress.

This point becomes even more apparent when we look just at the programs that the Republicans had slated for elimination in the Contract with America. Clinton not only prevented many of these programs from being executed, but as we show in a multivariate analysis, his favorite

Table 3: Budget Increases in Clinton's Favorite Programs

Program	1993 Outlays (1993 dollars)	1993 Outlays (2000 dollars)	2000 Outlays actual	Percentage Change above inflation
Adult Education	$305	$345	$470	36%
Bilingual and Immigrant Education	$237	$268	$406	52%
Education Research Programs	$162	$183	$319	74%
Special Education	$2,966	$3,352	$6,036	80%
Head Start	$2,776	$3,137	$5,267	68%
Education Technology	$23	$26	$769	2,859%
Federal Work Study	$617	$697	$934	34%
Dislocated Worker Assistance	$517	$584	$1,589	172%
JobCorps	$966	$1,092	$1,358	24%
Lands Legacy Initiative	$380	$429	$727	69%
Mass Transit	$3,774	$4,265	$5,785	36%
Solar and Renewable Energy	$249	$281	$315	12%
Energy Conservation and Efficiency	$592	$669	$745	11%
U.S. Global Change Research	$1,323	$1,495	$1,701	14%
Water/Wastewater Grants and Loans	$508	$574	$631	10%

NOTES: Outlays are in millions of dollars adjusted to 2000 dollars. Source: Outlays reported in Moore and Slivinski (2000), originally from OMB, Budget of U.S. Government

programs actually received budget increases. The Contract-inspired 1995 House budget called for the elimination of more than two hundred government programs, including three entire cabinet agencies (Education, Energy, and Commerce). We focus on the ninety-five largest targeted programs in order to test the effect of a Clinton "imprimatur" on a program's expected budget outlays. We identify a program as a Clinton favorite if he mentioned it in a State of the Union address or in the *Economic Report of the President*.[38] A simple bivariate looks at the average percentage change in budget outlays between 1995 (first budget with Republican majority) and 2000 (last budget of Clinton's presidency) is shown in figure 4.

We estimate three different multivariate models: model 1 predicts the 1995 budget outlays for the largest ninety-five programs on the

Figure 4: Average Percent Change in Budget Outlays 1995–2000 for Targeted Programs

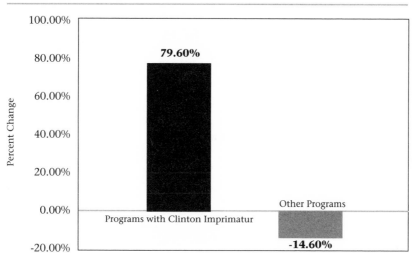

Republican's "hit list"; model 2 predicts the 2000 budget outlays; model 3 predicts the *percentage change* in outlays between 1995 and 2000.[39] The results in model 1 show that the effect of a Clinton imprimatur on the program's expected 1995 budget (in 2000 dollars) is positive and significant; similarly, in model 2 we see that the effect of a Clinton imprimatur on the predicted 2000 budget is also positive and significant. Clinton programs had, on average, 1995 budget outlays of nearly $3,000 million (in 2000 dollars) more than non-Clinton favorites, and $3,300 million more in 2000 budget outlays. In contrast, if a program was in one of the three departments targeted for elimination, its expected budget dollars were less than programs not in those departments. We know that the Republican leadership preferred these programs to have no budget at all, yet we find that Clinton's programs were not only saved, but their budgets were actually increased.

We next turn to effect of a Clinton program on the percentage change above inflation between 1995 and 2000 for these same programs. Because the dependent variable now refers to a percentage, rather than an absolute number, the analysis is standardized with respect to the size of the program. We again find that, on average, programs that Clinton deemed as important show a positive and significant change—so their budgets increased between 1995 and 2000. These findings suggest that when Clinton wielded his veto pen, he did not back down on his key programs.

To further determine whether the budget policy outcomes more closely reflected the preferences of Clinton or the preferences of the Republican Congress, we can do a quick comparison of Clinton's proposed budget outlays with the actual Congress-approved budget outlays on these ninety-five targeted programs. We find that Clinton's proposed 2000 budget for these ninety-five programs correlated with the final approved budget at .99—almost perfectly. We know that the Republicans wanted these programs to all have zero budgets, yet Clinton's proposed budget outlays that were greater than zero clearly came closer to the final approved budget.

Granted, it is always more difficult to kill a program than to create one (Rauch 1999).[40] Scholars have long noted the difficulty of extinguishing government programs and agencies—though some antiquated programs like the Bureau of Mines and the Travel and Tourism Administration were actually shut down under the Republicans' clock. However,

Table 4: Regression Analysis of Budget Outlays for Programs Slated for Elimination in Contract

	Model 1: 1995 Budget Outlays	Model 2: 2000 Budget Outlays	Model 3: Percentage Change 1995–2000
Constant	930.2	1001.8	-212.2
Commerce Dept. Program	-747.6	-820.4	219.6
	(1552.2)	(1734.4)	(1750.7)
Education Dept. Program	-1600.5*	-1694.4*	581.5*
	(792.3)	(885.4)	(941.5)
Energy Dept. Program	-903.2	-1001.8	112.2
	(2591.2)	(2895.4)	(2925.2)
Clinton Pet Program	2999.8***	3315.8***	2506.2***
	(908.3)	(1014.9)	(1216.1)
N	95	95	95
Adj. R-square	.09	.09	.02

NOTES: * p< .05, ** p< .01, *** p < .001

Clinton was not only able to be a moderator of Republican attempts to cut programs, but he was also able to propose and pass new programs. Figure 5 shows a few of the new programs (and their budgets during Clinton's presidency) that a Republican-controlled Congress still funded.

An alternative explanation for Clinton's policy success was that he only proposed policies that he knew he could win. In other words, Clinton was aware of the institutional constraints and proposed policies accordingly. And this largely seemed to be the case with regard to new policymaking. In his second term especially, Clinton picked his new policy proposals wisely—for example, Clinton tackled welfare reform because it was a policy that could be moved, while healthcare reform was not.

Conclusions

We have argued that given the distribution of preferences in the 103rd and 104th Congresses and the supermajority institutions of the filibuster and the veto, neither President Clinton nor the Republicans in the 104th Congress could move legislation as far left and right (respectively) as they

Figure 5: Clinton Initiated Policies

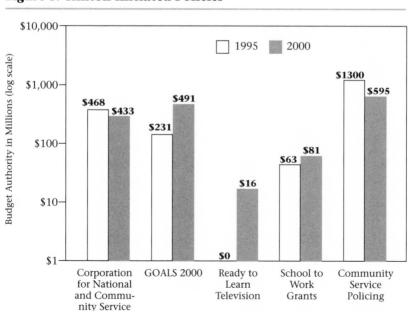

preferred. Setting aside the impeachment issues over the 105th and 106th Congresses, the president and the Republican Congress managed to legislate without shutting the government down. In short, over the last two Congresses of the Clinton presidency both sides seemed to understand the constraints under which they worked. Clinton could not get policies too far to the left and the Republican Congress could not legislate the Contract over the Senate filibuster and the veto.

Given these constraints, how did the president fare? In the 103rd House he did pass a budget further left than Republicans desired, but the failure of his healthcare legislation, the stimulus package, and a series of other issues such as gays in the military led to the first fully Republican Congress since 1954. The president's use of the veto and his management of public opinion in the 104th Congress thwarted the Republicans' euphoria of late 1994 and early 1995. Becoming the first Democrat reelected since FDR, Clinton turned what looked like a sure-fire "Carter-esque" one-term presidency into a landslide victory over Senate majority leader Bob Dole. His personal victory did not transfer to the Congress as Republicans maintained majorities, albeit decreasing majorities in the 105th and 106th Congresses.

In the last section of the paper we argue that—given the constraints —and the Republican leadership's policy preferences, Clinton's policies did very well. We looked at programs the Republicans wanted to eliminate and at the programs that the president favored and compared their budget growth. In almost every instance, the results indicated that the president's preferences were more closely adhered to than were the Republican leadership's preferences. Undoubtedly, the president's choices were somewhat endogeneous—he likely chose areas where he could win, and we simply cannot build that into the model. Nevertheless, leadership over policy is always about choices, and our analysis shows that Clinton's choices in his first term overestimated what he could achieve. In contrast, his choices in the 104th Congress were superior to Republican choices, especially in regard to the 1995–96 budget battle. The last two governments in regard to policy (excluding impeachment) were characterized by lower expectations about what was possible, yet even here the president's favored programs were better funded than either inflation or overall growth would predict. Moreover, programs and departments that the 104th Republican Congress sought to eliminate were not only not eliminated but funded at increased levels.

Overall our view is that more attention should be paid to the electoral results in the Congress with special attention focused on the crucial median House and Senate members, the filibuster pivot in the Senate, and the veto pivots in the Congress. This element of elections and super-majorities yields, within limits, a plausible range of policy change. Determining a plausible range of policy change will, over the long haul, yield much more objective and accurate assessments of presidential leadership in the area of legislative policy.

Appendix

The estimates of legislator preferences were of two types (Brady and Volden 1998): (1) Americans for Democratic Action scores (adjusted and not adjusted), (2) Multiple measures of liberal—conservative dimensions including COPE (labor scores), LCV (environmental scores), C of C (business scores), and fifteen other measures. These scores were averaged across the eighteen measures and ranked such that lower scores are conservative and higher scores are liberal. Additionally, the median senators and representatives were computer for *each* of the eighteen measures to verify that these measures were comparable. For example, Senator Sam Nunn (D, Ga.) was in the median group on seven of the eighteen issues while Rep. Charles Wilson (D, Fla.) was in the median group nine times. When the analysis of members at the median is used, the findings are that Democrats with three or more median rankings were primarily from southern and border states (75 percent) with others being from the Midwest and Southwest. The preference orderings of the senators in the 103rd are shown below as an example.

Preference orderings of Senators (103rd), ADA Scores

Left of Median		Right of Median		
Wellstone	100	Ford	60	
Metzenbaum	100	Byrd	55	
Feingold	100	Hollings	55	
Sarbanes	95	Chafee	55	
Leahy	95	Exon	50	
Levin	95	Johnston	45	
Lautenberg	95	Nunn	45	
Kohl	95	Specter	45	
Boxer	90	Roth	45	
Kennedy	90	Cohen	40	<-2/5th pivot

Harkin	90		Breaux	40
Akaka	90		Packwood	35
Moynihan	90		Heflin	35
Kerry	90		Shelby	35
Bradley	90		D'Amato	35
Murray	90		Danforth	35
Moseley-Braun	85		Kassebaum	25
Simon	85		Bond	25
Wofford	85		Stevens	20
Mikulski	85		Murkowski	20
Pell	85		Gorton	20
Mitchell	85		Grassley	20
Glenn	85		Coats	20
Baucus	85		Simpson	20
Inouye	85		Burns	20
Feinstein	85		Domenici	20
Riegle	80		McCain	15
Biden	80		Brown	15
Bumpers	80		Smith	15
Conrad	80		McConnell	15
Sasser	75		Faircloth	15
Dodd	75		Hutchinson	13
Daschle	75		Warner	10
Kerrey	75		Thurmond	10
Robb	75		Mack	10
DeConcini	75		Pressler	10
Durenberger	75		Lugar	10
Campbell	75		Dole	10
Rockefeller	70		Coverdell	10
Bingaman	70		Gregg	10
Pryor	70		Helms	10
Boren	70		Bennett	5
Graham	65		Kempthorne	5
Lieberman	65		Lott	5
Matthews	65		Hatch	5
Hatfield	65		Craig	5
Dorgan	65		Wallop	5
Bryan	60		Gramm	5
Reid	60		Nickles	5
Jeffords	60		Cochran	0

4 African Americans and the Clinton Presidency

Reckoning with Race, 1992–2000

DARLENE CLARK HINE

In this chapter, Prof. Darlene Clark Hine examines why, as she argues, "the vast majority of African Americans consider President Bill Clinton to have been the most beneficent occupant of the executive branch of the federal government in its history." To account for such widespread support, Professor Hine examines various areas of public policy as well as important, but often ignored, symbolic politics. With his positions on affirmative action, Haiti, and welfare reform and his cabinet appointments, President Clinton was able to secure widespread approval from the African American community. Further, such approval was not merely limited to Bill Clinton himself, but carried over into a much broader support for the Democratic Party. As Professor Hines discusses, the support that President Bill Clinton nurtured and received from African Americans translated into more diffuse party support as African Americans became integral Democrats during the 1990s.

> It is a peculiar sensation, this double-consciousness, this
> sense of always looking at one's self through the eyes of
> others, of measuring one's soul by the tape of a world
> that looks on in amused contempt and pity.
> —W.E.B. DuBois, 1903

> What was done cannot be undone. But we can end the
> silence. We can stop turning our heads away.
> —William Jefferson Clinton, May 16, 1997

The vast majority of African Americans consider President Bill Clinton to have been the most beneficent occupant of the executive branch of the federal government in its history. The Arkansas native amply rewarded, in substantive and symbolic ways, black Democrats for their unwavering political support and voting loyalty in the 1992 and 1996 elections. During his first administration African Americans composed fully one-quarter of his cabinet.[1] His friend Vernon Jordan chaired the transition team in 1992. The interplay of the material improvements and symbolic advances that many African Americans, especially members of the black professional class, enjoyed during the 1990s complicates any assessment of Clinton's presidency. Did these positive developments represent a maturation of black political power or did they reflect the largesse of the charismatic Bill Clinton and the leadership of the Democratic Party? How did Clinton's mastery of symbolism politics, his manipulation of rhetorical, moral, and political power, frame black people's expectations and explain their overwhelmingly positive evaluation of his tenure as chief executive? How can black interest, mobilization, and participation in presidential politics be sustained and enlarged since Clinton?

Symbolism Politics

The high approval ratings a national black constituency accorded Clinton throughout his presidency merit analysis if we are fully to understand the importance of race-sensitive policies to black electoral mobilization and the social factors that shape black participation in the political affairs of this country. The U.S. presidency is endued with inordinate moral authority, and the chief executive commands great symbolic power as well as considerable material capital. Max Weber in his essay "Class, Status and Party" defined power as "the chance of a man or a number of men to realize their own will in communal action even against the resistance of others who are participating in the action."[2] Law professor Derrick Bell addressed the importance of symbols in black history and culture: "Symbols have been the mainstay of blacks' faith that some day they will truly be free in the land of freedom." He insists that "most whites and lots of black folks rely on symbols to support their belief that black people have come a long way since slavery and segregation to the present time."[3]

Still, while many Americans acknowledge that African Americans have overcome disfranchisement and dispossession; too many others, in spite of a plethora of individual positive symbols, according to a study by the National Opinion Research Center at the University of Chicago, harbor convictions that black people collectively remain intellectually inferior, less patriotic, and insufficiently motivated as compared to white Americans. Ironically, these same Americans assigned identical negative characteristics to white southerners.[4] In a metaphysical and metaphorical sense, black Americans, even more so than Bill Clinton, a representative white southerner, had something to prove as he took the oath of office in January 1993.[5]

Bill Clinton became a proficient practitioner of the politics of symbolism, and this talent proved to be enormously appealing to some African Americans. During the eight years of his tenure, President Clinton successfully engaged in symbolism politics to reckon with America's legacy of race discrimination and racial violence. At pivotal junctures Clinton acknowledged and apologized for some of the government's more egregious miscarriages of justice and unscrupulous policies that had debased black citizens. The core of this essay links the past to the present with a focus on the symbolic importance of events such as Bill Clinton's apology for the Tuskegee Syphilis Experiment, which began in 1932 and ended forty years later, his rescinding of the dishonorable discharges of black Navy dock workers during World War II, his support of affirmative action, and his intervention in Haiti. These actions, combined with the Race Initiative, which he appointed historian John Hope Franklin to chair, illuminate why the majority of black Americans supported Clinton. This support was never absolute, although it was always overwhelmingly positive. Black members of the group that journalist Ellis Cose referred to as "the privileged class" remained outspoken in their objections to major Clinton policy initiatives, most especially to his support of the crime bill and the welfare-reform bill.

Black Presidential Politics

Only a bifocal lens permits simultaneous examination of black Americans' political negotiations and Bill Clinton's strategies to secure black allegiance. The black political agenda since the waning of the classic Civil Rights Movement consisted of, among other things, two non-negotiable demands. First, African Americans desired unfettered access to, and greater inclusion within, the nation's economic, social, educational, and political institutions. Second, and as important as this quest for "universal freedom," was respect long denied and recognition of their humanity.[6]

That Bill Clinton accepted black people as fully human and was committed to rectifying the nation's racist past is beyond question. Black political scientists Hanes Walton and Robert C. Smith described Bill Clinton in a praise song: "Clinton is arguably the first authentically non-racist, non-white supremacist president in American history. . . . Clinton is as free of racist and white supremacist thinking as any white person can be."[7] Still, at critical junctures during his eight years in the White House, even this astute and gifted politician felt compelled to respond to some black demands in order to retain their support, especially when particular policies failed, such as his proposal for a comprehensive plan to guarantee universal healthcare and the bungled Lani Guinier nomination that sparked considerable dismay within black communities. It was at these moments that Clinton's symbolism politics proved most effective in containing black popular alienation and disaffection.

To assume that black Americans lacked viable alternatives other than to remain steadfast Democrats is to obscure the potency of black political power. Likewise, to attribute black voting behavior to emotional attachments and sympathy, appearance, regional identity, musical tastes, and/or religious affiliation is to distort the political record. As novelist Ralph Ellison said of Lyndon B. Johnson, "I cannot so easily ignore the changes that the President has made in the condition of my people and still consider myself a responsible intellectual."[8] Ellison summed up the impact of black patronage appointments on the record of the southern-born president whom Richard Dalleck called the "flawed giant": "He [Johnson] has changed inescapably the iconography of federal power, from his military aides to the Cabinet, from the Federal Reserve Board to the Supreme Court."[9] Louis Martin (1912–97), founding editor of the *Michigan Chronicle,* editor of the *Chicago Defender,* and deputy chairman of the Democratic National Committee (1964), was arguably the mastermind of black presidential politics during the 1960s and 1970s. Affectionately referred to as the "Godfather of Black Politics," he served as advisor to three post–World War II Democratic presidents—John F. Kennedy, Lyndon B. Johnson, and Jimmy Carter. In this capacity Martin influenced Johnson's appointment of African Americans to key cabinet, judicial, and ambassadorial posts.[10]

Louis Martin's work, the growth of the black judiciary, and the rise of black elected officials in the 1970s facilitated the expansion in black political focus and strategy to include appeals to the federal judicial and legislative branches of government and to the executive office. After two decades of Martin's stealth-like influence and subtle coalition building, black Americans understood more fully the substantive and symbolic power wielded by presidents.[11] But they also learned something even more portentous. As Martin put it, "We were moving beyond this business of appointments being the thing that black America was keenest about."[12] Careful cultivation of a Democratic president, especially one of southern origins, and a stronger liberal-progressive Democratic Party paid great dividends. Indeed, black leaders deemed it essential to put into the White House a Democratic president as a prerequisite to the preservation of civil-rights gains. Actually, any Democratic president would provide more support for the relentless struggle for respect and equality of opportunity that African Americans desired than a Republican one.[13]

In an Ellison-like analytical vein it is illuminating to note the ways in which Clinton used the power of his presidency to open space for a new race discourse in America and in so doing moved the country further along the path to acknowledging race wrongs. Yet, it is also essential to place the origins of black people's political acumen and reverence for Bill Clinton within the historical context of the 1960s Civil Rights and the 1970s Black Power Movements. Thus, not only is it important to appreciate what Bill Clinton did to earn black loyalty and admiration, it is necessary also to nudge attention to what they did to prepare for and make possible Clinton's ascendancy.

After the passage of the Voting Rights Act of 1965, black popular interest in electoral politics mushroomed as the idea that a black person could become a viable candidate sunk root. But it was the three Democratic presidential bids of African Americans, congresswoman Shirley Chisholm in 1972, and the Rev. Jesse Jackson in 1984 and 1988, that signaled the popular transformation in black political mobilization and noticeable increases in the number of black registered voters.[14] By the middle of the 1990s the black electorate had become truly national, all of the southern states with the exception of Arkansas sent at least one black congressman to the U.S. House of Representatives. Thus, the presidential victories Clinton achieved in 1992 and 1996 also reflect the triumph of black political power. Black people now knew that whenever black politics failed to deliver, or proved insufficient or was nullified, then Republicans—Richard Nixon, Ronald Reagan, George H. W. Bush, and George W. Bush—moved into the White House. They also now knew that Republican presidential control spelled white backlash and stunted aspirations in spite of the fact that Reagan on November 2, 1983, signed a law designating the third Monday in January to honor Martin Luther King Jr.

Democratic occupants of the executive branch in the post–Civil Rights era provided a small but growing cadre of black professionals an enhanced visibility that translated into greater access to corporate, governmental, and academic opportunities and positions. In 1964 there were only 103 black elected officials in the nation; by 1994 there were nearly 8,500. Forty-one African Americans served in Congress by 1996. These professionals possessed symbolic value to the larger black community as testaments to black ability and achievement. Vernon Jordan confided that he was proud to chair Clinton's transition team in 1992 because, "As far as we have come, many blacks still thrill at the sound of 'the first' one of our own to hold this position or that position—and rightly so."[15]

In the Clinton presidency, Jocelyn Elders and David Satcher served as the first black female and male surgeons general. Regardless of how their tenures ended, each broke new ground and disrupted long-standing barriers of professional exclusion.[16] The University of Pennsylvania law professor Lani Guinier may not have become in 1993 an assistant attorney general for civil rights or the civil-rights enforcement chief in Clinton's administration as he had proposed, but she was shrewd enough to exploit the bungled nomination to land a position in 1998 as the first black woman tenured professor at Harvard Law School. She deserves applause for her agency and her adamant refusal to play the role of hapless victim of Clinton's perfidy.[17] Indeed, Lani Guinier so effectively transformed her ordeal into a bully pulpit that she became a beacon, and a metaphor, for all black women.

For a plethora of reasons, too numerous for the scope of this presentation, Clinton remains a revered figure among the majority of African Americans. Under his watch, American businesses created ten million new jobs, and many black people found employment, some for the first time. Many black women did particularly well. The 2000 census reported that women owned 38 percent of African American–owned businesses, a larger percentage than that of any other minority group and more than the nation's business community as a whole of which women owned only 26 percent. Still, the census reveals that minority firms account for only 15 percent of all businesses in the nation. It is important to underscore the need for a more nuanced understanding of popular black America's support for Clinton. An exploration of black politically progressive practice and internal socio-economic stratification would complicate the reigning caricature of Bill Clinton, the first black president.[18] Clinton's "real" and symbolic significance to black America is much too complicated to be captured in a joke.

Issues and Relationships

In this section I identify a few of the substantive issues and symbolic events that shaped, and illuminate the tensions within, the mutually beneficial relationship between President Clinton and black Democrats, radicals, and progressives who composed both the privileged and the laboring classes.

HAITI—1994

In 1994 Randall Robinson, president of Trans Africa, commenced a twenty-seven-day hunger strike in order to pressure President Clinton to provide safe haven for thousands of Haitians who had fled their homes in the aftermath of the military overthrow of the democratically elected president Jean-Bertrand Aristide.[19] In the three years following Aristide's December 1990 election and overthrow, the Haitian military killed approximately five thousand civilians. Robinson's protest secured the support of the Congressional Black Caucus, led by California congressman Ronald V. Dellums. Although Clinton had initially refused to abandon the policy adhered to by his predecessor, he responded to the black leadership's demand that he end the practice of automatic repatriation of Haitian refugees.

President Clinton went even further and appointed William H. Gray III, current president of the United Negro College Fund, his special advisor and charged him to implement the revamped Haitian policy. But Robinson remained skeptical, confiding, "We have won an important round, but is the victory illusory?" He took solace in one thing, "I do know one thing, Gray is a brilliant politician."[20] Robinson's faith was not misplaced. On September 19 Clinton displayed his willingness to use the power of his office to restore Aristide to his presidency. Robinson exulted, "President Clinton is demonstrating great political courage and resolve." In spite of little support in the House of Representatives or the Senate, Clinton ordered American troops into Haiti. As the sixty-one planes loaded with paratroopers headed for the Caribbean island, the Haitian military ruler agreed to step down and accepted exile. On October 15, 1994, Robinson shared in the Restoration Day festivities in Port-au-Prince, Haiti.

AFFIRMATIVE ACTION—1995

President Lyndon Johnson first used the term "affirmative action" in a 1965 executive order that required federal contractors to "take affirmative action" to guarantee that job seekers and employees "are treated without regard to their race, color, religion, sex, or national origin." Much of the credit for compliance with affirmative action belongs to Republican president Richard Nixon. The process of setting goals and timetables to achieve full compliance with federal civil-rights requirements appealed to large corporations and accounted for the early success of affirmative-action initiatives. Though it has produced more litigation, the issue of affirmative action in employment has been less controversial than that of affirmative action in college admissions. State higher-education institutions from California to Texas to Michigan occupy the center of the controversy both because they are narrowly bound by the Fourteenth Amendment's prohibitions on racial discrimination and because they represent the gateways to upward mobility for millions of Americans, white and black.[21]

Few civil-rights policies in the late twentieth century have proved more controversial. Many white Americans argue that it runs contrary to the concept of achievement founded on objective merit and is therefore reverse racial or sexual discrimination. In the wake of several restrictive U.S. Supreme Court decisions and the growing strength of Republican opposition, Clinton took a stance that won him enormous praise in the black community. He declared, "Affirmative action has been good for America. . . . We should reaffirm the principle of affirmative action and fix the practices. We should have a simple slogan: Mend it, but don't end it. . . . Remember we're still closing the gap between our founders' ideals and our reality."[22] Veteran political analyst Carl T. Rowan lost all pretense of cool. He effusively proclaimed that "his [Clinton's] firm assertion that 'affirmative action has been good for America,' this son of once–Jim Crow Arkansas gave an address that ranks with Lincoln's Emancipation

Proclamation, Martin Luther King's 1963 'I have a dream' address, and President Lyndon Johnson's 1965 speech at Howard University."[23]

THE WELFARE REFORM BILL—1996

By far the harshest criticism Clinton received from black progressives and radicals came on the heels of his signing the Personal Responsibility and Work Opportunity Act in 1996. The loss to the Republicans of the U.S. House of Representatives in the 1994 midterm elections restricted the influence and cut the power of the Congressional Black Caucus. Only two (congressmen Albert Winn of Maryland and Sanford Bishop of Georgia) of the thirty-five black Democrats in the House approved the Welfare Reform Bill. Had Democrats retained control, it is unlikely that Clinton would have signed this legislation that Georgia congressman and Civil Rights Movement veteran John Lewis called "heartless, mean-spirited, low-down and dangerous."[24] Lewis did not take lightly his stance on this occasion or when he opposed the Crime Bill. He confessed that "standing against my own party and president was a politically difficult decision to make."[25]

The legislation combined Clinton's own ideas with others espoused in the Republicans' Contract with America blueprint for conservative changes. The main target of the Personal Responsibility Act was Aid to Families with Dependent Children (AFDC), a program created in 1935 as part of the Social Security Act to prevent children from suffering because of the poverty of their parents. The conservative "welfare reform" measure ended guarantees of federal aid to poor children, turning control of such programs over to the states along with allocations of block grants. The act denied benefits to legal immigrants, reduced food stamp appropriations, and limited families to five years of benefits. It also required most adult welfare recipients to find employment within two years.

Pennsylvania State University black studies professor Clyde Woods attacked Clinton's action and recounted the deplorable state of poor black children's lives in Mississippi. He noted that, "One out of every three children in Mississippi lives in poverty. Additionally, the state pays the lowest benefits in the USA: $120 a month for a mother and two children. Subsidized or free school lunches are received by six out of ten children in Mississippi, for some of these children this lunch is their only meal of the day. None of these harsh realities prevented Clinton from approving Fordice's experiment with the lives of 50,000 destitute families on welfare, 82 percent of whom are African Americans."[26] Historian Robin D. G. Kelley called it "the most draconian measure of the late twentieth century . . . signed not by a Republican president but by a self-proclaimed liberal Democrat."[27]

Actually, Clinton's support of the welfare act was consistent with his centrist ideology, and it was politically astute. His stance immunized him from Republican attacks on the issue and did little to erode his support among popular African Americans. The debate over welfare policy receded to the back burner during the 2000 election campaign and disappeared completely after George W. Bush took office, superseded by the emphasis on tax cuts for the wealthy.

TUSKEGEE SYPHILIS—1996

On May 16, 1996, five of the participants in the United States Public Health Services' study of untreated syphilis, 1932–72, journeyed to Washington, D.C., to attend a special meeting at the White House. Over six hundred men who had been part of the study had died. Herman Shaw served as spokesperson for Charlie Pollard, Carter Howard, Fred Simmons, and Frederick Moss. He declared, "This ceremony is important because the damage done by the Tuskegee Syphilis Study is much deeper than the wound any of us may have suffered. It speaks to our faith in government."[28] David Satcher explained the faulty science and immorality that lay behind the study. "The USPH Study of untreated syphilis in the Negro male was wrong for many reasons. The participants were never informed about the purpose of the study, never asked to give their informed consent to participate in the Study and were intentionally misled about receiving treatment."[29] Demonstrating a compelling mastery of symbolism politics, Clinton stated, "No power on Earth can give you back the lives lost, the pain suffered, the years of internal torment and anguish." But there was something that only Clinton could do. He apologized: "We can look you in the eye and finally say on behalf of the American people, what the United States government did was shameful, and I am sorry." He added, "I apologize and I am sorry that this apology has been so long in coming." And he declared, "I am sorry that your federal government orchestrated a study so clearly racist. That can never be allowed to happen again."[30] But it is significant that Clinton ended with an acknowledgment of the men's humanity and power: "Only you have the power to forgive."[31]

PORT CHICAGO—1999

The Port Chicago Naval Base is located north of San Francisco. On July 17, 1944, in the worst home-front disaster of World War II, an explosion at the base killed 320 American sailors, of whom 202 were black ammunition loaders. In the following month 328 of the surviving ammunition loaders were sent to fill another ship. When 258 of these men refused to do so, they were arrested. Eventually the navy convicted fifty men of mutiny and sentenced them to terms of imprisonment ranging from eight to fifteen years. The navy later reduced the sentences to seventeen months for those with good behavior. President Truman released all the men from prison, but neither he nor the navy acknowledged that the felony conviction, charges of treason and cowardice, and the loss of all veteran benefits shrouded their lives. The NAACP's Thurgood Marshall filed a brief on behalf of the fifty men arguing that they had been railroaded into prison because of their race, but to no avail.

Inspired by a book written by sociologist Robert Allen, *The Port Chicago Mutiny*, two Bay Area congressmen, George Miller and Ronald V. Dellums, launched a decade-long lobbying campaign to clear the names of the fifty black sailors. In December 1999 their efforts bore fruit when Bill Clinton pardoned former-sailor Freddie Meeks of Los Angeles, one of the three remaining sailors convicted of mutiny. Meeks, in an interview, expressed his gratitude to Bill Clinton, "I knew we had a good president and I figured he would do the right thing, and he did the right thing with this pardon. . . . I appreciate it very much."[32]

Conclusion

> Some day the Awakening will come, when the pent-up vigor of ten million souls shall sweep irresistibly toward the Goal, out of the Valley of the Shadow of Death, where all that makes life worth living—Liberty, Justice, and Right—is marked "For White People Only."
> —W. E. B. DuBois, THE SOULS OF BLACK FOLK, 1903

The Civil Rights Movement succeeded in dismantling legal and political barriers to black freedom. One of the driving forces behind the conservative resurgence of the 1980s was a reaction to the gains of black America. During the 1990s President Bill Clinton helped to counter this assault against the whole edifice of laws and court decisions and governmental aid to the poor and dispossessed. While the country made significant strides toward understanding and rectifying the racial wrongs of its past, the problems of economic deprivation and continued discrimination remains. Still, Bill Clinton raised the bar so high in the appointment of

African Americans to his cabinet and to key positions of power within the federal government that when his successor, George W. Bush, appointed Colin Powell to be secretary of state and named Condoleezza Rice the national security advisor hardly a brow was raised.

Perhaps the most significant transformation that occurred under Clinton's presidential watch was that black people became integral Democrats. To most observers and pundits they may have seemed just another special-interest group, especially given the blindness of intractable racism. But, slowly, inexorably, black people became something more as Clinton demonstrated his respect and acceptance of black humanity. So the party became a potent marker of black identity. If black people do not vote the Democratic Party ticket, Democrats lose elections. Black people, therefore, must assume the lead in forming coalitions with other segments of the party and must bring into greater operational harmony this often unwieldy conglomeration of conflicting interests. The future depends on it. Bill Clinton spoke directly to the importance of the black vote and about his desires in an interview with radio show personality Tom Joyner. To Joyner's question about what he would like historians to say about him, Clinton replied:

> I want them to say that I helped to take America into a new era, that I really prepared America for a global economy; a global society; for increasing diversity at home; for responsibilities in a world where there was no Cold War, but we had a lot of challenges from terrorism, from racial and ethnic and religious wars. I want them to say that I did create an America of dramatically increased opportunity for all people, an America where we were coming together more in a spirit of unity, an America that was a leading force for peace and freedom and prosperity in the world. That's what I want them to say.[33]

In this chapter I have tried to balance a sort of upstairs (the black privileged class)/downstairs (the black working and working poor class) approach to understanding black people's reaction to the Clinton's presidency. I am wary that revolutions can and often do go backward, yet heartened by the reality that freedom is a constant struggle. Clinton reaffirmed this commitment to struggle most effectively in the minds of the popular black community by refusing to cave in during his impeachment. He got up every day and went to work. In spite of it all, however, words Martin Luther King Jr. uttered many decades ago resonate loudly as I reflect on the unfolding legacy of the Clinton presidency. The country is today even more divided along class and race lines. And King's words demand attention: "When millions of people have been cheated for centuries, restitution is a costly process. Inferior education, poor housing, unemployment, inadequate health care—each is a bitter component of the oppression that has been our heritage. . . . Justice so long deferred has accumulated interest and its costs for this society will be substantial in financial as well as human terms."[34] Clinton helped to put America on the road to restitution; where we end up, however, is the challenge of the next century.

5 Clinton, Fulbright, and the Legacy of the Cold War

RANDALL B. WOODS

In this chapter, Professor Woods examines the foundations of President Clinton's foreign policy as well as the unique developments on the international stage that made foreign policymaking during the 1990s uniquely complex and uncertain. Professor Woods contends that because of the singular events of the 1990s, and in particular the end of the Cold War and the accompanying rise in both ethnic and religious conflict, the Clinton administration forged an activist international policy—yet a policy that was also pragmatic and centrist. Further, Professor Woods argues that to thoroughly understand President Clinton's foreign policy, one must understand the lessons that Bill Clinton learned while working with one of his acknowledged mentors, Senator J. William Fulbright. Professor Woods argues that many of President Clinton's international views can be traced back to this early relationship. Ultimately, however, Professor Woods argues that President Clinton faced such unique international developments that the experiences and lessons learned from Senator Fulbright were not always applicable in a world that appeared to be increasingly full of hatred and animosity toward the United States.

In a 2000 article in *Foreign Affairs,* international-relations scholar Stephen Walt surveyed current opinion concerning the foreign policy of the previous eight years: "'It's the economy, stupid.' Back in the 1992 campaign, that one line told us that Bill Clinton did not intend to be a great foreign policy president," Walt wrote. "As his second term ends, most pundits agree that this is one promise he has kept. Critics on the right argue that he is too eager to accommodate a rising China, too blind to Russia's corruption and cronyism, and too slow to use force against states like Yugoslavia or Iraq. On the left, liberals bemoan Clinton's failure to prevent the genocide in Rwanda, his tardy response to the bloodletting in the Balkans, and his abandonment of his early pledge to build a multilateral world order grounded in stronger international institutions. Even pragmatic centrists find him wanting, deriding his foreign policy as 'social work' that is too easily swayed by ethnic lobbies, public opinion polls, and media buzz."[1] According to Walt, all these judgments were too harsh. In the end, he concludes, "The foreign policy of the Clinton administration has been well suited to an era when there is little to gain in foreign policy and much to lose."[2]

Not surprisingly, the architects of the Clinton-era diplomacy see their policies as nothing less than revolutionary. According to Sandy Berger, Clinton's national security advisor, the men and women who succeeded the Bush foreign-policy team faced a crisis in leadership: "In 1992, the United States was widely seen as unlikely to sustain its global engagement in the absence of an overriding threat. It was lagging competitively. U.S. alliances were in jeopardy, with their missions undefined and with new threats—from the Balkans to a nuclearizing North Korea—being inadequately addressed. Japan and western Europe were considered increasingly likely to forge separate identities outside their alliances with America. U.S. foreign policy had barely come to grips with the emerging challenges of a globalized world, from the volatility of markets to the proliferation of weapons to the spread of disease."[3] The Clinton team, Berger asserts, responded in spades: "As the first president who has understood the global economy," the national security advisor claimed, "Bill Clinton has led the greatest world trade expansion in history—from $4 trillion to $6.6 trillion a year." Believing that "local conflicts can have global consequences," Clinton devoted himself to peacemaking, rejecting those who contended that America should do nothing about foreign wars unless it was directly threatened. There was an emphasis on nonproliferation—the Agreed Framework with North Korea that from 1994 froze the production of plutonium for nuclear weapons in the North.

Like the American people, Clinton and his advisors cared deeply about human rights but were careful not to involve the United States militarily in situations over which it had little or no control. What Berger and other Clintonites touted, then, was a pragmatic, activist foreign policy in which Washington attempted to use American power to keep the peace and foster economic and social justice at home and abroad.

As a historian, I am not so much interested in value judgment as I am in cause and effect, in placing the Clinton policies in a longer and larger perspective, in seeing patterns and connections. Like other decision makers, President Clinton responded not only to immediate circumstance and traditional interest groups but also to his own experience and education. In this regard, I think that J. William Fulbright, one of the president's acknowledged mentors, is particularly important.

In 1992 Bill Fulbright's former mailroom boy and protégé, William Jefferson Clinton, was elected president of the United States. Fulbright, who for thirty years had chaired the Senate Foreign Relations Committee (SFRC) and struggled to shape an alternative Cold War foreign policy for five administrations, was absolutely delighted. Actually, he had been quite pleased with George Bush, declaring him to be one of the most knowledgeable men ever to be in charge of American foreign policy; but Clinton was an Arkansan, a Rhodes scholar, an educated, pragmatic, interested man who had opposed the war in Vietnam. The election of his protégé seemed a redemption to Fulbright, a repudiation of the anti-communist true believers he had struggled against since the dawning of the Cold War, a fitting response to those who had heaped aspersions on Arkansas through the years, a last laugh on his old nemesis, Lyndon Johnson. Although rumors concerning Fulbright's intervention in his behalf to keep him out of the draft had caused Clinton difficulty during the presidential campaign, the president took pains to acknowledge his debt to the former junior senator from Arkansas and to embrace him publicly. In May 1993, at a gala ceremony in Washington, Clinton presented an overwhelmed Fulbright with the Medal of Freedom. Following a massive stroke, the Arkansan died in his sleep at one o'clock in the morning on February 9, 1995. President Clinton delivered the eulogy at a moving ceremony in Washington National Cathedral.[4]

Arguably, Clinton, the first post–Cold War president, could have had no better mentor than Bill Fulbright. Indeed, because he served his apprenticeship under a foreign-policy expert who embraced the concept of cultural relativity, who refused to see the communist world as simply an evil monolith, who genuinely believed in the notion of multilateralism in both economic and strategic matters, Bill Clinton seemed well prepared to head the foreign-policy establishment during the 1990s. But, it should be noted, the Clinton policies were sometimes as much a reaction to as a reflection of Fulbright internationalism. In part this was because one individual represented the executive branch and the other the legislative, but also because there was more idealism and less moralism in one than the other.

At the close of World War II and the dawn of the Cold War, Fulbright perceived the central problem of U.S. foreign policy to be how to preserve Anglo-American civilization from destruction. Appalled by the bombing of Hiroshima and Nagasaki, he decided that the world was far too dangerous a place for the members of the Atlantic community to simply go their own way. As part of a universal effort to control the forces of nationalism and fascism, the western democracies would have to surrender a portion of their national sovereignty within the context of an international collective security organization. Only in this way could aggression be nipped in the bud and eventually the socio-economic roots of war be eliminated. Subsequently confronted with the reality that neither his country nor its wartime allies were willing to relinquish their freedom of action within a regional association of nations, much less an international one, Fulbright resigned himself to working toward the rehabilitation of Western Europe and the containment of Soviet and Chinese communism. Thus did he support not only the Marshall Plan—which, according to John Gaddis, represented the most perfect conflation of American ideals and self-interest in the postwar era—but military aid to Greece and Turkey, foreign aid in general, and limited intervention into foreign societies threatened by communism. He did not, however, buy into the globalist assumptions inherent in the Truman Doctrine, agreeing with George Kennan that America's response ought to be commensurate with its power and with the actual threat to its interests, economically and strategically defined.[5]

During the Eisenhower years Fulbright sensed a rigidity and moral absolutism in American policy that hindered America's drive for competitive coexistence with the Soviet Union; he criticized Dulles and Eisenhower not only for their strident anti-communism but also for their unimaginative and inflexible approach to combating America's enemies. Their emphasis on military aid and alliances, he charged, allowed the Soviet Union under Nikita Khrushchev to identify itself with anti-colonialism and through pragmatic aid programs and support of indigenous nationalist movements to win the battle for the developing world.[6]

Frightened by the resurgence of the radical right that began with the establishment of the John Birch Society in 1959 and mightily impressed by Khrushchev's conciliatory visit to the United States that same year, Fulbright moved beyond competitive coexistence and embraced the concept of détente. He was well pleased with the Kennedy administration's plans for a flexible response to the communist threat and, following the Berlin and Cuban Missile Crises, with its willingness to make a fresh start with the Soviet Union. Indeed, he greeted the signing of the nuclear test-ban treaty as nothing less than the dawning of a new age. Though he continued to be troubled by the structure of foreign aid and the vast sums spent on the military-industrial complex by Secretary of Defense Robert McNamara, the new chairman of the Senate Foreign Relations Committee had every reason to believe that Kennedy's flexibility and the search for détente would continue under Lyndon Johnson. Fulbright's famous 1964 speech, "Old Myths and New Realities" was designed to point the nation and the administration further down that road.[7]

With the burgeoning of the military-industrial complex, the penetration of the military by the radical right, far-reaching covert operations by the CIA, and the onset of the Vietnam War, however, Fulbright decided that the United States was acting in ways that were counterproductive of its strategic and economic interests. The powerful chair of the Senate Foreign Relations Committee came to believe that the very liberal internationalist philosophy that he had espoused from 1944 through 1964 was the primary culprit. America's obsessive anti-communism had produced a foreign policy that supported right-wing military dictatorships in the name of freedom and democracy.[8]

By the summer of 1969 Fulbright had concluded that, like Lyndon Johnson, Richard Nixon had become a prisoner of the radical right, the military-industrial complex, his own psyche, and other forces of which he was only dimly aware and which he could not control even if he had wanted to. The country was frightened and exhausted, afraid to lose in Vietnam, but increasingly convinced that it could not win. The liberal internationalism of the Kennedy-Johnson years was dead, thoroughly discredited by events in Southeast Asia. The void in American foreign policy was being filled by the true believers, vested interests, and political opportunists who had a stake in the continuation of the war in Vietnam, the perpetuation of the Cold War, and the maintenance and expansion of the network of bases and commitments that it had spawned. If Congress did not act, the nation would be dragged into one foreign adventure after another until, morally and financially bankrupt, it disappeared from the face of the earth like other empires before it.

With the activism of the Kennedy-Johnson years in disrepute, Fulbright reasoned, the best bet for checking the right-wing radicalism spawned by the Cold War and extricating America from Vietnam was traditional conservatism. From the summer of 1969 until the Arkansan's departure from the Senate in 1975, the Constitution served as the principal rallying point in his campaign to end the war and contain the burgeoning American empire. Only that hallowed document, he perceived, offered sufficient political protection for those who were sure to be accused of endangering America's national security. Carefully, meticulously, Fulbright and his chief of staff, Carl Marcy, built support for the notion that first the Johnson and then the Nixon administrations were making international commitments and involving the country in future wars without its permission or even its knowledge, and in so doing were violating the basic law of the land. The movement that began with passage in 1969 of Fulbright's national commitments resolution was transformed into a relentless juggernaut by Cambodia, Kent State, and Watergate. It culminated in 1973 with passage of the War Powers Act.[9]

As chairman of the Senate Foreign Relations Committee, then, Fulbright continually decried the power of the military-industrial complex and worked to limit its influence. He denounced unilateralism and insisted that the United States embrace and work through international organizations. He recognized that there were limits on American power—and interests—and called on the executive to define those interests carefully and apply American might only when and where they were threatened. The proper course for policymakers was asymmetrical containment of threats, not global policing; he stood for a foreign policy of restraint. Above all, Fulbright argued that pragmatism rather than ideology, rationality rather than prejudice should be the watchwords for American diplomats.

Bill Clinton assumed the presidency at a time unique in the history of American foreign relations. The end of the Cold War left the United States in a position of unquestioned preponderance. Its economy was 40 percent larger than its nearest competitor, and its defense spending equaled that of the six next highest, many of which were Washington's close allies. The United States led the world in higher education, scientific research, and advanced technology. As it faced the last decade of the twentieth century, then, America possessed great power and freedom of action but no overriding enemy and no clear idea of its objectives. "Thus the central paradox of unipolarity: the United States enjoys enormous influence but has little idea what do with its power or even how much effort it should expend," Stephen Walt observed.[10] An important byproduct of this preponderance was that most Americans lost interest in foreign affairs. Two-thirds of the Republicans elected to Congress in 1994 reportedly did not possess passports. Nativists in Congress would cut the budget allocation for international affairs, attempt to sanction foreign firms trading with Cuba, hold UN dues hostage to extremist views on family planning, and drag its heels in financing key U.S. commitments to the International Monetary Fund and Middle East peace process.[11] The diplomatic problems that Clinton faced seemed radically different from those confronting Fulbright's generation. Future conflicts promised to be not only international but intranational. Religious hatreds, sectarianism, and tribalism, which frequently transcended national boundaries, had replaced the Cold War as the principal threats to peace. These conflicts would pit governments against their own populations as often as government against government. Globalization would be the byword of the 1990s, but as Sandy Berger observed, "It can expand access to technology that enriches life—and technology that destroys it. It can equalize economic opportunity—and accentuate economic disparity. It can make dictatorships more vulnerable to the spread of liberating ideas—and democracies more vulnerable to the spread of terrorism, disease, and financial turmoil."[12]

Like most presidential candidates, Bill Clinton in 1992 had spoken in only the most general terms about the diplomatic course he would follow if he were elected. Not surprisingly, he had promised to address the problems of the post–Cold War era. The United States, he said, should provide aid to the former Soviet Union to help it down the road to democracy and free enterprise. Indeed, there were Wilsonian overtones to his foreign-policy statements. Advancing democracy should be the object of "a long-term Western strategy," he said. At the same time, the president emphasized that the focus of future foreign policy would be the global economy.[13] America would have to learn how to compete peacefully with Japan and the German-led European community. To the dismay of conservatives, the new president declared that, given the culmination of glasnost and perestroika, there was no further need for an ever-expanding defense establishment. The would-be administration's economic program envisaged cuts in the defense budget of $123.9 billion between 1994 and 1998. And, finally, Clinton seemed to echo former president Jimmy Carter in calling for an American-led campaign to ensure respect for human rights. Indeed, during the presidential campaign he had blasted the Bush administration for not doing more to stop the sectarian conflict then raging in the former Yugoslavia.[14]

As the world was to learn, the Clinton administration would advance five major foreign-policy goals: (1) to shrink the military-industrial complex and use the "peace dividend" to advance social and economic security in the United States; (2) to reduce the risk of major war in Europe, East Asia, and the Middle East, largely by remaining militarily involved there; (3) to reduce the threat posed by weapons of mass destruction (WMD); (4) to foster a more open and productive world economy; and (5) to attempt to build a world order compatible with basic American values by encouraging the growth of democracy and by acting forcefully to curb major human-rights abuses. These goals were hardly controversial; indeed, they were virtually indistinguishable from those of both Bushes.[15]

As far as creating and distributing a peace dividend, Clinton proved as good as his word. Following the election, Secretary of Defense Les Aspin announced the scrapping of Star Wars, and the administration began dismantling or scaling down 92 overseas bases and 129 domestic installations.[16] Clinton's 1994 budget promised to reduce the federal deficit $140 billion by 1997. The Clinton budget marked the first decline in defense spending since the Cold War began. The president and his advisors believed that for the United States to play its proper role in world affairs there would have to be unity and economic strength at home. Thus his emphasis on civil rights, welfare reform, and healthcare for all.

In regard to his second objective, Clinton had to limit America's direct military role and encourage key allies to bear a heavier burden because domestic support for overseas military operations was fragile. But he deserves credit for holding NATO together at a time when its principal reason for being—the Cold War—was waning. Under American leadership, NATO assumed the broader role of guaranteeing peace and security throughout Europe. As Sandy Berger would later boast: "In Europe, we revitalized NATO from a static Cold War alliance to a magnet for new democracies, with new partners, members, and missions."[17]

In Asia the reaffirmation of the Japanese-American security treaty in April 1995 defused Japanese concerns about a continued U.S. military presence and constituted a powerful symbol of America's continued engagement in the region. When Communist China began menacing Taiwan in an effort to intimidate the island into accepting Anschluss, the

Clinton administration reassured the Asian democracies by stationing its Pacific fleet in the Taiwan straits. And, perhaps most important, Washington showed a willingness to confront an increasingly bellicose North Korea.[18]

In many ways, the end of the Cold War for Europe was a mixed blessing. And it was here, the continent of primary interest to the United States throughout most of its history, that the Clinton foreign policies were to be put to their greatest test. Much of Eastern Europe had toiled under the yoke of communist totalitarianism for forty years, but at the same time Soviet-sponsored authoritarian regimes had held fierce ethnic and religious rivalries in check, especially in the volatile Balkans. In 1991 with the collapse of the communist regime, Yugoslavia, a federation that included the states of Serbia, Montenegro, Croatia, Bosnia Herzegovina, Slovenia, and Macedonia, broke apart. Slovenia and Croatia declared their independence. When Bosnia Herzegovina attempted to break away from Yugoslavia, war erupted between the Serb and Croatian minorities in Bosnia on the one hand and the Bosnian government, which was largely dominated by Muslims, on the other. The Croats wanted to merge with Croatia and the Serbs with Serbia. Both groups were Christian. Neither wanted to be part of an independent Bosnia ruled by Muslims. Over the next three years tens of thousands of people died as first the Croats and then the Serbs, aided by the army of the Serbian republic under the leadership of nationalist Slobodan Milosevic, secured control of large parts of Bosnia. During these campaigns the Serbs engaged in "ethnic cleansing" in which thousands of Muslims were raped, tortured, and killed. The Muslims and Croats conducted their own ethnic-cleansing campaigns but on a much smaller scale. The United Nations inserted some twenty-four thousand peace-keeping troops into the combat zones and negotiated one cease-fire after another only to see all of them collapse in the face of the blood-and-soil nationalism of the Balkans.[19]

As President Clinton came into office, the pressure on him to intervene militarily to relieve the Serbian siege of Sarajevo and to stop the bloodshed in general became intense. He insisted, however, that the Bosnian nightmare was a matter for NATO and the UN, and that the members of those organizations in closest physical proximity to Bosnia, namely France and Germany, should take the lead. Privately, the Clinton administration had decided that it would intervene in Bosnia only when and if the parties involved showed a willingness for peace. Despite its professed sympathy for human rights, the Clinton administration was afraid of becoming bogged down in another Vietnam-type conflict. In

1995 after years of bloody fighting and ethnic cleansing, and a crushing economic embargo imposed on Yugoslavia by the UN, the Serbs (pressured by Milosevic who had been forced by international pressure to do a turnabout), Croats, and Muslims agreed to a cease-fire and to Bosnia-wide elections for a parliament and a three-person presidency. The Dayton Accords (named for the Ohio city where the negotiations took place) were to be backed by a sixty-thousand-person NATO force, including twenty thousand American troops.[20]

Fulbright not only approved of Clinton's handling of the Bosnian situation, there is reason to believe that the president actively consulted his mentor during the early stages of the crisis. During the Vietnam conflict, Fulbright had argued repeatedly that the United States had neither the duty nor the ability to impose a settlement on a nation within which there was no consensus, especially on the vital issue of war and peace. Moreover, if those nations most proximate to the crisis and hence most affected were not willing to risk blood and treasure to resolve it, it ill behooved the United States to do so.

The Clinton administration intervened in Bosnia only with great reluctance. The new regime inherited another situation, however, in which the United States was already deeply involved. Late in 1992 the Bush administration authorized a U.S.-led but UN-sanctioned military intervention into the East African state of Somalia. During the 1980s first Moscow, then Washington had poured weapons into this poor but strategically located nation of five million persons in an effort to win the support of dictator Mohamed Siad Barre. When the Cold War ended, he fled, but Somalia teemed with weapons. What ensued was a civil war between rival clan leaders, President Ali Mahdi Mohammed and Gen. Mohammed Farah Aydid, that impoverished and brutalized the country, creating hundreds of thousands of refugees and mass starvation.[21] Although a similar situation existed in Sudan, the American media chose to focus on the swollen bellies and fly-covered corpses in Somalia. The Bush administration caved into public pressure and on December 3 received UN Security Council approval for military intervention. A week later twenty-eight U.S. troops landed in Mogadishu, the capital and scene of much of the fighting. The expeditionary force set up a relief network but did not disarm the clansmen who withdrew to await events.

President Clinton pledged to stay the course in Somalia, and he proved as good as his word. In June 1993, a price of twenty-five thousand dollars was placed on General Aydid's head, but he remained at large. When a U.S. helicopter was shot down by Somali militiamen, killing many of its occupants, and a further eighteen Americans died in a fire-fight in October, the United States began to lose heart. During spring 1995 the last of the U.S. and UN troops withdrew. The military situation remained unresolved, but mass starvation had ended, and the semblance of a national economy had once again emerged in Somalia. No doubt Bill Fulbright would have argued that Clinton should have known better. Anyone who had lived through the Vietnam era should have realized the folly of sending American troops to settle a civil war in a nation in which no U.S. vital interest was involved. Indeed, where Fulbright would differ most with Clinton was probably over human rights. The former chair of the SFRC had been openly critical of Jimmy Carter. The deployment of American power to influence how other regimes treated their citizens would take the nation down a dangerous path. It was the kind of moral, cultural imperialism that had led the United States into a disastrous war in Southeast Asia. But Fulbright could have consoled himself with the realization that at least Clinton did not take ten years and fifty thousand dead to learn his lesson.[22]

Like most of its predecessors, the Clinton administration perceived Latin America and specifically the Caribbean basin as the area most vital to the U.S. national interest. The poorest republic in the Western Hemisphere, Haiti had suffered under one autocratic regime after another throughout the nineteenth and twentieth centuries. With the support of a tiny business and planting elite, these brutal dictators had exploited and oppressed the nation's peasantry. In 1991 the cycle appeared to be broken with the election of Jean-Bertrand Aristide, a Catholic priest and social activist. Aristide, however, soon ran afoul of the military and the plutocracy. Late in the year he was driven into exile in the United States.[23]

For three years the military regime of Gen. Raul Cedras imposed a reign of terror on Haiti. Paramilitary thugs tortured and killed Aristide supporters and those suspected of opposition to the government. The United States imposed a blockade in an effort to bring down Cedras and restore Aristide to power, but the embargo only further impoverished rural peasants and the urban poor. Finally, President Clinton ordered military intervention. Before U.S. troops could land, however, former president Jimmy Carter persuaded Cedras to step down voluntarily. As a consequence, American troops occupied the country without resistance. Late in 1994 President Aristide returned to Haiti, and that unfortunate republic once again started haltingly down the path toward democracy and reform.[24]

Fulbright had opposed Lyndon Johnson's intervention into the Dominican Republic in 1965—indeed, the open breach between the two men dated from that incident—and by the end of his career he regarded himself as a staunch noninterventionist. But there were limits. Although he had opposed the Bay of Pigs operation, the chair of the SFRC had advocated a U.S. invasion of Cuba during the Cuban Missile Crisis. Clearly, he believed that the Caribbean was an area vital to U.S. interests and that the exercise of American power there was not only necessary but appropriate. To his mind, as to Clinton's, the physical survival of the United States took first precedence and the self-determination of indigenous societies second. Where the two men differed was over the use of force. Both would agree that authentic national security warranted military action, but in regard to the second, Fulbright refused to equate national self-determination with democracy and so could see no reason under any circumstances for U.S. military intervention.

As far as international economics was concerned, Bill Clinton was as committed to free trade and American participation in a global economy as his Republican predecessors. With a great deal of effort he pushed through Congress the North American Free Trade Agreement (NAFTA), which provided for the gradual elimination of tariffs and other trade barriers between the United States on the one hand and Canada and Mexico on the other. What was envisioned was a vast North American free trade zone in which goods and capital would flow freely across borders, allowing Mexico, the United States, and Canada to produce and export those goods and services that they produced most efficiently. Mexican petroleum, agricultural products, and cheaply produced manufactured goods would enjoy new access to U.S. markets while Mexico would be open to American technology. Protectionists in the United States complained that U.S. manufacturers would move their operations to Mexico to take advantage of cheap labor thereby increasing unemployment in the United States. The Clinton administration replied that every blue-collar job lost in the United States would be replaced by a new white-collar one. That argument prevailed. The president also skillfully handled the Mexican peso crisis of 1994. When Congress balked at funding a support package to Mexico, Clinton used his executive authority to take money from the Exchange Stabilization Fund.[25]

Clinton's philosophy, of course, fit in perfectly with Fulbright internationalism. While a Rhodes Scholar, Fulbright had studied under Robert McCollum at Oxford. The Scotsman was a classic English liberal, a disciple of both Adam Smith and Woodrow Wilson; Fulbright ardently supported every trade liberalization act to come before Congress. He and Clinton were part of the multi-lateralist revolution in American foreign policy that began with the passage of the Reciprocal Trade Agreements Act under Franklin Roosevelt. For both men foreign aid should be primarily non-military, designed to get impoverished nations up to speed and enable them to compete economically in an interdependent world.

Bill Clinton's second inauguration in January 1997 took place amid increasing tensions in the Middle East. In Israel Prime Minister Benjamin Netanyahu headed a political coalition which included the right-wing Likud party and which was dedicated to implementing as little of the peace accord with the Palestinians as possible. With armed clashes between Israeli security forces and Palestinian youth on the increase once again, the Clinton administration came under intense pressure from human-rights activists to force the Israelis to halt new settlements in occupied territory and to implement the peace accords, and from American Zionists to lend all aid and support to Netanyahu in his struggle against Palestinian nationalists. After months of nerve-wracking diplomacy, Washington persuaded Netanyahu and PLO chairman Yasser Arafat to attend a conference at the Wye River Plantation in Maryland. There in October the parties signed the Wye River Memorandum, an agreement that promised the further redeployment of Israeli forces from 13 percent of the West Bank, which would put 18.8 percent of the region under Palestinian control. Future withdrawals were to be negotiated in the final status talks that were set to be concluded by May 1999. For its part, the Palestinian authority promised renewed efforts to control terrorism and to nullify provisions in the Palestinian charter that called for Israel's destruction.[26]

Both Clinton and Fulbright had experienced the Six Day War and its aftermath. Both regarded the situation in the Middle East as a tragedy in which there were no villains, only victims. And both believed it imperative that the United States use its influence to secure a just and lasting peace for the region. In 1970 Fulbright had called publicly for a land-for-peace deal to settle the Arab-Israeli conflict. Under his plan, Israel would retreat behind its pre-1967 borders in return for full Arab diplomatic recognition and a great-power guarantee of Middle East borders. He was denounced publicly by the government of Golda Meier and American Zionists. Indeed, Fulbright came to believe that it was his stand over the Middle East rather than Vietnam that cost him his Senate seat in 1974. Clinton was much more sensitive than Fulbright to pro-Israeli sentiment in the United States, but he did everything in his power to encourage

moderates in Israel itself. And, in fact, the blame for rejecting a comprehensive land-for-peace deal during the Clinton administration lay with
Yasser Arafat rather than the president and Ehud Barak.

While the Clinton administration wielded the olive branch in the Arab-
Israeli conflict, it was forced to employ the thunderbolt in its ongoing
confrontation with Iraq. In January 1998 Saddam Hussein denied UN
inspectors access to a number of suspected weapons sites. U.S. forces were
sent to the region, but a military strike was averted when UN secretary-
general Kofi Annan worked out an agreement in February so that so-
called "presidential sites"—locations Saddam had declared off-limits to
foreigners—would be open to inspection.

Mindful of past deceptions by Baghdad, Clinton warned that if Iraq
reneged on the agreement, "then the United States . . . would have the
unilateral right to respond at a time, place, or manner of our own choosing." His resolve was tested in late fall, when Saddam again refused to
cooperate with the inspectors in an attempt to pressure the UN to end
crippling economic sanctions on Iraq. After failed negotiations, the
United States and Great Britain unleashed a major air bombardment.
American and British planes blasted several presidential sites. The bombing seemed to have little effect on Baghdad's intransigence, however.
Meanwhile, France, Russia, and China, anxious for trade with Iraq, led
the way in calling for a lifting of UN sanctions. Bill Fulbright had supported the Gulf War, although without enthusiasm. U.S. and Western
European dependence on Middle East oil coupled with the threat posed
to American security by weapons of mass destruction were enough to
convince even this staunch noninterventionist that the use of force was
necessary.[27]

As chair of the Senate Foreign Relations Committee, Fulbright had
championed the original Nuclear Non-Proliferation Treaty and had
fought the Nixon administration tooth and nail over its determination
to maintain nuclear superiority over the rest of the world. Given globalization, the impoverishment of the Soviet Union, and the emergence of
chemical and biological weapons, non-proliferation was an even more
compelling issue for Clinton than for the presidents Fulbright had
served. In this area the Clinton administration's most conspicuous achievement, in addition to containing Iraq, was the protracted effort to dissuade North Korea from acquiring nuclear weapons. The administration
briefly considered a preemptive strike in 1994 but cooler heads prevailed.
Following protracted negotiations, North Korea agreed to cease plutonium production at the Yongbyon research reactor, and the United

States, Japan, and South Korea agreed to provide North Korea with two light-water reactors for its power needs.[28]

It should be noted that Clinton's efforts to halt the spread of WMD in other areas ran afoul of a Republican-dominated Congress and the military-industrial complex. The perspective embodied by former congressman and secretary of defense Melvin Laird was still alive and well in the person of chair of the House Appropriations Committee Dick Armey. The White House failed to persuade the Senate to ratify the Comprehensive Test Ban Treaty in October 1999.[29] This constituted a severe blow to the long-standing American effort to slow nuclear proliferation, rekindled foreign concerns about American unilateralism, and made it easier for China, India, and other nascent nuclear powers to develop weapons as sophisticated as those of the United States. The administration also failed to dissuade India and Pakistan from testing nuclear weapons in the spring of 1998, and responding to charges that he was soft on defense, the president signed the National Missile Defense Act of 1999.

Observers of the Bosnian crisis of the mid-1990s predicted that the wave of nationalism and ethnic cleansing could not be contained within that province. They were right. The increasingly autocratic Slobodan Milosevic was able to retain power in the former Yugoslavia, now reduced to Serbia and Montenegro, primarily by appealing to Serbian ultranationalists, by propagandizing, and by isolating his countrymen from the outside world. Shortly after coming to power he had ended the autonomous status of Kosovo, a province in the southwest part of Serbia made up of 90 percent ethnic Albanians and 10 percent ethnic Serbs. As Serb military police continued to harass the Albanian majority, intellectuals, youths—many of them jobless—and farmers grew increasingly disenchanted with the peaceful approach of the Democratic League of Kosovo (LDK) headed by Ibrahim Rugova. Following a bloody Serb crackdown in the central Drenica region, Albanian nationalists turned to the burgeoning Kosovo Liberation Army (KLA), which was pledged to winning independence for the province through force of arms.[30]

In July 1998, Serbian police and the Yugoslav army launched a massive attack on rural areas in an attempt to destroy the KLA's base of support. Thousands of homes in more than four hundred villages were looted and burned, approximately 350,000 people were displaced, and at least 1,000 Kosovar Albanians killed. Religious differences made the violence particularly ferocious. The Albanian Kosovars were Muslim while the Serbs were Orthodox Christian. The latter were determined, among other things, to protect the numerous historic and religious sites in Kosovo.[31]

By September, NATO, concerned about instability on its southeastern flank and under increasing pressure from human-rights advocates, decided to intervene. Under threat of air assault, Milosevic signed an agreement with U.S. envoy Richard Holbrooke that provided for the stationing of two thousand unarmed foreign observers in the troubled province and the gradual withdrawal of Serb police and military personnel. But instead of pulling his forces out, Milosevic decided sometime in early 1999 that the only way the KLA could be destroyed and Kosovo preserved for Serbians was to drive a majority of the Albanian population out, thus creating more of an ethnic balance. In March and April some sixty thousand Serb police and soldiers systematically rounded up and expelled ethnic Albanians from Kosovo, driving them into Albania or Macedonia and in the process threatening to destabilize those countries. In April, after Milosevic refused NATO's repeated demands to cease and desist, the alliance, led by the United States, launched around-the-clock air attacks on Serb positions in Kosovo and on Serbia. The assault only hardened Belgrade's resolve.

The Clinton administration, supported by Germany and France, refused pleas to introduce ground troops. That Russia, a traditional ally of Serbia, was adamantly opposed to the bombing but particularly the deployment of NATO ground forces had much to do with the alliance's position. While NATO bombers destroyed much of Yugoslavia's infrastructure, Serb forces drove more than one million of Kosovo's two million ethnic Albanians out of the province. But expulsion was only part of the ordeal the Kosovar Albanians had to endure. Serb forces systematically robbed the refugees, burned or shelled their houses, selectively raped the women, and executed some ten thousand young men. In late May 1999 the Hague international tribunal indicted Milosevic as a war criminal. In June, Belgrade finally admitted defeat and began pulling its troops out of Kosovo. The Allies divided the region into five districts and prepared occupation forces. As the regime in Belgrade teetered on the brink of collapse and Kosovo's one million plus refugees prepared to return home, the Clinton administration was receiving grudging approval from even its harshest Republican critics. Not a single American life had been lost in the operation.[32]

It is difficult to compare Fulbright and Clinton's foreign policy views first because for Fulbright the single most destructive force in American society during his lifetime was anti-communism. It polarized the populace, produced the military-industrial complex, threatened the world with nuclear annihilation, and bred such disasters as the war in Southeast Asia. Obsessed with a society that was obsessed with the Cold War, Fulbright continuously battled against what he considered the nefarious fruits of that conflict. He urged his countrymen to opt for multilateralism rather than unilateralism, to reject intervention and embrace the concept of cultural relativity, to promote economic interdependence rather than protectionism, to make idealism rather than moralism the basis of their foreign policy. In downplaying the threat posed by the Soviet Union and Communist China, Fulbright dreamed of a multipolar world in which education and economics rather than armaments and nationalism dominated international affairs. And a comparison is difficult second because Clinton was president and Fulbright was not. Nevertheless, Fulbright's influence on his protégé was clear and unmistakable. Anticommunism was not the force in Clinton's world as it was in Fulbright's, although some would argue that it had only metamorphosed into religious fundamentalism, nativism, and protectionism. But its symptoms were. Clinton pledged to reject unilateralism and exert American power through international institutions.[33] He shrank the military-industrial complex. He avoided intervention in the Balkans until the warring sides had exhausted themselves and there was clearly a will to peace. In the Middle East, in the Balkans, in Northern Ireland, Clinton demonstrated his conviction that it was in America's interests to use its economic and political influence, if not its military might, to secure peace and stability. In economic matters the younger Arkansan was no less a multilateralist than the elder.

And yet as president, Clinton could not enjoy the consistency that Fulbright could as senatorial pundit. There were certainly failures and inconsistencies.

In retrospect, Clinton's handling of the Kosovo situation appears less than a model of far-sighted statecraft. By issuing an ultimatum at the Rambouillet conference that Serbia was certain to reject, Washington most likely provoked what could have been an avoidable war. Moreover, Clinton and Secretary of State Madeleine Albright badly underestimated Milosevic's resolve and were caught off guard when NATO's bombing campaign led him to accelerate the expulsion of Albanians in March 1999.

Indeed, the Clinton administration proved unable to deal effectively with both supernational and subnational threats to U.S. security. The supernational threat took the form of a growing globalization of grievance networks, including the transnational network of terror groups active from South and Central Asia to southern Russia to the Middle East and Africa. All shared a messianic hatred of open, tolerant societies. The subnational threat is the challenge to the nation-state from the potential disintegration of ethnically diverse societies. The Clinton administration, like its predecessor and successor, had no real answer to the question: How does the United States balance legitimate demands for self-determination against the danger of unleashing new grievances?

Relations with Russia declined but that was primarily because of continuing economic difficulties and weakness of political institutions in Russia. The United States could have done more to hasten transition from communism to capitalism and totalitarianism to democracy, but the real missed opportunity was America's failure to support large-scale privatization in 1991–92.

The Clinton administration pledged to rely on international institutions, to embrace "assertive multilateralism," but in the end Clinton acted as one would expect of the leader of the world's only remaining superpower—relying on international institutions when it suited the nation's interests and prejudices, and criticizing or ignoring them when it did not. For example, he used force against Serbia without explicit Security Council authorization. Moreover, as the world's sole superpower, the United States showed little interest in agreements that limited its freedom of action. The American military opposed the land-mines treaty and the international criminal court, and Clinton proved unwilling to incur the Pentagon's wrath by supporting them. Indeed, in many instances his policies represent a clear departure from Fulbright internationalism. As an idealist, Fulbright had consistently stressed reliance on the United Nations and other supernational entities. For him the process would lead to the greater good. For Clinton as for most chief executives—and for most moralists—processes were to be manipulated for the greater good.

Depressingly, 9/11 and its aftermath seem to pose a threat to the Fulbright-Clinton legacy. The war on terrorism has given a fillip to the military-industrial complex. Though the United States is working to build a world-wide anti-terror coalition, the Bush administration clearly will resort to unilateral action if it thinks such action is warranted. The door to xenophobia and superpatriotism stands wide open. So far the country has refrained from equating Islam with terrorism and Arabs with enemies, but the constant need for justification—demonizing the enemy—in the face of ongoing national mobilization will be tempting.

6 Rightward Currents

Bill Clinton and the Politics of the 1990s

DAN CARTER

In this chapter, Professor Carter examines the national political context in which President Bill Clinton governed. Through a rigorous discussion of various public policies supported by President Clinton (such as healthcare and welfare reform) as well as the changing political environment in the United States, and in particular, the Republican takeover of Congress in 1994, Professor Carter argues that President Clinton found himself presiding over a country that had been (for decades) slowly but consistently moving to the conservative end of the ideological continuum. In fact, according to Carter, "The essential realities underlying the political system in the 1990s were the ideological, political, and economic advantages held by the Republican opposition. . . . The tide of American politics was moving steadily to the right." Such political constraints forced President Clinton to adopt unique style of governing "from the middle" that allowed substantial gains in some areas of public policy but may have left the Democratic Party in disarray.

Those who seek to measure the success and failures of a presidency should always remember the old proverb "If wishes were horses, then beggars would ride." Franklin Roosevelt came to the White House in 1933 in the middle of an economic crisis that gave him broad support for almost any action he wished to undertake. Lyndon Johnson drew energy from the creative upheaval of the Civil Rights Movement and political momentum from a nation mourning the assassination of John F. Kennedy. In 1980, Ronald Reagan was the beneficiary of more than two decades of broadening opposition to the liberal politics of the post–New Deal era. But Bill Clinton was elected in a moment of political disequilibrium, to head a political party that was ideologically and politically divided and to head a nation far more united on what it did not want—more of the same—than what it wanted. The difficult task, from this brief vantage point, is to assess the political successes and failures of his presidency in that context of opportunity and constraint.

Creating Policy—And a Compelling Story Line

Like every modern president, Bill Clinton came to the White House with an agenda that he believed would guarantee his place in history. The presidents with the greatest reputation were those who had taken "bold stands to upend the existing order," he told his principal speechwriter, Michael Waldman. However, Clinton recognized the "packaging" of those accomplishments as well as the actual achievements established a president's place in history. Ronald Reagan was the prime example. He had acted cautiously even as he claimed to act boldly against big government. Reagan, Clinton concluded admiringly, "had a story line."[1]

For more than a decade, Democrats had struggled to respond to the growing conservatism that Reagan represented. Clinton, a moderate border-South governor, had no desire to return to what he saw as the discredited policies of traditional liberalism. But he believed that the Republican Party, by embracing a knee-jerk anti-government ideology, had overreached itself in the 1980s in the same way liberals had in the 1960s. Voters were hungry for a new, middle ground between the policies of left and right.

On the eve of the 1992 presidential campaign, a number of political leaders and observers had also argued that there was a new vital center waiting for fresh leadership. In his best-selling 1991 book, *Why Americans Hate Politics,* E. J. Dionne emphasized what he believed were the ways in which the new left of the 1960s and the new right of the 1980s had conspired to "wage war against public life" by creating a political system that abandoned the "practical concerns of the broad electorate."[2]

The "moralism" of the 1960s left and its hypersensitive attention to individual liberation meant that liberals were insensitive to the growing sources of alienation among (predominantly) white, middle-class Americans. The tax revolt was not simply a reflection of selfishness, argued Dionne, and concerns over rising welfare rolls and crime rates should not have been dismissed as covert racism, nor should the Sixties liberals have been so quick to ignore complaints about inefficient government bureaucracies and to label calls for traditional family values as veiled bigotry.

Dionne was equally critical of the new conservatism of the 1980s: its intolerance of gays, its hostility to equality for women, and its insensitivity to the ongoing problems of poverty, particularly among African Americans. Worst of all, he found, was the right's "indifference to economic inequality." Reagan and his advisors had promised tax relief on work, savings, and investment, but at the end of the 1980s, it was clear that the vast majority of the tax cuts had been lavished on the wealthy. Working and middle-class Americans had actually seen their taxes go up as a consequence of increases in social security payroll taxes and state and local taxes.[3]

What was needed—and what the American people wanted—insisted Dionne, was a new "language of common citizenship" that blended "conservative values such as self-help and hard work, and the liberal values of generosity and tolerance." In practical terms, this meant moving away from an emphasis upon affirmative action for minorities and programs specifically targeted for the poor. Instead, political leaders concerned about developing a new vital center of American politics should focus on broad programs such as education and expanded job training that would heavily benefit the poor and minorities without appearing to single them out for special treatment. Dionne argued that such "universal programs" were far more likely to draw the support of broad segments of the American political electorate.[4]

Dionne's ideas echoed those of the Democratic Leadership Council (DLC), an unofficial party organization founded in 1985 by elected Democrats. Most members of the DLC, representing dwindling white Democratic constituencies in the South and border South, argued that the national party had become associated with a "tax and spend" liberalism, welfare policies that led to dependence rather than employment, an obsession with the civil rights of lawbreakers, an "adversarial stance toward mainstream moral and cultural values," and a hostility toward national defense that left the United States vulnerable in dealing with its foreign foes.[5]

Bill Clinton, a leading member of the DLC, sought to put a more positive emphasis on the message as he focused upon "opportunity and responsibility." On the campaign trail he promised, if elected president, he would (1) revitalize a sagging economy through a combination of tax cuts for the middle class and "investment" programs in job training and education; (2) institute universal healthcare coverage for the more than thirty-five million uninsured Americans; (3) reform the welfare system by giving recipients the skills that would allow them to break the cycle of dependency, and (4) overhaul the federal government to make it leaner and more efficient.[6]

While Clinton often sought to emphasize his difference from the "big government" approach of earlier Democratic candidates, the goals he sought were traditional ones for a Democratic president. He sensed that, while voters might oppose government in the abstract, in practice they passionately defended such government-led programs as social security, Medicare, the GI Bill, and aid to education. Clinton's policies were an attempt to reconcile the public's schizophrenic attitude toward government in such critical areas as universal healthcare and welfare reform.

Politics and Governance in the Clinton Administration

CASE STUDY ONE: HEALTH CARE, 1993–94

Harry Truman had called for universal healthcare as part of his Fair Deal, and the issue surfaced again in the Johnson administration before the Vietnam War brought such ambitious social policies to a halt. With the burgeoning budget deficit of the Reagan years, there seemed little appetite for revisiting the issue. Quite apart from the ideological opposition to increased government involvement in the healthcare system, conservatives (and some liberals) had argued that expanding universal healthcare would be so expensive it would bankrupt the country.[7] By the 1992 election, however, more than thirty-eight million Americans lacked access to insurance (70 percent of them in working families making less than thirty thousand dollars a year), and concerns over healthcare had begun to surface in polls and focus groups. In the economic downturn of the early 1990s, many middle-class Americans were concerned that they might lose their jobs, and thus their healthcare, which was usually tied to employment.

Clinton, along with many other healthcare experts, argued that the existing system was itself part of the problem of spiraling costs. The uninsured sick lacked the benefits of early detection and preventive treatment, which meant that they showed up in emergency rooms where delayed diagnosis often resulted in heroic and expensive procedures. At the same time, the jerry-built system of private insurance systems had made little effort to contain costs beyond jettisoning clients who were considered financial risks.[8] As Clinton argued in his September 1993 speech introducing his healthcare proposals, the American system "takes 35 percent more of our income than any other country, insures fewer people, requires more Americans to pay more and more for less and less, and gives them fewer choices."[9]

What was equally important was Clinton's belief that the passage of universal healthcare legislation would establish his historical legacy and strengthen the Democratic Party's base among lower-income working-class voters (who were often uncovered by health insurance) and middle-class voters who were fearful they might lose access to healthcare because of events beyond their control. The week after Clinton introduced his health plan in September of 1993, a Gallup Poll showed the public supported his proposal nearly two to one.

Seven months later, the nation's voters were ready to abandon the Clinton plan by a similar margin and Senate Democratic majority leader George Mitchell confirmed what had become obvious: the administration effort to radically transform healthcare in America was over.[10]

The Clinton plan had failed to keep the support of the American people, argued conservative opponents, when it became apparent that it was an intrusion of "big government" into a problem best solved by limited legislation to encourage incremental improvements that, in turn, could only come from the workings of the free-enterprise system. Apart from ideological convictions, there was always a partisan edge to this opposition. Irving Kristol, the chief Republican strategist in the campaign against the bill, argued that the Clinton health plan was a "serious *political* threat to the Republican Party" which might very well "revive the reputation of . . . the Democrats . . . as the generous protector of middle-class interests."[11] Republicans should "defeat the Clinton plan root and branch," using the healthcare fight as a "model for routing contemporary liberalism and advancing an aggressive conservative activist agenda."[12]

Kristol's uncompromising opposition to the Clinton plan quickly spread through the broad network of conservative organizations that had come into being in the 1970s and 1980s. From ideological trend-setting publications like the Heritage Foundation's *Policy Review* to mass magazines such as *Reader's Digest,* opponents followed a remarkably similar script: The Clinton plan was a bureaucratic nightmare, it would be too expensive, it would reduce the choice of most Americans, and it would lead to rationing and ultimately to European-style medical socialism. All of these characterizations were reinforced and amplified through radio talk shows (Rush Limbaugh attacked the plan almost daily during late 1993 and 1994), advertisements by smaller insurance and healthcare corporations opposed to the plan, and literature distributed by conservative grass-roots organizations such as the Christian Coalition.[13]

The irony, as Theda Skocpol pointed out in her careful analysis, was that the Clinton plan was "*a compromise* between market-oriented and government-centered reform ideas." And it was a compromise shaped by the fact that Clinton believed he had to develop a universal healthcare system without increasing the massive budget deficit he had inherited from the Reagan and Bush administrations. Ultimately the Clinton plan involved a complex mixture of cost controls (centering around the encouragement of health-management plans), mandates for employers requiring them to insure their workers, the "pooling" of individuals to prevent companies from excluding those who were unhealthy, and some government subsidies for those who remained uncovered under the new plan. It was a complicated program because the healthcare system was enormously complex, but—if anything, Skocpol concluded two years later—the "Health Security Plan" originally devised would have led to "significantly less governmental involvement than we have now."[14]

Skocpol's analysis (and that of other advocates of the Clinton plan) coincided with the view of many administration insiders (including Hillary Clinton) that the measure failed because of Republican partisanship and the skillful misrepresentation of the plan by partisan and selfish economic interests. Defenders of the Clinton plan were particularly indignant over the famous "Harry and Louise" television spots produced by healthcare opponents, which dramatized the main arguments of the plan's opponents. To defenders of the Clinton proposal, they were a symbol of the ruthless willingness of special interests and right-wing ideologues to mislead the American public.

It was true that these skillfully produced ads often misrepresented the plan and vastly exaggerated the role of government bureaucracy, and they were seldom countered by liberal lobbying groups. (The American Association of Retired Persons focused its efforts on preserving Medicare and stayed on the sidelines while organized labor, still smarting after the bruising battle over the passage of NAFTA, gave only half-hearted support to Clinton on this issue.) The key problem for the proponents of universal healthcare, however, was not Harry and Louise or even the factual accuracy or inaccuracy of opponents of the Clinton healthcare plan. It was the receptivity of middle-class voters to the arguments, true or untrue. In retrospect, it seems clear that most voters were apprehensive, but not yet desperate, about the future of their healthcare. And their uneasiness was heightened by their loss of faith in the effectiveness of the national government. The Clinton administration's fundamental misjudgment lay in overestimating the willingness of the 85 percent of Americans covered by health-insurance and health-maintenance organizations to make financial sacrifices or run the risk of healthcare rationing for the 15 percent—most of them working class—who were uninsured.[15]

CASE STUDY TWO: WELFARE "REFORM" AND THE CHANGED POLITICAL CLIMATE,1995–96

The Republican sweep in 1994 under the banner of the Contract With America was the backdrop for the next major domestic policy struggle: welfare reform. For conservatives it was the ideal issue on which to wage the next battle with traditional liberalism and the culmination of a campaign against welfare entitlements that had begun in earnest in the early 1970s as liberals and conservatives fell back upon battle lines shaped by ideological—even philosophical—differences in their conception of human nature and the role of government.[16] William Julius Wilson's 1987 study, *The Truly Disadvantaged,* was particularly influential in trying to shift the argument away from the issue of the "underclass" (which had become a theme of liberals and conservatives) in order to focus on the economic changes of post-1960 urban America that had left behind an entire generation of individuals who lacked access to jobs and skills and thus the ability to take advantage of any opportunities that might become available. Men, particularly black men, had lost access to well-paying or even modestly supportive blue-collar jobs as the growth of the suburbs and the isolation of inner cities led to the spatial separation of low-income urban Americans from the jobs that were available. While these forces had a particularly devastating effect upon minority communities, they applied to whites as well. "Underclass" culture, which was too often marked by collapsing family structures and antisocial criminal behavior, was not a manifestation of innate depravity or a sudden moral collapse among the poor. It was a direct response to the structural changes created by the new post-industrial economy. And the only solution was a broad program of government intervention emphasizing the creation of private- and public-sector jobs even as the disadvantaged were helped to acquire basic educational and job skills and support for families during the transition from welfare to work. In a key departure from some earlier liberal prescriptions that emphasized income redistribution, Wilson shared the conservative view that welfare without work led to a debilitating culture of dependency.[17]

Conservatives also emphasized the dangers of dependency and the importance of work, but they worked from a different script that bore many similarities to the arguments that had supported the Elizabethan poor laws. George Gilder's best-selling 1981 book, *Wealth and Poverty*, had provided the new and very conservative administration of Ronald Reagan a rationale for attacking federal welfare programs for the poor. In a striking departure from the rhetoric of the previous fifty years, Gilder explicitly embraced the desirability of income inequality. Only the absence of a governmental safety net and the threat of abject poverty would lead the current poor (who were "refusing to work hard," he argued) to abandon their profligate ways and follow the time-tested formula for success. The poor "must not only work, they must work harder than the classes above them." Poverty was a direct consequence of inherent moral weakness, exacerbated by a perverse welfare system that rewarded the indolent and discouraged the ambitious.[18]

Charles Murray's *Losing Ground: American Social Policy, 1950–1980*, published three years later, had an even greater impact. Gilder was essentially a right-wing polemical moralist, but Murray's book was filled with charts and tables, one of the first of dozens of carefully crafted social science works that would emerge in the coming years from conservative think tanks. (Murray was a fellow of the newly created Heritage Foundation.) Despite the scholarly apparatus, the argument was little different from Gilder's. Murray described a world in which teenage girls had illegitimate babies only to collect welfare payments, young men refused to take responsibility for their bastard children, and the poor deliberately refused to take "entry level" positions because they could always fall back upon the welfare largesse of taxpayers. Since the Great Society, welfare had become a program of rewarding the "least law-abiding," the "least capable," and the "least responsible" among the poor. The only solution was to scrap the "entire federal welfare and income-support structure for working-aged persons, including AFDC, Medicaid, Food Stamps, Unemployment Insurance, Worker's Compensation, subsidized housing, disability insurance and the rest."[19] When Murray's book appeared, it was greeted with outrage by traditional welfare scholars who saw it as nothing more than right-wing ideology masquerading as scholarship, but it quickly became the foundation for a broad and sweeping attack by conservatives on the notion of federal assistance for the poor. By the 1990s such arguments had become almost universal among conservative thinkers. (During the 2000 presidential campaign, George W. Bush said his "favorite book" was *The Dream and the Nightmare: The Sixties Legacy to the Underclass* by Myron Magnet, a book that was a popularized distillation of thirty years of conservative anti-welfare arguments.)[20]

Welfare reform was always interwoven with the nation's racial history. A 1994 CBS/*New York Times* poll found more than half of white Americans believed that blacks made up the majority of the poor; another 31 percent thought that the total number of black and white poor were "about equal." A similar percentage thought that most welfare recipients were black. In fact, African Americans made up about 30 percent of those Americans living below the poverty line and approximately one-third of those receiving means-tested government assistance. (Even in the AFDC program only 36 percent of recipients were African American despite the fact that this program was almost entirely associated with black recipients in the minds of white Americans.)[21] Although most conservative opponents of federal welfare programs sought to avoid explicit racial justifications for their view, the powerful association of welfare with (what many white voters believed was) a vast black urban antisocial and criminal underclass inevitably gave a boost to their movement.[22]

Beleaguered defenders of federal welfare programs argued plaintively that the voters had been "hoodwinked" by conservatives. It wasn't just that Americans constantly exaggerated the number of black and Hispanic means-tested welfare recipients, they also erroneously believed that AFDC costs were exploding. It was true that the number of AFDC recipients continued to rise during the 1980s and 1990s, but the major increases had taken place in the 1960s and the cost of this most controversial welfare program actually *declined* 15 percent between 1975 and 1995 as a consequence of the 50 percent cut in the level of support payments.[23] But welfare defenders missed the point. The struggle had become more about philosophical and ideological convictions than budgetary realities.

In his 1992 campaign for the presidency, Clinton had promised to "end welfare as we know it," and he initially spoke with some specificity about his plans for getting people off the welfare rolls and into the work force. But (though this was not spelled out in detail), Clinton's plan with its job retraining provisions and transitional support policies for welfare recipients—healthcare, day care for children, and income supplements— would have initially cost *more* than the existing system.[24] His advisors quickly learned from voters' focus groups that welfare reform was an issue with "no traction." Instead the campaign focused more and more on one theme—"It's the Economy, Stupid"—with healthcare as a side issue. After the election, concerns over the budget and fights over healthcare and NAFTA made welfare reform even more of a non-starter as a major legislative priority.

The overwhelming 1994 success of Republicans under the banner of Newt Gingrich's Contract with America transformed the political landscape. When the 104th Congress convened, an invigorated congressional Republican majority made "reforming" federal welfare policy a top priority. The first Republican welfare measures were soon caught up in complicated maneuvering over the budget as Clinton vetoed the federal budget because it included what he described as a radically punitive revision of the nation's welfare system. It was Clinton's veto that led an overconfident Newt Gingrich to shut down the national government. In the aftermath, the majority of voters blamed the shutdown on the Republicans, but the setback did nothing to dampen the party's commitment to press the issue. While Republicans maintained tight party discipline, the Democratic Party was marked by divisions between liberal Democrats supported by traditional party constituencies (labor, minorities, and advocates of maintaining and expanding entitlement programs) and the moderate wing whose main constituency was an increasingly conservative middle class.

Supported by a substantial number of Democrats, Republicans came back the following year with a largely unchanged legislative proposal, which they astutely labeled the "Personal Responsibility and Work Opportunity Act." While Clinton vetoed two versions of the Republican plan, he made no effort to craft a Democratic alternative and insisted that he continued to "strongly support time limits, work requirements, the toughest possible child support enforcement, and requiring minor mothers to live at home as a condition of assistance."[25] A third version of the measure, unchanged in the essentials, arrived on his desk in the late summer of 1996 just three months before the fall elections at a time when Clinton's political fortunes had improved as he moved to the right (or triangulated, as advisor Dick Morris kept insisting).

In accepting or rejecting the Republican measure, Clinton confronted a choice between defending his traditional Democratic constituency or taking an unpopular position that might well jeopardize his reelection. The third bill included minor increases in the budget for job retraining and restored entitlement to healthcare for children, but it retained deep cuts in food stamps, eliminated emergency medical benefits to legal immigrants, and—as had been the case of all three Republican bills—ended welfare as an entitlement.[26]

While the Republican bill was extraordinarily punitive in its details, it was difficult to explain to voters why these details were so critical since Clinton's original proposal had also called for stringent time limits and work requirements. In the end, the political calculations proved decisive. Accepting the bill would strip Republicans of one of their most effective campaign issues and guarantee Clinton's reelection; the worst aspects of the bill, insisted the president, could be corrected in future legislation.

On August 22, 1996, Clinton signed the Republican welfare bill in a Rose Garden ceremony. In some respects, the president's embrace of welfare reform in 1996 and his successful reelection that fall show his ability to bounce back from the bruising defeat of his healthcare proposal. Viewed from the traditional liberal wing of the Democratic Party, it was a chronicle of the president's (and their party's) betrayal of the fundamental interests of poor and working-class Americans. But it is also a story that, in many respects, follows directly from the conservative transformation of American politics in the 1970s and 1980s.

The Changing Political Landscape, 1968–92

The rise of this conservative movement had its roots in the three decades before the Goldwater campaign, drawing upon two powerful and interrelated impulses. The first was an unambiguous defense of laissez-faire capitalism. During the 1930s, most Americans seemed to accept the argument that the federal government had an obligation to protect the American people against those whom Franklin Roosevelt described as a "malefactors of great wealth" by regulating and controlling these financial interests. At the same time, the establishment of a limited national welfare system—symbolized most concretely by the Social Security Act of 1935—represented a new and expanded role for the national state. But a vocal and articulate minority of Americans maintained their hostility to the liberal Democratic ideals. Apart from their complaint that the welfare state led to idleness and undermined the work ethic of its recipients, business defenders of laissez-faire capitalism were quick to argue that the heavy hand of government—with its stifling red tape and burdensome taxes—thwarted the wealth-producing force of individual entrepreneurs. A second conservative impulse came from the linkage of the welfare state (and the Democratic Party that created it) with fears of international communism. Since the Bolshevik Revolution, American conservatives had warned of the threat of international communism, but in the aftermath of World War II, their arguments fell upon more receptive ears.

Conservative intellectuals, led by the Austrian-born economist and social philosopher Frederick Hayek brought these two arguments together during the late 1940s and early 1950s by arguing there was a practical affinity between any liberal political movement like the New Deal and the forces of totalitarianism. Communism and German National Socialism were simply the mature results of all forms of "collectivism." As he argued in his brief, but influential 1944 book, *The Road to Serfdom,* any attempt to control the economic freedom of individuals inevitably led (as his title suggested) to serfdom—and to barbarism.[27]

The National Review, founded in 1954 under the editorial leadership of William Buckley and bankrolled by wealthy business conservatives, soon became the crossroads through which a new generation of intellectual conservatives passed. In the years that followed, there would be other magazines and other conservative institutions created, but *The National Review* remained, in many ways, the Mother Church of this new movement.

Academics and the media tended to focus attention on the new conservatism's most bizarre forms such as the paramilitary Minutemen or Joseph Welch's John Birch Society. The title of three influential works of this period give some sense of "establishment" attitudes toward these ideas: *The Radical Right,* edited by Daniel Bell; Arnold Forster and Benjamin Epstein's *Danger on the Right;* and Richard Hofstadter's *The Paranoid Style in American Politics.*[28] Despite such scorn from mainstream liberals, however, the burgeoning suburban development of post-war America created the setting in which a new conservative movement would flourish. In her study of Orange County, California, in the 1950s and 1960s, historian Lisa McGirr has given us a portrait of this emerging constituency: the "Suburban Warriors" of the new conservatism. Mainline political pundits of the 1950s had often described these new political activists as "anti-modern." While it is true that they often rebelled against what they saw as the excesses of change, they were in fact products of suburban prosperity, "winners" for the most part who had benefited from the government-led Cold-War prosperity of the 1950s and 1960s. Many of McGirr's subjects, in fact, had worked in the burgeoning defense industries of Southern California.[29]

These middle- and upper-middle-income families had escaped what they saw as the unpleasant and dangerous public spaces of decaying central cities and retreated to a controlled environment of malls and private automobiles. (The advent of cable television and video rentals even ensured private entertainment space within their homes.) In these new communities there was little space for or interest in a "public sphere."

Economic pressures intensified this suburban revolt. During the 1960s and 1970s, rising real-estate assessments for private homeowners, dramatic increases in inflation, and tax-bracket creep at both the state and national level led directly to California's Jarvis-Gann initiative— Proposition 13—which passed decisively and set the stage for further demands for tax reductions across the nation. From the perspective of these new suburbanites, secular humanists and liberal social engineers demanded ever higher taxes and offered only the charm-less attraction of unruly public spaces and expensive public programs for (these new conservatives felt) the undeserving poor.[30]

The ideology of this new right centered around traditional conservative demands of the 1950s: rolling back communism abroad, rooting out Reds at home, and lowering taxes by shrinking the "welfare state." But there was also a distinctly religious and "traditionalist" aspect to these new "suburban warriors." The decade was a period of astounding religious resurgence; by the best estimate, the number of Americans who described themselves as regular churchgoers increased more than 70 percent. And most of that growth could be attributed to Catholics and Evangelical, culturally conservative churches such as Southern Baptists who were profoundly unsettled over the social "liberalization" of society.[31]

In part, the movement remained largely invisible (except in its more extreme forms) because it took place at the community level. Suburbia became the setting for new forms of community mobilization as energized networks of middle- and upper-middle-class conservatives organized neighborhood meetings, showed "anti-communist" movies, launched petition drives to block sex education in the local schools, elected school-board members who would guarantee the adoption of "pro-American" texts, and (in the case of Los Angeles) select a school-board superintendent who barred discussion of the United Nations in the classroom.[32]

The political resurgence of American conservatism came in the 1960s in an almost inevitable response to Lyndon Johnson's Great Society programs. Although liberals might deride the timidity and limitations of the Johnson agenda, from the Office of Economic Opportunity to the National

Endowment for the Arts and the National Endowment for the Humanities to the creation of Medicare and Medicaid, the 1960s marked a substantial expansion of the New Deal welfare state. Conservatives attacked the Great Society on both fiscal and philosophical grounds. It was too expensive, they charged, and it discouraged initiative by giving the poor "handouts" rather than forcing them to find work on their own. And Johnson, by aligning the executive branch with the Civil Rights Movement, ignited a powerful white backlash, a political reaction that was not restricted to the South. Well before the 1960s, white urban working-class and white-collar voters in northern industrial cities reacted with hostility to the in-migration of African Americans.[33]

During the 1960s this white backlash proved critical. If leading conservatives sought to distance themselves from the cruder forms of racism, the movement as a whole drew strength from opposition to the Civil Rights Movement as it emerged in the 1950s and 1960s. [34] Whatever Barry Goldwater's personal feelings on the issue of race, his opposition to the Civil Rights Act of 1964 was the logical culmination of a decade of fairly consistent conservative opposition to any federal action designed to protect the rights of African Americans, and in the years that followed there was a constant effort on the part of conservative political strategists to use white racial resentment to strengthen the Republican Party. As Republican strategist Kevin Phillips argued to Richard Nixon in 1970, "Negro-Democratic mutual identification" was a critical factor in the growth of the Republican Party in the South and the lynchpin of a national political realignment in favor of the GOP. With the Democratic Party becoming the "Negro party through most of the South," the Republicans would become the majority party in the region and attract disenchanted white working-class voters in the North as well.[35]

Traditional anti-statism, muscular anti-communism, an uneasiness over accelerating social change, and a hostility to federally supported civil rights may have furnished the foundations for the growth of conservatism, but the tumultuous and unsettling events of the 1960s made millions of Americans more responsive to conservative arguments: the race riots of the long hot summers of the decade, the angry street demonstrations that followed America's growing involvement in Vietnam, and the general sense that the United States was in the midst of a moral meltdown. Rising crime rates, the legalization of abortion, the rise of out-of-wedlock pregnancies, the increase in divorce, and the proliferation of "obscene" literature and films undermined traditional cultural values. Their own neighborhoods might be relatively calm, but through the immediacy of television millions of Americans felt directly menaced by the social and cultural upheavals of the decade.[36]

Anti-Washington rhetoric grew, for the federal government seemed complicit in these assaults on traditional American values. The United States Justice Department proposed that northern schools be integrated; the federal courts "pandered" to criminals and banned state-sponsored prayer from the schools even as it opened the nation's bookstores to "filth and pornography"; and the executive branch of government rewarded noisy special-interest groups even as they ignored the complaints of hard-working, tax-paying Americans, charged conservatives. A powerful new network of conservative talk-show hosts increasingly depicted federal bureaucrats from IRS agents to forest rangers to OSHA inspectors to EPA enforcement officers to BATF agents as power hungry, arrogant, jack-booted thugs intent on harassing honest tax-paying citizens with mindless and unnecessary red tape while diverting their hard-earned dollars to shiftless and lazy undeserving poor (and predominantly black) people.

Wealthy American conservatives also helped to transform the battleground of ideas. As late as the mid-1960s, American liberalism still shaped the parameters of public debate. Beyond *The National Review* (a magazine of decidedly limited circulation), the decidedly fringe publisher, Regnery Press, and the editorial pages of a few pro-business newspapers like the *Wall Street Journal,* one would be hard-pressed to find national outlets for doctrinaire conservative views. In the three decades that followed, however, the landscape of American intellectual debate drifted steadily toward the right.

Pittsburgh billionaire Richard Mellon Scaife, best known for spending more than two million dollars on the "Arkansas project" to uncover Clinton scandals and for his belief that the White House had arranged the assassination of Vince Foster,[37] had long played a critical role in bankrolling a sophisticated conservative infrastructure: think tanks like the Heritage Foundation, educational and litigational legal organizations such as the Pacific Legal Foundation and the Southeastern Legal Foundation, magazines, and college newspapers and publications. By 1998, Scaife alone had contributed more than $640 million (in 1998 dollars) to these conservative groups. Other wealthy donors like Colorado beer brewer Joseph Coors, oilman Fred Koch, Vicks heir H. Smith Richardson Jr., and former treasury secretary William Simon also recognized the powerful role their contributions might make in building a conservative infrastructure that would carry conservative ideas throughout the nation.[38]

During the Carter administration one of the last building blocks of the conservative movement fell into place. Evangelical Christians had built a powerful group of educational, publishing, and broadcasting institutions during the 1950s and 1960s. Alarmed over what they saw as an increasing drift toward a liberal secularism that undermined traditional values in American society, these groups had turned toward political activism. The Supreme Court's decisions in 1962 and 1963 outlawing official school prayers had long rankled evangelicals, but the Carter administration's demand that church schools (because they were tax exempt) undertake affirmative efforts to secure minority students ignited a new wave of activism. After 1978, under the leadership of evangelical activists like Marion ("Pat") Robertson and Jerry Falwell, religious conservatives mobilized around such hot-button issues as abortion, school prayer, and the teaching of evolution; and they increasingly channeled their new activism through the Republican Party.[39]

This tilt toward conservative Republicanism was particularly important in the white South. There is no evidence that the percentage of evangelical conservatives who go to the polls has increased significantly over the last three decades, but every survey shows that the percentage of Americans who describe themselves as religious conservatives has grown, reaching as much as 25 percent by some estimates.[40] By the mid-1990s, these white born-again Christians were voting Republican three or four to one, and half of them lived in the South.[41] During the 1980s and early 1990s, political scientists who studied voting behavior disagreed over whether to describe the changes among white voters in the region as "dealignment"—essentially the loss of support for Democrats—or "realignment." which would suggest a shift from the Democratic to the Republican Party. The election of 2002 seems to have settled the issue.[42]

The breakthrough for conservatives came in 1980 when Ronald Reagan swept into the presidency, decisively defeating incumbent Jimmy Carter by promising dramatic tax cuts, a rollback of the federal government, a new emphasis upon "market solutions" to social problems, a dramatic rebuilding of American military might, and a return to "traditional" American values. The eight years of the Reagan administration may have left some of the most committed conservatives dissatisfied, but ideological purists underestimated the extent to which the former California governor's optimistic rhetoric energized and inspired the conservative movement. Moving from a relentlessly negative portrait of bureaucratic waste and governmental ineptitude, Reagan offered Americans an optimistic solution to all the difficulties they faced: the marketplace. Laissez-faire had been the backbone of American economic conservatism for more than a century, but the former Hollywood actor proved remarkably successful at promoting it as an uplifting and painless path to the future. "Individual greeds add up to general gain," Garry Wills would later write, so long as the nation was spared the stifling hand of government. "The Market thus produces a happy outcome from endless miseries."[43]

As Bill Clinton would say with grudging admiration: Ronald Reagan had a story line.

In reality, the middle class remained the principal beneficiaries of government entitlement programs. As Robert Reich, Clinton's first secretary of labor noted in 1997, the "truly big entitlements are Medicare and Social Security [as well as] the mortgage-interest deduction . . . a $55-billion-a-year housing subsidy mostly benefiting the middle class and the wealthy. . . ."[44] But for many traditionally Democratic voters—the so-called "Reagan Democrats"—their party had become a vehicle of grasping minorities who demanded their hard-earned tax dollars for welfare and took their jobs away from them through affirmative action.[45] Even when race was not the paramount issue, a hostile attitude toward the federal government had come to permeate the thinking of many of these traditionally Democratic voters. As late as the 1990s, voters who identified themselves as Democrats remained slightly more numerous than Republicans, but as a group of political scientists persuasively argued in 1992 in *The Myth of the Independent Voter,* more and more Americans who claimed they were "independent," in fact, were consistently voting Republican. More importantly, the intensity and level of participation among Republican and Republican-leaning voters was higher than among Democrats and Democratic-leaning voters.[46]

Confronting the Challenge: Bill Clinton's Strategy

The essential realities underlying the political system in the 1990s were the ideological, political, and economic advantages held by the Republican opposition. Between 1968 and 1988, Republicans captured the presidency in five of the six elections; only the hapless Jimmy Carter managed a narrow victory in the wake of the disgraced Richard Nixon. Bill Clinton came to the White House in 1992 with 43 percent of the popular vote, the lowest support of any president since Woodrow Wilson in 1912. Numerically, Democrats still held a comfortable edge in the Senate (58–42) and in the House (258–177), but these numbers were illusory.

Even as Clinton captured the White House, his party lost ten seats in the House. The tide of American politics was moving steadily to the right.

From the 1970s Democratic Party leaders had been aware of the growing erosion of their electoral strength. George McGovern described the problem with considerable insight in the aftermath of his 1972 defeat. While Jimmy Carter generally ignored the Democratic Party whenever possible, Clinton made at least a half-hearted effort to rebuild his party. At times he seemed to see the Democratic Party primarily as a conduit for raising and spending money rather than mobilizing voters around issues; at other times he seemed to believe that his success depended upon articulating a persuasive message to the American people and strengthening and uniting his party in order to enact his legislative policies.

Critics claimed that Bill Clinton was never able to carry through on his campaign themes because of a lack of focus and discipline, but the more fundamental problem was the fact that these themes could never achieve the kind of over-arching simplicity of conservatives' call for less government and more reliance on market solutions. Clinton was the first president to attempt to address the problems of stagnant middle-class incomes and massive dislocation that stemmed from the domestic and international upheavals of the 1970s and 1980s, but his response was complex and hardly susceptible to the kind of sound-bites that increasingly shaped the news cycle, a cycle increasingly dominated, as one observer noted, by the "simpleminded, sensational, and cynical."[47] At the same time, his two major early legislative achievements—deficit reduction and the enactment of the North American Free Trade Agreement—did little to strengthen his own constituency. By the 1996 election, under the tutelage of Richard Morris—he was concentrating more and more on a narrow slice of middle-class suburban voters, and spending much of his energy trying to raise funds for his reelection campaign. In the political context of the 1990s, that strategy amounted to a rational choice, at least in the short run.

The Changing Composition of the American Electorate

Since 1960, the number of Americans who have confidence in the responsiveness and effectiveness of government has plummeted. The year John F. Kennedy became president, 60 percent of Americans agreed that one could usually "trust the government in Washington to do what is right." By 1990, that figure had declined to approximately 25 percent.[48] Political scientists studying voting behavior insist that a lack of confidence in government does not necessarily lead to a decline in voter participation. As a number of studies have shown, going back into the 1960s, voters who express confidence in government are no more likely (in fact they are slightly less likely) to go to the polls than those who are disenchanted. The problem is that most polls do not distinguish the nature of voters' confidence (or lack thereof) in the system. More affluent voters may feel hostile toward the national government because they feel that it is unnecessarily taxing them to support the less-deserving poor, while the poor working-class and lower-middle-class voters may feel that the federal government is in the hip pocket of wealthy special interests. Both may be disillusioned, but the nature of their disillusionment is quite different. The more fundamental finding of students of voting behavior is that individuals vote *if they feel they can change the system*.[49]

There may be many factors involved in voter turnout, but powerlessness, not cynicism, seems more important in leading individuals to abandon the system, and it is statistically indisputable that the greatest decline in voting turnout has been among low-income individuals, particularly those with a high-school education or less. Between 1972 and 1988, low-income voters declined approximately 10 percent, while the turnout of high-income voters was up more than 6 percent.[50] By the election of 2002, 72 percent of voters with family income of seventy-five thousand dollars or more (approximately 23 percent of the electorate) went to the polls; less than 39 percent of voters from households with family income in the bottom twentieth percentile (less than twenty-five thousand dollars) voted.[51]

It has been an article of faith among liberal activists that broadening the electorate to make it more representative of all classes would lead to a shift in American politics from right to left.[52] Not surprisingly, conservatives (who often share this assumption), have been less than enthusiastic about measures to increase voter turnout. Most politicians have found it necessary to publicly insist that they supported broader voter participation, although South Carolina's Republican senator Strom Thurmond bluntly argued that one of the dangers of a democracy was granting the suffrage to voters who would "vote themselves a share of the public treasury." Presumably this was one of the concerns of conservative columnist Thomas Sowell who argued that "loose election laws" and aggressive get-out-the vote campaigns "allow not only more voter fraud but also more uninformed and apathetic people to drag down the quality of the decisions that will shape our future as a nation."[53]

What is somewhat surprising in view of this widespread assumption is the argument of a number of political scientists that increasing voter participation would result in little change in electoral outcomes or in policy choices. In a 2001 article in the *British Journal of Political Science*, Benjamin Highton and Raymond Wolfinger deployed elaborate charts of survey data and mathematical formulas that purported to prove that the ideological differences between 1996 voters and non-voters were "relatively slight." Non-voters, Highton and Wolfinger have concluded, have been "well represented by those who vote."[54] But their own data shows that, on key "redistributive economic questions," the non-voting population was five to nine percentage points more "liberal" than those who cast their ballots, hardly an insignificant difference. Even by the most skeptical calculations, full participation in the 1992 presidential election would have widened Clinton's lead over George W. Bush by 1.3 percentage points; in 1996 it would have doubled his lead over Dole.[55]

Surely some of this decline among lower-income voters has to do with the perception that they are powerless in a system that is increasingly weighted to interests of capital.[56] In the 1980s conservatives had promised that lowering taxes for the wealthy and reducing the role of government (particularly in supplying public services for the poor) would result in a growing economy, which would in turn improve the lives of all Americans. By the beginning of the twenty-first century, however, it was the consensus of most economists that the United States had become the most unequal society in the industrialized West.[57]

Occasionally conservative hard-liners responded to these complaints by defending low wages as a necessary incentive to force the indolent lower classes to work, but most have insisted that economic inequality is either exaggerated or irrelevant since income is rising for all levels of society. These arguments were encapsulated in a series of op-ed pieces and editorials that appeared in the *Wall Street Journal* in the summer of 1995: "The Inequality Myth: Getting Richer (At Different Rates)," "The Rich Get Richer, and That's All Right," and "The Inequality Myth: What Wealth Gap?"[58] According to the statistics compiled by the Congressional Budget Office, however, the income of the poorest one-fifth of Americans fell 12 percent between 1980 and the end of the 1990s, while the top 20 percent saw its income rise by nearly 40 percent, and the top 1 percent of Americans saw their after-tax income grow by 120 percent. (The income of middle-income Americans—those between the fortieth and eightieth percentile—changed very little).[59]

"Show Me the Money"

According to the most thoroughgoing analysis of election financing, in 1976, the cost of all campaign spending—local, state, soft money, party, congressional, and presidential—was $1.26 billion. This figure rose to *$4.8 billion* in the 1996 election cycle, a figure significantly exceeded in 2000. Thus, during a twenty-year period when median household income in the United States increased approximately 10 percent, political spending went up 380 percent.[60] The amounts spent on lobbying have increased by even greater amounts. In the 1999–2000 cycle, the top three groups of industries alone—pharmaceuticals, insurance, and telecommunications—showered Washington with $510 million in lobbying and campaign contributions. Much of this "lobbying" was thinly veiled political advertising. For example, in the months leading up the election of 2000, pharmaceutical companies spent $65 million in "issue" ads, most of it attacking Democrats' proposals for their Medicaid prescription plan.[61] The month before the 2002 election, reports to the Federal Election Commission and to state election commissions profiled a political system still out of control: $14 million in Georgia on the Max Cleland–Saxby Chambliss Senate race, with another $55 million spent on the governor's and house races; $25 million in North Carolina on the Erskine Bowles–Elizabeth Dole campaign; $20 million in the Wellstone/Mondale-Norman Senate campaign in Minnesota. By the time the race was over, the candidates for Congress and the governorships had spent enough, one wag suggested, to bring the growing deficit under control.[62] Even if the Supreme Court upholds the Bipartisan Campaign Reform Act of 2002, it seems unlikely that the modest restrictions embodied in this legislation will stem the flow of money into the political system.

To be sure, most of the loudest complaints about the undue power of money in politics come from more "liberal" organizations such as Common Cause and the Center for Public Integrity. Conservatives—who have benefited more generally from this largesse—dismiss the importance of money in politics. And there are scholars—particularly political scientists—who have deployed complex models and mathematical equations to show that, in the words of Janet M. Grenske, contributions by political action committees "do not affect members' voting patterns." Others have also questioned the extent to which money plays a critical role in shaping specific policy.[63]

While journalists and liberal critics of the current system often oversimplify the relationship between electoral success, legislative outcomes, and campaign contributions and lobbying, it would seem to be counter-intuitive, and indeed a contradiction of the notion of self-interest that lies at the heart of conservative ideology, to suggest that (for example) the pharmaceutical industry expected nothing for the $300 million it spent on lobbying and campaign contributions in the twenty-four months leading up to the election of 2000. And the argument that campaign contributions have little impact on politics is contradicted by politicians who have seen the process from the inside. As former Republican senator Alan Simpson observed, "Who, after all, can seriously contend that a $100,000 donation does not alter the way one thinks about—and quite possibly votes on—an issue?"[64]

The problem with much of the social-science literature is that it overlooks the way in which an inability to gain access to large campaign contributions blocks candidates with alternative viewpoints. It is a demonstrable fact that organized labor and traditional liberal interest groups cannot match the funds available from corporate interests and conservative advocacy groups. Moreover, scholars intent on measuring the interaction of one or two factors (legislative votes and campaign contributions, for example) often oversimplify the complex interaction of money and politics by focusing upon final legislation outcome rather than the critical role played by legislators behind closed doors as they negotiate legislative language, formulate amendments, and work behind the scenes to shape the specific content of legislation. Surely no one could argue with a straight face that campaign contributions had nothing to do with the fact that an unnamed member of Congress anonymously (and secretly) inserted a provision in the 2002 anti-terrorist legislation protecting the Eli Lilly pharmaceutical company against vaccine lawsuits—an action which caused an uproar only because it was a cruder version of everyday political practices.[65]

In any case, the sense of the voters that both sides were implicated in the search for special interest money hardly worked to the benefit of liberal Democrats. While the Republican Party remained positioned to benefit most from this growing flood of contributions during the 1990s, Bill Clinton and the leadership of the Democratic Party aggressively sought to match their efforts by tirelessly appealing for campaign contributions from major business contributors. While he often insisted that he supported reining in campaign contributions, he also argued that he and his party could not engage in unilateral disarmament; he had to go out and raise these enormous sums of money in order to counter Republican advantages. Whatever the rationale, in the minds of the voters, there was little difference between the two parties as far as links between "special interests" and politics. Both parties were trapped in a subtle web of deference to their sources of campaign funds. And in supplying those funds, the role of labor and liberal special interests were declining while capital had become king.

Religious and cultural conservatives may rail and liberals may complain, but—as novelist George Packer astutely noted—the "economic half of Reagan's revolution was continuous with the cultural half of the '60s revolution." The attitude of most Americans (at least those who counted) has been relatively consistent. "Cut taxes, deregulate business, cut the welfare state (for the poor), but protect my economic interests and my freedom to do whatever I like." The 1960s and the 1980s were "both about freedom," Packer observed, "and they both won and we are left with the consequences."[66]

Bill Clinton may have been uncomfortable with the fundamental bedrock on which the politics of the last two decades rested: the notion that the nation's political future must permanently be held captive to the imperatives of the marketplace. But temperament and a keen sense of political realism made him shy away from raising fundamental questions about the desirability of a society built upon self-interest and self-gratification: the crowning glories of consumer capitalism. If self-interest was all that was at stake during the last thirty years, then many (though certainly not all) of the political outcomes during these years have an inexorable logic. Middle- and upper-income voters may be unsettled by reports that thirty-eight (now forty-one) million Americans have no health insurance. But the reality is that—as the Clintons learned in 1993 and 1994—providing healthcare for all Americans would require sacrifices. Even more occasionally, middle- and upper-income voters may be made uncomfortable by evidence that millions of individuals who left the welfare rolls have moved to minimum-wage jobs that offer only the most marginal of existences. Again, in terms of immediate self-interest, it has been economically advantageous to middle- and upper-income Americans to have a mudsill of poor, uneducated, and low-wage workers to perform the thankless, unskilled tasks of our growing service economy.

The liberal wing of the Democratic Party may have been disappointed in Clinton for his policies as well as the way in which his personal foibles allowed conservatives to discredit even his milder form of liberal politics. But it was unrealistic to expect him to embark on a grand design to reshape the American political system. At a time when election-year bromides often bear little relationship to the governance that follows, Bill Clinton's presidency proved (by today's political standards) relatively consistent with his campaign promises. On economic matters, he was a moderately conservative Democratic intent on working within a system in which conservatives had successfully "delegitimated" the notion of an activist government and the marketplace was king. A few members of the administration like Labor Secretary Robert Reich argued that Clinton should focus upon fundamental questions about growing economic inequality and the need for an activist federal government that would halt these trends. But most members of the Clinton administration were uncomfortable—intellectually and politically—with what seemed easily parodied as a class-based politics out of touch with the 1990s. Instead, temperament and political judgment argued for a modestly reconfigured shift of emphasis that accepted the new economy as a given and sought only to shift the balance toward the interests of the middle class. At best, under the terms of the "New Covenant," the massive insecurity of the poor and the working class would be tempered modestly and a new Democratic majority would be built upon recapturing the allegiance of swing middle-class voters. That strategy succeeded in reelecting Bill Clinton in 1996; it did little to rejuvenate the fortunes of a Democratic Party still adrift at century's end.

7 The Women's Movement Agenda and the Record of the Clinton Administration

DOROTHY MCBRIDE STETSON

In this chapter, Professor Stetson examines the support President Clinton received from women and women's groups. The facts are clear that the gender gap in presidential voting was the decisive reason for Clinton's victories both in 1992 and 1996, and President Clinton received substantial support from women throughout his eight years in the executive office. Was support for Clinton among women and women's groups, in the midst of sex scandals, rational behavior? Or as Professor Stetson asks, were women's groups being hypocritical after "ganging up on Clarence Thomas and even abandoning their long time ally Senator Robert Packwood over sexual harassment," and then "supporting someone who recklessly 'used' a female intern for sex and lied about it. Even more appalling, how could a feminist like Hillary Rodham Clinton stay with him?" The answer, according to Professor Stetson, is that women were neither hypocritical nor irrational. Professor Stetson argues that President Clinton's record across four policy areas (abortion, welfare reform, placing women in top governmental positions, and international prostitution) warranted the support that he received from women and women's groups.

By 1992, feminists had waited a long time for a presidential candidate who would promote a women's rights agenda and who actually had a chance of winning.[1] There was also the intriguing prospect that, for the first time, a candidate's wife promised to be an advocate for feminist goals inside the administration. Soon after the inauguration, feminist support for Bill and Hillary Rodham Clinton was rewarded. One of the first presidential orders was to rescind Bush administration bans on the use of federal funds for abortion counseling and family planning overseas. Then, as promised during the campaign, the president signed the Family and Medical Leave Act, which had been twice vetoed by President Bush. Despite missteps on gay rights in the military and healthcare reform, feminist support for Clinton remained strong.[2]

Women's movement organizations remained true to their leader throughout the second term, even in the face of persistent investigations of wrongdoing in Arkansas financial schemes and the subsequent sex scandals. With the press enjoying a field day of sensational reporting of Whitewater, Zippergate, and Monicagate, Pat Ireland, president of the National Organization for Women, publicly vowed to stay with their man. Press reaction was swift: How *could* feminists be so hypocritical? After ganging up on Clarence Thomas and even abandoning their long time ally Senator Robert Packwood over sexual harassment, here they were, supporting someone who recklessly "used" a female intern for sex and lied about it. Even more appalling, how could a feminist like Hillary Rodham Clinton stay with him? Editorials denounced a feminist double standard and the right-wing pundits, already expert at manipulating symbolic politics, gleefully jumped on the bandwagon to declare, once again, that feminism was a bankrupt ideology.[3]

The absence of any agreement among feminists themselves, let alone journalists and the American public, on what feminism means is one reason such a flurry of comment is possible. While in the 1970s, it was possible for the International Women's Year (IWY) Conference in Houston to present an agenda for promoting women's rights based on support from grass-roots women's organizations, by the 1990s, there was disagreement among activists on just about every aspect of that agenda.[4] Furthermore, rather than declining, the number of feminist organizations had vastly increased, reflecting recognition of the great diversity of identities and interests among American women.[5] Any journalist could find a self-proclaimed supporter of women's rights who would give a quote to advance just about any claim.

Despite these attacks, feminist backing for President Clinton remained strong throughout his second term.[6] Why? Like most voters, women's movement activists do not base their support on personalities or spouses, but on policies such as healthcare, child care, and social security. As Allen points out, even if many voters consider that a politician's personal life is a factor in determining his or her worth as a government leader, it is only one aspect of a career. Thus, it appears, many women in the long run followed this advice: "it makes sense to look at the whole picture—to weigh the political importance of the particular personal conduct against the value of the person's public political acts and see how the person's whole record looks in light of the political alternatives."[7]

The goal of this paper is to assess aspects of the policy record of the Clinton administration to see if it warranted such women's movement loyalty. It will not be possible to examine every aspect of the record that pertains to the feminist agenda or women's rights. Rather, this paper reviews four policy areas: representation, abortion, welfare reform, and trafficking in women. These represent a range of gender-policy dimensions and were selected because I have done extensive research on them as part of the cross-national research project of the Research Network on Gender, Politics, and the State.(RNGS)[8] Following a discussion of feminism and women's movement goals and activism in the 1990s, the paper will assess the role of the Clinton administration as an ally of the movement. The conclusion will consider some explanations for the findings.

Feminism and the Women's Movement in the 1990s

Most people who use the term *women's movement* do not provide a useful definition of the concept for empirical research or do not define it at all.[9] Here, I use the definition offered by Jane Mansbridge that defines the movement not in terms of individuals or organizations but as a discourse: "a set of changing, contested aspirations and understandings that provide conscious goals, cognitive backing, and emotional support for each individual's evolving feminist identity."[10] These contested ideas are the *movement;* the organizations and individuals who use and act on portions of feminist discourse are *representatives* of the movement or movement activists.

It is important to distinguish the ideas (feminism) from the actors (movement representatives) in our discussions of the women's movement. Usually, critics of women's movement's failings and fortunes repeatedly fail to recognize the difference. These authors of frequent feminist obituaries confuse the activities of organizations with the ideas that form the movement. Either may be united or divided, vibrant or in decline at the same time or at different times. In the 1990s, however, neither the ideas nor their advocates were in death throes. Feminist discourse was widespread, vibrant, and complex. Rather than declining, the organizations representing the women's movement were strong, active, and influential. They formed a Women's Lobby, an institutionalized presence in Washington, D.C., with more than 150 feminist organizations including litigation organizations, policy research centers, PACs, national membership organizations like NOW and AAUW. These organizations remain embedded in national and regional networks that easily form and stay in issue-centered coalitions and have institutionalized access to major policy arenas in Congress and the bureaucracy. Out in the states and municipalities, feminist organizations have diversified and proliferated at the grass-roots, often forming the foundation for sub movements on, for example, domestic violence and women's health issues. According to Barbara Ransby of University of Illinois/Chicago writing in *Signs,* the style of black feminist activism has especially emphasized "decentralized mobilization efforts, informal leadership, and flexible structures," certainly a style of organization often under the radar of the national press.[11] Furthermore, feminists are organized within a multitude of social institutions—as caucuses in legislatures, in churches and synagogues—as well as in the military, professional organizations, universities—especially women's studies programs—unions, and various social movements.[12] Disney and Gelb provide evidence that institutionalization has not led to deradicalization of the movement. Rather, the agendas of many organizations have expanded to include more feminist issues while retaining that unique combination of personal and political goals that characterizes the movement.

The strategy of institutionalized women's movement activists is, primarily, to have an impact on the government. Researchers typically use two measures of movement-activist success with respect to the state: procedural and policy content.[13] The procedural success is measured by increases in the presence of movement actors inside government in elected, appointed, and civil service positions and as accepted members of policy networks. The policy content goal aims to include the substantive claims of movement activists in specific policy decisions made by public officials. Procedural and policy-content indicators of movement success coincide with concepts of descriptive and substantive representation as well as process change.[14]

Feminism refers to the those ideas of the women's movement "involving challenges to patriarchy, assertions of women's rights to equality and justice, and critiques of gender-based subordination of women to men."[15] In the United States, feminism is often characterized by disagreement and debate.[16] Thus, although movement activists are all interested in advancing both procedural and policy goals, they differ over what substantive changes will improve women's position in relation to men. One major disagreement regards descriptive representation. Should feminists try to bring more women into Congress and the Cabinet, or only women who represent feminism? Is *any* woman preferred over a man who stands for women's rights?

It doesn't get any easier to reach agreement when it comes to policy content. Here the movement actors draw on two major schools of feminist thought.[17] One school—difference feminism—sees women as a distinct social group with special talents and needs that are different from those of men. The other—equality feminism—emphasizes the commonality between men and women and promotes equality of opportunity. This debate affects movement strategies relating to procedural or descriptive representation. For those who believe that women are a separate social group, including any women in a government institution would constitute a movement success. For those who focus on equality rather than difference, as long as there is a level playing field, women and men are interchangeable both as representatives or opponents of movement goals; thus they may be more likely to work only for including more feminist women. In studying the procedural successes of women's movement activists, the RNGS project looks at the incorporation of feminists in the policy-making processes as well as the presence of women in power. Here, too, this paper examines the Clinton administration record in bringing women into power. It will also note those appointees who have had connections with the feminist movement activism.

In studying the policy impact of the women's movement the RNGS project looks at the debates leading up to important policy decisions. Researchers gather evidence of gendering in the debates. *Gendering* refers to the language policy actors use to express how the policy problem and its proposed solutions will affect women in comparison to men. Policy debates may be about women's issues such as abortion and rape without being gendered. They may also be gendered without being feminist. Thus, to determine whether the movement has been effective by inserting gendered language into the dominant frame of debate on an issue, the frame must be compared with the definition of the issue offered by feminist movement activists. If the two are congruent and not in contradiction, then we conclude that the movement activists have been successful in influencing state action. Because of the divisions in feminist thought, women's movement activists may disagree about which gendered perspective will advance their cause. This paper looks at the relation between women's movement activists and the Clinton administration in gendering policy debates and content in debates on partial-birth abortion, welfare reform, and trafficking in women.

Political Representation

THE CABINET

Increasing the representation of women in the 1993 Cabinet was clearly a high priority for the Clinton administration. Nevertheless feminists put on the pressure during the appointment process, causing the president to accuse them of being "bean counters." Highlighted in the press was the struggle to find a woman who could get Senate confirmation as attorney general. The high-profile withdrawal of Zoe Baird followed by Kimba Wood over their employment of illegal immigrants and failure to pay social security taxes was a dismal start. Later it was revealed that a double standard was in play: Ron Brown, secretary of commerce, was allowed quietly to pay back social security taxes for his domestic help. However, Clinton did not give up; finding a single woman with no children—Janet Reno—finally brought the first woman to this high-level Cabinet position.

The first Cabinet set a record with five women. By the end of the second term, 40 percent of his cabinet-level appointments were women (twelve of twenty-nine), including the first woman secretary of state, Madeleine Albright. This was a dramatic increase in representation over previous administrations at this high level.[18] As for feminist presence, only two of the twelve had any documented association with women's movement organizations: Donna Shalala, secretary of health and human services had been a member of the Women's Caucus for Political Science and Alexis Herman, secretary of labor, was active in women's advocacy organizations before and after her appointment as director of the Women's Bureau of the Department of Labor in the 1970s.

THE COURTS

In the judicial branch, President Clinton repaid much of the debt he had to the women's movement lobby for their support by appointing Ruth Bader Ginsburg to the first vacancy on the Supreme Court. For the women's movement, this appointment had the same symbolic impact as Lyndon Johnson's appointment of Thurgood Marshall in the 1960s had for the Civil Rights Movement. Ginsburg was not only a feminist and a member of the NOW Legal Defense Fund board in the 1970s, but she led the ACLU Women's Rights Project to ban sex discrimination under the equal protection clause of the Fourteenth Amendment. Her success in *Reed v. Reed* (404 U.S. 71, 1971) and four later cases set the precedent for overturning most legislation that discriminates against women. As justice, she continued the development of equality doctrine with her decision in *U.S. v. Virginia.* (116 S.Ct. 2264, 1996). Still, at the end of the Clinton administration, there remained only two women among the "brethren."

With respect to lower-court appointments, Clinton had an opportunity to fulfill his campaign pledge to establish a government that "looks like America," appointing more women and minorities than ever before to the bench. He appointed eighty women to district and circuit courts, compared with Carter's forty, Bush's thirty-six, and Reagan's twenty-nine. There is little evidence, so far, that the increased representation of women has had any impact on the content of decisions which might indicate that more women means more feminist decisions.[19] These results don't tell us much about how many of these judges were feminists or had experience as movement activists; it may tell us more about the strong influence of legal culture over movement ideologies within the court system.

WOMEN'S POLICY AGENCIES

The establishment of women's policy agencies is a way to bring women and women's movement activists into policy networks. In the United States, such agencies are likely to be temporary and issue focused. An exception is the Women's Bureau of the Department of Labor established by statute in 1920 to advance the interests of working women. The statute mandates the president appoint a woman as director; President Clinton appointed a feminist, Karen Nussbaum, who had extensive experience in advocacy for women in labor unions. While there is not yet an extensive survey of women's policy offices in U.S. government over the last decades, it is likely that the Clinton administration was one of the most active.[20] The administration established the White House Office for Women's Initiatives and Outreach as a mechanism to develop support from women for the 1996 elections; it continued to operate through the second term. He also created the President's Interagency Council on Women (IAC) to implement the 1995 United Nations Beijing Plan of Action for women in the United States. Composed of women in top-level positions throughout the administration, the honorary chair was Hillary

Rodham Clinton, and it was housed in the Department of State under chair Madeleine Albright. The administration also established the Interagency Committee on Women's Business Enterprise and the deputy assistant secretary for women's health in the Department of Health and Human Services.

Partial-Birth Abortion Ban Act

Shortly before Clinton moved to the White House, the U.S. Supreme Court rendered a decision that shifted the frame of the abortion debate. Between 1973 and 1992, the top priority of the pro-life movement was to return to the states the constitutional authority, prohibited in *Roe v. Wade* (410 U.S. 113. 1973), to ban first trimester abortions. Despite appointment of a majority of anti-abortion Supreme Court justices by Republican presidents, in *Planned Parenthood v. Casey* (112 S.Ct. 2791. 1992) a majority of justices upheld the central ruling in *Roe*, that government could not place any undue burdens on the liberty of a woman to seek abortion up to the point of viability of the fetus. After *Casey,* both pro-choice and pro-life activists changed strategies. The pro-choice movement, a combination of feminists, family-planning organizations, and health professionals, focused on gaining better access to abortion services. The pro-life movement sought to change the dominant discourse on abortion from a matter of women's rights versus fetal rights (pro-choice versus pro-life) to an assault on the abortion procedure itself as a criminal act.

They started with a campaign against a relatively new procedure, a variation of the dilation and extraction surgical procedure for second-trimester abortions. The D&X had been developed as an outpatient procedure. As such, it provided a safe alternative to standard second-trimester abortion procedures performed in hospitals, and it had been made necessary because, under pro-life pressure, most hospitals refused to allow any abortions. Prodded by the National Conference of Catholic Bishops, the National Right to Life Committee distributed articles renaming the procedure "partial-birth abortion" and claiming that by killing the "nearly born" child in the birth canal, partial-birth abortion was three seconds from infanticide. With a Republican majority in both houses of Congress after 1994, pro-life legislators introduced a bill that absolutely banned this procedure.

With this proposal, its supporters sought to redefine the abortion issue to remove any reference to women's rights and liberties in the policy debate and focus instead on a direct attack by doctors on the unborn, or as they called it more frequently, the "nearly born." Opponents of the ban countered this initiative by trying to refocus attention, if not on women's rights, at least on women's medical treatment. Eventually, they gave up on opposing the ban and worked for an exception to the ban for the health and safety of the mother.

The bill passed both houses of Congress in 1995; not a single feminist pro-choice voice had been heard during the committee hearings on the bill. Women were represented in the debates only in terms of references to their body parts: uterus, cervix, birth canal. In other words, the debate in Congress was not gendered, nor did women participate. When President Clinton vetoed the act in 1996, however, he used the White House Office of Women's Initiatives to introduce women whose lives or fertility had been spared through a D&X procedure into the debate. In addition, he reiterated his position that he would not sign the ban unless it provided an exception for women's health. With this public act, President Clinton gendered the debate on the partial-birth abortion ban. After that, pro-choice groups were invited to participate in hearings. However, Congressional pro-life advocates refused to insert the women's health exception fearing it would be a loophole permitting widespread use of this procedure. So, the ban passed again in 1997, and Clinton vetoed it again.[21]

The Clinton vetoes meant that, in the end, the law was unchanged; this served the policy goals of women's movement activists on the issue. Even more significant, however, was his ability to stymie the pro-life plan to redefine the abortion issue in such a way as to remove women's interests and women themselves as legitimate players in the debate. Nevertheless, by focusing only on an exception to the ban, rather than an outright rejection of the effort to criminalize medical procedures, the frame of the abortion debate had narrowed and further constrained the range of claims for women's rights within the debates on abortion issues.

If there is one issue where the Clinton administration remained steadfast in support of the women's movement, it was the abortion issue. He was able to reverse all the pro-life rules that had been spread through twelve years of Reagan/Bush. However, it is a testament to the power of the pro-life right and the Catholic leadership that, despite the administration's commitments to women's right to choose, it was able to develop an emotional, symbol-laden, and largely incorrect description and pass it off as regular, widespread medical practice, causing even long-standing abortion-rights allies in Congress to waver and vote for the ban. Many pro-choice advocates had warned that, through the gradual banning of all abortion as illegal killing of the unborn, the partial-birth abortion ban would be the beginning of the end of legal abortion in the United States. Only the Clinton administration's and the Supreme Court's adherence to a definition of the abortion issue that weighs women's rights and health against the rights and health of the fetus prevented what many pro-choice advocates had predicted.

Welfare Reform

As a candidate, Bill Clinton promised to "end welfare as we know it." Probably more than any other pledge, this statement defined the candidate as a New Democrat, the U.S. leader of the Third Way. Traditional liberals were appalled. Still, it was a popular position because a majority of Americans opposed Aid to Families with Dependent Children (AFDC), the welfare policy in place since the 1930s. This program entitled parents (mostly single mothers) to financial assistance as well as medical care and food stamps. Politicians had sought for decades to put welfare recipients to work, without success. One reason for this failure was that the policy issue was defined primarily as a support for poor children with an emphasis on family needs. Thus, any work programs gave generous exceptions for women with small children.

This definition began to change in the 1980s. First of all there was the New Federalism of President Ronald Reagan: to shift many social policies to the states with the federal government providing only block grants. Then, the Family Support Act of 1988 (FSA) responded to requests by governors for permission to experiment with pilot programs for moving welfare recipients to work. As governor of Arkansas, Clinton was one of the most active governors in developing alternative policies to the failed AFDC: with a combination of job training and healthcare support, Arkansas required welfare clients to work in jobs after two years on assistance, providing community work if private jobs were not available. As part of the package, FSA also required states to provide some child care and strengthen child-support enforcement.

By 1990, the frame of welfare reform debate had changed to focus on moving people off welfare rolls by helping them become economically self-sufficient. In this way, the policy would reduce poverty, not perpetuate it. Before the 1992 election, Democrats in Congress convened hearings, planning to expand the FSA approach. Although this was a switch in their focus, neither the congressional Democrats nor candidate

Clinton advocated abolishing AFDC and its entitlement. Yet that is exactly what the House Republicans were considering. Although before 1994 they were outnumbered, they proposed a major shift in the frame of debate on welfare, claiming that AFDC itself was the problem because it perpetuated dependency, rewarded laziness, encouraged teenage pregnancy, and penalized marriage. They wanted to get rid of it altogether.

Engrossed in a brutal battle over healthcare, it took President Clinton two years after the election to introduce a welfare-reform bill. With another nifty slogan—"Make Work Pay"—the administration's goal was to make welfare mothers economically self-sufficient, following the successful pilot program developed in Arkansas. This approach would maintain AFDC entitlements and a strong role for the federal government but introduce some modest time limits and a few punitive measures. Government would still take responsibility for assuring that welfare recipients had adequate support in terms of education and training, child care, and child-support enforcement to be successful in their new jobs.

This approach was driven off the tracks by the Republican victory in 1994 elections and the Contract with America. With the majority in both houses of Congress, the conservatives took control of the welfare-reform debate and proposed a bill that fit their definition of the problem. Although they gave lip service to National Governors Association demands for decentralization and state flexibility, their bill included a set of federal regulations—disincentives intended to wean welfare recipients from the state dole. These were family caps (no additional financial support for children born of parents on welfare); requiring welfare recipients to work; no benefits for unmarried mothers under eighteen ("if they can't live with parents, then they should be in group homes or put in orphanages or up for adoption"); requiring them to name the fathers of out of wedlock children to get payments; forcing fathers to pay support and participate in work programs; lifetime limits on welfare eligibility; denying assistance to both legal and illegal immigrants.

After this, the only role the Clinton administration had was to try to soften the punitive approach in the Republican bill. At first, women's rights activists worked with the administration. Both were forced into a reactive mode. In their testimony they tried to present an image of welfare mothers that countered the Republican vision of teenage girls getting pregnant and expecting the government to support them and of adult mothers and grandmothers who were incapable of maintaining their families and raising their children to be self-sufficient. Like the

Democrats, the women's rights groups portrayed women as struggling to live, seeking work but lacking education and adequate training. It was a tough battle. The Republicans had control of the debate and they knew that, given his boastful pledge to end welfare, President Clinton needed some sort of welfare-reform bill to look credible in the 1996 campaign. It was not a situation conducive to compromise.

As work on the bill neared completion, with only a few modifications of the most punitive aspects, the Women's Lobby turned its attention to President Clinton, demanding that he veto the bill and save the entitlement program for the poor. NOW even mounted a hunger strike in front of the White House to bring attention to its demands, but to no avail. With the election looming, the president saw no other choice than to sign whatever bill was sent and promised his disappointed feminist supporters to work for "modifications" in the law in future Congresses. NOW president Patricia Ireland warned that Clinton would feel the feminist wrath in the 1996 presidential election. Whether feminists boycotted is difficult to say; we do know the election produced majority support among women for the president and a large gender gap.

Can we chalk up welfare reform as a defeat for the women's movement? Well, not entirely. While the women's movement activists were fairly unified in support of maintaining a federal guarantee of support for poor mothers, they were not in agreement about welfare reform.[22] Furthermore, it had not been a high-priority issue on the women's movement agenda. The mainstream organizations, such as NOW, American Association of University Women (AAUW), and the Federation of Business and Professional Women's Clubs (BPW) became active in 1994, forming a lobbying coalition, but their members never took to the issue the way they had rallied for abortion rights. The feminists in Congress, many of whom had close partnerships with the Women's Lobby organizations, were divided on the Republican bill. The major question dividing them was the provision requiring work for welfare mothers. A new organization found itself somewhat on the margins of the mainstream feminist position on welfare. The Women's Committee of 100, declaring that "a war against poor women is a war against all women," demanded the preservation of AFDC entitlement with the goal of allowing poor mothers to do the work of mothering with their own children, just like the mothers of more affluent families do.[23] Thus, the women's movement activists opposed the Republican bill that Clinton signed, but they were not united on an alternative.

Inside Congress, the Congressional Caucus for Women's Issues (CCWI) took an interest in the welfare-reform issue in the early 1990s. And, although the Gingrich House withdrew all support for such legislative organizations, leaders continued to work on the issue. The CCWI included all women in Congress. They were sensitive to the divisions among women on various issues. In the case of welfare reform, the CCWI focused almost entirely on funding for child care for welfare mothers seeking employment and on strengthening enforcement of child support. The White House Office of Women's Initiatives worked with CCWI on their proposals, but neither group actively sought to retain AFDC entitlements demanded by various feminist groups.

Trafficking in Women

Changes in international relations brought the issue of trafficking of women and girls for prostitution to the government agenda. The end of the Cold War and increasing global trade led to a dramatic increase in the number of women transported by organized-crime organizations from Eastern Europe, Asia, and Latin America to the West, including to the United States. In 1998, President Clinton issued a directive: "Steps to Combat Violence Against Women and Trafficking in Women and Girls." He gave responsibility for carrying out this directive to the President's Interagency Council on Women (IAC), housed in the State Department under the chairmanship of Secretary of State Madeleine Albright. Work groups were established including a task force at the Department of Justice. A three-part policy was devised: prevention through research, to gather information on the problem; protection, focusing on social services for victims; and prosecution, to strengthen criminal penalties and enforcement. The IAC turned to a Clinton Senate ally, Democrat Paul Wellstone to introduce the bill to authorize the new policy. At the same time, Rep. Chris Smith, Republican of New Jersey and chair of the Subcommittee on Human Rights, developed his own bill. He had become aware of the problem of trafficking while a delegate to the Organization for Security and Cooperation in Europe (OSCE). His approach was to use U.S. foreign-policy power for moral good; his bill provided the president with powers to sanction foreign governments that contribute to the trafficking problem. President Clinton and the State Department opposed such a punitive approach.

Proponents of both bills agreed on the need for a redefinition of the trafficking issue. Up to this time, the federal authorities had defined the problem in terms of immigration. When confronted with a case of forced prostitution of foreign women in the United States, they treated the victims as illegal aliens and a top priority was to return them to their countries of origin. In doing this, they routinely deported the only witnesses to the coercion involved in trafficking. The new bills defined the issue as one of human rights and focused on the traffickers as the wrongdoers. They defined the crime in terms of the force, fraud, or deception used by organized gangs to capture or entice women and girls to leave home and travel to Western countries, often expecting to find work and a better life. Instead they often ended up without passports or documents, in brothels, in debt and forced to service many men sexually. Bill sponsors made analogies between trafficking and slavery or involuntary servitude. Soon, they expanded their definition of trafficking to include all forms of coerced labor.

Fourteen women's rights groups formed an informal coalition to lobby Congress on the trafficking issue.[24] Since Senator Wellstone was the point man for the Clinton bill the coalition approached him with its proposals. They were old *amis de combat;* Wellstone was a staunch supporter of the women's rights agenda and a key ally in advancing the reauthorization of the Violence Against Women Act up for consideration in 1999–2000. The feminist coalition sought a change in the administration's bill. It was based on a distinction between voluntary prostitution and coerced prostitution, punishing only the perpetrators of coercion. The feminists asserted that all prostitution was exploitation; this view reflects the radical feminist ideology.[25] They argued that if a procurer or pimp brings women into the United States for prostitution this should be penalized. The administration bill would leave untouched traffickers bringing women into the country to work in the sex industry (pornography, strip clubs, escort services) as long as they did not use force or deception.

When Wellstone was unmoved by their plea, they brought their case to the president's IAC, specifically the office charged with implementing the president's anti-trafficking directive. The meetings between the feminist coalition and the IAC staff were not cordial. IAC officials were aware that there was a split in the women's movement and international feminism over whether prostitution is by definition exploitive or whether it is, in the absence of violence, a conventional form of work. The IAC not only rejected the radical feminist claim, it worked in Congress to degender the debate; that is, to expand the definition of trafficking to all persons coerced into any labor. Thus the administration bill made no explicit reference to sex trafficking of women and girls.

The feminist lobby finally turned to Rep. Chris Smith. The Republicans had the majority in Congress and as a committee chair Smith was in a position to move a bill through the legislative process. The women's lobby did not consider Smith a friend. A strong Catholic, he had been a staunch pro-life advocate in abortion debates. At the same time, he favored infusing a moral stance in U.S. foreign policy and was appalled at the testimony of victims of trafficking and their suffering. In introducing his bill penalizing trafficking, specifically in women and girls for prostitution, he sought to further his moral position. It turned out that Smith's socially responsible religious position coincided with the radical feminist view of prostitution as sexual exploitation. Thus, Smith was receptive to requests for revisions to his bill to incorporate the feminist coalition's definition of the issue. Over the opposition of the IAC and the Clinton administration, Smith's staff worked out a compromise with the feminists—a two-tier definition of trafficking:

> Sex trafficking: "the recruitment, harboring, transportation, provision or obtaining of another person for the purpose of a commercial sex act."
> Severe sex trafficking: "a commercial sex act induced by force, fraud, or coercion or in which the person induced to perform such act has not attained 18 years of age."[26]

This distinction was more symbolic that instrumental policy; only severe sex trafficking would be subject to criminal sanctions in the new law. At the same time, the symbolic policy was more than the Clinton administration had been willing to allow. Smith's bill ultimately went into effect as the Trafficking Victims Protection Act of 2000 (PL 106-386) in October 2000 with little opposition. The language of the act was gender neutral and included the administration's demand that it cover all forms of coerced labor, not just sex. The preamble did recognize that women and girls are the principal victims of trafficking.

The IAC remained unmoved by claims for a radical feminist definition of prostitution and trafficking, and the feminist activists were perplexed by the lack of support they received from the Clinton administration. IAC's official explanation appealed to imperatives of U.S. foreign policy. During the late 1990s, the United Nations was debating a protocol on trafficking to be a supplement to the UN Convention Against Transnational Organized Crime. Some U.S. allies (for example, the Netherlands) had already changed their laws to decriminalize prostitution as sex work and made clear distinctions between coerced and voluntary prostitution; the IAC officials claimed it would be an insult to them if the United States went ahead and criminalized all forms of prostitution at the time of these debates. The final debate on the protocol took place after the enactment of the Trafficking Victims Protection Act. In December 2000, the protocol was adopted in Vienna.[27] In doing so, a majority of nations supported the radical feminist definition of prostitution as, by definition, exploitation; silent during the debate, the U.S. delegate voted for the final version.

Conclusion

In 1999, women's rights organizations stood by their man, President Clinton, despite his involvement in sex scandals. Given the policy record of his administration, was this support warranted? Was Clinton an ally of feminists? And, would things have been different with another leader, a Republican, in the White House? Based on this review of political appointments and the debates over the partial-birth abortion ban, welfare reform, and trafficking in women, the answer is a qualified yes to all questions.

On two issues, political representation and abortion, the Clinton administration was a strong supporter of feminist claims. The president made a conscious effort to put more women in appointed office, and women joined the Cabinet and the judiciary in record numbers. He appointed a feminist to the Supreme Court. Given the dramatic increases in women's representation in comparison with Republican administrations, there is little doubt that women would not have been so successful if a Republican was in the White House during the 1990s. It is certain that there would not be a feminist like Ginsburg on the Supreme Court.

With respect to abortion, the Clinton administration was absolutely steadfast in support of the women's movement position. Without Clinton, the pro-life strategy to criminalize abortion procedures would have been completely successful at the federal level. The two vetoes prevented that; Clinton's women's policy offices regendered the abortion debate after efforts by pro-life congressional leaders to remove women entirely from the discussion. Still, the pro-life movement made gains during the Clinton administration by narrowing the scope of the debate and thus the range of claims allowed. Even with a united Women's Lobby and a steadfast President, the pro-choice movement remained on the defensive.

Clinton's role in the debates over welfare reform was much less satisfying for the feminist activists. For one thing, he had taken a leading role before becoming president in moving the welfare-reform debate away from the women's movement focus on the well-being of poor mothers and their children and toward a requirement to move people off welfare into jobs. Changing the welfare system drastically was part of Clinton's definition of himself as a New Democrat. With respect to the Republican determination to abolish AFDC entitlements, Clinton agreed with the feminists in preserving it. Halfway through the debate, however, the administration lost control of the issue and was unable to save the entitlement. While Clinton might have invested more political capital in seeking to save AFDC, it is certain that there was no Republican who could have or would have saved it either.

With trafficking, Clinton disappointed the feminist activists not only by not helping them reach their objectives but also by working against them to develop a bill that considered sex trafficking as just another form of coerced labor. Thus, the activists turned to a Republican congressman whose views on the issue were more compatible with theirs. It is very likely that a Republican in the White House would have been even more supportive of the feminist views of the issue than the Clinton Democrats.

These findings illustrate the imperfect fit between American liberalism, usually associated with the Democrats, and women's movement feminism. When the third-wave women's movement organized in the 1960s, it was not associated with any political party. There were feminists active in both parties, and they worked together on specific policy campaigns as well as in the National Women's Political Caucus to bring more women into power. When the right-wing conservatives, especially the pro-life movement, became dominant in the Republican party with the rise to power of Ronald Reagan, women's movement activists turned increasingly to find support for their demands in the Democratic party. Thus, from the defeat of the Equal Rights Amendment in the early 1980s on, feminists depended on Democrats, and a few "liberal" Republicans to further their agenda in Washington. With the dramatic shift to the right in Congress after the 1994 elections, both the feminists and the Clinton administration were in a defensive mode on abortion and welfare reform. And, apart from a few "Old" New Deal Democrats left on Capitol Hill, they found little support for retaining AFDC and its entitlement.

It is also important to keep in mind the divisions within feminism. The Clinton administration was a dependable ally on issues where movement activists were most united: political representation and abortion rights. The "inside" feminist in the White House—Hillary Rodham Clinton—was especially important in pushing for women appointees to the Cabinet and the courts as well as the strong and steadfast pro-choice stance. On welfare reform and trafficking issues, however, feminists were divided. They differed over work requirements for welfare recipients as well as to whether prostitution inherently exploited women or was, at times, a viable option for work. It is those issues where the Clinton White House disappointed the Women's Lobby activists.

The trafficking issue raises questions about the alliance between liberalism and feminism, especially on sexuality issues. In 1999–2000, the active women's movement coalition adhered to a radical feminist definition of prostitution. While not the only feminist position, it is a dominant one among activists in the United States. This collides with traditional liberal position of choice and consent in matters relating to sexuality (at least among consenting adults). If prostitution and pornography are defined as exploitation and oppression of women, it is logical to appeal for help from the government in preventing and punishing the abuse. Such a view counters the liberal acceptance of a wide variety of free sex speech and action under the consent test free from government interference. The very concept of privacy that many consider to liberate men and women sexually is under attack by the radical feminist proposals. Since the nineteenth-century social-purity movement through the anti-pornography campaigns of the 1980s, feminists seeking protection from sexual exploitation of women usually find political allies, not on the U.S. left but on the right. Thus it was in the late 1990s when the Clinton administration's women's policy office, chaired by Hillary Rodham Clinton, worked to derail the women's movement campaign for punishment for sex traffickers. On this issue, they were more attached to liberalism than to the feminist lobby.

8 Clinton's China Policy

JUNE TEUFEL DREYER

In this chapter, Professor Dreyer examines President Clinton's evolving foreign policy toward China. The shooting of unarmed demonstrators in Tiananmen Square during late spring of 1989, and the subsequent criticism associated with President George H. W. Bush's alleged coddling of China, promised that President Clinton would be forced to take difficult positions toward a nation that represented both substantial human-rights violations and vast economic potential. During President Clinton's first year in office, he was faced with nearly all the major problems associated with China and American foreign relations—trade, intellectual property rights, human rights, weapons, and Taiwan. Professor Dreyer argues that while President Clinton was initially a strong supporter of human rights, he soon followed in the paths of his predecessors by granting most favored nation trading status to China amid substantial criticisms. Professor Dreyer discusses and contrasts the first and second Clinton administrations and the evolution of the strategic partnership approach adopted by President Clinton during the second term. She concludes by arguing that much of President Clinton's foreign policy, as well as the stated goals and ultimate success in reaching those goals, was quite similar to many of President Clinton's contemporaries.

Candidate Clinton

A s the 1992 presidential campaign worked its way toward November, debates over China policy were conspicuous by their absence. This was not because the actions taken by the incumbent president, George H. W. Bush, were considered particularly successful. His response to the party- and government–ordered shooting of unarmed demonstrators in and around Tiananmen Square[1] in June 1989 had been tepid at best. Deng Xiaoping, leader of the People's Republic of China (PRC), refused to accept the president's telephone calls. Bush's hesitation about announcing sanctions against the PRC did not resonate well with the moral outrage of the American population, not to mention his political enemies. When it was later revealed that the president had dispatched not one but two secret missions to Beijing, the first one just days after the massacre and the second featuring television footage of the American envoys sipping champagne with what the press called "the butchers of Beijing," there was still more criticism. The president's explanation that quiet diplomacy could achieve more than recriminations struck his many critics as unconvincing. A typical reaction, as expressed by Human Rights Watch member Holly Burkhalter in spring 1992, termed Bush's approach of coddling China while whispering occasional criticism "an abject failure."[2] However, in the words of a *New York Times* article of the time, although "the president had demanded little of China, the candidates showed little interest in discussing it."[3]

An exception to this occurred in August, when candidate Clinton, in a major address to the Los Angeles Council on World Affairs, declared

> From the Baltics to Beijing, from Sarajevo to South Africa, time after time this president has sided with the status quo against democratic change, with familiar tyrants rather than those who would overthrow them; with the old geography of repression rather than a new map of freedom.[4]

He vowed to link the PRC's human-rights record to its receipt of trade privileges by the United States. Despite this alliterative rhetoric, nominee Clinton actually said very little about China or anywhere else in the Far East. This author tried to elicit a policy statement on China and Asia by calling Clinton's campaign headquarters in Little Rock, Arkansas, every week or two. She was initially told, several times, that such a statement would be forthcoming shortly, then, also several times, that it had been postponed, and, finally, just before the election, that plans to issue a statement had been called off. Given that the campaign's major slogan had been "It's the Economy, Stupid," this was not startling although somewhat surprising nonetheless.

As little as Clinton had said, it was enough to raise the hopes of those who were disappointed by Bush's policies. Across the Pacific, however, the PRC leadership was plainly worried. In October, they were described as "horrified" by the prospect of his election.[5] Considering that only a few months before, incumbent Bush had greatly angered the Chinese by agreeing to sell 150 F-16 fighter planes to Taiwan, this is a telling comment. John Kamm, a business consultant and director of a project to promote dialogue on human rights in China, predicted a very tense, delicate relationship whoever won the White House, save that Sino-American relations would probably go downhill a bit faster if Clinton won.[6] Stapleton Roy, the U.S. ambassador to Beijing, was portrayed as aware that if Clinton were elected, the embassy might have to switch course.[7] Other sectors of the bureaucracy were also expecting change. Following Clinton's election, the Department of Commerce scheduled interagency hearings in the expectation that it would be better positioned to overcome the Department of Defense's strong opposition to the sale of crop-duster aircraft to Iran and satellites to the PRC before Bush left office than after.[8] The two agencies were in fact able to reach a tentative agreement to allow the export of the jets.[9]

The president-elect appeared to soften his stance slightly when, a day after meeting with the man he had just defeated, he suggested that Bush's policies were showing signs of reducing human-rights and trade violations.[10] But in a well-publicized speech at American University, Clinton, though endorsing the broad thrust of Bush's trade policies, made continued trade growth with the PRC contingent on progress in human rights. The State Department's final annual report on human rights under the Bush administration indicated that there was much room for progress, enumerating a lengthy list of abuses that had occurred in 1992.[11]

The First Term

Clinton's first year in office saw him tested on most of the major outstanding issues between the United States and the People's Republic, including trade, intellectual property rights, human rights, weapons pro-liferation and Taiwan.

Initially, there were some signs that China's leaders were amenable to a degree of cooperation with the new administration. One factor may have been Beijing's desire to host the 2000 summer Olympic games. Western journalists reported that their normal "tails" had stopped trail-ing them in mid-January. They believed that a desire to elicit more favor-able coverage ahead of the arrival of the Olympic Committee was the reason. If so, party and government must have been disappointed as the journalists wrote articles describing the construction of a brick wall to hide slums from the committee's view and vagrants banished to the sub-urbs. In a particularly poignant story that was widely reported, a men-tally impaired young man who apparently did not understand commands to keep out of sight was beaten to death. In another gesture thought to be meant as a goodwill gesture to the new president, the Chinese leader-ship released two prominent political prisoners in February. One had been in solitary confinement for over twelve years; another had been imprisoned since the 1989 demonstrations at Tiananmen.[12]

While public commentary concentrated on trade and human-rights issues, U.S.–China relations actually encompassed a broader range of topics. Although these garnered few column inches in the press, they were arguably of greater importance. The administration wanted Beijing's help in urging moderation on the North Korean government, since P'yongyang was believed to be close to deploying nuclear weapons. The president also wanted China to join a voluntary halt in nuclear testing, to stop the proliferation of weapons and military-related technology to rogue states, and to agree to a peaceful settlement of its differences with the Republic of China on Taiwan.

These moderating factors notwithstanding, Clinton's actions indi-cated that he took his campaign promises seriously. In April, he met with the exiled leader of Tibet, the Dalai Lama, at the White House. Bush had done so as well, though somewhat less publicly. Since Beijing views the Dalai Lama as a separatist who wishes to set up an independent Tibetan state—the lama's protests to the contrary notwithstanding—the Chinese press reacted with predictable anger.[13] Rhetoric linking extension of the PRC's most favored nation (MFN) status to improvement in human-rights abuses continued, and garment maker Levi Strauss pledged that it would not make direct investments in China and would reduce its use of mainland contractors because of the country's poor human-rights record. One other large U.S. manufacturer, Timberland, had already pulled out of the PRC after the Tiananmen incident.[14]

In a well-thought-out and carefully timed countermove, the Chinese government announced a month before the deadline for renewal of MFN that it would order a billion dollars worth of U.S. products, including such high-end commodities as airplanes, cars, telecommunications equipment, and oil. The clear intent of this move was to show the value of the Chinese market since the deals would collapse if the low tariffs guaranteed by MFN were terminated. The lobbyists for companies whose profits would potentially be impacted descended on Washington, predicting dire consequences if MFN were not renewed. Others estimated that exports to the PRC had created about fifteen thousand jobs in the United States, and that U.S. consumers would be adversely affected if MFN were canceled since the relatively inexpensive items China exported to the United States would be effectively cut off.[15] Even Hong Kong governor Chris Patten, despised by the mainland government for his efforts to introduce democratic government to the colony, flew to New York to plead for renewal. Patten was motivated not by sympathy for the PRC but by the realization that termination of MFN would adversely impact Hong Kong's economy as well as that of mainland China.

Opponents of MFN renewal had an equally well-timed response, citing indications that China might be shipping M-11 missiles to Pakistan in contravention of an agreement made under the Bush administration. When the agreement was announced, it had been hailed as a triumph of Bush's "quiet diplomacy." Nor, they pointed out, had the PRC met other important criteria such as allowing all dissidents to leave the country, opening its markets, or permitting inspection of its prison facilities. Moreover, since the PRC consistently exported far more to the United States than it imported, its manufacturers would suffer more than those of the United States if MFN were canceled.

Proponents of MFN, including some diplomats, countered, oddly, by saying that the PRC was not *openly* flouting agreements—why secrecy would render the breach of contract less objectionable is difficult to understand—and that human-rights advocates were too quick to criticize China.[16] The *New York Times,* heretofore a champion of human rights for the oppressed, took a somewhat less assertive editorial stance. It suggested that Clinton should encourage reform-minded PRC forces by carefully linking trade privileges to "achievable human rights objectives," conveniently neglecting to specify either which rights were achievable or which were too difficult for the administration to achieve.[17]

The administration, buffeted by business interests on the one hand and human-rights advocates on the other, saw an obvious way out: persuade the Chinese to make improvements in human rights in order to allow Clinton to extend MFN. The assistant secretary of state for East Asia and the Pacific, Winston Lord, was dispatched to Beijing to convey this message. Lord, who had accompanied Henry Kissinger on his historic mission to the PRC in the early 1970s, warned the Chinese leadership that Clinton needed some positive actions on human rights if he were to fend off Congress on the issue of trade privileges. There is no indication that he received any.[18] In the end, Clinton renewed MFN, stipulating that the PRC would have to make "overall progress" in several areas of human rights for any subsequent renewal. These would, he said, be carefully monitored over the coming year. Reaction to the conditional renewal was generally favorable. The president had come up with a solution that almost all could live with.[19] A London newspaper opined that the agreement proved that "pressure works on Peking"; the West's hand with China had never been stronger.[20] To be sure, there were dissenters: an arms-control advocate, for example, was unhappy since the agreement linked trade to human rights alone rather than encompassing proliferation issues.[21] The Chinese press, angry at Clinton's arrogance in imposing any conditions at all, spewed vitriol.

The reaction from a Hong Kong newspaper, the *South China Morning Post,* was gleeful. It opined that Governor Patten, whom the mainland regularly castigated in creatively vulgar language, must be pleased to see that now it was "Slick Willie" being described as "a strutting whore . . . condemned for a thousand years . . . a spoiled brat."[22] In a more thoughtful treatment, another *SCMP* article analyzed the president's decision as owing more to the state of his administration's standing in Washington than it did to Beijing's progress in human rights. After only five months in the White House, still part of the traditional "honeymoon" period when the press and public tend to give a new president the benefit of doubt on policy questions, Clinton's approval rating stood at a bare 36 percent. This was well below that of any predecessor at a comparable time. Fifty percent of those polled expressed disapproval of his job performance. Clinton's expensive haircut on the runway of the Los Angeles airport had tied up traffic for hours, his tax bill had passed the House of Representatives by a bare six votes, and he had been indecisive on Bosnia, deficit reduction, healthcare reform, and gays in the military. When the American media fall out of love with their president, the author observed, they do it totally—making the wounded president easy prey to special-interest and protectionist lobby groups. This, the paper felt, was exactly what had happened to Clinton. Noting that he had "tacked" Tibet, which numbers an impressive list of entertainment celebrities among its backers, onto the list of conditions for renewal, *SCMP* characterized the MFN decision as "owing more to Hollywood-style public relations and a knee-jerk reaction to the news of the day than a well thought-through policy towards a huge trading partner."[23]

If the president hoped that MFN renewal would soothe Sino-American tensions, he was mistaken: other issues quickly crowded to the fore. In August, the United States charged the PRC with transporting the ingredients for chemical weapons to Iran. Having no legal basis to seize or inspect the ship believed to be carrying the suspect chemicals, the Americans resorted to shadowing the vessel with military ships and planes. The Chinese, denying that any such cargo was aboard, protested America's harassment tactics. After three weeks of intense negotiations, an agreement was reached to have the ship, the *Yinhe*, dock at the Saudi port of Damman—at least one other country having previously denied docking permission—and its contents inspected. No trace of the suspect chemicals was found.[24] Beijing denounced the United States as a "self-styled world cop" and demanded an apology and compensation. A source familiar with the incident later told the author that American intelligence had received correct information that the chemicals were to be transported, but that the *Yinhe* did not take the materials aboard despite what had been entered on the bill of lading. Hence no apology or compensation was rendered, thereby giving the Beijing government a grievance to exploit.[25]

In the same month, the administration charged the PRC with violating an international arms-control agreement by shipping sensitive military technology to Pakistan and announced that it would bar American exports of almost a billion dollars in high-tech goods to the PRC over the next two years. The Chinese government protested, arguing that the range of the missile in question, the M-11, was under the range covered by the Missile Control Technology Regime and threatened to reconsider its commitment to the treaty. The Chinese foreign minister also pointed out that Washington, not Beijing, was the world's largest arms exporter.[26] Another grievance had been added to the growing list.

In September, the Olympic Committee announced that Sydney, Australia, rather than Beijing had been chosen as the site of the 2000 Summer Games. The Chinese government seems to have set itself up for the disappointment, perhaps reasoning that if it won, the celebration would have been worth the substantial advance preparations and if it lost, it would have yet another issue to criticize the United States over. To allow schoolchildren to stay up late for the expected happy news, next day's classes had been canceled and bands, fireworks, and large-screen public television coverage arranged. The sense of disappointment was keen, even being expressed in racist terms. Cooler heads must have realized that both Japan and South Korea had previously hosted the games, but cooler heads were not much in evidence at the time. Even Senior Minister Lee Kwan Yew of Singapore was sympathetic to the PRC, saying that although the apparent reason for the turn-down was human rights, the real reason was political: to show Western political clout. America and Britain wanted to "cut China, an emerging power, down to size."[27]

Clinton's harder line was denounced by business interests in the United States and retaliated against by the PRC. Immediately after sanctions stemming from the sales of M-11 missiles to Pakistan were announced, aerospace officials began to press the administration to soften their effect. For example, they argued, the sanctions would unfairly penalize America's satellite industry from selling goods that would not be used for military purposes.[28] As if to underscore their argument that, if the PRC were not able to purchase what it wanted from the United States, it could find other customers, there were a spate of stories about Israel selling high-tech weapons to China.[29] A new round of political repression began the day after the Olympic Committee's decision to award the 2000 Summer Games to Sydney. Journalists were arrested on charges of leaking "state secrets" and dissidents subjected to secret trials.[30] In October, China exploded another nuclear device, rejecting Clinton's call against breaking the informal testing moratorium. The administration's subsequent order to resume American tests in 1994 was criticized within the United States as constituting a dangerous escalation.

Clinton then took a number of steps that could be construed by the Beijing leadership as indicating that he was overly anxious to improve Sino-American relations. Assistant Secretary of State for Human Rights John Shattuck was sent for a week of talks, followed by Agriculture Secretary Mike Espy. Shattuck stated that, although the United States would have to terminate MFN on human-rights grounds if it were up for renewal during his October visit, he felt that if there were "significant progress" between then and the June 1994 deadline for renewal, he was confident that the PRC's MFN status could become permanent. Espy added that high-level visits would "increase and intensify" with the goal of improving relations. It was reported that National Security Advisor Anthony Lake had completed a review of the administration's China policy that presented Clinton with recommendations for improving ties.[31] A new buzzword, "enhanced engagement,"[32] emerged, though no one appeared to know what it meant apart from the administration's hope for a less tension-laden relationship with China. Administration officials warned that if the United States treated China as an enemy, then it would surely become one. They did not appear to be aware that Beijing had regarded the United States as the PRC's number one enemy since 1989, choosing to cite instead the pleasanter words of Chinese officials at ceremonial gatherings of high-ranking officials. Consonant with not wishing to treat the PRC as an enemy, Clinton officials also made efforts to improve military-to-military contacts with the People's Liberation Army (PLA), arguing that the PLA's influence in setting China's political agenda outweighed the importance of sanctions imposed after the revelation that M-11 missiles had been sold to Pakistan. It was time, they said, to put the PLA's repression at Tiananmen behind us and move the relationship forward. Assistant Secretary of Defense Chas Freeman expressed his belief that military isolation had "taken its toll in terms of mutual understanding"[33] and stated that Washington now saw China as a potential partner.[34] Doubters noted that, though Shattuck's delegation had given Chinese officials a list of political detainees, he had been evasive when pressed to clarify what constituted enough human-rights progress to ensure a renewal of MFN trade status.[35] And there was no conclusive evidence—unless one accepts the word of the not always reliable Hong Kong press—that the PLA had a major role in China's political decision-making. Former secretary of state Alexander Haig, visiting Beijing to introduce his new boss, the president of United Technologies, asked rhetorically, "How dare [the United States] go around telling the rest of the world that it must live up to American standards on human rights? . . . Tiananmen is a long way behind us" and accused the administration of driving the next generation of Chinese leaders toward "jingoism" and "anti-Americanism."[36] This, of course, rested on the assumption that the next generation of Chinese leaders would espouse the authoritarian values of the present generation. Since many of the PRC's younger dissidents feel that Washington should press their government to institute rule of law and democratic reforms, this contention is not necessarily valid.

In a goodwill gesture on the eve of the Seattle meeting of the Asia Pacific Economic Cooperation (APEC) forum, Clinton announced an agreement to sell the PRC a sophisticated $8-million supercomputer. Sought for some time by the PRC, the transfer had been blocked under the Bush administration after it discovered that Beijing had broken its promises to Washington by exporting M-11 missile components and technology to Pakistan. Disagreeing with the administration's contention that use of the supercomputer would be monitored to prevent its diversion to military uses, a Pentagon expert on nonproliferation described technical difficulties involved in implementing safeguards, adding that "if the Chinese manage to use the supercomputer in a weapons program, no one's going to go in there and pull the plug."[37]

Those who hoped that the new slogan of enhanced engagement or the sale of the supercomputer would ease the Seattle summit were disappointed. What Clinton got was a stern lecture from PRC president Jiang Zemin on the right of sovereign states to set their own policies without interference from outside powers and the lack of relevance of U.S. values in the Chinese context. In an editorial entitled "China Stiffs the President," the *New York Times* commented that, while Clinton had toned down his rhetoric and loosened restrictive policies in an effort to be sensitive to Chinese considerations of "face," Jiang had offered no gestures of his own to protect Mr. Clinton's political position.[38] The *Los Angeles Times* noted the contrast between the actual forty-degree temperature in Seattle and the freezing nature of the Jiang-Clinton talks.[39]

In early 1994, the first State Department human-rights report done under the new administration described the PRC as having made no significant progress on human-rights abuses. Three days later, however, Jiang Zemin, meeting a congressional delegation led by House majority leader Richard Gephardt, said that the PRC would try to meet Clinton's concerns about human rights. Gephardt came away feeling that, for the first time, the Chinese leadership was "very serious" about resolving the most contentious issues between it and the United States. The International Red Cross reported that its representatives and PRC officials were discussing opening Chinese prisons to inspection for the first time since the communist government assumed power in 1949. And in early February, the Beijing government released three political prisoners.

Those who saw a trend in these developments were quickly disabused of such a notion. A week after the prisoners were released, the government began a new, and severe, crackdown on Christianity. The prison inspection talks did not result in actual visits to prisons. And, in what was interpreted as a clear signal to the United States, China's most famous dissident, Wei Jingsheng, was re-arrested for a day just before Secretary of State Warren Christopher was to visit. The Christopher mission did not go well. Reminding his hosts that the date for certifying progress in human rights was fast approaching, the secretary was confronted with what one analyst called an avalanche of vitriol.[40] He was told bluntly that the PRC's human rights behavior was none of America's concern, and prominent dissidents were arrested publicly during his visit. A *Washington Post* columnist commented that it was fortunate for the secretary that Washington was so absorbed with Clinton's alleged involvement in the unfolding Whitewater scandal that "the astonishing debacle he brought upon himself and his administration" had not received greater attention.[41] Just after the secretary's departure, Chinese foreign minister Qian Qichen declared that both the United States and the PRC lived quite well for twenty-three years without trading with each other and could do so nicely again. Beijing would not yield on the human-rights issue, and President Clinton had "enmeshed himself in a web of his own spinning" over the June deadline he had set for China to make overall significant progress on human rights or else lose its favorable trade status with the United States.[42]

As human-rights groups marshaled their supporters to urge the administration to hang tough on its commitments, Wei Jingsheng was re-re-arrested in a well-publicized incident that the Beijing government clearly intended to signify that it, too, would be tough. Wei was arrested in April in broad daylight by no less than seven carloads of public security agents—numbers far beyond what was needed to apprehend a lone, unarmed man. Moreover, Wei's health had been badly impaired by more than a decade of malnourishment in a solitary confinement punctuated only by savage beatings. The White House responded simply that it was "deeply troubled." On the other side of the MFN issue, legions of business leaders, lobbyists for industry, and trade organizations were predicting the consequences of withdrawal of the PRC's privileges in terms described as "near apocalyptic."[43]

In late May, Christopher gave Clinton a report on the PRC's human-rights record that effectively provided the administration with a legal argument for renewing MFN. China had, said the report, complied with two conditions that the administration had said were mandatory: it had resolved all outstanding emigration cases, "made progress" in allowing the United States to inspect prison-labor factories and was "taking steps to implement" a bilateral agreement to prevent the export of goods made with prison labor to the United States.[44]A few days after receiving the report, arguing that remaining engaged with China was a better policy than cutting off billions of dollars in trade, Clinton renewed MFN. He further announced that henceforth he would decouple trade from human rights: in the future, policy toward China would rely more on diplomacy and less on brinksmanship. Over time, the new policy would nurture democracy, maintain a "strategic relationship" with Beijing and achieve more progress in human rights.[45] This act finalized what had been known for several months. Clinton's transformation from crusader against coddling to enthusiastic engager had taken barely a year.

Although howls of betrayal were loud,[46] business leaders were pleased, as were many others who had wearied of the annual debate over MFN, which always resulted in renewal, irrespective of Beijing's words and deeds. The decision easily survived congressional efforts to overturn it. What did not show signs of easing were U.S.-China relations. The November 1994 midterm congressional elections saw major gains for Republicans, who became the majority party in both House and Senate, thus further complicating the Clinton administration's ability to negotiate with the Chinese.

Decoupling human rights from trade did not mean that either issue went away, and other issues came to the fore as well. Nineteen ninety-five began with U.S. trade representative Mickey Kantor threatening to impose steep tariffs on Chinese goods unless Beijing stopped violating intellectual-property rights. These violations, in such areas as films, computer software, and music, were estimated to cost American businesses and, by extension, the balance of payments, over a billion dollars a year. After protracted and bitter negotiations, a copyright agreement was reached under which the PRC promised, among other things, to devise and carry out an enforcement policy on intellectual property rights within the next three to five years, set up task forces in various cities and provinces to curb infringements, raid factories involved in illegal manufacturing and retailers who were selling pirated goods, and revoke factories' operating licenses for repeated offenses. The U.S. representatives described their Chinese counterparts' approach as more businesslike and less political than in the past, perhaps indicating a more mature approach to the contentious issues under discussion.[47] That this new approach did not necessarily yield positive results became obvious within a few months, as production facilities that were closed after repeated violations reopened under new names or moved to new locations to do the same business. With corruption and local protectionism rampant in the legal system, factory owners could also simply pay officials and police not to notice the nature of the goods that factory employees were turning out.

In June, Chinese police arrested human-rights activist Harry Wu, a naturalized American citizen, when he entered the PRC to try to gather information on prison camps. After several months of diplomatic negotiations between the two countries, Wu was tried, convicted, and expelled, thus removing the major impediment to allowing first lady Hillary Rodham Clinton to attend a high-profile international women's conference being hosted by the PRC.[48] Also in June, the Central Intelligence Agency informed the administration that the PRC had delivered important components of missile systems to Iran and Pakistan. The dozens and perhaps hundreds of missile guidance systems and computerized machine tools that were supplied to Iran would enable Tehran to improve the accuracy of its missiles as well as to build such missiles on its own. There were concerns that these missiles would exceed the payload limits and range of the missile accord that China had promised to uphold. Pakistan had received the components of M-11 missiles. Loath to impose the sanctions that these revelations would entail, the administration appeared reluctant to deal with the report, saying that the evidence it presented was not conclusive.[49]

By far the most explosive event in Sino-American relations also came to a head in June. Lee Teng-hui, the president of the Republic of China on Taiwan, had received his Ph.D. degree from Cornell in 1968. Clearly one of the most distinguished alumni of that distinguished institution, he had been invited to receive Cornell's outstanding alumnus of the year award. The State Department would have to issue Lee a visa to accept the award. Beijing, which regards Taiwan as a breakaway province, forcefully represented its opposition to the State Department and received Warren Christopher's personal assurances that Lee would not be granted a visa. Since the secretary knew that Taiwan had strong bipartisan support in both houses of Congress and that Congress not only controlled the State Department's budget but also had to approve ambassadorial appointments, Christopher's decision to give such assurances is inexplicable. A visit that could have taken place almost unnoticed soon turned into high political theater. Criticism filled the press. It was noted that virtually every law-abiding person who wishes to enter the United States receives a visa. Proponents of the visit pointed out that Clinton had even entertained some quite unsavory visitors, such as the head of the terrorist-affiliated Irish Republican Army, at the White House. Why, then, they asked, should the democratically elected president of a friendly state be excluded? Should any foreign country be allowed to determine the visa policy of the United States? In April, the House voted 396–0, and the Senate 97–1, to back issuing a visa to Lee. The State Department issued the visa. International media coverage was now focused on what would normally be a low-key ceremony that was chiefly of interest to the

Cornell community. Lee went to Ithaca in June and gave an acceptance speech that strongly hinted at his country's independent status.

Beijing, claiming it had been betrayed by the United States, was infuriated. It retaliated sharply. In July and August, the mainland military twice bracketed Taiwan with missile tests, causing major disruption to shipping in the heavily trafficked international waterway between the two states. The Taiwan stock market, one of the busiest in Asia, plunged; its citizenry was terrorized. The PLA also began a series of war games, which looked as if they might be the precursors of an armed invasion of the island. In addition to indicating its anger over the Lee visit, Beijing appeared to be trying to disrupt Taiwan's March 1996 presidential election, which Lee, as the incumbent, was favored to win. The Clinton administration, perhaps wishing to avoid escalating an already tense relationship with mainland China, confined itself to calls for calm. In the eyes of critics, this simply emboldened Beijing to further provocative behavior. Sending the aircraft carrier *Nimitz* on an unpublicized visit through the Taiwan Strait did not deter the PRC—when its itinerary became known, the administration explained that the carrier was diverted due to bad weather.

Other news from China created no better impression of its government than did the military threat to Taiwan. *The Dying Rooms*, produced by the British Broadcasting Corporation, included graphic videotape footage of abandoned children who were warehoused under shocking conditions, with some being deliberately allowed to starve to death. The Beijing government announced its intention to "supervise" the dispersal of financial news, leading suspicious investors to worry that "supervise" might be a euphemism for "censor" or "manipulate." There were more revelations of Chinese weapons proliferation to rogue states. In the midst of these concerns and of escalating cross-strait tensions, an American ship, the USS *Bunker Hill,* made a port call in Qingdao, the first such visit since the suppression of the Tiananmen demonstrations and only the third warship port-call since the PRC was founded in 1949.

Taiwan's many and bipartisan congressional supporters fumed as the military exercises looked as if they might escalate into an actual invasion. Wishing to prevent this, members of Congress contemplated legislation that included an explicit U.S. military commitment to Taiwan. At that point Clinton, hoping to forestall Congress from taking this rather drastic step, ordered two aircraft-carrier battle groups, those of the *Nimitz* and the *Independence,* to sail toward the area, where they took up positions not far from the Taiwan Strait.[50] A mainland-controlled Hong Kong newspaper warned that the carriers would be "buried in a sea of fire" if they entered the strait.[51] But the exercises were called off early with bad weather given as the explanation. Taiwan's presidential election was carried out as scheduled, with Lee winning by an impressive margin that he claimed gave him a mandate to continue the policies to which Beijing had so strongly objected. No praise is due Clinton for support of Taiwan's democracy: he sent the carriers only when convinced Congress would take even stronger action. Moreover, he took immediate steps to placate Beijing, assuring the PRC's government, in writing, that he would not support Taiwan independence, that he did not support "one China, one Taiwan," and that he did not support Taiwan's membership in any organization for which statehood was a criterion. This was done secretly; it became known only in July 1998, when Clinton iterated the same phrase in answer to a question posed during a Shanghai call-in show. When the predictable furor over his "three noes" broke out in the United States, the administration explained disingenuously that this represented no change in past policy.

Clinton's placatory policy continued. With regard to proliferation, the administration agreed in May 1996 to accept the Chinese government's explanation that its officials had no knowledge that equipment for the production of weapons-grade uranium had been sold to Pakistan. Moreover, it pointed out, the sum of money involved had not been great. Additionally, Beijing's leaders had promised that it would never happen again.[52] Critics were skeptical that a country so concerned with security that it meted out severe jail sentences to individuals for merely speaking with foreign reporters could not track the movements of the components of nuclear weapons. They also pointed out the absurdity of the argument that little money had changed hands—would proliferation not be proliferation even if the materials had been transferred free of charge? Finally, if the Chinese leadership had not known that the material had been sold to Pakistan in the past, how could American authorities be sure that they would know if it happened in the future?

In the same month, a sting operation the Federal Bureau of Investigation had been carrying out on illicit Chinese arms shipments to the United States had to be aborted just short of capture of the higher-level culprits. A leak from the State Department was suspected. A report by the CBS program *60 Minutes* raised the question of high-level administration involvement. Given the allegations of scandal that had swirled around Clinton even before his election in 1992, critics found no difficulty accepting this explanation. One of the lower-ranking people arrested insisted that the Chinese government had known all along what was happening.[53] A subsequent investigation revealed that Wang Jun, son of a leading general and the head of one of the weapons-exporting companies targeted by the sting, had been entertained at a White House coffee and contributed to the president's reelection campaign. The Chinese attitude throughout was intransigent. In April, for example, Prime Minister Li Peng announced a $1.5 billion order for Airbus jets, strongly hinting that European leaders' less aggressive support of human-rights issues had been a decisive factor in choosing Airbus over U.S.-made Boeing jets.[54]

Later in the year, it was announced that China had become the chief contributor to America's trade deficit, surpassing Japan for the first time on record. The growing imbalance in U.S. trade with the PRC, which grew larger each year, was to become another thorn in the administration's China policy.[55]

Clinton's capitulation to the Chinese had been swift. A *San Francisco Chronicle* editorial entitled "America: The Pushover Country," accused him of "out-Bushing Bush" in coddling China.[56] Nor, others pointed out, did abandoning the link between human rights and trade appear to be helping American businesses compete. The U.S. trade deficit with the PRC was increasing rapidly, and the administration appeared uninterested in redefining the basic economic relationship between the two countries.[57] As spring gave way to summer, confrontational statements from the PRC ebbed. Suspicious persons concluded that China was trying to ease the now complaisant Clinton's chances for reelection; the exceptionally naïve thought that "a new China consensus" had been achieved in which America was finally dealing with the PRC in a realistic fashion.[58]

The Second Term

Despite the scandals that continued to swirl around him, Clinton easily won reelection and his China policy continued in the same vein. The president admitted that his policy of constructive engagement had failed to engender progress on human rights but said that he believed it was the correct policy nonetheless.[59] Critics charged that he had sold out U.S. policy interests in exchange for campaign contributions from individuals in or closely associated with the Chinese military, arms dealers, and intelligence organizations. An internal Justice Department review found that the FBI and federal prosecutors "mishandled" highly classified intelligence on accusations that China improperly tried to influence American elections.[60] Senator John McCain, Republican of Arizona, stated that there was "at least an attempt to suborn the foreign policy of the United States," while White House special counsel Lanny Davis countered that there was no connection whatsoever between the contributions and policy positions taken by the president.[61] A letter written by alleged middleman Charlie Trie and turned over to a Senate investigative committee could be interpreted as linking a U.S. pledge to stay out of China's internal affairs (that is, not intervene in a Taiwan confrontation) to continued campaign contributions.[62] And, as pointed out by the *Wall Street Journal*, after the visits of these foreign donors, "there was a radical about-face in the Clinton MFN policy toward China, and export controls on high-technology sales to China were eased."[63] In both this and a scandal involving lax security at scientific-research facilities that enabled the Chinese to obtain state-of-the-art weapons technology, the president's supporters tended to see coincidence where his critics believed there was conspiracy. They conceded that changes in policy had occurred but saw them as the outcome of the administration's desire to please two often opposed domestic constituencies, business and human-rights, rather than donors associated with the Chinese government. They also pointed out, correctly, that lax security in high-technology research facilities had long pre-dated the Clinton administration. A number of scientists argued forcefully that the free flow of information and personnel was the best way to advance scientific knowledge for the betterment of all humanity, regardless of national boundaries.

Other Clinton appointees interviewed for this chapter expressed similar views. By the president's second term, stated a Commerce Department official, there was no grand strategy. China policy became "don't rock the boat; this may be the best we can do." Concessions were not consciously made to the Chinese who, he judged, had already in the early 1980s brilliantly manipulated the American agricultural community to reduce bars to their textiles. Meanwhile, the official found his work hamstrung by statutes that were "hammers rather than scalpels," in the face of which even the president could not really do much. U.S. decision making on China became one of lowest common denominators due to the American conviction that no policy should be enacted unless everyone agreed.[64] A Democratic strategist agreed, terming Clinton's policy "thoughtless and ineffective—just like that of his predecessors." What some people saw as consciously thought-out changes in policy he attributed to the turnover among officials, with different people interpreting policy guidance in different ways.[65]

This perhaps explains the background of the administration's choice of "strategic partnership" to describe its China policy in Clinton's second term. The president appears to have been motivated by a belief that the best way to modify the PRC's belligerent behavior was to draw it into a condominium with the United States in order to ensure post–Cold War stability in international relations. Warren Christopher's successor as secretary of state, Madeleine Albright, used the term during her April 1998 visit to China when the two sides officially opened a hotline between the two countries.[66] The phrase "strategic partnership" became the administration's mantra over the next two years and continued regardless of how dissonant the policy was from reality. Despite the scandals over campaign contributions and theft of technology, Clinton cited the strength of the partnership as justification for his June 1998 visit to China where, as mentioned above, he publicly stated the "three noes" he had secretly promised the PRC leadership in 1996. An angry Congress passed nearly unanimous resolutions supporting Taiwan, infuriating China. Beijing became still more upset when a congressional select committee issued a report detailing China's theft of American weapons technology.[67] In May 1999, an American plane accidentally bombed the PRC's embassy in Belgrade while attempting to end the Yugoslav government's ethnic cleansing of Kosovo. Mobs of Chinese citizens, encouraged by their government, attacked the U.S. embassy. The Chinese media questioned how there could be a strategic partnership with a nation that committed such dastardly deeds. U.S. ships were forbidden to visit Chinese ports, and even the Special Administrative Region of Hong Kong. Commentators now had fresh evidence for their oft-repeated claim that American offers of friendship were but a thin cover for its real aim: to encircle and contain the PRC.[68]

In early 2000, Beijing finally accepted the administration's apology, along with its check for $28 million in compensation.[69] Hong Kong began to agree to visits by American naval vessels, albeit on a case-by-case basis. Gen. Xiong Guangkai, known for his hard-line views, was received with honor in Washington. The administration continued to dichotomize its strategic options as isolation versus engagement, seemingly unwilling to admit that there were policy positions intermediate between the two extremes. In wry recollection of the U.S.-China policy that prevailed at the turn of the nineteenth century, the Open Door, critics made pained references to its reincarnation as the "Open Doormat" policy. Undaunted, Clinton continued to insist that trade would solve all, or at least most, problems: economic development would inexorably lead the Chinese people to press for political freedoms. Arguments that communism did not seem to be dying in the PRC but rather mutating into a new form that abandoned economic centralism while continuing to repress freedom of political expression were either ignored or denounced as the flailings of China-hating isolationists.

According to both the State Department's 2000 human-rights report[70] and United Nations high commissioner for human rights Mary Robinson,[71] China's human-rights situation was in fact deteriorating. Reports of arms proliferation continued. A Department of Defense study that indicated the PLA's military capabilities had increased to the extent that Taiwan was unlikely to prevail against a mainland attack was suppressed, presumably because its release would oblige the administration to sell more arms to Taiwan and hence anger Beijing.[72]

Clinton stayed his course. Administration spokespersons continued to warn against regarding China as an enemy,[73] and to overstate the significance of small victories, such as agreements on intellectual-property rights and the occasional release of political prisoners. Human-rights activists termed the latter "hostage diplomacy": Beijing could count on the administration interpreting its freeing a dissident or two as justification for some concession it wanted. The administration also continued to maintain that the PRC's entry into the World Trade Organization would hasten positive change in the country.[74] After the final congressional vote to do so, most members who voted yes stated that they believed the argument.[75]

Conclusion

His criticisms of Bush for coddling dictators notwithstanding, Clinton came into office lacking a well-thought-through policy on China, or indeed on Asia in general. During his first year in office, he seemed to be sincerely trying to use America's economic power to modify the PRC's behavior with regard to outstanding issues between the two countries, including human rights, intellectual property rights, trade, Taiwan, and proliferation. Apparently the president had not anticipated Beijing's ability to use the lure of its own market to enlist U.S. business interests to help it to resist attempts to use the trade lever against China. By 1994, there had been an abrupt about-face. Clinton seemed intent on establishing friendly relations with the Beijing government with scant regard for the consequences to U.S. interests. No link between pro-PRC policy decisions and Clinton's acceptance of campaign contributions from individuals with close ties to the highest levels of the Chinese government can be definitively established. But the amount of questionable contributions involved, when added to the high profiles of some of the donors, certainly creates the appearance of suspicion.

At the close of the president's eight years in office, all the problems in China policy he had hoped to solve not only remained but had arguably been worsened. Proliferation continued, as did violations of intellectual-property rights. Beijing's pressure on Taiwan had intensified. The trade deficit with the PRC continued to widen, and human-rights abuses showed no improvement. Judged by the standards Clinton had himself set forth at the time of his election, the president's China policy had failed. Scandals aside, Clinton's China policy differed little in essence from that of his predecessor, George H. W. Bush. Had Clinton not set higher goals for his administration, this failure would seem less stark.

9 Clinton Foreign Policy and the Revolution in the East

ROBERT LEGVOLD

In this chapter, Professor Legvold discusses how the Clinton administration responded to the end of the Cold War and how difficult it was to forge a guiding foreign-policy paradigm following the collapse of the Soviet Union. As Professor Legvold summarizes, "George H .W. Bush presided at its dawn, but Bill Clinton was the first U.S. president to have the responsibility for shaping this new reality, for giving sustained answers to the two key questions: To what purpose and in what manner?" Professor Legvold evaluates the changing relationships between the United States and Russia during the 1990s and the many constraints facing both nations. With close attention to President Clinton's evolving strategies, Professor Legvold ultimately concludes that while the Clinton administration had limited success in "warming the Russian people to their U.S. 'partner in reform,'" its achievements were large given the considerable political constraints both in the United States and the international arena.

Bill Clinton's eight years in the presidency form a critical interlude between two worlds: the Cold War, closed and fast receding from popular memory, and a new, shapeless landscape shadowed by the global forces of supranational capital, technology, mobile humanity—often desperate humanity—and terror, a landscape pocked with ethnic conflict and local humanitarian disasters. During these years, two fundamental challenges qua opportunities faced the president and his foreign-policy teams. First, how to influence the transformation of what had been the other half of a bipolar world—the "East," the once forbidding cluster of Marxist-Leninist adversaries. It had three parts: helping to shape the character and conduct of Russia and the other fractured pieces of the former Soviet empire as they struggled to build new political and economic orders and find international identities; coping with the rise of an economically resurgent but politically unreconstructed China; and managing the perils associated with the lesser relics of a faded socialist past, particularly North Korea.

The other challenge came less well-etched, lifting and settling like fog around what were taken to be the new core questions—what was to become of the United States' Cold War alliances, particularly NATO; how far should the United States go in invigorating and then relying on multilateral institutions, including the United Nations; and how ambitious could and should the United States be in bailing out failed or failing states? Behind these questions loomed the second challenge: to make the most of the United States' emerging primacy. By almost any measure of power—military, economic, technological, and even cultural—the United States stood like a colossus amid the collapsed remnants of the old world. To what purpose, however, should this historic preponderance be put? And how should it be wielded (for the manner of its use would be as important as the ends sought)?

To understand the successes and failures of the Clinton administration in dealing with the first challenge—the focus of this essay—one must have a sense of the second challenge, because it both transcends and suffuses the first. Beginning with the Clinton administration, responding to primacy has come to be the very essence of U.S. foreign policy and the single most important phenomenon in the international relations of the new century. George H. W. Bush presided at its dawn, but Bill Clinton was the first U.S. president to have the responsibility for shaping this new reality, for giving sustained answers to the two key questions: To what purpose and in what manner?

Before Clinton ever entered the White House, columnists had begun trumpeting the arrival of American hegemony, the earliest of them often advocating the vigorous use of American power to impose outcomes serving U.S. national interests (as they chose to define them).[1] True, at this early stage, before the phrase "the sole superpower" or "the indispensable nation" tripped lightly from the lips of a widening circle of politicians and publicists, many people worried more that in the hazy uncertainties of a post–Cold War world the American public would flee into narrow self-preoccupation, particularly, as the country suffered through the early-1990s economic recession.[2] Nor were most commentators impressed with Bush's limp effort to define the moment and set the country's foreign-policy course. Coming out of the Persian Gulf War, the president had said that the war was about "more than one small country; it is a big idea; a new world order," with "new ways of working with other nations" in order to achieve the "peaceful settlement of disputes, solidarity against aggression, reduced and controlled arsenals and just treatment of all peoples."[3] He and his people, however, never gave content to the concept of "a new world order" and did even less to sketch the U.S. role in bringing it about.

In these initial years, not all members of the foreign-policy intelligentsia accepted axiomatically a leadership role for the United States. Some celebrated American ascendancy precisely because it could free the United States from what they saw as an unnecessary responsibility for world order—from the false conviction that the United States needed to be militarily present everywhere lest disorder in this or that quarter undermine the values we espouse and the economic intercourse we depend upon.[4] On the contrary, the United States' near invincible power made it safe (for the United States) to leave it to other countries to assume order-creating roles within their own neighborhoods. But few among the wider circle of opinion or policymakers thought in these terms.

Rather, the awkward and half-engaged argument was soon over how openly and unapologetically the United States should throw its weight around. Again, Charles Krauthammer provided the extreme argument, but he only said aloud and more pointedly what a sizable part of the Congress and conservatives more generally thought. "America Rules: Thank God; Who Else Should Call the Shots? China? Iran? The Russian Mafia?" went the title of one his articles in 1997.[5] "Nothing of significance gets done without us," he boasted. "Until the Americans arrive in Bosnia, the war drags on. When America takes to the sidelines in the Middle East, nothing moves. We decide if NATO expands and who gets in. And where we decide not to decide, as in Cambodia—often held up as an example of how the UN and regional powers can settle local conflicts without the U.S.—all hell breaks loose." Good that it should be so. Without the "dominance of a benign power" disorder is inevitable. "Why? The modern world, interconnected as it is today, can exist in only two states: reasonably structured or chaotic." If it is to be the former, "the structure must be established and maintained by a leading world power." Those who shy from unipolarity should think again. "Multipolar systems," he warned, "do not evolve into happy Elks clubs."

Precisely how a "reasonably structured" world was to be achieved and how the United States should exploit its preponderance to make it possible, however, remained sketchy, acquiring more vivid form only when it came to Saddam Hussein's Iraq and the Korea of Kim Jong-Il. Looked at more closely, it turned out that the purpose of hegemony was to maintain hegemony, at least, in the first instance. An assertive U.S. role in Europe and Asia, backed by its nonpareil military, would discourage other states, even friendly ones like Germany and Japan or groupings like the European Union, from challenging U.S. preeminence in the security sphere. American power was to give the United States a free hand, and a free hand was designed to leave the United States unconstrained by the inconveniences of multilateralism as well as the fecklessness of allies and the carping of China, India, often Russia, and much of the Third World.

In the spring before Clinton's election, senior civilian officials in the Pentagon had begun drafting the quintessential version of the hegemony-for-hegemony's-sake argument. It appeared in what they hoped would be the *Defense Planning Guidance for the Fiscal Years 1994–1999*. According to reports at the time, the document committed the United States to ensure that other states could not challenge "our leadership" or seek "to overturn the established political and economic order." Mechanisms should be kept in place "deterring potential competitors from even aspiring to a larger regional or global role."[6] Clinton and his incoming team did not share this aspiration, and after a semi-embarrassed flurry of denials from defense officials, the idea disappeared from sight.

President Clinton, his secretary of state, Warren Christopher, and his national security advisor, Anthony Lake, believed as heartily as those at the other end of the spectrum in the necessity of U.S. leadership. They also sensed as distinctly as more hawkish voices the reality of the United States' growing political weight. But, while doubtless committed to protecting this primacy, they tended to see it as the lubricant for a more liberal international order—one fostering the growth of democracy, sensitive to the pain and violence inflicted by inhumane or disintegrating regimes, and open to the free play of global economic forces.

To the extent that they accepted the more classical notion of primacy's significance, it was less to counter and manage the power of potential competitors than to incur the responsibility of holding the ring in Europe and Asia, where the United States' presence helped avoid the return of old rivalries while fostering new paths to security. Their conception of primacy not only made multilateralism compatible, but integral. U.S. strength could render multilateral institutions such as the United Nations more effective, and these institutions could help to diffuse the burden, while giving other states a sense of responsibility, particularly for addressing disorder in their own regions. Thus, the new Clinton administration came to office proclaiming its commitment to "assertive multilateralism." In the ritual juxtaposition used to measure U.S. foreign policy under different presidents—between Wilsonianism and Realpolitik, liberalism and realism—the Clinton approach appeared to place it at the liberal end of the spectrum. Indeed, Clinton the candidate had decried "the cynical calculus of pure power politics" as "ill-suited to a new era."[7]

In any case, the evocations were sufficiently pronounced to trigger the reflexive opposition of those at the other end of the spectrum. The United States under Clinton, they would charge with increasing fury, was misusing, worse, squandering its advantage. It was too soft or self-deceived to say upfront that the United States held the upper hand, that its predominance was a good thing, and that "as the strongest power" it would "act with or without the others, and then [ask] its partners whether they will join."[8] This criticism, however, was about how power should be used, not about the aims for which it was to be used. On that score, the critics too objected. They pilloried the administration for letting itself get sucked into a series of so-called "humanitarian interventions," in Bosnia, Somalia, and Haiti, do-good exercises where, by their light, the United States had no vital interests at stake.[9]

The argument, as it took shape in the 1990s, however, obscured the fundamental issues at stake and, in the process, made it difficult to sort out criteria by which to distinguish what the administration should and should not have done from what it could and could not do. Nearly a half century ago, Arnold Wolfers contrasted states in pursuit of "milieu goals" with those seeking "possession goals."[10] By the first he had in mind efforts to shape the international setting and, hence, the context of policy. By the second he identified the traditional desire of states to control territory and the behavior of others. Wolfers did not mean to suggest that states sought one kind of goal to the utter exclusion of the other, but he believed one or the other had to dominate. As a "realist," he was convinced states had to worry first about how they were doing *within* an environment, and only as an afterthought how they might alter that environment.

Bill Clinton presided over a foreign policy that privileged milieu goals. He sought to promote democratic values in other societies because he accepted the theory that democracies do not fight one another and, therefore, that an international order dominated by democratic states would be a more peaceful one. He believed the promotion of economic development and the reduction of inequality among societies added justice to international politics, and a more just international order was essential to peace and stability. He supported, albeit inconsistently, so-called "humanitarian interventions" on the grounds that unattended misery inflicted by governments on their own people would degrade the international environment, eventually making it less safe for all. He devoted considerable energy to preventing the spread of weapons of mass destruction because a world with multiplying nuclear powers was a more dangerous world and so too a world in which terrorists could get their hands on chemical or biological weapons. And he pushed for, again not without retreats, a more open trading and investment regime not only because it served U.S. interests but because it promised a prosperity "raising all boats" and, hence, weakening one important source of conflict. Above all, according to one of his closest advisors, he sought to create "an overarching architecture of cooperative structures as opposed to the traditional dynamic of balance-of-power competition."[11] Hence, in displacing rivalry with community, he genuinely cared about strengthening international institutions—global, regional, trans-regional, and sub-regional—although not to a degree paralyzing U.S. action.

At root, Clinton's severest critics disbelieved in the pursuit of milieu goals—at least if they were ever allowed to rival "possession goals." Hence, without rejecting out-of-hand criticism of human-rights abuses in China, much less in Cuba or North Korea, they objected to "crusades" that threatened to undermine the United States' strategic stakes in the relationship with China. Even more strongly did they object to propagating American theories of democracy, if this dragged the United States into indiscriminate "nation building" around the world. In particular, they assailed the idea of humanitarian intervention because it committed the United States in places where it had no vital interests. While they cared about limiting the spread of weapons of mass destruction, theirs was not a general concern, but one tied to specific governments such as Iraq, Iran, and North Korea. And, while they shared the Clinton administration's belief in a more open international trading system, their stake was more in the advantages this would afford the United States than its ameliorative effects in international politics, and they eyed suspiciously efforts to strengthen the WTO regime at the expense of U.S. autonomy. When it came to the tradeoffs between, on the one hand, stronger international regimes to deal with the environment, genocide, regulation of the commons, biological weapons, or protecting children and, on the other hand, U.S. autonomy, they insisted on autonomy.

There, of course, were more than two sides to the foggy foreign-policy debate over U.S. primacy and its proper use, but these two perspectives set its terms. Alas, because the true, deeper stakes at issue remained unarticulated and probably unrecognized, three unhappy consequences followed. First, because within the policymaking community no one framed the issues in fundamental terms, no one, including senior figures within the administration, had a basis for judging the scale of the emerging historical opportunity. Realpolitik-types were right to argue that reengineering the international setting (whether to make the world safe for democracy, to thicken the web of international law, to prevent nuclear proliferation, or to manage regional conflicts) would not be easy even for the most powerful state. But with the end of the Cold War a unique circumstance arose that made the enterprise less fanciful. For one of the rare moments in the last three hundred years of international politics, strategic rivalry among the major powers disappeared. None of them defined any of the other major powers as a primary security threat; none strained to amass military power against another; and none labored with alliances intended to thwart aggressive designs assigned to another.

As a consequence the normal competitive dynamic that makes milieu goals a luxury dissipated. In fact, without the kind of compelling adversary expected by the realist school, focusing on the rough-and-tumble of international politics to the exclusion of building a sounder general environment made no sense. The Clinton administration felt its way toward a more transcendent foreign policy at a time when relations among major players favored this approach more than ever before, rendering U.S. primacy more potent in this context (and more vulnerable in any other).

Alas, the same could not be said of the domestic setting. With the end of the Cold War, the collapse of the Soviet Union, and the rapidly forgotten threat of nuclear winter, the world seemed a far less dangerous place, and the American public lost interest. By every measure of public opinion, support for an ambitious foreign policy rapidly waned. Elections, particularly the November 1994 election, produced a Congress not only unwilling to spend money on foreign undertakings but hostile to increased U.S. commitments of any kind. An uninterested public and a "nativist" Congress left the field to special interests, which by their nature obstructed a coherent, broad-gauged foreign policy.[12] Thus, what the international setting permitted, the domestic setting proscribed. Bill Clinton's core foreign-policy failure resided in his inability to square the two, and then, in the face of this failure, the ease with which he yielded to domestic political constraints.

The Clinton foreign policy would be weakened by a further characteristic that ultimately added to the administration's disadvantage in dealing with resistance at home. In a foreign-policy speech to Freedom House in October 1995, Clinton asserted, "To use the popular analogy of the present day, there seems to be no mainframe explanation for the PC world in which we're living. We have to drop the abstractions and dogma, and pursue, based on trial and error and persistent experimentation, a policy that advances our values of freedom and democracy, peace and security."[13] Experimentation and trial and error, however, were not a good idea, and the lack of an articulated and consistent conceptual framework to guide policy made the task abroad more unmanageable and the reception at home more unforgiving.[14]

A second unfortunate consequence flowed from the constricted meanings attached to U.S. primacy in the 1990s. By overlooking the larger possibilities built into the original Clinton foreign policy, the debate diverted attention from a hard-headed assessment of the real, as opposed to the imagined or misconceived, limitations of the policy. Democratic peace theory may or may not be true, but Clinton's belief in it ought not to be faulted as simply Wilsonian idealism. Rather the problem was with getting from here to there. Instead of feuding over the merits of democracy building as a path to peace, U.S. interests would have been better served by concentrating on the potential tensions and ruptures likely to be sparked by the harsh transition to democracy in the post-socialist states. How should the United States have acted to cushion or counter these effects? Similarly, rather than standing for or against humanitarian interventionism as an idea, again, better that the discussion focus on the practical matter of determining when and how to get involved. How might criteria have been designed to distinguish cases where national interest, the threat to peace, and moral outrage warranted intervention from other less compelling cases? And how might policy have been designed for so-called full-cycle planning (from crisis prevention to peacekeeping to peace building) rather than merely adorned with an "exit strategy," devised not to make policy more effective but simply more palatable? Rather than arguing over the perils and annoyances of multilateralism versus the ease and effectiveness of unilateralism (or the other way around), it would have been better had more energy gone into reconciling the two, into finding ways by which one could serve the other.

Third, and most fundamentally, the failure to recognize the underlying contrast in goals perforce guaranteed the failure to see a primary threat to U.S. primacy. Put starkly, preponderance in the absence of milieu goals risked de-legitimizing U.S. primacy. It was not unilateral U.S. behavior alone that assured rising resentment among other states, even friends, and attempts on their part to cut the United States down a peg or flout its leadership, but unilateralism in pursuit of narrow, self-interested goals. Slowly and the hard way, the United States would learn over the last stages of Clinton's leadership and the initial phases of George W. Bush's that, while preponderant U.S. power could not be compromised, its effectiveness could be. For the United States to convert its overwhelming advantages into increased policy efficiency, it needed to give primacy legitimacy. Various commentators had different, often oblique, ways of framing the issue. Joseph Nye spoke of combining the United States' "soft" power (the impact of its ideals and culture, education system, and the like) with its "hard" power (military and economic resources directly under the control of government).[15] Others stressed the importance of good citizenship; that is, that the United States should be seen as assuming its fair share of commonly recognized international responsibilities.

Ultimately, however, while the forms of power used and the manner of their use clearly mattered, the decisive consideration turned on the ends served. Primacy would be a wasted asset if it was marshaled to assure U.S. security at the expense of others, to wall the United States off from common obligations undertaken by the rest of the international community, or to impose transparently self-serving outcomes viewed as unwarranted or harmful by other key actors. Legitimized by a readiness to put U.S. power to work to help stabilize critical regions in peril; keep the historic post-communist transformations from exploding or grinding to a halt; and create rules and agencies guarding against the destruction of the environment, the flow of drugs and disease, and the terrorizing of populations, U.S. primacy would not only have a better chance of enduring by generating fewer counter currents, but also of being vastly more productive. Not that in the process U.S. self-interest should be sacrificed. The trick was to locate and highlight the juncture where national interest intersected with bettering the international setting, and to worry less about how good works threatened the unhindered pursuit of national interest. It was a trick Clinton wanted to master, but could not. He left foreign policy to a successor less interested in trying.

The Clinton Administration and the Revolution in the "East"

The effects of U.S. primacy and the desultory effort to master them eventually encased all of U.S. foreign policy. Clinton, however, did not begin by stressing U.S. ascendancy. Indeed, he did not begin by featuring foreign policy. His was to be a presidency focused on domestic issues. The great geopolitical contest had ended, and no new challenge demanding a president's attention had appeared in its place. Clinton could afford to speak loftily and somewhat off-handedly about a "new world" "more free but less stable"—a world "we did so much to make" and "must continue to lead." "While America rebuilds at home," he said in his first inaugural, "we will not shrink from the challenges, nor fail to seize the opportunities, of this new world. Together with our friends and allies, we will work to shape change, lest it engulf us."

If one challenge stood out against this rather shapeless background, it was Russia. Even before entering office, Clinton had said that, if his administration failed to "come up with a decent policy and aggressively pursue it," the Russian problem "will swarm us and I might have to spend all my time on foreign policy."[16] Warren Christopher devoted his first major foreign-policy address to the topic. "Helping the Russian people to build a free society and a market economy," he proclaimed, is "one of our highest foreign policy priorities." It is, he said, "the greatest strategic challenge of our time," for "bringing Russia—one of history's most powerful nations—into the family of peaceful nations will serve our highest security, economic, and moral interests."[17]

Eight years and two administrations is not a long time, but the distance between the simple, high hopes of Clinton and his people at the start of his first administration and their weariness and misgivings at the end of his second is immense.[18] U.S. policy traveled this distance in roughly three phases. First came a period of easy, unquestioning hope, accompanied by an ambitious, energetic commitment to the Yeltsin regime and Russian reform. Gradually this phase, which I call the period of "strategic partnership," dissolved into a more ambiguous phase, and U.S. policy fell back to managing a "mixed relationship," one marked by seriously contentious as well as genuinely constructive elements, yet one still predicated on the importance of Russia's successful transition to democracy and markets. The third and last phase emerged after the Russian financial crash of summer 1998. Uncertainty over Russia's capacity to succeed with reform now overshadowed hope, and the relationship was allowed to drift, battered by mounting sources of friction. U.S. policy toward Russia grew increasingly agnostic, both with respect to the country's political future and the urgency of the United States coping with Russia's various foreign policy discontents. Although in the administration's last year, the grimmest apprehensions had eased, and the effort to move ahead on issues like national missile defense and the ABM treaty resumed, the lethargy and controversy had taken its toll.

When Bill Clinton arrived in the presidency in 1993, a year after the collapse of the Soviet Union, the United States had already enthusiastically embraced the new Russia. Six months into its existence, at the June 1992 summit, President Bush went out of his way to underscore that this meeting was not "between two powers that are struggling for global supremacy but between two partners striving to build a democratic peace."[19] To codify the new relationship, he and Yeltsin signed, along with twelve other agreements, a Charter for American-Russian Partnership and Friendship. The document brimmed with fulsome references to their shared ideals of democracy and commitment to the rule of law, human rights, and fundamental freedoms; it evoked their special responsibilities as permanent members of the UN Security Council for maintaining international peace and security and, more than that, for building "a democratic peace that unites the entire community of democratic nations"; and it promised broad U.S. support for the reform effort in Russia.[20] Yeltsin, in the months before the summit, had talked of a "democratic zone of trust, cooperation and security" among the states of the Northern Hemisphere and a "strategic alliance" stretching from "Vancouver to Vladivostok." The charter echoed the idea. Pledging their countries' determination to strengthen the "Euro-Atlantic Community" (wherein Russia was clearly located), the two leaders based their commitment on the conviction "that security is indivisible from Vancouver to Vladivostok."

These were not mere rhetorical flourishes. Both men fairly bubbled with optimism over the prospects for U.S.-Russian relations. Bush, after signing a variety of accords, including far-reaching cuts in strategic warheads, spoke of a "new partnership," bringing it "within our power to alter forever our relationship so that it becomes the greatest force for peace, a democratic peace, that the world has ever known."[21] Yeltsin boasted of doing more in five months to cut nuclear weapons than the two sides had been able to do in the prior fifteen years and then in an off-handed swagger urged that the two countries meet the reduction deadlines even faster than required by the treaty.[22] Bush dwelled on the various measures being taken to promote economic ties, "and this," he said, "is just the beginning of what surely will become one of the largest two-way trading relationships in the entire world."[23] Yeltsin outdid him. The IMF credits that the two sides were discussing would help, but foreign investment would make the difference, and dramatically so, for, as he enthused, the flow "will not be a matter of tens of billions of dollars, but hundreds of billions of dollars."

Yet, in fact, the actions, rather than the words of the Bush administration bespoke another set of considerations. For much of the new Russia's first two years of existence, the administration had hung back, offering rhetorical support for its effort to build democracy and markets, but only token material support. In fall 1991, as the Soviet Union was crumbling and Yeltsin began outlining the scale of change to come, Bush left it to the Department of the Treasury to determine how the United States would engage. Secretary of the Treasury Nicholas Brady's answer was, modestly. He and his colleagues were far more concerned with ensuring that Russia and the other new states would assume responsibility for the Soviet debt than they were with what the United States should do to facilitate economic reform within these countries.[24]

In this respect the Bush administration responded to Yeltsin's reform much as it had to Gorbachev's perestroika: a commendable undertaking, but the United States would consider putting resources into it only after the Russians had proven they could make it work. In the case of Gorbachev, their coldness toward "grand bargains" had arisen from a genuine conviction that it would be money down a hole. In the case of Yeltsin, their niggardliness had the reinforcement of election-year considerations—a mounting budget deficit, recession, and the unpopularity of foreign aid. Only when Richard Nixon in March 1992 assailed the administration for doing too little and raised the specter of "losing Russia," a charge echoed by candidate Clinton, did Bush cobble together a package of aid measures, most of it bits and pieces of previously committed funding from G-7 nations and international financial institutions.

The Clinton administration's approach differed markedly. In the second of only three foreign-policy speeches given during the campaign, Clinton had accused Bush of being "overly cautious on the issue of aid to Russia," and that for political not policy reasons. "Let me be clear: our nation can afford this," he said. "This is not an exorbitant price to pay for a chance to create new American markets and anchor a revitalized Russia firmly in the democratic camp."[25] Thus, Clinton came to office touting the importance of getting behind reform in Russia. Indeed, Russia represented the largest and most concrete case in point for a new president convinced that a more democratic world would be a safer one. Thus, Yeltsin's Russia quickly emerged as the cornerstone of early Clinton foreign policy. It would not be smooth sailing.

In March 1993, less than three months into his first term, Clinton faced a critical choice when Yeltsin impetuously declared martial law as he attempted to roll over an increasingly obstreperous political opposition. Or so it seemed, for Yeltsin never actually followed through with his declaration. Clinton, however, before learning of the Russian president's retreat, lent him unreserved support. The administration had decided on a "partnership with Russian reform," and Yeltsin was the steed on whose back the chances of reform traveled.

Clinton now made it a priority—perhaps *the* priority of his foreign policy—to rally support for Russia and its increasingly embattled leader, cajoling the Congress to do more, pressing the G-7 nations to come up with a large aid package ($28.4 billion), and pushing for the rescheduling of inherited Soviet debt. He wanted this in time to help Yeltsin prevail in a referendum on reform that Yeltsin had called for late April. "We do this," the U.S. president said April 1, on the eve of his first summit with Yeltsin, in what would be the most complete and carefully considered speech on the Russia subject in his two terms in office, because Russia "must be a first-order concern."[26] It must be, because "the world cannot afford the strife of the former Yugoslavia replicated in a nation, as big as Russia, spanning eleven time zones with an armed arsenal of nuclear weapons that is still very vast." Unless the United States and the rest of the West acted, he exhorted, four historic opportunities may be squandered: first, a chance to enhance national security and avoid the danger of Russia seized again by tyranny or sunken in chaos; second, a chance to turn Russia from "an adversary in foreign policy" to "a partner in global problem-solving"; third, a chance to enhance the West's economic well-being by turning defense spending to more productive use; and, fourth, a chance to invest in an "inherently rich nation" that, when reformed, can contribute greatly to global economic growth.

The Clinton administration, at this point, was working with a clear and very fundamental syllogism. It started from the proposition that "no relationship is more important to the long-term security of the United States than our strategic relationship with Russia."[27] Next it assumed that for this "strategic relationship" to succeed so must reform within Russia. For, were reform to fail and dictatorship to return or anarchy to emerge, the consequences would be, in Secretary of State Christopher's word, "appalling." "The shadow of nuclear confrontation could return. Our 'peace dividend' would be cancelled. Cooperation in foreign policy would vanish. And the worldwide movement toward democracy would suffer a devastating setback."[28] Thus, it followed, the United States should "do all we can now to help Russia's reformers succeed." The alternative was to "stand aside" and "take our chances," which, Christopher and his president argued, would be, first, to forfeit a "rare chance to shape a more peaceful world" and, second, to risk replacing the investment needed now with vastly greater expenditures should things go wrong.

The argument rested on several assumptions, some of them unarticulated, and one or two almost surely unconscious. First, in linking the benefits of a new U.S.-Russian relationship to successful reform within Russia, Clinton and his people took it for granted that the alternative to successful reform was either a return to tyranny with presumably the aggressive foreign-policy pathologies characteristic of Russia's authoritarian past or a descent into anarchy with all of its perils. Not much thought was given to a deeply troubled reform that left Russia in limbo. Second, the threat to reform came from the relics of the Communist past and the new primitive nationalists on the right ready to make common cause with them, not from the inherent flaws in Yeltsin's conception of reform or the strategy for its implementation. Hence, the administration's support for Yeltsin was not merely large and real, but uncritical and virtually unconditional.[29]

When the confrontation between Yeltsin and his opponents boiled over in September 1993, and Yeltsin dissolved the parliament and then two weeks later, amid mounting violence, laid siege to it, the administration squirmed a bit but, as the Russian expression goes, "looked through its fingers." Christopher explained to a Russian audience that "the United States does not easily support the suspension of parliaments.

But these are extraordinary times."[30] The steps taken by Yeltsin "were in response to exceptional circumstances. The parliament and the constitution were vestiges of the Soviet communist past." This was a "battle between reform and reaction." It was, one should hope, "the last gasp of the old order in Russia."

Third, the administration saw no reason to question the direction of Yeltsin's foreign policy. Yeltsin and his team, it was assumed, wanted out of deep conviction to build ever closer relations with the West—above all, with the United States. If anything threatened to disrupt this natural course of events, it was the danger that cruder, more unreconstructed elements, Yeltsin's opponents, could yet come to power. Hence, the circle was closed: Support for reform was support for Yeltsin and support for Yeltsin was support for Russia's partnership with the West.

This, in turn, depended on a fourth assumption, one that was not much discussed at the time and, indeed, perhaps not much thought about. From the start, not merely the Clinton administration but all Western leaders implicitly assumed that Russia's evolution toward liberal internationalism, begun under Gorbachev and embraced by Yeltsin, was now part of the natural order of things. This new orientation featured a conception of security that de-emphasized military threat, stressed the interdependence of nations, supported multilateral institutions, emphasized great power cooperation, and, in particular, argued for the merger of democratic aspiration with enlightened foreign policy. All this was seen not merely as the choice of particular leaders, but as a logical stage in Russia's development.

Before the year was out, however, the second assumption, making Yeltsin one with reform, was suddenly jarred; and then, more slowly, over 1994, the third and fourth assumptions too began to fray. In December 1993, parliamentary elections were held in Russia, and the results stunned more than the Clinton administration. Out of nowhere Vladimir Zhirinovsky's semi-fascist, semi-lunatic movement won more than 20 percent of the vote, outpacing any other party. Candidates associated with reform and democracy took a beating, while the Communist party and its allies, far from fading into history, proved that their angry criticism of Yeltsin's reforms had increasing public sympathy.

For the Clinton administration the election outcome was unsettling enough, but, scarcely had the president returned from the January 1994 Moscow summit, than Yeltsin, who had just promised him to stay the reform course, happily accepted the resignation of key reformers and began reaching out to the anti-reform opposition.[31] Moreover, even before the elections, the whitest of the knights in the Yeltsin foreign policy entourage, Foreign Minister Kozyrev, adopted a noticeably more churlish attitude toward Russia's new neighbors, while insisting on Russia's duty or right—a distinction he blurred—to keep the peace throughout the former Soviet Union. After the elections, Russia's foreign policy hardened on a number of issues, beginning with the Bosnian conflict but also on Russia's intention to do business with whomever it pleased, including Iran and China. By fall 1994, as the issue of NATO enlargement gathered momentum, aspects of U.S.-Russian discord suddenly were major and deep.

U.S.-Russian relations were moving into a second phase. Slowly the tone and emphasis in U.S. policy too changed. The shift was not abrupt, and it did not lead to a wholesale reconsideration of premises or a dramatic recasting of policy. Clinton, Christopher, and the others let talk of a "strategic partnership" with Russia lapse, and they referred more often to the risk that Russian politics could spin off in the wrong direction. They also began to put more emphasis on the pain that reform had caused the Russian people and the need to achieve tangible results giving them some reason for near-term hope. But the priority attached to the relationship remained unchanged. Progress on reform remained an imperative. The inference that the United States and Russia would continue to cooperate on the most important issues remained intact. And Yeltsin remained the figure at the center of U.S. policy.

One saw the new edge to U.S. policy most clearly in a speech by Clinton's recently appointed secretary of defense, William Perry, in March 1994. Instead of a "strategic partnership," he called for a "realistic, pragmatic partnership based on mutual interests."[32] "Mutual interests," however, might not prevail. "The new Russia," he said, "will have interests different from our interests." Even with allies, and he chose to mention France and Japan, "we have rivalry and competition alongside our partnership, and so it will be with Russia." That, he said, is the best case. "Reality No. 2" was a worst-case and "we must be prepared for it," for it is possible that "Russia will emerge from the turbulence as an authoritarian militaristic nation hostile to the West."[33] How then to react? Perry urged a "flexible and open-ended" approach, preferably still "on a course which is beneficial to Russia," but one at the same time, at least with respect to defense programs, with a "hedge against the possible negative outcomes." Yet, in the end, he came back to the administration's core proposition: Because Russia was so significant, because "the difference between the best possible outcome and worst possible outcome is so important," the United States had to make "the strongest possible effort to try to influence it to a positive outcome."

The Clinton administration had always had its critics, people who from the start thought its policy too "Russo-centric," too unguarded, and too amateurish. The idea of strategic partnership was, to use Zbigniew Brzezinski's characterization, entirely "premature."[34] Gradually they were also coming to see the policy as too focused on Yeltsin and the reformers. Clinton and his people, however, remained convinced that Yeltsin was the necessary axis of U.S. policy, despite his sometimes wobbly course, precisely because he seemed the only political force capable of protecting a reform option. When a Russian television viewer suggested to Clinton, following his TV address during the January 1994 Moscow summit, that he was "supporting not so much the reforms in Russia but the personality of President Yeltsin," Clinton defended himself by stressing that Yeltsin was an elected president and the only one the country had. While he, the U.S. president, should meet with and listen to other Russian democratic voices, "in the end, I still have to work with your president."[35]

By 1995 the U.S.-Soviet relationship had taken on a very different character from the brave enthusiasm of the early years. While the leaderships in both countries continued to value the relationship and to see it as a central focus of policy, no longer did they assume a natural convergence of interest and a growing camaraderie between their two countries. Both continued to emphasize their common stake in advancing strategic nuclear-arms control; impeding the proliferation of nuclear weapons; fighting terrorism; cooperating against organized crime, the flow of drugs, and other malignant traffic; and working together to help contain regional violence from Bosnia to Afghanistan. But they went about this agenda prepared simultaneously for increasingly frequent dissension.

Real as the reasons for cooperation were, so were the conflicts. Two years earlier when the Clinton administration objected to the sale of cryogenic rocket technology to India, the Russians had obliged them by scaling the deal back. Now the administration's far more strenuous objection to the sale of nuclear power facilities to Iran, with the Congress in the background threatening all measure of sanctions, prompted a firm rebuff.[36] START, far from swiftly entering into law, malingered in both parliaments, a convenient target for Russian politicians who wanted to vent their spleen over U.S. offenses. Most important, NATO enlargement had swelled into a bulky, raw subject of discord.

Leadership on both sides, whatever their unease, chose to handle the evolution to a mixed relationship as constructively as possible. They tried to keep the emphasis on the positive side of the relationship and to approach the growing sources of tension and discord with as much restraint as possible. Their choice versus the alternative was in full form by the 1995 summit, held immediately after the Moscow commemoration of the fiftieth anniversary of the end of World War II.

By this time, Moscow's position on plans for NATO's enlargement had hardened into non-negotiable opposition. The U.S. Congress and Speaker Newt Gingrich, in particular, were threatening that either Russia cancel plans to build a light-water nuclear reactor at Bushehr, Iran, or the Congress would block any proposed economic assistance to Russia. And the Russian government was objecting often and vigorously to the course of U.S. and NATO policy in Bosnia, particularly, to what it viewed as one-sided, anti-Serbian measures.

Rather than let these and other differences dictate the character of the relationship or risk creating a destructive synergy, Clinton, Yeltsin, and their foreign-policy teams worked hard to keep their increasingly turbulent agenda under control. In Moscow they went out of their way to stress what the two could accomplish if they worked together, exerted themselves to give a push forward to several key arms-control projects, and sought to circumvent several contentious issues, such as the planned sale of nuclear reactors to Iran, by assigning them to the Gore-Chernomyrdin commission for further study. In short, the essence of U.S. policy during this second phase was to feature the still constructive portions of the agenda and to approach areas of disagreement with as much flexibility as possible; that is, to seek mutually acceptable accommodations rather than draw a line and insist that Russia yield to U.S. concerns. This, in turn, meant that the administration committed itself to fending off forces within Congress less interested in pursuing a positive-sum approach to the relationship.

The Yeltsin leadership adopted essentially the same approach. It too had to cope with parliamentarians who wanted Russia to resort to ultimatums and a take-it-or-leave-it stance on key issues. The fact that the Russian government responded to the increasingly mixed relationship in ways mirroring the U.S. administration's helped to fortify the administration's choice. This, however, would not have been enough, had Yeltsin and his people also not remained committed to pursuing their objectives, particularly those in dispute with the West, by playing within the rules.

For example, long before 1995 Russian officials had come to see the 1990 Conventional Forces in Europe treaty as maladapted to the new security requirements facing their country, particularly from the south. However, rather than unilaterally abrogate the agreement, as some within the military advocated, Yeltsin and his team chose the longer and more cumbersome path of preserving the treaty while seeking adjustments to it. Similarly, by 1994 the Russians had grown increasingly impatient with Western policy toward Saddam Hussein's Iraq. Again, however, rather than defect from the sanctions regime imposed on Iraq by the West—although, here too, there were voices in favor of doing so— Yeltsin and his people preferred instead to intensify their diplomacy directly with Iraq and indirectly with Jordan in hopes of persuading Saddam to comply with UN requirements. Or, to take a third example, although the Yeltsin leadership, particularly his minister of atomic energy, disagreed with U.S. objections to the sale of nuclear reactors to Iran, rather than dismiss the Americans, they agreed to let a sub-group of the Gore-Chernomyrdin Commission study the issue and, if the U.S. could show that the facility was likely to aid a nuclear-weapons program, to reconsider their decision. All of these actions are what I mean by "playing within the rules," and it was important that, when more aggressive Russian politicians had no qualms about letting U.S. concerns be damned, the national leadership chose this other way.

Over 1996–97, the contentious side of the relationship gathered momentum, impelled, in particular, by bitter Russian resistance to the planned enlargement of NATO. In the process, another new, damaging influence began to emerge. Across a swelling portion of the political elite, the conviction grew that the United States, far from having Russia's best interests at heart, saw Russia's weakness as a moment of opportunity. From the beginning a noisy minority had insisted on a conspiratorial view of U.S. aims. Many in this camp simply extended their original bilious notion that the United States, abetted by either an unwitting or a treasonous Gorbachev, had destroyed the Soviet Union. Now, however, mainstream elite opinion began to argue that what once was seen as misguided U.S. policy was actually malevolent policy. That is, that the United States intentionally sought to use this moment to reduce Russian influence and substitute its own, particularly in Russia's immediate vicinity.

Slowly every aspect of U.S. policy in the former Soviet Union was beginning to be viewed through the prism of strategic rivalry: the U.S. effort to promote alternative pipeline routes for Caspian Sea oil and gas; its engagement in Uzbekistan, Georgia and Ukraine; its Baltic "Action

Plan"; the nature of PfP exercises; and on and on. NATO expansion served as the centerpiece of this effort, the decisive step that like a spectroscope revealed the overall pattern in U.S. policy. At a minimum, the vast majority of the Russian political elite were no longer ready to give the United States the benefit of the doubt.

Although this harder, more suspicious attitude had invaded policy-making circles as well, particularly with Evgeny Primakov's appointment as foreign minister in January 1996, still the Yeltsin leadership did not abandon its basically constructive approach to the increasingly mixed relationship. Some around Clinton, notably his senior Russian specialist, Strobe Talbott, commented on change, but for the most part, neither the president nor other key policymakers seemed to worry much about the corrosion taking place at deeper levels of elite opinion in Russia or to find reason to question the solidity of its Russia policy.[37] Reinforced by the tendency of Yeltsin and his people eventually to give—or seem to give—ground on the most serious issues of discord, including NATO expansion, the administration continued to accent the positive. It continued to hope for the best, and it continued to avoid facing, with anything other than perfunctory caveats, the prospect of a derailment of either Russia's slow advance forward or of U.S.-Russian relations.

The collapse of Russia's financial markets on August 17, 1998, ushered in the third and ultimate phase of the Clinton policy toward Russia. To be clear, rarely does a significant shift in policy depend on a single event, and in this case, the roots of the change had been growing for some time. The drama of August, however, forced the Clinton administration to admit to itself that the premises of prior policy were sorely compromised and maybe even turned to dust. Maybe economic reform was a failure or fated to fail. Maybe in this circumstance Russia really would stumble from its tortured path toward democracy into who knows what abomination of tyranny or disorder. And, therefore, maybe the administration's hopes of containing and managing the frictions continuously whipping at the relationship rested on nothing solid.

Uncertainty rather than a clear alternative vision now enveloped policy. The August economic crisis occurred only a few weeks before the next scheduled Clinton-Yeltsin summit. To make matters worse, Yeltsin chose to deal with the economic crisis by dismissing the government, thus precipitating a political crisis over the choice of a new prime minister—a political crisis that had the potential of turning into a constitutional crisis if a now-emboldened Duma rejected his preferred candidate a third and final time. Clinton, neck-deep in his own political crisis, arrived in the middle of this.

Preparations for the summit on both sides had been half-hearted and last-minute—an awkward aside for distracted leaders.[38] Compared to the prior five presidential meetings between the two men, particularly their summits at Vancouver (1993) and Moscow (1995), this one was strikingly listless. The two leaders managed to concoct a very small list of two new cooperative projects: one agreement to exchange information on ballistic-missile launches anywhere in the world detected by either country's early-warning system, the other an agreement by each to degrade fifty tons of plutonium. But more than ever these were items hastily plucked from the shelf to provide the summit with some minimal sense of accomplishment. Yeltsin also announced that the two sides had agreed "on paper" to set up in southern Russia "a joint center for control over missile launches," but symptomatically, this idea, which came from the Russian side, had not been shared with any of the relevant Russian bureaucracies, including the military, and they quickly buried it.[39]

Not quite sure what to say, the president settled on a combined pep talk ("We know these are tough times for you; America too has been through tough times; we know you have the talent and courage to prevail, if you but stick to your dreams") and instruction on the imperatives imposed by the modern global economy.[40] He exhorted Russia to proceed with tax reform, strengthening property rights, creating a strong banking sector, and the like—all the things needed to improve the atmosphere for investment. This he told the Russians was not because the United States meant to impose its own particular agenda but "because these are the imperatives of the global market place, and you can see them repeated over and over and over again. You can also see the cost of ignoring them in nation after nation after nation." Correct in itself, it was not a message with much resonance as long as the United States seemed increasingly disengaged from the hard, practical choices Russia had to make.

A clearer sense of the administration's shaken hopes and queasiness emerged a month after the president's return. Secretary of State Albright, speaking before the U.S.-Russian Business Council in Chicago, confessed that "a true and lasting transition to normalcy, democracy, and free markets in Russia is neither inevitable nor impossible. It is an open question, the subject of a continuing debate and struggle."[41] She hoped that the new Primakov government would do the right things—spurn easy but foolish economic measures threatening to send Russia spinning toward hyperinflation or toward renewed state control of prices and capital flows—but she was not so sure: "We can only wonder if some members of Primakov's team understand the basic arithmetic of the global economy."

To this point Russia and the United States "had been able to advance our cooperation where our interests converge and to manage our differences honestly and constructively." "The question now is," she went on, "whether that cooperation can continue." Can it, she asked in an echo of Talbott's earlier, lonely observation, when "there are many voices in Russia who want to shift the emphasis in Russia's interaction with America and our allies from one of partnership to one of assertiveness, opposition and defiance for its own sake."

Talbott himself, a few weeks later, sounded the same theme. "Is Russia a troika-wreck waiting to happen?" he asked after citing Gogol's famous metaphor.[42] "Maybe, but not necessarily," came his hedged response. "For the last decade or so, despite zigs and zags," he said, Russia had been moving toward "a normal, modern, prosperous, democratic state—at peace with itself and its neighbors, a full member and beneficiary of an increasingly interdependent world." "The question of the last several months is whether Russia has in some fundamental way shifted course, heading at break-neck speed back to the future or over the precipice." It was not a question that he would have asked even a year earlier or, had someone else put it to him that he would have answered with so many "ifs" and alternatives.

The Russian troika, however, did not whirl over the edge. Primakov's government maintained a steady course, resisted the temptations feared by the administration and, blessed with rising oil prices and a boost to domestic production from a devalued ruble, actually achieved modest (3.5 percent) economic growth in 1999. Russia's escape allowed Clinton and his team to cut short their morose hedging, but it failed to restore the relationship to its pre-August 1998 status. On the contrary, no sooner had the uncertainties surrounding the August crisis eased than the mounting crisis over Kosovo began to do its damage. At its end, U.S.-Russian relations were in poorer shape than any time since the dying phases of the Cold War.

Kosovo reverberated so violently in U.S.-Russian relations because it came as a culminating event. After three years of slowly accumulating resentments and major stress over NATO expansion, Russian indignation was an explosion waiting to happen. Still, in both intensity and thrust, the Russian reaction imposed a new and far heavier burden on the relationship. Not only did the Russian leadership and virtually the whole of the political elite object to NATO's action and circumvention of the United Nations, they took the war as proof of the threat that NATO posed to their country. If NATO permitted itself to act unilaterally in the Balkans, nothing, they argued, would stop it from doing likewise in or around Russia.[43] As a measure of how far the deterioration had advanced, liberal, normally Western-oriented politicians made the argument nearly as bitterly as hard-line nationalists.

Although NATO's campaign against Serbia was a joint undertaking, Russia's enraged intellectuals and politicians focused their frustration on the United States. Kosovo, in their mind, represented one more instance of the Americans deciding in their own highhanded fashion what needed to be done and herding the Europeans into conformity. With Kosovo Russia's dashed hopes for some kind of limited but constructive partnership with the United States hit bottom. This is not to overlook the helpful role that Russia played in the war's diplomatic endgame or to argue that the two sides, even at this low point, were incapable of cooperating. But the general tenor of the relationship was now more inauspicious than at any time since Clinton first entered office.

On the U.S. side, the president and his advisors were fully aware of Russian anger and of how much of it was directed at the United States, but in their shifting scheme of priorities, dealing with Moscow's displeasure no longer had much urgency. This too was a measure of how far the relationship had slipped. Instead policy toward Russia responded increasingly to domestic political impulses. Domestic factors, of course, played a role in the administration's approach to Russia all along, and, as the relationship drifted though the second "mixed" phase, the president and his team had grown noticeably less willing to draw down political capital in fighting those in Congress eager to sanction Russia for transgressions such as the aid allegedly provided Iraq's missile program by Russian companies.

Reluctance to do battle with the Congress, however, now veered toward a deeper anxiety. By fall 1999, on the eve of U.S. presidential elections, the administration suddenly grew alarmed that Russia's problems could be turned against it if the Republican opposition succeeded in blaming it for much of what had gone wrong. In August a money-laundering scandal involving the Bank of New York spotlighted the problem of corruption in Russia. Although scarcely a new issue, its appearance on U.S. shores gave critics of the administration a handle, and they seized it to launch their attack. Congressional Republicans organized a series of hearings into Russian corruption and the degree to which carelessness on the U.S. part had contributed to the problem.

The brouhaha in turn fed a spate of press commentary on the theme, "Who lost Russia?" The answer being readied by the critics, of course, was the Clinton administration. In committee hearings and on op-ed pages, they belabored the administration for naively and myopically embracing Russia's liberal reformers, ignoring the obstacles to transplanted Western models, and overlooking the distortions and criminality that their chosen allies were either too incompetent or unwilling to counter. The House leadership sanctioned a special advisory group, under Rep. Christopher Cox's leadership, to investigate the administration's mishandling of Russia policy. The subtitle of the glossy result, issued less than two months before the 2000 election was "How the Clinton Administration Exported Government Instead of Free Enterprise and Failed the Russian People."

In part because "Who lost Russia?" was a foolish way to phrase the issue and in part because Republican critics did not have a clear alternative course to recommend, the would-be campaign fizzled. Still, at the time, the White House reacted with considerable nervousness, marshaling defensive arguments before the Senate and House committees and appealing to a range of potentially sympathetic commentators in the outside community to weigh in with the press and Congress. The longer term effect was to make U.S.-Russia policy a neuralgic subject for the administration and Vice President Gore, the party's standard-bearer in the presidential election. The objective was to keep Russia out of political discourse and away from the campaign. In short, to render Russia a non-issue.

Events, however, did not fully cooperate. Roughly at the same time that the debate over U.S. policy was stirring, Yeltsin and his new prime minister, Vladimir Putin, launched the military assault on Chechnya. Clinton and his people were not eager to see more wreckage in the U.S.-Russian relationship, but the scale of military excess and a prudent regard for the potential public reaction in the United States compelled them to criticize sharply Russian actions. They also, however, resisted steps to punish the Russians, including the use of the IMF for this purpose. Even so, Clinton's face-to-face appeals to Yeltsin and then Putin produced emotional explosions from Yelstin and steely dismissals from Putin.

As the Clinton and Yeltsin eras drew to a close, the administration treated Putin's arrival as a potential opportunity to restore some momentum to the relationship, particularly in the area of arms control. Albright's quickly scheduled trip to Moscow three weeks after Yeltsin's surprise December 31 announcement was intended to test the possibility, and away from the limelight, policymakers redoubled their diplomatic efforts to achieve agreement on several stalled arms-control matters, including national missile defense. Hopes were that, after the March 26 elections, the new Russian regime would move more swiftly and decisively than its sclerosed predecessor had. When Clinton paid his fifth and final presidential visit to Moscow in June 2000 and tried to draw Putin out on these issues, the new Russian president was politely but conspicuously unresponsive. "Clinton," writes Strobe Talbott, "felt patronized. It was no mystery what Putin's game was: he was waiting for Clinton's successor to be elected in five months before deciding how to cope with the United States and all its power, its demands, and its reproaches."[44]

The U.S.-Russian relationship began the new millennium a very pale shadow of the high-profile, high-optimism affair that had prevailed only eight years earlier. No one any longer treated the issues at stake between the two as at the core of their respective agendas, save for perfunctory references to the safekeeping of nuclear weapons. George W. Bush, the Republican presidential candidate, explicitly challenged the wisdom of pretending Russia ought to be in the forefront of U.S. foreign-policy priorities.[45] Clinton, who treated Russia as his most important foreign-policy success in the first year of his first administration spent the last year of his last administration trying not to discuss the subject. In few quarters, including the administration and, even more so, the Congress, did anyone any longer rouse themselves to broad-gauged assessments of the state of the relationship and what should be done. When on rare occasion others did undertake the task, the results tended to be discouraged and critical. The emphasis was on the mistakes made by both sides; expectations for the future were modest.[46]

Rethinking Clinton's Policy toward the Former Soviet Union

How good or bad the Clinton policy was depends on one's measuring stick. Unfortunately the one used in most instances by the administration's sharpest critics is generally the wrong one, doing justice to neither the administration nor, worse, the issues at stake. To argue that the administration spoiled reform in Russia by pumping massive funds in the direction of its favorite reformers without asking questions, other than to impose misguided macroeconomic stabilization conditions, rather misses the point.[47] And so too the nested set of related charges: That by looking the other way while the process of privatization was

hijacked by special interests, the administration fostered widespread corruption in Russia and then coddled Russian leaders when they failed to
address the problem. Or that they paid no attention—that they even
justified—Yeltsin's anti-democratic, anti-constitutional measures to crush
opposition or cling to power. Or that they allowed Russia's aid to Iran's
nuclear program to go unimpeded but for half-hearted protests.

Aside from the inaccuracy of these accusations, which in almost all
cases is considerable, the argument is wrong for two reasons: First, while
the Clinton administration could and should have improved policy at
the margins, it simply was not within its power to prevent Russia from
walking on the wrong side of reform. It could and should have refused
Yeltsin uncritical support when he let the constitutional crisis of 1993
come to a head and then resolved it with force, but this would not have
rectified the politically strategic error that the Russian leader had made
at the outset in failing to solidify institutional support for reform. It
could and should have found a better balance between the critical but
narrow macroeconomic criteria that it attached to its lending and the
need for broader and more basic institution building prerequisite for
reform, but even had it, nothing could have ensured the reform process
against the hidebound and often destructive political context enfolding
it. It could and should have been sooner alert and sterner in reacting to
the criminalization of the state occurring parallel to the changes that it
celebrated, but no external force could have prevented the widespread
corruption that has attended the collapse of socialism and the building
of capitalism everywhere. And the list could be extended. In the end,
however, had it done all these things, almost surely the state of Russian
politics, the condition of its institutions, and the results of reform—in
short, the odd and often dispiriting mix of success and failure—would
still have turned out roughly as it did.

Second, the argument misses a more critical consideration. In the
end, the slow deterioration in U.S. relations with Russia was less the problem than a manifestation of a more fundamental shortcoming. From the
outset the West, Americans and Europeans alike, had framed the Russian
challenge in a fashion that made the Russia problem more difficult and,
simultaneously, the obstacles to a sustainable policy, greater.

The root of the problem stemmed from an analytical failure at two
levels, albeit an understandable failure, given the mood of the day and
the constraints imposed by domestic politics in the United States. First,
analysts and policymakers paid far too little attention to the broader and

more complex post-Soviet environment shaping the Russian challenge. Second, failing in that respect, they were in no position to think through the implication of developments within this larger context for the peace and well-being of Europe, Asia, and the world beyond. From these two oversights, a chain of consequences followed.

To turn to the first of these analytical failures: because Western governments—for in this the Clinton administration was scarcely alone—from the start, chose to deal with Russia and other parts of the former Soviet Union in disembodied fashion, rather than as an integral problem, they obscured the most serious challenges the post-Soviet space raised for international security, particularly in Europe and Asia. Russia understandably was the focus, but only as an object of Western concerns (such as, managing nuclear weapons, rallying Russian support in the Middle East and Balkans, and liquidating the last institutional traces of the cold war in Europe) or as an object of Western hopes (turning a cold-war adversary into a democratic, market-oriented partner). Russia was not approached as only one piece—granted, a very large piece—of a complex network of relationships, processes, and problems in what was once the Soviet Union.

As a result, three things occurred. First, Russia was torn from its context. Even the West's entirely justified concern with promoting political and economic reform in Russia was never pursued in connection with Russian reform's close dependence on reform in the other post-Soviet states. Similarly, to the extent the West made the remainder of the post-Soviet space a factor in its policy toward Russia, it was to discourage Russia's neo-imperialist temptation, not to consider how disorder in this sphere was likely to influence Russian behavior, let alone impinge on security in the larger international setting. They ended by featuring Russian behavior rather than the source of the trouble.

Second, most other parts of the post-Soviet space were treated either as a residual of U.S. policies toward Russia or as fragmentary and subordinate challenges: Ukrainian nuclear weapons, Caspian Sea oil and gas, Islamic extremism in Central Asia. None of the sub-regions or key players in them was treated whole and the dynamics within and among them framed other than in fragmented fashion. In the case of the Caucasus, little or no effort was made to understand, let alone address, the complex nexus among internal conflict, troubled reforms, regional violence, oil, and the intricate role of outsiders that included not just Russia, but Iran, Turkey, Israel, Greece, the United States, NATO, and the EU. In the case of Central Asia, few focused on the meaning of the rise of a new Inner Asia, with Central Asia at its core, where four nuclear powers interacted, the problems of separatism in the Chinese borderlands overlapped the sources of instability in four of the five Central Asian states, and political and economic transitions made little headway. The policy agenda was reduced to energy, Islamic extremism, and drugs, with the Americans saving a corner of theirs for pressing the faltering process of democratization.

Third, and most consequential, because U.S. policy disaggregated the post-Soviet space and dealt with Russia accordingly, the United States was in no position to contemplate the link between trends within this vast hinterland and the rest of Europe or Asia, much less to develop strategies for managing these effects. Rather than seeing the larger phenomena that individual events and troubles represented, Western policymakers treated them in isolated terms or ignored them altogether.

For example, the violence that erupted across southern portions of the former Soviet Union in 1992–93 represented no general challenge from Western perspectives. Taken separately a Tajik civil war held no particular importance for Europe or the United States. Nor did the violence in southern Ossetia. Or in Abkhazia. Or Transniestr. Not even in Karabagh, until oil and gas entered the picture in the mid-1990s. With minor but telltale exceptions, no one in Western policymaking circles thought of these conflicts as instances of a more general and dangerous phenomenon: not merely regional instability stirring in the debris of a collapsed empire, but as a pathology leading to the widespread destabilization of territory on the fringes of Europe, if synergies developed among these conflicts or if several of them began to merge with longstanding conflicts to their south. Nor did policymakers pause long over the risk that, as these conflicts propagated and then festered, the dynamics surrounding them would harm, not help Russia's relations with the West.

True, in the first year of the Clinton administration, senior policymakers did argue for a more active U.S. role in mediating regional conflicts in the post-Soviet space. The recommendation figured in what was to be Presidential Decision Directive 13, a document intended to strengthen the U.S. commitment to UN peacekeeping and to spell out the basis on which the United States would do more to contain the pattern of post–Cold War conflict. Those most concerned with U.S. policy toward Russia reasoned that the United States should help limit conflict in the post-Soviet space, first, to eliminate ammunition for Yeltsin's domestic opponents; second, to prevent local conflicts from spreading to

Turkey and South Asia; and, third, to deny Russia's military a pretext for intervening in neighboring states.[48] The idea was quickly crushed, the victim of a groundswell of public and congressional opposition to U.S. involvement in UN peacekeeping, particularly, in the wake of the U.S. debacle in Somalia, the culminating stage of which occurred during the period PDD 13 was under review.[49] For the remainder of the administration it remained a limited backwater of activity. No one at senior levels of the administration wanted to make it an important dimension of U.S. policy in the former Soviet Union or to salvage a sound idea from the visceral sentiments now stirred by Somali-like efforts.

A second example goes to the heart of the problem of Russia, the post-Soviet space, and European security. Because the Europeans and the Americans approached Russia and the region in disaggregated terms, the objective of policy was predetermined, but sub-optimally for European security. The objective became the piece-meal solution to squeaky wheels (Polish insecurity, the Hungarian and Czech desire not to be left behind, and Bosnian-style tragedies). Russia figured in policy as an obstacle to be overcome, and Ukraine and the Baltic States, as unresolved issues to be temporarily finessed. Had the Europeans and Americans thought in more comprehensive terms, the challenge would have been to integrate security in the post-Soviet space with European security, and the frequently uttered notion of an undivided Europe—of European security from the Atlantic to the Urals—would have emerged as the working objective.

Justified as NATO enlargement was in response to the piecemeal agenda, it surely would not have been the means by which the integration of post-Soviet and European security was resolved. Far from enhancing security among the post-Soviet states, the expansion of NATO and its open-ended sequel scrambled the security issues among Russia, Ukraine, Belarus, Moldova, and the Baltic States for the remainder of Clinton's term in office. Eventually the Russian dimension of the problem eased, two years after Clinton left office, and the new Russian president, in the wake of September 11, threw Russia's lot in with the West. Even then, however, the new mechanism and new agenda organized around the new NATO-Russia Council and a focus on the struggle against global terrorism, the threat from the spread of WMD, and regional conflict still left security west of the Urals decoupled from security in the remainder of Europe. The unresolved problem of mutual security among Belarus, Moldova, Russia, and Ukraine remained unsolved.

If the first analytical failure stemmed from an impoverished notion of how Europe's two halves should be related to enhance all-European security let alone how the dynamic within Inner Asia might one day dis-rupt Asian security, the second analytical failure had to do with the con-ception of security itself. Or, more precisely, with the little systematic thought given to the link between political and security trends within the post-Soviet sphere and trends far beyond.

In a hierarchy of threat the most fundamental and gravest is the clas-sical threat of war arising from great-power strategic rivalry. While war in Europe seems an impossibility and war among great powers in Asia an improbability, the emergence of strategic rivalry, its prerequisite, is far less remote. I will return to the subject. Second in the hierarchical order comes war among lesser powers, which, if armed with nuclear weapons as India and Pakistan, poses a threat scarcely less frightening than the first category. The third kind of threat, intrastate tension, often focused on ethnic or minority grievances, likely to explode, perhaps with the risk of spilling over into violent interstate conflict. Fourth on the list is the threat posed by "failed states." And, fifth, what might be called the prob-lem of "lethal leakage": the flow of noxious products (disease, drugs, crime, and worst, nuclear materials) should these "exports" no longer be within the control of home governments.

They are a hierarchy not only in terms of gravity but also in terms of one category's relationship to the next. The top three are linked by the risk of escalation: violent intrastate conflict often crosses borders and becomes violent interstate conflict; war between lesser states may draw in outside powers, including the major powers; and local wars that draw in major powers evoke the possibility of great power conflict. Or, in the other direction, the bottom two threats contribute to the degeneration of an international environment. That is, while not an immediate threat to security of major powers understood in traditional terms, they do degrade the international community's sense of well-being and threaten the welfare of even the most stable and prosperous states.

One does not have to study this list long to realize that then and now developments within and among the post-Soviet states embody more of these threats than virtually any other region in the world. That, however, is not how policy planners in Europe and the United States behaved—then and now. Neither the Clinton administration nor its suc-cessor made the configuration of threat potentially emanating from the post-Soviet space a systematic focus of policy. The problems on which the Clinton administration focused (facilitating Russia's troop with-drawal from the Baltic States, impeding the transfer of nuclear technol-ogy to Iran, securing nuclear weapons and materials in the former Soviet

Union, constructing multiple pipelines out of the Caspian basin) were strands of larger, interconnected problems. Sometimes the problems addressed were very important, such as democracy building and market reform, the unresolved Karabagh crisis, and the fallout from NATO enlargement.

Yet, they too were but fragments of four overarching, linked sets of issues: first, the problem of mutual security among major post-Soviet states and the potential role, for good and ill, of key states on the outside (China, Japan, the United States, and the Europeans); second, energy both as a factor in the international politics of the post-Soviet space and an important component in the energy security calculations of others from China to North America; third, the problem of regional instability in the post-Soviet space, particularly, in the south, and its potential fusion with active or latent disorder in neighboring regions; and, fourth, the immense challenge of the post-socialist transformations underway not just in Russia but the dozen other new states, the way these interacted, and their effects on the international politics of the region and of the region with the outside world. To return to an idea introduced earlier, scarcely anywhere else could one find a linked sets of issues more central to the character of the emerging international order—that is, a more important set of "milieu goals." Had the Clinton administration remained serious about using U.S. primacy to help fashion a more democratic, stable, and safe sequel to the Cold War, a broad, systematic approach to these four challenges raised by not merely Russia but all of the former Soviet Union would have been the place to start.

Failing that, several things followed. First, the administration had difficulty rallying public support for its policy in Russia and the other new states, largely because it could not convey the stakes justifying a deep U.S. engagement. One suspects it could not, because, having settled for a lesser, fragmented version of the challenge, it had not persuaded itself of the scale of the stakes involved. Clinton, in his first major address on Russia policy, the address to the Naval Academy on April 1, 1993, outlined the challenge and the opportunity as well as any Western leader before or after, but its spirit soon dissipated, and he made no further effort to build on the speech's grand appeal by subsequently spelling out its conceptual implications.

Second, because the administration's framework of analysis was constricted, it tended to overlook or underestimate incipient trends likely to make the four core challenges more difficult. The first of these were the early traces of strategic rivalry between Russia and the West within the post-Soviet space, particularly, between Russia and the United States. As noted at the outset, one of the truly remarkable features of contemporary international politics has been the absence of strategic rivalry among the great powers. For one of the rare moments in the last three hundred years of the modern state system, relations among the great powers were not dominated by maneuvering for strategic position, military competition and a preoccupation with military balances, or the organization of rival alliances. In Clinton's second term, however, this began to change. Broad portions of the Russian political elite by 1995–96 had come to see the United States as Russia's rival in the regions surrounding it.

While a crude misreading of the administration's ultimate intent, the misperception grew because aspects of policy could easily be misread and because the administration made little effort to counter it. Thus, for example, U.S. spokesmen often represented the struggle to build oil and gas pipelines out of the Caucasus as of strategic importance not only to block an Iranian option but also to weaken Russia's capacity to pressure its neighbors to the south. When in November 1999 the governments of Georgia, Azerbaijan, Kazakhstan, and Turkey agreed to support construction of the Baku-Ceyhan route, Secretary of Energy Bill Richardson described it "as a major foreign policy victory"—a "strategic agreement that advances America's national interest."[50] Nor, after 1994, did the Clinton administration hide the fact that it sought closer relations with Islam Karimov's Uzbekistan (a regime originally treated as anathema because of its abuse of human rights) as a counterbalance to Russia in Central Asia. And a good many aspects of U.S. or NATO relations with Georgia, Azerbaijan, and Ukraine could easily be interpreted as directed against Russia.

Russian politicians, however, wove these random threads into a large, coherent design, viewed as a attempt to roll back Russian influence and replace it with that of the United States and NATO. Russian observers looked at the disparate elements of Western policy—Partnership for Peace exercises in the Crimea, military training for Kazakh officers, NATO discussions with Ukraine, U.S. oil and gas initiatives in the Caucasus and Central Asia, and so on—and imagined a broadly coordinated, aggressive strategy intended to weaken Russia's role, trim its power, and oblige it to follow the foreign-policy lead of the United States and NATO.

Eventually Putin, by shifting the basis of Russian foreign policy, cut short the competition brewing between Russia and the United States across Eurasia. In downplaying traditional security concerns—such as the state of military balances, NATO's significance, and geopolitical joust-ing—and stressing instead international economic trends and the need to make Russia a part of modern global forces, he diminished the signifi-cance of the United States and NATO's activities in the region. Were it not for this fundamental adjustment on his part, he and those he forced to go along would never have reacted with the equanimity they did to the arrival of U.S. military power in Central Asia and the Caucasus in the months after September 11.

While Bill Clinton had encouraged Russian leaders to adjust their foreign-policy agenda in the direction Putin eventually took, during his time in office he did relatively little to avert trends pushing toward greater Russo-American competition in Russia's immediate neighbor-hood. The Bush administration, although the beneficiary of Putin's shift, has been even less attuned to the potential for its resumption, should the two sides mismanage the interplay between Russian interests and the United States' increasing military role in the post-Soviet space.

The shrinking agenda and constricted focus of the Clinton admin-istration led its senior figures to underplay another potentially impor-tant contextual development in the vast Russian-Eurasian sphere. A growing tendency toward polarization within the region accelerated during Clinton's second term. What were weak clusters of states coa-lescing to cope with practical economic and border problems were beginning to precipitate out into more durable alignments with strong security overtones. The collaboration among Russia, Belarus, Armenia, Kazakhstan, and Kyrgyzstan constituted one pole. Initially organized as a customs union, it has gradually been viewed by Moscow, Minsk, and others as a framework within which to deal with emerging security threats. Increasingly the line-up among Georgia, Ukraine, Uzbekistan, Azerbaijan, and Moldova (GUUAM) formed another pole as the group took steps to address their version of the security threat, one that for the most part was the flip side of the first group's fears.[51] The polarization, however, continues at many levels. The strategic dialogue among Armenia, Greece, and Iran is another manifestation. So too the counterpart col-laboration among Azerbaijan, Turkey, and Israel.

In the first instance, this trend did not owe to things done or not done by the Clinton administration or the European allies. Russian actions, a long, unhappy history, and a variety of other causes were at its root. This, however, did not change the fact that the trend was unhealthy for the region and, were it to deepen, how much it would eventually complicate matters throughout Europe and Asia. Had the

Clinton administration continued to focus on the broad milieu goals proclaimed at the outset, had it then recognized the ways in which the problem of mutual security within the post-Soviet space constituted a critical concrete instance of these goals, the president and his people would have thought more about the implications of the polarization occurring among the post-Soviet states. Alongside, they would presumably have also have calculated ways to damp down the trend.

Instead, in the absence of a process fostering mutual security within the post-Soviet space, the lines forming within the post-Soviet space began to take on an invidious overarching aspect. Thus, for example, Russia's security ties with Armenia were neither pursued (by Moscow) nor interpreted (by others) as merely addressed to narrow regional interests. Russian defense planners made no secret of their stake in the relationship as a partial defense against NATO, and they conducted military exercises accordingly. On the other side, Azerbaijani leaders attempted to use Russian-Armenian cooperation to justify collaboration with NATO, suggesting, as Haider Aliev's former national security advisor did, that Baku would happily provide the Western alliance with military bases.[52] Similarly, Russian commentators refused to see GUUAM in limited terms; it must, they assumed, have the quiet backing of the United States and NATO. Nearly every collaboration within the region, with or without foundation, acquired a larger implication, insinuating the involvement of Western or other outside powers.

Neither the United States nor Western Europe could be expected to solve problems created by Russian paranoia nor should they have avoided useful involvements simply for fear that Moscow might misrepresent them. But it was in their interest to play their hand in a way that did not deepen the competitive trends already at work in the region. This they did not do. As with strategic rivalry, the tendency toward polarization has lost some of its momentum as a result of Putin's altered agenda and turn toward the West. But it has not disappeared, nor will it soon, and, therefore, farsighted U.S. and allied leadership would do well to pay attention, looking for ways, at a minimum, not to add to the trend and, better, to impede it.

What then is the verdict on Clinton's foreign policy and the revolution in the "East?" And how should this be judged in the larger context of the course Clinton set for the country as it struggled to fit its role to the growing preponderance of its power? Ultimately historians are likely to write well of Clinton for rallying to the cause of reform in Russia and the other post-Soviet states. They may say that his administration saw the protagonists within Russia in too black-and-white terms or that its recipes were not always well designed. They will certainly suggest that it oversimplified the challenges facing Russia, and, in particular, that it underestimated—not to say, simply overlooked—the complex way that Russia's tortured domestic development would blend with foreign-policy frustrations to burden U.S.-Russian relations. And, if an objective of policy should have been to encourage the Russian people to embrace reform and warm to their U.S. "partner in reform," historians will add that the Clinton administration fell short.

In the end, however, these shortcomings do not outweigh the sheer significance of enlisting in the effort. Warren Christopher was right when he characterized the change underway in the former Soviet Union as "the greatest strategic challenge of our time." Had the United States stood back and watched, or placed its wagers timidly, or haggled over every detail before acting, the fault would have been far greater. For all the rockiness of the process, Russia managed in a decade of independence to destroy the old system, close the door to even a partial return to the past, preserve stability amid the change, and at the turn of the new century, produce a leadership ready to take "ownership" of reform. That is, a leadership that understood the necessary next steps, did not deceive itself over the difficulties ahead, and charted a steady course. The West had more than a small hand in this, and within the West the Clinton administration played a leadership role.

10 The Clinton Show

Notes on a Postmodern President

RANDY ROBERTS

In this essay, Professor Roberts discusses the unique societal constraints that influenced the Clinton administration. He argues that the celebrity-worshiping Hollywood culture dominant in the contemporary United States has changed not only how presidential candidates must campaign and govern but also what we, as citizens, expect from our leaders. Our very conception of leadership, he argues, has been dramatically altered by our postmodern society. Professor Roberts discusses the many ways in which the television culture has permeated both the oval office and the body politic. In the contemporary paradigm of "celebrity-equals-success," we expect both actors and politicians to be constantly changing (actors changing characters and roles while politicians change positions and policies); to do otherwise would be boring, unentertaining, and therefore, a failure. Professor Roberts asks, "To say that Clinton is a character (or characters), that one might dislike him in a particular role but love him as pure theater, is another way of saying that he is postmodern. . . . And was that not what his audience, his fellow boomers, wanted?" Professor Roberts also details the changes in President Clinton's public appearances, rhetoric, and presence—all carefully crafted by once-Republican political strategist Dick Morris. Professor Roberts concludes by examining how the attack media have now made the presidency one of the longest running and most popular (and therefore successful) contemporary reality television programs.

January 20, 1961. Snow everywhere, and bone-deep cold. Snow on Holy Trinity Church, where president-elect John F. Kennedy had attended mass that morning. Snow along the route to the White House where he and Jackie had gone to meet and have coffee with President and Mrs. Dwight Eisenhower. Snow along Pennsylvania Avenue, his last stretch before taking the oath of office. Snow still on a few of the twenty-thousand people who huddled against the chilly wind before the East Portico of the Capitol, waiting patiently for the inauguration. Only a patch of grass, scraped of snow and spray-painted green, seemed to escape the arctic look of Washington, D.C.

Now it was his turn. The older generation had had its say. Poor old, tired Robert Frost, defeated by gusty winds and cloudless-sky glare, had reached into his bag of poems rather than fail to read the one he had written for the occasion. And the other men, those of Joseph Kennedy's generation, draped in long coats and wrapped in scarves, many clutching down hats, looked like antiques from another century, as old and brittle as Frost himself. But not Jack Kennedy. He was Hollywood perfect. The cold, the glare, the snow—props to make him look even more handsome and manly, props to bring a squint to his eye and draw a contrast between him and them. No overcoat, no scarf, and certainly no hat—in his Camelot men thought nothing about scampering around in freezing temperatures in their shirtsleeves. His generation, after all, had come to maturity during the Great Depression and done the real fighting in World War II. And so his turn was their turn.

Kennedy knew this, instinctually. His inaugural address was an open challenge to his generation. Leadership of the most powerful and influential nation in the world was now theirs. "Let the word go forth from this time and place, to friend and foe alike, that the torch has been passed to a new generation of Americans born in this century, tempered by war, disciplined by a hard and bitter peace, proud of our ancient heritage, and unwilling to witness or permit the slow undoing of those human rights to which this nation has always been committed." The image words were all there—"tempered," "disciplined," "proud," "committed." As the first president born in the twentieth century, Kennedy recognized the significance of the moment. Historian Thomas C. Reeves caught the atmosphere: "Standing in the freezing weather hatless and coatless, erect and seemingly fearless, JFK personified for many the hopes and dreams for future national greatness."[1]

*   *   *

Fade to January 20, 1993. A clear, cold winter day, the sort that made spectators squint into the sun for a look at the new president. Once again the guard is changing. William Jefferson Clinton, "Bill" to everyone in Arkansas and the United States, stood where Kennedy had stood exactly thirty-two years before, affirming the same oath that Jack had affirmed. Like Kennedy, Clinton recognized that his was not just another inauguration; it was the passing of the torch from one generation to the next, from Kennedy's Depression–World War II–Cold War generation to his. In his address, Clinton reflected on "the mystery of renewal" and the need for each generation of Americans to "define what it means to be an American." Magnanimous at the moment when magnanimity comes the easiest, he thanked President George Bush and his crowd "whose steadfastness and courage triumphed over depression, fascism, and communism." The phrase "the Greatest Generation" was not yet common currency, so he did not dwell on the accomplishments of the outgoing generation. Instead he addressed his people, the Baby Boomers, born after the war, raised in the shadows of the Cold War and "unrivalled prosperity," but now, sadly, inheriting an economy "that is still the world's strongest but is weakened by business failures, stagnant wages, increasing inequality, and deep divisions among its own people." He spoke, at long last, as the first of us, the largest, if not the greatest, generation in the nation's history, to whom all history had pointed, conditioned to deny aging, alter faces and bodies with an eye toward perfection, and expect a twelve-step program to solve any problem. Bill, his hour come at last, was destined to be a different breed of president.[2]

In his inaugural address Clinton openly embraced the ideas of change and reinvention. He spoke in his opening remarks about "the vision and courage to reinvent America," then paraphrased Thomas Jefferson's notion that the nation needs "dramatic change from time to time." In fact, eight times in the fourteen-minute speech, Clinton spoke about the need for change and renewal, a leitmotif that writer William Safire noted echoed Abraham Lincoln's Gettysburg Address. But what sort of dramatic change did he envision? What agenda did he articulate for America? On these and many other matters, he was ominously vague. In the end his speech was more pastiche than a new vision. If it echoed, distantly, Lincoln, it absolutely resounded with the touchstones of the old and new Democratic Party, stirring memories of Jefferson, Franklin Roosevelt, John Kennedy, and Martin Luther King. Clinton's concluding remarks, delivered perfectly, showed how well he blended rhetorical images into a pleasing brew: "From this joyous mountaintop of celebration we hear a call to service in the valley. We have heard the trumpets. We have changed the guard. And now, each in his own way and with God's help, we must answer the call."[3]

Reading the address a decade after the inauguration, one senses a man reaching for greatness without a clear vision of what it entails. The images are all there—Jefferson's notion of perpetual revolution, Roosevelt's faith in experimentation, Kennedy's call for sacrifice, and King's grand mountaintop—but the substance seems a bit chimerical. Certainly most inaugural addresses and great public speeches are more style than substance, but the finest have at least a fresh and unified style. Roosevelt was always purely Roosevelt, just as Kennedy was quintessentially Kennedy, and of course King was identifiably King. But Clinton's address was different, and its rapid succession of images, its nimble movement from one popular touchstone to the next was faintly disturbing, almost like a good idea that was not fully articulated. Yet the address did signal a new type of president, one not fully committed to any agenda or single sets of ideas. As the next eight years would demonstrate, William Jefferson Clinton was America's first postmodern president.

For a biographer and a cultural historian, the central question regarding Bill Clinton is his place in American culture. To be sure, there are other, and perhaps more important, questions to be asked about his presidency. Did the changes he championed and the legislation he saw enacted represent real successes, blown opportunities, tragic failures, or unconscionable betrayals? Or some combination of the above? Did his foreign-policy decisions inch the world toward peace or war? Did they bring America more respect or scorn? And what about his impact on his own party? Did he forge a new, more vital Democratic Party, or did he cut the heart out of the party? Or, put differently, is his Democratic Party the best hope for the twenty-first century or a shadow of Reagan's Republican Party? Fair and good questions all, but I find myself more interested in others. Who is Bill Clinton? What does he represent? What does he portend? Has he created a new model for future presidents? I'm interested in fitting Clinton—the man and especially the phenomenon—into the orbit of modern culture. I contend that he and his presidency represent a radical departure; in fact, that he signaled the coming of age of the postmodern, celebrity president and presidency.

I'm no theorist and make no assumptions that academic buzzwords have any universally recognized or distinct meaning. And few families of words are more slippery or subject to personal definitions than "postmodern" and its many stepchildren. For me, the most concrete way to define postmodern man is place the term into a historic and cultural context. In the last two hundred years Western man's vision of himself has undergone several fundamental and undeniable changes. The Romantic era, the age of Lord Byron, Percy Bysshe Shelley, and Samuel Taylor Coleridge, put man in the center of the universe. Man became a product of himself, not God, and his ideas, his broodings, his angst, and his accomplishments were his alone, not divinely inspired or heaven sent. If in the early nineteenth century the Romantics put man in the center of the universe, in the mid-nineteenth century the Victorians made man heroic, almost a mortal god. Suddenly he was capable of greatness, able literally to change the course of mighty rivers and bend the world to suit his designs. He was Gordon in Khartoum using his life as a weapon; Stanley combing central Africa for and finding Livingstone; Burton searching for the source of the Nile. Nothing was beyond his reach.

Victorian poets captured the mood nicely. Robert Browning in "Andrea del Sarto" (1855), the poem he considered his finest, wrote the lament of a great craftsmen who lacked a great soul, an artist who lacked the drive to reach his fullest potential. Del Sarto's tragedy is that he knew he had the substance of greatness within him. "Ah, but a man's reach should exceed his grasp, / or what's a heaven for?" he muses. The failure to strive is the only true tragedy. Alfred Lord Tennyson, the voice of the Victorian conscience, knew as much. In "Locksley Hall" (1842), he writes of a jilted lover, a man who lost the woman he loved to a man with more money. He had every reason to brood romantically over his great disappointment, and he does—but not at length. He is, after all, a soldier, and at the very mid-point of the poem he realizes, "I myself must mix with action, lest I wither by despair." He hears the bugle, the call to action, and he turns his back on Locksley Hall and the memories: "Let it fall on Locksley Hall, with rain or hail, or fire or snow; / For the mighty wind arises, roaring seaward, and I must go."

The scientific discoveries and philosophic speculations that gave birth to naturalism called into question the Victorian notion of man, and

World War I laid waste to it. The great gash that ran from the English Channel through Belgium and France to Switzerland could not be sutured with the thread of Browning and Tennyson. On the Western Front man's reach had exceeded his grasp again and again and again— and it was a horror unimaginable. The millions who died, the millions more who had their bodies and minds shattered, testified that man was anything but a mortal god. They paid the ultimate price for modernism.

Modernism was dominated by shattered men, weak, timid, pathetic, impotent, grave, lonely, isolated, tiny men. Modernism has had many squeaky, scratchy voices, but one of the earliest and certainly the finest and most definitive was T. S. Eliot's. In "The Love Song of J. Alfred Prufrock" Eliot creates an almost perfect hollow man, the logical cultural conclusion to Shakespeare's indecisive Hamlet. In a poem that is a veritable CliffsNotes for modernism, Eliot captures the essence of the modern man in the lines, "There will be time, there will be time / To prepare to face to meet the faces that you meet." The central idea is that modern man has no face at all; he is a succession of masks, situational facades that serve this need or that.

The notion that modern man lacked a center has been echoed throughout mid-twentieth-century psychology and social science. Sociologist David Riesman's *The Lonely Crowd: A Study of the Changing American Character,* first published in 1950, paints modern Americans in distinctly Prufrockian colors. Mid-nineteenth-century Americans— Victorian Americans—Riesman argues, were by and large "inner-directed." Inner-directed individuals had only one face, as constant as a "psychological gyroscope." Their "inner" sense was "implanted early in life by the elders and directed toward generalized but nonetheless inescapably destined goals." The growth of a centralized and bureaucratized society, one shaped by wealth and greater social interaction, created a different personality type. Riesman maintains that in America an "other-directed" personality emerged. He was spawned in the upper middle classes of American cities, a man, compared with his "inner-directed" ancestors and Europeans, who was "shallower, freer with his money, friendlier, more uncertain of himself and his values, more demanding of approval."[4]

The other-directed man, it almost goes without saying, is directed toward others, seeking the approval and receiving his directions from others. "While all people want and need to be liked by some of the people some of the time," Riesman writes, "it is only the modern other-directed types who make this their chief source of direction and chief area of sensitivity." Although Riesman employs the writings of Erich Fromm, C. Wright Mills, and Arnold Green among others, to delineate and detail the other-directed individual, he might just as well have simply quoted Eliot, for other-directedness is tantamount to wearing "a face to meet the faces that you meet." In the century-long journey from "inner-direction" to "other-direction," Americans lost character and gained personality. They learned that to get ahead they had to get along and that nobody got ahead by being oddballs or odd-ducks. The secrets to success: conformity and performance.[5]

The desire to be liked and to conform to the expectations of others led the other-directed individual to chose masks to suit the occasion, and none was by any means indicative of the person who wore it. Masks were worn for effect, and sometimes even to conceal the face—or lack of a face—beneath. In his delightfully insightful study *Life the Movie: How Entertainment Conquered Reality,* Neal Gabler suggested the importance of the other-directed modern person: "To an inner-directed individual—say, a nineteenth-century American farmer—the idea of creating an image for the benefit of others would have had absolutely no meaning. He didn't dress to be a farmer or design his home to look like a farmhouse, and he didn't self-consciously perform in ways that would have signified to others that he was a farmer. He dressed like a farmer and acted like a farmer not for effect but simply because he *was* a farmer." This was a very different thing from dressing Ralph Lauren farmer-chic and eating prairie haute cuisine.[6]

The idea that modern man lacked an essential, unchangeable core became one of the hallmarks of modernity, achieving by mid-century the status of an undeniable truism. Sociologist Erving Goffman explained how "life itself is a dramatically enacted thing." Psychologist Robert Jay Lifton advanced the notion that the modern "protean self" had to be flexible and infinitely changeable simply to survive the realities of modern life. Fellow psychologist Kenneth Gergen essentially agreed with Lifton, arguing that the modern "pastiche personality," one created and defined by relationships with others, militated against the development of a core identity. In an age where "image is everything" and "notion lasts forever," personality adaptation was as necessary to survival and success as water and an education. Modern life, in short, had assumed the form of the hit early-twenty-first-century television reality show *Survivor.*[7]

The leap from concepts of modernity to post-modernity was a shorter jump than most postmodern cultural theorists and critics contend. Once again the emphasis is on the lack of the core self. Michel Foucault, one of the leading postmodern theorists, wrote about the "decentering of the subject," which, said in another way, is the same thing as the de-emphasis of the individual. It is a reaction to—or deconstruction of—the autonomous self. The individual only exists within the context of a time and a place, and he or she is endlessly illusive, shifting shapes like an amoeba and breaking apart and reconstituting like mercury. Foucault and the boldest postmodernists radically challenged western thought, denying the Enlightenment and Romantic ideal of man. Where Riesman advanced the idea that nineteenth-century and twentieth-century man represented different personality types, Foucault attacked the entire western notion of personality.[8]

In modernist thought, the Eliot, Riesman, et al. view of man is drearily depressing, and it has given birth to an endless stream of poems, novels, and films to commit suicide by. But in the realms of popular culture, and especially celebrity culture, the postmodern variation of modernism is anything but depression. It offers a rich, exciting cornucopia of choices. To mix metaphors—and why not?—postmodern theorists have created a whole new ball game, one in which each player gets to invent the game and play by his or her own rules. The winner is the person who manipulates the absolute freedom of choices the best. It doesn't matter who you are, it matters only who you say you are and how well you can play the part. Image *is* everything.

It has long been fashionable, if somewhat churlish, for cultural curmudgeons to complain endlessly about the vacuity of modern celebrity-based culture. Historian Daniel Boorstin's often-reprinted definition of celebrity—"The celebrity is a person who is known for his well-known-ness." —is as meaningless as it is memorable. He is correct that modern celebrity is often not the result of some heroic action or significant achievement but rather something that is carefully constructed. In Boorstin's view, newspaper and magazine editors and television executives create celebrities. The celebrity "has been fabricated on purpose to satisfy our exaggerated expectations of human greatness." In the use of the passive voice and the assumption that the celebrity is something of a pawn, Boorstin robs the celebrity of both agency and his central place in modernity and post-modernity. Far from being trivial, celebrities were the first to understand that if image is everything not everyone has the ability to create, manipulate, and market unique images. Celebrity takes talent.[9]

Modern celebrities created personas then molded them to fit their lives. Humphrey Bogart was the moody, cynical reluctant hero who did the right thing almost against his better judgement. John Wayne could also be reluctant, but only because he took longer to see the lay of the land, not because of any cynicism. James Dean was the tortured rebel hero who had good instincts but was usually too conflicted to do the right thing. On screen and off screen, these and a handful of other iconic hero celebrities played their roles with exquisite certainty, even to the point of dying in type. But if they wore a mask, they only wore one mask. Wayne never played Dean, and Bogart never played Wayne, just as Marilyn Monroe never played Bette Davis. Any icon who blurred persona was persona non grata.

Postmodernism has weakened the rigid nature of iconic persona. Where once celebrities were known for only one mask, now they were permitted, even expected, to change masks regularly. The classic case, of course, is the career of dancer/singer/actress Madonna. She first attracted public notice in the late 1970s as a rebellious teen pop star. Dressed in mix-and-match cast-off goodwill clothes, fake pearls, and crucifixes, she caught the attention of the media and gained a popular following. By the mid-1980s she had begun to reconstruct her persona, this time as muscular, cross-dressing, expensively-attired, stylized star in the mold of Marlene Dietrich or Greta Garbo, at once both sexual and unapproachable. In the 1990s she continued to change her persona and, it seemed, her very identity. She became increasingly androgynous and surrounded herself with she-men and he-women who blatantly challenged sexual lines. Then from the radical edge of polysexuality she moved back toward the mainstream as a torch singer and contented mother.

Who was the real Madonna? Was she the sadomasochistic drag-queen impersonator or the thoroughly modern mom? Were her changes genuine or commercially motivated? How, it might be asked, could one woman appeal to straight and gay men, feminists and anti-feminists, working-class teenagers and designer-conscious wealthy women, and almost every ethnic minority in America? The point is that it really didn't and doesn't matter. She realized that reality—whatever that means—was not the issue. As she said about her documentary *In Bed with Madonna* (a.k.a. *Truth or Dare*, 1991), "You could watch it and say, I still don't know Madonna, and *good*. Because you will never know the real me." This was as much a statement of postmodern personal liberation as boxer Muhammad Ali's 1964 assertion, "I know where I'm going and I know the truth, and I don't have to be what you want me to be. I'm free to be what I want." In a postmodern world freedom means not having to say this is me.

*　*　*

The freedom of invention and re-invention—deconstruction and reconstruction—that Madonna's career symbolized would have been alien to Americans in the 1950s and 1960s, and certainly unimaginable in the nineteenth century. But in the late twentieth century, a world shaped by Vietnam and Watergate, energy shortages and economic transitions, black comedy and irony, cultural confusion and ambiguity, her various transmogrifications were hardly surprising. Even her attempts to shock lost their shock value and were greeted with an air of curious ennui. "What next?" became just "Next." Postmodern Americans—as most cultural critics agreed—having been fed an endless diet of sordid scandals, inflated hype, and apocalyptic warnings, had become jaded, and the cry for the next course often began before the last had been consumed.

It was, to say the least, a difficult time to be a politician. Such traditional political attributes as concern, consistency, and compassion—respect for various constituencies, willingness to stay the course, and faith in the system—struck many baby boomers and their children as "BORR-RING." But the time had come for them to take office, and Bill Clinton was their first president. Biographer David Maraniss got it right in the title of his biography of Clinton. Bill Clinton was "first in his class," not the best student or athlete, not the brightest or best-looking, but the first to reach the White House, the first to raise the flag of the baby boomers above the rose garden. And Maraniss's attitude toward Clinton was also right for the late twentieth century: "Clinton became not a politician but a character. Whether he was doing something admirable or questionable, I would say the same thing to myself: Well, that's Clinton. In that sense, I came to like him even when I disliked him and dislike him even when I liked him. . . . He is a big character, whether he is acting big-hearted or small."[10]

To say that Clinton is a character (or characters), that one might dislike him in a particular role but love him as pure theater, is another way of saying that he is postmodern, that he is about style over substance, performance over accomplishments. And was that not what his audience, his fellow boomers, wanted? In a world so crowded with fifteen-minute famers that most had their moments trimmed to mere seconds, President William Jefferson Clinton had to compete for attention with O. J. Simpson, Madonna, Donald Trump, Michael Jackson, Mike Tyson, Mike Jordan, Princess Di, and so many other flash-in-the-pan and accidental celebrities. In the celebrity sweepstakes being the president of the United States, the most powerful man in the world, was only important if he did something really cool, like swim naked in the reflecting pool or kick ass in a political pie-eating contest. The brutal struggle for the spotlight sent filmmaker Mike Nichols into despair: "Metaphor has left art and gone into current events. Who in the fuck is going to compete? Where is there a hero who can fall from greater heights than Michael Jackson? Where is there a more naked rivalry than between Tonya Harding and Nancy Kerrigan? What couple can you write about that is a stronger metaphor about relations between the sexes than the Bobbitts?"[11]

Perhaps it was inevitable that it was exactly in this hyper-competitive world of celebrity that Clinton had his greatest political impact. Before Clinton presidents had been good or bad, successes or failures, but they had not really been celebrities. Even John Fitzgerald Kennedy, unquestionably the most glamorous president, though he achieved cult status in death, had not quite reached celebrity status in life. Celebrity photographer Phil Stern snapped a most telling picture of Kennedy. It is a simple black-and-white photograph taken at JFK's 1961 inaugural showing Frank Sinatra lighting a cigarette for Kennedy. Stern's focus is on Sinatra's face; the singer's hands and the new president are completely out of focus. Even at Kennedy's moment of triumph, Stern's lens sought out the ranking celebrity.[12]

But until the end of the twentieth century presidents lived pleasantly unconcerned about becoming celebrities. In the last century there were essentially two presidential models: the good man and the political innovator. The good man president, popular during much of the late nineteenth century and occasionally in the twentieth century, set a high moral tone for the nation. He was generally not know for his intellect or ideas, but rather for his solid, forthright, and decent nature. William McKinley and Calvin Coolidge, and to a slightly lesser extent Harry Truman, Dwight Eisenhower, and Jimmy Carter, exemplified the type. Political innovator presidents are men who seek office in order to change America. This is not to say that some were not also men of integrity and character, because several were—and others were not. Rather, their raison d'être were their ideas. Theodore and Franklin Roosevelt, and especially Woodrow Wilson, Lyndon Johnson, and Ronald Reagan, personified the second category. But the good man and the political innovators had one thing in common: they were what and who they were. Whether they liked them or disliked them, Americans had a fairly accurate read on them. Americans were never in doubt about the goals of Theodore

Roosevelt, Woodrow Wilson, or Ronald Reagan. They never questioned the integrity of Calvin Coolidge, Dwight Eisenhower, or Jimmy Carter. And most probably never fully trusted Franklin Roosevelt, Lyndon Johnson, or Richard Nixon.

Oddly, the most intriguing presidents were the most politically and biographically slippery ones, but in postmodern America even those presidents had lost much of their fascination. Nixon at his worst seemed less compelling than O. J. Simpson. As celebrities they lacked proper range. Their personalities and their public images were too set in stone. Missing was that most precious celebrity quality—the ability to surprise. The pages of *People* magazine dramatized the fate of politicians in the celebrity sweepstakes. Begun in 1974, *People,* more than any other publication, tracked the ups and downs of celebrities, and its covers marked who was hot and who had staying power. Not surprising such mercurial figures as Princess Diana, Elizabeth Taylor, John Travolta, Madonna, and Cher appeared the most often on the magazine's covers. Editor Richard Stolley had a simple set of rules for a successful cover: "Young is better than old. Pretty is better than ugly. Rich is better than poor. TV is better than music. Music is better than the movies. Movies are better than sports. Anything is better than politics. And nothing is better than a celebrity who has just died."[13]

From the time Bill Clinton emerged as a serious presidential contender in 1992, he clearly did not conform to the traditional presidential models. He was most decidedly not a moral exemplar. Revelations about his draft imbroglio—his stated intention to serve in a ROTC program and his reneging on his promise after receiving a high draft lottery number—called into question his basic honesty. And multiple allegations of his extramarital affairs raised serious questions of his basic morality. Nor had he developed a reputation as a political innovator with a fresh, far-sighted vision for America. He was a popular governor from a small southern state that had a long history of suspicion and resentment of any liberal, activist politicians. Given Arkansas's conservative tendencies and Clinton's ambitions, he found it wise to camp in the center of the political spectrum. Where once he struck the pose of a McGovern liberal, now he made friends with Tyson Foods and other business interests, cultivated the favor of the Stephens investment house, and rooted hard for the Razorbacks in all athletic contests. At the same time he won friends in the state's African American community and became a thoughtful voice in the Democratic Leadership Council, an organization that labored to pull the Democratic Party toward the modern vital center. Reporters insisted that Clinton was bright, articulate, and likable, that he had a gift for understanding the nuances of policy and genuine feel for poor and disadvantaged Americans, but they did not mistake him for Woodrow Wilson or Ronald Reagan. Clinton had no grand vision, and his political compass lacked a true north.

But a faithful political compass—just as the inner-directed individual's "psychological gyroscope"—was not packed in the postmodern person's baggage. In Arkansas, Clinton learned that to survive he had to keep changing shapes and adopting the issue du jour. Elected governor in 1978, he made a political mistake when he raised fees for automobile licenses, a move that cost him his 1980 reelection bid. The 1980 loss to Republican Frank White is crucial to understanding who Bill Clinton was and who he became. After the election he turned to his political strategist Dick Morris to revive his career. Morris, in effect, gave Clinton an elementary biology lesson: survival of a species—or, as the case may be, Clinton's political career—depended on adaptation and evolution. To win he had to change. Morris told him to apologize for raising taxes, a political act of contrition. Though Clinton resisted the idea, he did tell Arkansas voters that he was "really sorry for that," adding, "When I was a boy growing up my daddy never had to whip me twice for the same thing."[14]

Morris also advised Clinton to devote more time to raising money and spending it on television advertising. As far as Morris was concerned, newspaper coverage was too unreliable, subject to the perceptions and opinions of journalists. Television was a direct pipeline to the voters. And the camera loved Clinton. He exuded warmth, friendly ease, and a folksy charm. Unlike previous political campaigns, where expensive television advertising was saved for the last weeks of the race, Clinton began his television spots ten months before the election. The strategy worked. He seemed invulnerable to attacks from both his political opponents and the press. Assaults on his record were useless. He had been big enough to apologize, voters reasoned. And voters saw him so much on television— and liked what they saw—that negative press coverage had little impact. Clinton was back on track. He returned to the governor's mansion in 1982 and proceeded to win three more terms in office.

Morris's strategy—which became Clinton's as well—was driven by constant, issue-oriented polling. He wanted to know how his candidate was doing at all times and what issues were the most important. He wanted his charge to not so much lead the electorate but to follow it, championing the issues that the majority of Americans believed were the most important. It was not a strategy suited to every politician. It demanded not only the willingness but the ability for reinvention; the politician had to be able to express and sell sincerity regardless of the issue or the circumstance. More than any previous administration, the Clinton White House employed frequent and wide-ranging polling, leading one authority to label the Clinton approach a "permanent campaign." The polls themselves, however, did not prevent Clinton from political blunders or overreaching his grasp. Early in his first term someone in his administration blundered by ordering ham as the main course at a reception after the dedication of the Holocaust Museum in Washington. And, even more seriously, his mishandling of the Travel Office issue and especially healthcare reform cost him politically. But he always recovered. And in his ability to recover he defined the postmodern presidency.[15]

Reviewing Clinton's first term in office, *New York Times* writer Todd S. Purdum captured both Clinton and his leadership style: "One of the biggest, most talented, articulate, intelligent, open, colorful characters ever to inhabit the Oval Office can also be an undisciplined, fumbling, obtuse, defensive, self-justifying rogue. His strengths and weaknesses not only spring from the same source but could not exist without one another. In a real sense, his strengths are his weaknesses, his enthusiasms are his undoing and most of the traits that make him appealing can make him appalling in the flash of an eye." Searching for one word to define Clinton proved difficult. Purdum relied on the overused "paradox." Former Clinton advisor George Stephanopoulos preferred "kaleidoscope," which suggests an endless number of different patterns and shapes. Others have hinted that he was just too ready to move whichever way the wind blew to be hemmed in by one metaphor. Clinton's attraction and problem was that baby boomers saw something of their best and worst in him, sensing that the sum of his—and their—great talents might produce nothing important.[16]

Following the same theme, Bruce Miroff, a gifted political scientist and observer of presidential style, contends that Clinton's greatest political strength was his apparent lack of a core character. Reporters, Miroff noted, found him a "slippery" politician who "habitually played games with the truth" and treated most people like disposable objects. He lied, he evaded, he sidestepped. He mastered the art of semantics, constructing worlds where nothing seemed as it was or was as it seemed. "[A] simpler or more honorable political figure would likely have been crushed by the defeats Clinton has suffered and constrained from pursuing the opportunistic and shape-shifting strategies that Clinton has followed to recover from them," Miroff writes. "Character, in the traditional sense of the word, would likely have made Bill Clinton into another Jimmy Carter."[17]

That may be true, but it also too harsh, criticizing Clinton because he was what his background and his times had conspired to make him. Perhaps another way of assessing Clinton is to view his two terms as president as a complex television program with elements of pathos, comedy, farce, and drama, one where characters came and went, rose to near stardom and fell in disgrace, and played a variety of different roles. Think along the lines of a *West Wing* created and written by Larry David and Larry Flynt. How else can you explain the endless twists and characters, from Gennifer Flowers to Lani Guinier, George Stephanopoulos to Dick Morris, and Newt Gingrich to Monica Lewinsky? And through it all the First Family, facing every sort of political and personal trial. Such an idea might sound facetious, but it is not. In postmodern America the lines between reality and fiction, comedy and tragedy, serious and fatuous have become hopelessly blurred. The Clinton White House, America's first great reality television program, conditioned baby boomers to think that far from being BORR-RING politics could be great theater. Whatever Clinton's successes or failures as a leader, politician, or human being he had the ability to fascinate, titillate, and surprise his audience. And no matter what the situation or the topic, he had the knack of projecting sincerity. He made Americans believe that he believed whatever he was saying. In short, he was the perfect actor, the ideal postmodern politician, and the first celebrity president.

People magazine, which would jettison its traditional attitude toward politics and politicians to cover The Clinton Show, hinted that something different was in the political wind when it featured the Clinton family on its July 20, 1992, cover. In the "exclusive," pre-convention, fluffy story, Clinton, with seemingly sincerity, went beyond the traditional Democratic candidate's mantra of being for a whole bunch of things and against mighty few and entered into the realms of postmodern discourse. Dressed in faded jeans and exhausted from the rigorous campaign, Clinton ranged broadly over political and personal subjects and in the end demonstrated that the personal was political and the political was personal. On the campaign trail, for example, Clinton had insisted that young, pregnant females had the right to have abortions without their parents' permission. In the *People* interview, however, he and Hillary discussed how they had "hung tough" against allowing their twelve-year-old daughter Chelsea to get her ears pierced. The implications —abortion without their consent was permissible but ear piercing was a family decision—was not lost on some of the magazine's readers. But such wild, illogical swings came to characterize his The Clinton Show.[18]

The swings also generated interest, creating a sort of water-cooler buzz for The Clinton Show. Actually, in the nine years that *People* actively covered him—ranging from six months before his election to six months after he left office—Clinton appeared in the magazine's pages over 150 times. Very few of the articles—four to be exact—dealt directly with policy issues, though many more touched on one hot subject or another. Most of the coverage labored to construct one or another image of Clinton. Oddly, the two most prominent faces of Clinton featured in *People* were the president as family man and the president as celebrity. Roughly two-fifths of the pieces centered on Hillary, Chelsea, Bill's brothers and brothers-in-law, or family friends. The emphasis in most of these pieces was on the Clintons' strong sense of family values. Roughly another two-fifths of the coverage focused on Clinton's star power, his rock 'n' roll roots, and his legions of celebrity supporters. From Shirley MacLaine, Goldie Hawn, Bonnie Raitt, and Barbara Streisand to Danny Devito, Warren Beatty, Dustin Hoffman, and Jack Nicholson, the cream of Hollywood consistently appeared in photographs with or extolled the virtues of Bill Clinton. At one 1992 preelection gathering Streisand sang a new verse of "It Had To Be You":

> George Bush and Dan Quayle
> They golf and they sail
> One doesn't look good, the other can't spell
> Those fellas won't do. . . . It has to be you.[19]

The majority of the other pieces dealt with Clinton's various scandals, generally slanting toward discussions about how he and Hillary were coping with the "problems." Once again, the editors of the magazine lumped Clinton's infidelities with those of other celebrities. Elizabeth Hurley and Hugh Grant, Kathie Lee and Frank Gifford, Donald and Ivana Trump, Kevin and Cindy Costner, Bill and Hillary Clinton— they all had to learn how to overcome the occasional potholes in married life. Just as other non-celebrity couples had, too. As the articles made clear, celebrities and presidents were just people. The scandals, however, always seemed divorced from the political arena. It was all part of The Clinton Show, or as one *People* article dubbed it, "As the White House

Turns." Far from being seen as the president of the United States, Clinton was seen more as an actor playing the president of the United States in a weekly series, or even a daily soap opera.[20]

Viewed as a series, The Clinton Show clearly had three seasons. In the first season the fresh, bright politician from the South showed up in Washington, D.C. and learned some lessons in hardball politics that were not taught at southern schools. He was full of good intentions, but every move he made became twisted by conservative opponents. His attempt to reach out to gay Americans became mired in the gays in the military fight, and his effort to reward women stagnated in the Lani Guinier confirmation fiasco. The medical lobby and its Republican supporters derailed Hillary's work on healthcare reform, and other opponents created scandals over the Paula Jones accusations and Whitewater without substantial evidence. By 1994 his poll ratings had dipped to 40 percent, leaving him defenseless in the mid-term elections. Conservative Republicans, led by Newt Gingrich, who looked and sounded like a Hollywood heavy, appeared on the verge of ruining Clinton and shattering his vision for America. Like any good series, the first season ended with a cliffhanger. Was Bill dead in the water?

The second season saw the emergence of a new Clinton. In a postmodern, Madonna fashion, he was literally re-made. The architect for the new Clinton was his old crony, pollster and advisor Dick Morris. Clinton the man and politician was different. Early in his first term he had cultivated a Hollywood look, going so far as to get a two-hundred-dollar hair cut in Los Angeles by "hair guru" Cristophe. After the Republicans' 1994 victory, Morris instructed Clinton to look more Republican. In 1992, Morris said, the candidate was "America's buddy." "Down-to-earth, riding buses to campaign events, conducting town meetings, eating at McDonald's, going one-on-one with people, appearing on MTV, and playing the saxophone—he was a regular guy. 'But now,' I told the president, 'it's time to be almost the nation's father, to speak as the father of the country, not as a peer and certainly not as its child.'" The new image started with Clinton's wardrobe. Morris told him to scrap his favorite light-colored suits and patterned ties and wear navy suits and "bright-red power ties." Look the part was the message.[21]

And the message fit the look. The idealism and generally left-leaning tilt of his administration was shoved into the same storage closet as his Carolina-blue and cream sports jackets. Morris's instructions were look Republican, act Republican. The Republicans, Morris outlined in an early May 1995 memo, had five basic messages: "1. Fiscal/Economic

2. foreign/defense 3. racial 4. crime 5. social." "When Republicans are Reduced to Only Social Message, they lose," Morris wrote. That basic principle—or lack of principle—became the heart of the Clinton comeback. First, Morris told Clinton to "[g]ive absolute political priority to making a deal" on balancing the budget and deficit reductions. Second, use foreign policy to demonstrate toughness. Third, "neutralize the crime issue" by supporting more police and longer sentences. Fourth, "counter" Republican racial appeals with affirmative-action plans and immigration restrictions. The plan, Morris emphasized, would take everything from the Republicans except such social issues as abortion and guns. And no Republican could possibly ride into the White House on those minority issues. At the bottom of his agenda Morris penciled "check mate!"[22]

Morris's "leave them with only 20 percent" mantra became Clinton's blueprint for saving his presidency. Working closely with the Republican opposition in Congress, he pushed through legislation for a balanced-budget, tougher sentencing and more police, and conservative welfare reform. And for good measure, he bombed Serbian positions in Bosnia. Supporters of Clinton explained his actions using such phrases as "locating the common ground," "finding the dynamic center," "forging a third position," or some such heroic wording, as if he were blazing a trail through some unexplored wilderness. Many of his former Democratic friends, however, felt betrayed, suggesting that he was simply "fast-forwarding the Gingrich agenda" for his own political advancement.

Following Morris's polling, Clinton led Americans by finding out what they wanted to hear and then telling it to them. If he confounded Democrats, he bewitched Republicans even more. They had the nearly impossible chore of finding a popular issue that Clinton had not co-opted. A Republican authority on criminal justice put it nicely: "We say habeas corpus; they say sure. We say prisons; they say sure. We say more firearm prosecutions; they say sure." Never had a president so radically changed the emphasis and direction of his presidency. Never had a president made so many Americans wonder, "Who is that guy?"[23]

If the second season of The Clinton Show ended with a miraculous Hollywood comeback, the third season introduced—or, perhaps, re-introduced—another role for the president. Now dressed in blue suits, his hair graying but perfectly cut, his face losing the last of its chubbiness, Clinton had never looked more handsome or presidential. He looked like Charlton Heston playing the president. The combination of conservative policies and personal compassion fit him well. It looked as if his second term would finally free him to move toward real statesmanship. He certainly looked statesmanlike. But instead his second term turned into a farcical soap opera, a sometimes compelling, sometimes sad, always-unseemly E. E. Cummings tale of he said she said.

Thinking about the Monica Lewinsky season of The Clinton Show is a bit like recalling the best season of *Dallas* or *Survivor.* They seemed fascinating enough at the time but they lost all their interest once you knew the ending. Each step in that season, from the accusations and the finger-wagging indignity of Clinton's assertion that "I did not have sex with that woman" to the later parsing of words with Kenneth Starr and the impeachment hearing, echoes down the darkest alley of our history. In a battle that would allow no winner, only losers, it all had to end badly, and did. In fact, it ended even worse, with the barely explicable pardon affair, in its own way every bit as seedy as the Lewinsky affair.

And in the end, after The Clinton Show left the air and the best and brightest journalists and television commentators of the hour had their say, have we come any closer to the heart of Bill Clinton? I don't think so, which is in itself the perfect ending for a postmodern presidency. We know well only that we don't know well.

Conclusion

President Clinton

A Pragmatic and
Defensive Player

TODD G. SHIELDS,

JEANNIE M. WHAYNE,

AND DONALD R. KELLEY

Caveats and Cautions

As noted in the introductory chapter of this volume, our early investigation into the Clinton presidency has provided important insights into the administration and the politics of the 1990s. Not all of our participants agreed with one another; in fact, throughout our conference, disagreements were intense. We were pleased, however, to see substantial congruity emerge among the overall conclusions. Regardless, the interdisciplinary nature of this program created an eclectic panorama of theoretical and methodological work, and the fact that common themes ran through the conference attests to the importance and potential contributions of such a unique approach to studying politics and public figures.

It is important, however, to recall some of the limitations of our approach, particularly before we begin to discuss overall themes. First, our evaluation is admittedly early and without complete information. Further, we expect that as documents become available and scholars have more time to identify and digest new information, evaluations of both the politics of the 1990s and of the Clinton administration will be reexamined and altered. We recognize the potential problems associated with such drastically divergent perspectives and methodologies employed by our contributors. We must be careful not to overlook important conclusions masked by different units of analyses and designs. We believe, however, that the potential benefits of such an eclectic approach are well worth the efforts—such diversity in scholarship has led to unintuitive conclusions about this important part of history and the first two-term Democratic president since the Great Depression.

Our final caveats reflect the enormous complexity of evaluating presidential accomplishments and the singular context of the 1990s. The former task has been well documented by both historians and political scientists who struggle to assess what "performance" in the oval office means and, if we can define it, how it can be measured without bias or ideological prejudice. Of course, the difficulty of the goal is not sufficient reason to abandon the pursuit.

The latter task—understanding presidential performance during the turbulent and complicated political setting of the final decade of the twentieth century—has been less discussed. Scholars will most certainly evaluate and attempt to understand such a unique decade for many years. It is obvious that the world underwent dramatic transformations during the Clinton years—the explosion of technology, growing conservatism across the United States, increased ethnic and religious hatred around the world, and continued gaps in the standard of living between the developed and developing nations. These complexities render the difficult task of evaluating presidential performance even more intractable and do not readily facilitate comparisons between presidential administrations.

Politics of the 1990s

Even a brief examination of the 1990s and the accomplishments of the Clinton administration demonstrates the difficulties of understanding both the politics of the decade and the president's performance. It was clear even before Clinton's 1992 presidential election victory that the United States was undergoing substantial change. The early signs of the "information-based-high-tech" economy were obvious, and the nation seemed ready for a new generation of leadership. The 1992 campaign itself demonstrated the effectiveness of new electoral strategies, raising campaign standards and demonstrating both Bill Clinton's enthusiasm and ability for campaign politics. The Clinton campaign boldly demonstrated its commitment to reaching younger generations by answering questions on MTV and playing saxophone on the popular *Arsenio Hall Show*. He appeared equally at ease answering questions about Elvis Presley or world trade. His extensive use of polling, focus groups, and targeted media—along with insightful use of cultural symbols and music, such as the now inextricably linked Fleetwood Mac song "Don't Stop Thinking about Tomorrow" in the 1992 campaign—became the new standards in campaign tactics. In fact, even the 2000 presidential election bore the fingerprints of candidate Bill Clinton as both the Republican and Democratic candidates avoided the traditional nightly news media for the more popular, and soft-hitting, venues of David Letterman, Larry King, and Oprah.

Traditional American institutions and voting patterns were also changing at a rapid pace. The political parties were becoming increasingly polarized along ideological lines,[1] women were regularly voting at higher rates than men,[2] and congressional norms were disintegrating quickly, often in the direction of increasingly bitter disagreements and partisan attacks.[3] After twelve years of Republican rule under presidents Reagan and George H. W. Bush, accompanied by an economic downturn to which there appeared little relief (or fresh ideas) from the incumbent administration, the time may have been ripe to elect another Southern Democrat, but this did not mean that governing would be as easy as campaigning.

Success and Failure in the 1990s

Further changes across the United States during the 1990s included record economic expansion, which continues to be one of the primary public memories of the decade. In fact, February 2000 represented 107 consecutive months of economic expansion, the longest economic growth in United States history. The robust economy was used to reduce the national debt, create new jobs (an estimated twenty-two million from 1993 through 2000), experience five straight years of real wage growth, the longest consecutive increase since the 1960s, improve household income for the first time to over forty thousand dollars, and reduce unemployment and poverty rates among both adults and children. Workers were granted up to twenty-four unpaid hours of leave each year for school and childhood education, as well as up to twelve weeks of unpaid leave to care for seriously ill family members (or new children), all through the Family and Medical Leave Act. Even crime rates fell during the 1990s, and among the most dramatic declines were the drop in murders and gun violence. From 1993 to 2000, the murder rate fell more than 20 percent to the lowest level since 1967, and gun violence declined by more than 35 percent.

In the international arena, the Clinton administration worked to decrease trafficking in women and children; forgave $500 million in African debts, financially assisted the struggling economies of Mexico, Japan, and Brazil; and worked to strengthen international trade through support of NAFTA, GATT, and other trade agreements.

Of course, accompanying these domestic and international achievements were the growing lists of scandals, policy failures, and security threats. The most prominent of these were the accusations of financial misbehavior in the Whitewater investments, prolonged investigations by Kenneth Starr, the Monica Lewinsky affair (and accusations of others), questions surrounding ethical and legal campaign fundraising practices, and the number and substance of presidential pardons during the final days of the administration. Ultimately, the Clinton administration was forced to accept much less than its initial goals in several areas of policy, most notably in healthcare reform and homosexual rights. In the international arena, reforms in Russia were certainly not going as well nor as quickly as the Clinton administration wanted; China appeared to be increasingly hostile, flexing military muscle by conducting military maneuvers off the coast of Taiwan prior to that small nation's democratic elections (as well as reported theft of designs for high-tech weapons systems from American laboratories); and the first Gulf War seemed far from over as Saddam Hussein refused to allow full access to United Nations weapons inspectors.

Admittedly, this brief discussion of the success and limitations of the policy goals and achievements of the Clinton administration is far from complete. Regardless, it begins to demonstrate the enormously difficult task that faced our contributors—to rely on their own particular areas of expertise and methods to begin an initial evaluation of the Clinton administration. In the remaining pages of this chapter, we begin to identify common themes running through the contributions as well as provide some of our own insights from our perspective here in Arkansas.

Making Sense of the 1990s

In order to encourage each participant to follow his or her own unique methodological and intellectual preferences, we simply asked each to reflect on the Clinton administration and discuss his or her own areas of interest. We admitted that we wanted to facilitate interdisciplinary discussions and did not wish to place confining boundaries on topics or methods. The result was exactly what we wanted—an eclectic view of the Clinton presidency, an evaluation filled with complexity, praise, and criticism. As we anticipated, the investigations took dramatically divergent approaches to the study of the presidency: some focused nearly exclusively on President Bill Clinton himself, others placed more emphasis on national changes and the contemporary political landscape in the United States, while others examined the dramatic changes in the international political environment.

Focusing on the President, Moderate and Pragmatic

While nearly all participants, in varying degrees, evaluated aspects of the Clinton administration by examining the president himself, a few investigations focused specifically, although not exclusively, on the experiences, personality, and behaviors of William Jefferson Clinton. For example, Betty Glad arrives at the conclusion that President Clinton has a remarkable ability to empathize with others, even with those whom he may disagree or dislike. As a result, she argues that he is an accommodator who seeks to find areas of agreement between ideological and political factions, even when not necessarily in his own best interest.

These tendencies became clear to the American public as early as the 1992 primary season. Gov. Bill Clinton did not represent a traditional New Deal Democratic liberal. Rather, he chose to present himself as a combination of liberal and conservative policies, an ideological position he followed throughout his years in office, albeit with substantial adjustments following the 1994 congressional elections. For example, he supported socially liberal policies like gays in the military, abortion rights, and universal healthcare, but he also supported more conservative programs like welfare reform and the addition of thousands of policemen patrolling the streets in high-crime areas through the COPS program. Overall, President Clinton's tendency to gravitate toward the ideological middle, or perhaps adopt a pragmatic approach to a generally liberal paradigm, can be seen throughout many of his top priorities. Speaking to this general tendency, Glad writes, "the bottom line for Bill Clinton was not that he believed in big government, but that unlike his opponents on the right, he believed in some government." The substantial change from the substance and degree of government intervention espoused by FDR's New Deal policies and the "business-friendly" liberalism expressed by President Clinton should not be overlooked.

While the characterization of ideological moderation, accompanied by both an economic downturn in 1992 and unprecedented business growth in 1996, helped to ensure that candidate Bill Clinton was a formidable opponent during election years, they proved less helpful in President Clinton's attempts to govern from the middle. Again, as Glad concludes, "The problem for Clinton as president was that he had no stable coalition on which he could rely for the success of his programs. The neo-liberal doctrine was one calculated to win over swing voters. . . . Both the Democratic and Republican political parties had become increasingly ideological, and legislative proposals in the middle would stir up partisan juices. Moreover, there was no alternative interest-group structure in the middle on which Clinton could rely."

Training with Senator J. William Fulbright

Regardless of the difficulties surrounding an attempt to govern from the middle of the ideological spectrum, Bill Clinton's experiences with the former-senator J. William Fulbright may have prepared him well for the dramatic changes in the international environment following the end of the Cold War. As Randall Woods argues, "Clinton, the first post–Cold War president, could have had no better mentor than Bill Fulbright. . . . Bill Clinton seemed well prepared to head the foreign-policy establishment during the 1990s." Because of Clinton's early experiences with the importance of multilateralism and cultural understanding and, perhaps, in combination with his own personal leanings toward compromise and cooperation, he was well prepared to reject standard stereotypes of Russians, the Cold War, and the communist threat. In fact, as Woods argues, Senator Fulbright and President Clinton both opted for "pragmatism rather than ideology" in American diplomacy. As in domestic politics, however, such an approach left President Clinton open to critics on both the left and the right.

Quoting Steven Walt, Woods writes, "Critics on the right argue that [Clinton] is too eager to accommodate a rising China, too blind to Russia's corruption and cronyism, and too slow to use force against states like Yugoslavia or Iraq. On the left, liberals bemoan Clinton's failure to prevent the genocide in Rwanda, his tardy response to the bloodletting in the Balkans, and his abandonment of his early pledge to build a multilateral world order grounded in strong international institutions." Similarly, Bob Legvold argues that Clinton's reliance on pragmatism rather than ideology in foreign policy, or in Clinton's words abandoning "abstraction and dogma" in favor of "persistent experimentation," resulted in the appearance of an administration without a consistent conceptual framework to guide foreign (or domestic) policy, open to attacks from those more ideologically committed.

Overall, our contributors suggest that in many ways Bill Clinton was well prepared for the office of the presidency and that his limited experiences in foreign policy, associated with being governor of a small southern state, were aptly compensated for by mentoring from Senator Fulbright, which helped to create a leader ready for compromise and flexibility in a changing international environment. To those with uncompromising ideologies, Clinton's flexibility and willingness to "experiment" left him open to criticism from both Democrats and Republicans. The president's tendency to run to the ideological middle, often exemplified by his mix of support for some liberal social policies and conservative economic policies, and his case-by-case approach on the international front helped candidate Clinton appeal to swing voters, reshaping the image of Democrats and liberals. Recall that these were labels that inflicted substantial damage to Gov. Michael Dukakis's campaign for president in 1988. Unfortunately for Clinton, his success with swing voters did little to help him forge a coalition of interest groups, lobbyists, and attentive publics committed to an ideologically mixed approach to foreign and domestic policy. In fact, his eclectic approach to policy contributed to the dismay of the left and ire of the right—which leads to the second theme of our conference: more often than not, Clinton found himself playing defense in both the domestic and international arenas. And, not unlike his experiences as governor of Arkansas, he found greater success playing a defensive position.

A Defensive Player

LEARNING TO PLAY DEFENSIVELY IN ARKANSAS

Before we discuss President Clinton's abilities as a defensive player, it is important to examine his rise to the governorship of Arkansas and the experiences that influenced him along this path. In 1973 Bill Clinton, a recent graduate from Yale Law School, returned to northwest Arkansas where he took a faculty position teaching law at the University of Arkansas (Hillary Rodham Clinton joined the faculty in 1975).[4] Prof. Bill Clinton had little ambition for academics and focused his attention on building grassroots support for his future political career rather than on scholarship and academic publishing. After just one year as a professor, he ran for an open seat in Arkansas's third district against a Republican named John Paul Hammerschmidt. He lost the 1974 race and learned, early on, that he was too liberal to appeal to the many conservatives living in the northwest corner of Arkansas. He also learned a second and more lasting lesson: how to react defensively to a conservative public and a successful Republican challenger. His next campaign, in 1976, was for attorney general, which he won easily, by 56 percent in the Democratic primary. He found greater statewide appeal by moderating his policies and building support among women and minorities, a strategy that he would use consistently throughout his political career.

Attorney General Bill Clinton ran for the governor's office in 1978 and became the second-youngest governor in Arkansas history at the age of thirty-two. His first term as governor proved difficult. Governor Clinton took office anxious to ameliorate the problems facing citizens of Arkansas, and his zeal spread across many policy areas. As Diane Blair wrote, "Clinton's first regular session was action-packed and highly successful as he proposed and persuaded the lawmakers to enact an ambitious and wide-ranging legislative package initiating new programs in economic development, education, conservation, health, and roads."[6]

Unfortunately for the young governor, most of the money used to finance the improvement of Arkansas roads came from substantial increases in vehicle registration and license fees that proved unpopular across the state, and particularly loathsome in rural areas.[7] Adding to Governor Clinton's problems was President Carter's choice to inter thousands of Freedom Flotilla Cuban refugees in Arkansas. Ultimately, the young Governor Clinton faced intense and eventually successful opposition during his 1980 reelection campaign. Conservative Republican Frank White opposed Clinton's liberal activism and his tax-and-spend policies, campaigning that what Bill Clinton did not understand was that "the people of Arkansas want a good lettin' alone."[8] White also used video footage of rioting Cubans to charge Clinton with endangering the safety of Arkansans in order to placate the liberal President Carter. In fact, Clinton remained publicly quiet on the issue because he feared that openly attacking the president would reawaken memories of Governor Faubus's 1957 resistance of integration.[9] Journalist David Maraniss contends that "Clinton would be given high marks for his performance under pressure in dealing with the Cuban refugee crises, but his close friendship with Carter, which became strained in private but did not break in public, was held against him by Arkansas voters. It was also used to great advantage by Republican challenger Frank White and his handlers, who replayed footage of the Fort Chaffee riot to associate Clinton with images of disorder and bad times."[10] Historian Ben Johnson concluded that "Bill Clinton's political demise and recovery was an object lesson for moderate Southern Democrats in the era of Ronald Reagan."[11]

White's tenure in the governor's mansion was short lived, however, as Bill Clinton quickly earned his reputation as the "comeback kid." His return to public life taught him yet another lesson in playing defensively as a progressive facing a much more conservative electorate. Clinton displayed his ability to react carefully and successfully to the attacks and strategies of his conservative opponents by changing the tone of his 1982 gubernatorial reelection bid by moderating his policies and narrowing his policy focus to school reform and jobs. He also took the bold move to apologize for his mistakes during the first term, convincing the electorate that he was indeed a moderate and ideologically acceptable to the Democratic, yet conservative, citizens of Arkansas. In February 1982, after receiving a great deal of advice from both Dick Morris and Betsey Wright, Clinton aired television ads apologizing for the mistakes he had made during his first term in office, stating that "when he was growing up his daddy never had to whip him twice for the same thing."[12]

Clinton's apology, however, was not the only reason for his reelection success. His claims of moderation were made more credible by the actions of Gov. Frank White. During Frank White's two years as governor, his conservatism was clear and, in particular, his commitment to social conservatism was pronounced. One of the most obvious examples of this was Act 590, which mandated that students in biology classes were to be told that existing species had not evolved after the beginning of the universe. The American Civil Liberties Union filed suit, and the subsequent notoriety was reminiscent of the 1925 Scopes trial in Tennessee.

The proceedings even reached the attention of national political players, including the television evangelist Pat Robertson. With these connections in the minds of Arkansas voters, Clinton was able to re-invent himself as the true moderate, particularly in comparison to his opponent. As John Brummett argues, "after a stormy two-year term . . . he came back two years later pleading for a second chance as a reinvented listener, coalition builder, and moderate."[13] According to Ben F. Johnson, Clinton's 1982 "reinvention" campaign was typical of other candidates running as moderates across the South.[14]

During Clinton's second term in office, he focused on education and jobs. With greater moderation and focus, he successfully ran for reelection in 1984, 1986, and 1990, promising on the campaign trail not to leave the office early in order to run for the presidency, which many in Arkansas insightfully perceived was Governor Clinton's ultimate objective.[15]

LEARNING TO PLAY DEFENSIVELY IN WASHINGTON

In October 1991 Governor Clinton announced his candidacy for the presidency, running against incumbent Republican president George H.W. Bush. As mentioned in several chapters of this volume, Clinton's blend of pragmatic liberalism and his willingness to adopt ideologically moderate positions on many economic policies found substantial support among an electorate weary of twelve years of Republican control of the White House. Clinton's campaign theme of "It's the Economy, Stupid" combined with his business-friendly Democratic label, hit a chord among many voters and the comeback kid won the 1992 presidential election. President Clinton's honeymoon, however, didn't last long. Once in office, the apparently moderate candidate Clinton emerged as the more liberal President Clinton who supported gays in the military, increased taxes, and universal healthcare, awakening the powerful medical and insurance giants who successfully portrayed President Clinton as another tax-and-spend liberal. The similarities to Clinton's first term as governor are striking. His liberal activism ignited the passions of conservatives across the country, but in particular in the South, and as a result, President Clinton, just like Governor Clinton, was quickly and effectively criticized as being too liberal for mainstream voters.

In many ways, President Clinton's endorsement of ideologically liberal social policies did not find tremendous support across the nation as the country was moving increasingly toward the ideological right. As Dan Carter argues, the growing tide of conservatism across the nation reacted intensely to the president's support of liberal policies, and a cadre of hungry, conservative, and well-financed candidates announced their intentions of running for Congress in 1994. Certainly not all, but many of these impassioned and battle-ready congressional upstarts were from the South. With low approval ratings hovering around 46 percent during the 1994 November midterm elections, Bill Clinton found that substantial public support can be lost in less than two years from the White House as easily as from the governor's mansion.

Political scientist Paul Frymer argues that the southern origin of many of the members of the 1994 congressional revolution was no accident. He points out that Clinton's liberalism made it more difficult for conservative (and moderate) southern Democratic senators and representatives to separate themselves from the liberal image of the national Democratic Party, which they had done successfully for many years. President Clinton, however, was one of their own—a southern Democratic governor espousing liberal social policies consistent with the maligned "progressive" agenda associated with the northeastern Democratic Party leadership. No longer could southern Democratic senators and legislators easily disassociate themselves from the national party. According to Frymer, "Democratic House members from conservative districts were not as successful in distancing themselves from the more liberal views of the party's president . . . health care and other Clinton programs changed the perception that conservative voters had about their Democratic House members. . . . Southern Democratic House members had more difficulty preventing national party politics from entering into their campaigns as many were pressured for the first time into voting with a Southern Democratic president that many had supported in 1992. In the South, many conservative Democrats who ran unopposed in 1988 were targeted and defeated in 1994."[16]

In this respect, Clinton may be partly responsible for the ease of which southern Republicans broke years of Democratic dominance in the South. In fact, Clinton's home state elected its first Republican senator in 1996 and continues to have a Republican in the governor's mansion. Similar to when he was governor, President Clinton had to play defensively and alter his image or the conservative Republicans in Congress would have been able to block his initiatives and prevent a successful reelection bid in 1996.

Following the advice of political advisor Dick Morris, President Clinton, acting in ways similar to his comeback victory against Gov. Frank White in 1982, began to alter his image from a liberal to an ideological moderate. Shifting focus away from his prior support of liberal domestic policies, President Clinton began to focus his (and the public's) attention on foreign policy and more conservative economic initiatives, such as welfare reform. Perhaps most importantly, he began to portray himself as an ideological moderate in comparison to the conservative, and increasingly caustic, Republican congressional leadership. As Brummett argues, "In this drama from Arkansas, the protagonist gets off to a bad start on the job, appearing too much a liberal for the tastes of the mainstream . . . then, always adaptable and reactive, he sets out to slide to the political center, recruit experienced advisers, and reinvent himself while the pundits ponder whether he's a liberal or a moderate, an old Democrat or a new Democrat."[17]

Governing from the Middle

While governing from the middle and playing defensively against a conservative Congress was not easy, President Clinton was able to forge policy successes. For example, according to the analyses by Brady and Hillygus, Clinton was a successful defensive player in domestic politics. According to their analysis, he was not only able to increase budgets for his favorite programs but also to limit and even block many of the congressional leadership's agenda items contained in the Contract with America. As Brady and Hillygus state, "It is quite clear that President Clinton was able to work within the institutional constraints created by a Republican-controlled Congress. . . . Many of Clinton's programs actually had budget increases." In particular, funding for educational technology increased over 2,000 percent above inflation from 1993 to 2000, and funding for Head Start increased 68 percent above inflation during the same time. Finally, funding for the Dislocated Worker Assistance program increased 172 percent above inflation from 1993 to 2000. As in his second term as governor, Clinton found some of his greatest successes in the policy areas of jobs and education.

Support from Women and African Americans

The changes in the Clinton administration following the 1994 Republican revolution were similar to those of Bill Clinton's second term as governor in other ways as well. According to Maraniss, Clinton relied heavily on Betsy Wright and her strategy to reach out to women and minorities with "special letters for black supporters."[18] The support that Clinton received from women and minorities in the 1982 reelection bid was vital to his recapturing the governor's office as well as keeping that office until his bid for presidency. Much has been written on the gender gap in presidential voting in both 1992 and 1996 as Bill Clinton received the lion's share of support from women and minorities while Republican candidates George H. W. Bush and Bob Dole received significantly less. The voting patterns of women are particularly troubling for Republican candidates given that women now vote at rates higher than men and constitute about 52 percent of the population in the United States. In fact, the gender gap increased to 10 percent in 1992 and a historic high of 14 percent in 1996. Overall, Bill Clinton was able to successfully build and keep support from minorities and women, who were ballast for his strength both as governor and president.

In light of all the scandals surrounding women and the Clinton administration, how did he retain such loyalty among this voting block? According to Dorothy McBride Stetson, it was because of Clinton's willingness to support and appoint women to top governmental positions, his unwavering positions on abortion, child care, and social security, his moderate position on welfare reform, and his efforts to stop international trafficking in women.

Similarly, with respect to President Clinton's support among African Americans, Darlene Clark Hine argues that as president, "The Arkansas native amply rewarded, in substantive and symbolic ways, black Democrats for their unwavering political support and voting loyalty in the 1992 and 1996 campaigns." Further, according to Hine, Clinton was a successful practitioner of "the politics of symbolism, and this talent proved to be enormously appealing to some African Americans. During the eight years of his tenure, President Clinton successfully engaged in symbolism politics to reckon with America's legacy of race discrimination and racial violence. At pivotal junctures Clinton acknowledged and apologized for some of the government's most egregious miscarriages of justice and unscrupulous policies that had debased black citizens."

For example, Clinton apologized for the Tuskegee Syphilis experiment, rescinded the dishonorable discharge of black navy dock workers during World War II, supported affirmative action, and intervened in Haiti when there was, arguably, little foreign-policy advantage associated with such risks. Similarly, Stetson argues that Bill Clinton's appointment of Ruth Bader Ginsberg to the Supreme Court "had the same symbolic impact [for women] as Lyndon Johnson's appointment of Thurgood Marshall in the 1960s had for the Civil Rights Movement." Overall, both Hine and Stetson argue that President Clinton delivered on his promises to African Americans and women. This is not to say that many of his supporters were not tormented by the scandals, but it is to say, as Hine and Stetson suggest, that Clinton's supporters balanced the positives and the negatives.

Playing Defense against an Aggressive Media

President Clinton's earlier gubernatorial rival Frank White was very successful in using the media to unseat Governor Clinton in his first reelection campaign in 1980. But President Clinton would find the attack advertising he faced in his 1980 gubernatorial reelection bid mild in comparison to the scandal-hungry media he would face as president during the 1990s. Again, however, the defensive player Bill Clinton reacted to the changing environment and eventually withstood the storm.

In retrospect it seems clear that changing technology, primarily the proliferation of satellites and the Internet, fundamentally changed the manner and substance of the news that citizens received during the 1990s. Increasingly, newspapers, typified by the widely circulating *USA Today,* adopted promotional strategies and layouts similar to television news (for example, color pictures, brief stories, bullet points, less substantive sophistication) at the same time that management of newspapers and news magazines lost competitive share to new media outlets like cable television and partisan news sources. In fact, the niche marketing of partisan news over the Internet led many cable television stations to package their news to particular partisan audiences resulting in liberal news versus conservative news, abandoning the more traditional standards of objectivity and fairness in reporting. The proliferation of news outlets also changed the way the media covered elected officials and, eventually, changed how representatives and presidents attempt to lead the nation. As Ken Bode argues, "the Clinton presidency coincided with an explosion of new media sources which completely transformed the culture of news and information. Lyndon Johnson and Richard Nixon may have been pilloried by the press, but the media of their day was staid by comparison. There was no CNN, MSNBC, or Fox News Channel, and the supermarket tabloids had not yet discovered the fusion of politics and sex." Similarly, Randy Roberts argues that these changes in media and popular culture corresponded to a generational shift as baby boomers craved increasingly rapid-fire-shock-jock entertainment from not only the media but also from their leaders as well. He argues that, "It was, to say the least, a difficult time to be a politician. Such traditional political attributes as concern, consistency, and compassion—respect for various constituencies, willingness to stay the course, and faith in the system—struck many baby boomers and their children as 'BORR-RING.' But the time had come for them to take office, and Bill Clinton was their first president. . . . In a world so crowded with fifteen-minute famers that most had their moments trimmed to mere seconds, President William Jefferson Clinton had to compete for attention with O. J. Simpson, Madonna, Donald Trump, Michael Jackson, Mike Tyson, Mike Jordan, Princess Di and so many other flash-in-the-pan and accidental celebrities. In the celebrity sweepstakes being the president of the United States, the most powerful man in the world, was only important if he did something really cool."

Once it became obvious that the traditional news media had been replaced by programs like *Crossfire* and *Hardball,* where the audience appeal rests more on the decibel levels of the verbal combatants than actual substance, President Clinton worked defensively to circumvent the traditional news outlets. As Ken Bode notes, "Bill Clinton went through the entire 1996 presidential campaign without holding a single press conference." Instead, he took his message through alternative media avenues such as Oprah, Imus, Donahue, and Larry King. Of course, these outlets do provide important information to their viewers, but they are a fundamentally different news source from traditional news media, and the type and format of information that reviewers receive from these shows is also dramatically different. As one of President Clinton's pollsters claimed, "On the popular culture talk shows, you go directly to people, but more importantly it was a format in which you could talk about biography, you could talk about your life, which you didn't get the opportunity to do on *Face the Nation.*"

President Clinton and his administration found other ways to circumvent the attack media that proved quite effective as well. They gave priority to local reporters from outside the Beltway, they located strong supporters and allowed them greater access, flying them to Washington for privileged interviews with the president or vice president. They also permitted access to radio talk-show hosts who proved to be less acrimonious than the hypercompetitive national Washington news reporters. In the feeding frenzy of contemporary scandal-driven media presidents and presidential hopefuls are forced to find ways to get their messages out to the public through venues that are not packaged in gossip and where news sources are more likely to allow candidates and presidents to present their arguments without caustic attacks.[19] President Clinton has demonstrated that playing defensively with the news media is now a fundamental aspect of the contemporary executive branch.

Defensive International Player

President Clinton's defensive proclivities are not confined to American politics, culture, or media. In fact, in the area of foreign affairs we see this same pattern of initial idealism and policy initiatives that met with less than expected results, and the Clinton administration reacting, receiving advice from experts, reevaluating policy (or in Clinton's word, "experimenting"), ultimately changing course, and then often achieving substantive policy goals.

But in all fairness, perhaps the word "defensive" is a bit too strong in this context. There is, however, a case to be made in the run-up to the reelection bid in 1996 and throughout the impeachment-ridden second term that some foreign-policy initiatives were motivated by the desire to redirect public attention away from his domestic political troubles—for example, increasing pressure to end the war in Bosnia that resulted in the Dayton Accords, unsuccessful attempts to reanimate the Middle East peace process, and the response to Serbian actions in Kosovo. Not unlike that of other chief executives, Clinton's foreign policy is perhaps better characterized as "reactive," that is, based on the administration's response to events largely beyond its control. While Legvold's argument that the Clinton administration preferred to *think* in terms of "milieu goals," that is, to craft new institutions and/or multilateral procedures for coping with the new and admittedly poorly understood post–Cold War world— its *actions* fell short of these auspicious aspirations. In part the problem was rooted in the very nature of the foreign-policy team which was led by a secretary of state and national security advisor best described as highly competent technicians rather than strategic thinkers. And certainly Clinton himself possessed little of a strategic vision that would inform and give direction to the broader thrust of American foreign policy. To the extent that early shibboleths such as "assertive multilateralism" found concrete form in Bosnia, Kosovo, Somalia, and Haiti, they were implemented with little initial appreciation of the lowest-common-denominator limitations of multilateralism or the real-world military and political risks of such interventionism, however humanitarian its motivation.

On a less critical note, any commentary on Clinton's foreign policy must acknowledge the unique historical setting of his tenure in office. In one sense, the tasks facing any president at this turning point in history were analogous to those facing Clinton's two most prominent Democratic predecessors in the twentieth century, Woodrow Wilson and Franklin Delano Roosevelt. It is not an understatement to observe that all three held office at a time when a new world order was in the making. Both Wilson and Roosevelt (admittedly with varying degrees of success) boldly addressed that task by attempting to create new, if incomplete and imperfect, supranational entities, the League of Nations and the United Nations. For our purposes it matters little that America rejected the former and that, because of the Cold War, the latter's mission was substantially reinterpreted. What matters is that both Wilson and Roosevelt acted boldly, reasoning that the collapse of the old world order gave them a tabula rasa.

Clinton had no such blank slate. To his credit, he attempted partially to fill the void through the reinterpretation of existing institutional mechanisms, the acceptance of seemingly inevitable realities, and the assertion (if not the faithful implementation) of an operational code of "assertive multilateralism." On the first point—the reinterpretation of existing institutions—he took the lead in the redefinition and enlargement of NATO and its growing role in peacekeeping and nation building. On the second—the acceptance of seemingly inevitable realities—he offered only slight amendments to the creation of the North American Free Trade Area and the acknowledgment that the American economy was inexorably tied to an increasingly global economy (a point that American business interests urged on him at every turn). And on the final point—the operational code of "assertive multilateralism"—Clinton acted with the best of intentions, learning (and pragmatist that he was, accepting and internalizing) the limitations of such interventionism that inevitably flow from the complexities of peacekeeping and nation building and the difficulties of coordinating such multilateral action on the part of nations with different agendas and internal political realities.

What Clinton did not do also was important, and it may be one of the lasting achievements of the foreign policy of his administration at least in the sense that he did not commit American foreign policy to a false start in what now retrospectively seem to be the relatively calms days of the pre-9/11 world. Simply put, he did not invent a new enemy, real or imagined. Given the long-established American proclivity to identify its role in the world in relation to its enemies, whether geopolitical or ideological, it must have been tempting to consider inventing a new world order defined in black-and-white, good-guys-and-bad-guys terms.

To be sure, finding a convincingly threatening enemy in the 1990s would have been a difficult task, although some tried to redefine the fracture points in terms of the apocalyptic struggle of cultures or, more mundanely, in terms of increasingly powerful (and potentially protectionist) economic blocs. Yet the arguments never took root, and to his credit, Clinton never sorted out the world in such simplistic terms even at the most embattled moments of his administration.

Perhaps inevitably, nearly all presidential administrations quickly realize that their simplistic portrayal of international affairs as candidates quickly yields to complexity of the real world once they reach the Oval Office. The Clinton administration was no exception. During the 1992 election, Clinton focused his campaign on the economy, and foreign-policy priorities did not appear central to his messages. It was clear to careful observers that power shifts in the world economy, as well as ideological and nationalistic uprisings would make foreign policy an important priority during the 1990s. For example, the challenges of forging successful relationships with China became evident during the 1980s. Bill Clinton's predecessor, George H. W. Bush, was not particularly successful in his dealings with China, and the June 1989 demonstrations in Tiananmen Square, and their aftermath, proved the difficulty of forging successful coalitions with a recalcitrant Chinese government. Bush continually argued that the key to improved relations with China was "quiet diplomacy" rather than confrontation. Candidate Clinton, however, disagreed. He argued that ignoring China's human-rights violations was tantamount to American support of governmental repression. Initially Clinton kept his campaign promises and tied foreign policy with China, and particularly the granting of MNF, or most favored nation trading status, to China's record on human rights. He soon found, however, that business interests and the economic health of the entire United States would be severely limited without this giant trading partner. President Clinton ultimately renewed MNF status and subsequently decoupled trading status and human-rights violations. As June Dreyer notes, the transformation of Clinton's foreign-policy emphases on the link between MNF and human rights to breaking the connection took "barely a year." Following the 1994 congressional elections and the Republican revolution, Clinton's policy on China, as in other policy areas, became more moderate and pragmatic, and by Clinton's second term the administration's positions on China became "don't rock the boat; this may be the best we can do."

President Clinton's initial dealings with Russia also proved difficult, but his flexibility and willingness to "experiment" led to a more moderate and pragmatic position in relation to the former Cold War enemy. Clinton provided substantial symbolic and financial support to President Yeltsin and his reform efforts. The corruption and cronyism that pervaded Russian politics and business soon led President Clinton to react defensively and forge a more moderate position. As Robert Legvold summarizes, "Eight years and two administrations is not a long time, but the distance between the simple, high hopes of Clinton and his people at the start of his first administration and their weariness and misgivings at the end of his second is immense." Clinton's initial hope for and commitment to Russian reform, and the importance of a reformed Russia to America's foreign-policy interests, evolved into a greater degree of skepticism, or what Legvold calls a "strategic" and "mixed relationship" containing a great deal of serious contention. Following the Russian economic downturn in the summer of 1998, Clinton's policy morphed again into a final phase of "agnosticism" and resignation that Russia would not reach the economic and political reforms for which the administration had initially hoped.

As in many other areas of policy, both domestic and foreign, President Clinton's willingness to adjust policy to achieve overall objectives does not mean that Clinton was without policy success. In fact, as Legvold concludes, "Ultimately, historians are likely to write well of Clinton for rallying to the cause of reform in Russia and the other post-Soviet states. . . . In the end [the administration's shortcomings] do not outweigh the sheer significance of enlisting in the effort. . . . Had the United States stood back and watched, or placed its wagers timidly, or haggled over every detail before acting, the fault would have been far greater. For all the rockiness of the process, Russia managed in a decade of independence to destroy the old system, close the door to even a partial return to the past, preserve stability amid the change, and, at the turn of the new century, produce a leadership ready to take 'ownership' of reform . . . the West had more than a small hand in this, and within the West the Clinton administration played a leadership role."

The Concluding Paradox: The Economy—No, on Second Thought, the World—Stupid

Whatever other conclusions one might draw about the eight-year tenure of William Jefferson Clinton, it is apparent that he initially intended to leave his mark primarily in the realm of domestic politics and policy reform. The admonition to focus on "the economy, stupid," was more than just an insightful election-year strategy. It also said something important about what the Clintons (the plural is intentional) and the circle of policy wonks around them thought to be the most important priorities of the day. In part because of his own limited foreign-policy experience as the governor of a small state and in part because the much-touted end of the Cold War promised the dual benefits of an undefined and relatively unthreatening world and a chimerical "peace dividend," Clinton came to the White House committed to attaching the highest priority to domestic policy choices. Even when he was forced to moderate his course because of opposition—a response, much noted in this volume, that characterized his earlier career in Arkansas—he and those closest to him were drawn to modern-day versions of issues that for decades had been close to the heart of the Democratic agenda. Given his "druthers"—a good southern phrase—Clinton would have gone into history as the president who led America along a course of liberal-to-moderate reforms in economic and social welfare policy.

In that sense, at least, Clinton's election hardly qualified as one of those historic "realignments"—that is, an election that both reshapes partisan identities and party alignments and shifts the policy agenda substantially to the right or left. To be sure, Clinton was the first two-term Democrat since FDR, and Republican victories at the legislative level in 1994 seemingly foreshadowed sweeping changes, although these two realities in many ways cancelled each other or, at the least, led to a more tempered relationship between the opposite ends of Pennsylvania Avenue. But neither of these developments came close to realigning the nature of American domestic politics.

Realignments, however, come in many forms. If the terrain of American domestic politics had shifted, albeit at less than tectonic dimensions, the world outside had witnessed the realigment of continents. The list enumerated more than just the end of the Cold War, the breakup of the Soviet empire and, eventually, the Soviet Union itself. It also included the creation of new trading blocs such as NAFTA, a serious and eventually successful acceleration of efforts for European unity, and the emergence of China as a major player on the world stage. It was in this venue that Clinton, to no fault of his own, was initially less at ease. A thorough internationalist, as befitted his association with Senator Fulbright, he nonetheless entered this milieu with a strategy—multilateralism—rather than a vision. The notion of a "new world order" was still very much a blank slate, as were the modalities of America's commitment to creating it. To be sure, we were a "hegemon," at least in the nominal sense that we were the single most powerful nation in terms of military and economic strength. But how or where we would wield that power was still open to question. To the extent that Clinton actually used that power—"used" in the literal sense that the president committed U.S. forces to action beyond American borders—he did so for reasons philosophically consistent with his domestic agenda: humanitarian and nation-building efforts in Somalia and Haiti, to the resolution of a seemingly endless internecine war in Bosnia through the Dayton Accords, and to the defense of an oppressed minority in Kosovo. Even his diplomatic efforts to support fledgling democracies in Eastern Europe and the former Soviet Union put him on the side of the angels, even slightly tarnished ones like Boris Yeltsin. And with the exception of Somalia, where "mission creep" led to overexten-sion and eventual overexposure, Clinton's policies enjoyed a remarkable degree of success. Far more success, it can be argued, than his domestic political agenda, especially since Republican victories from 1994 onward forced him into a defensive, rear-guard action to blunt the sharper edges of the Contract with America.

Therein lies the essential paradox of the Clinton administration. At least a prima facie case can be made that when the sound and fury die down and the scandals are placed into proper perspective (but not for-gotten), the Clinton presidency will be remembered more for its largely successful efforts to cope with the new and very confusing realities of the post–Cold War world than for its domestic policies. Much of this stems from the fact that the world beyond U.S borders was blank slate, a tabula rasa, at least in terms of the role that America would play. In one sense at least, Clinton's successor would have no difficulty finding an enemy; September 11, 2001, would sort out the world for George W. Bush, defin-ing enemies, friends, and missions. But for Clinton, no clear delineation of friends and enemies, no list of easy victories or quagmires were pre-sent. Largely checkmated in his efforts at domestic reform and fighting against the right-wing tide of American politics, the president was freer to indulge himself in foreign-policy initiatives that were at least philo-sophically in tune with the abandoned domestic agenda. The battlefield on which the struggle with the new Republican majority would be fought was clearly mapped and cluttered with mine fields. In contrast, the map of the world was, for the first time since the beginning of the Cold War, remarkably uncluttered, offering a blank slate crying out for redefinition. And for a president eager to make his mark on history, a blank slate was a good thing.

Conclusions

As we draft the final pages of this volume, we are quickly approaching the 2004 presidential election. President George W. Bush has served four years in the White House and continues to enjoy popular support, although a slow economy and ambiguous accomplishments in the war on terror and in Iraq suggest that the 2004 presidential race may be more competitive than initially predicted. Regardless, the Clinton presidency, and the politics of the 1990s more generally, continue to be revealed through the political debates that continue long after Clinton left office.

In retrospect it seems clear that President Clinton's efforts to reach a new generation of Americans, beginning in the 1992 presidential campaign, would dramatically agitate a large segment of the population interested in preserving a more traditional presidency. Bill Clinton is a product of the rock 'n' roll generation, forged in the political struggles of civil rights, the sexual revolution, and experimentation with drugs. While the current president has his own share of youthful indiscretions, his presidency symbolizes a commitment to a much different standard; he demands proper attire for meetings in the Oval Office, punctuality, reverent views of the executive office, and a patriotic paradigm of citizenship. President Bush maintains a tight working schedule, relies heavily on his appointed cabinet members and rarely works into the late hours of the night. The differences in the personal characteristics of forty-second and forty-third presidents of the United States are as dramatic as they are revealing of the two men who occupied the White House during the transition into the new century.

Once the walls of the Cold War finally crumbled and the baby boomers elected a president from their own generation, they ushered in a president quite different from previous executives. President Clinton was a blend of southern tradition, Hollywood, and a commitment to compromise. He refused to define the world in terms of good and evil. He would, in fact, see both in most situations and find both policy and people characterized by shades of gray rather than strict categories. These qualities, in retrospect, would virtually guarantee that while candidate Bill Clinton would attract support from across voting populations, President Clinton would be a lighting rod for the attacks of those fundamentally opposed to perceived slippery changes in issues and policies or for the apparently irreverent way that President Clinton approached American traditions and symbols. Even if President Clinton would ultimately receive the most intense opposition from conservatives, governing from the middle left him open for attacks from both the ideological left and right.

Challenging traditional American mores as basic as the proper role of the First Lady, President Clinton's promise of getting two-for one (meaning that Hillary Rodham Clinton would play a larger role in forging American policy than previous First Ladies) ignited backlash not unlike the ire raised in Arkansas when Governor Clinton's wife spoke of herself as Hillary Rodham rather than Mrs. Clinton. Further, President Clinton's close association with Hollywood resulted in a clash of traditional American values that evoked intense emotional reactions even from residents in Clinton's home state. It is telling that the governing style of President George W. Bush is nearly the opposite of the style and substance of the Clinton presidency. The intensity and closeness of the 2000 presidential election serves as a wonderful example of America's struggle with these competing visions, not only of policy positions and foreign priorities but also of governing approach and style—the important symbolic meanings of the presidency. As cultural values in the United States are so clearly being debated and as the population continues to age, the intensity of these dialogues will likely grow more intense. What is less clear, however, is the path that America will ultimately choose. The interpretation and conclusions regarding the Clinton administration, however, will be explicitly or implicitly an important part of these discussions.

We believe it is clear, as the eclectic approaches and contributions to this volume attest, that the Clinton administration did forge policy successes in several areas that were central to President Clinton's objectives, particularly in regard to employment and the economy. In the area of domestic politics, President Clinton is most likely to be applauded for the economic expansion that occurred during the 1990s. What will continue to be debated is the extent to which he was directly responsible. Regardless, it is clear that, at minimum, President Clinton, as well as the Republican-controlled Congress, provided a sufficiently stable environment for business to expand and for the information revolution to dramatically and irrevocably alter government, business, and life in the United States and the world. In addition, President Clinton will be remembered for presiding over substantial welfare reform and the dramatic declines in both the number of people living in poverty and the number of families receiving welfare during the 1990s.

Further, the enormous support that President Clinton received from women and minorities throughout the 1990s, even during the Lewinsky scandal and impeachment process, demonstrates clearly the support of these growing groups of American voters. Ultimately the support that President Clinton received from women and African American voters during the 1996 presidential election provided the justification for a change in strategy within the Republican Party. Throughout the entire 2000 presidential election, the Republican Party and George W. Bush consistently and adamantly emphasized "compassionate conservatism" and a new image of the GOP.

In the foreign-policy arena, the events of 9/11 and the rise of nationalistic groups willing to use terrorism to achieve objectives make the foreign-policy problems of the 1990s appear sedate in comparison. Regardless, President Clinton was the first president to take office following the collapse of the Soviet Union and the first leader to face the difficulties associated with the collapse of the Cold War paradigm. President Clinton will be applauded for his efforts to have facilitated the Russian transition to democracy and his attempts to improve, with varying degrees of success, human rights and lives around the world.

Of course, the Clinton Administration will also be remembered, and chastised, for eight years of leadership rife with scandal and controversy, ranging from extramarital affairs, questionable campaign fundraising practices, and executive pardons. Whether history will ultimately conclude that President Clinton's policy successes outweigh the controversies associated with the administration remains something we are yet unable to judge. What is clear from the contributors of this volume, however, is that president Clinton governed during a unique time in American history. There was growing conservatism across the United States during the 1980s and 1990s that resulted in the Republican takeover of both houses of Congress during the 1994 midterm elections. While the popularity of this conservative movement is widespread, the Democratic voting habits of women and the stronghold of the Democratic Party in the growing urban areas of the country remain important exceptions. The future role of Latino voters and the ability of the Republican Party to reach women and African American voters will be deciding factors in whether or not the conservative transformation of the country continues.

About the Authors

Ken Bode

Ken Bode has worked in two venues. In academics he received his Ph.D. from the University of North Carolina and taught at Michigan State University, SUNY-Binghamton. and DePauw University. He was dean of the Medill School of Journalism and the Knight Professor of Broadcast Journalism at Northwestern University.

In journalism, he was politics editor of *The New Republic* magazine, national political correspondent for NBC News, a senior political analyst and documentarian at CNN, and moderator of *Washington Week in Review* on PBS.

Presently Bode is the Pulliam Professor of Journalism at DePauw University and a contributing columnist for the *Indianapolis Star.*

David Brady

David Brady received his Ph.D. from the University of Iowa. He is the senior fellow and associate director for research at the Hoover Institution at Stanford University, a professor of political science and ethics in the Stanford Graduate School of Business, and a professor of political science at Stanford University, as well as former associate dean of Stanford University (1997–2001).

He is the author of several publications, including *Congressional Voting in a Partisan Era; Critical Elections in the U.S. House of Representatives; Revolving Gridlock: Politics and Policy from Carter to Clinton;* and *The 1996 House Elections: Reaffirming the Conservative Trend* as well as co-author of *Change and Continuity in House Elections* and *How the Republicans Captured the House: An Assessment of the 1994 Midterm Elections.* He has also had contributions appear in *The American Political Science Review.*

His honors include the 1995 and 2000 Congressional Quarterly Prize for Best Paper on Legislative Topic, the 1989 American Political Association Richard F. Fenno Award for Best Book on Legislative Topic, the 1992 Stanford University Dinkelspiel Award for Excellence in Undergraduate Teaching, the 1993 Stanford University Phi Beta Kappa Award for Best Teacher, and the Rice University George Brown Award for Superior Teaching.

His research interests lie in the U.S. Congress, congressional decision-making, U.S. election results, and the history of political parties in the United States.

Dan T. Carter

Dan Carter received his Ph.D. from the University of North Carolina-Chapel Hill. He is the Education Foundation Professor of History at the University of South Carolina. He won an Emmy and the 2000 Writers Guild of America Best Documentary of the Year for the documentary film *George Wallace: Setting the Woods on Fire* and was nominated for an Academy Award for *Scottsboro: A Tragedy of the American South*. His publications include *The Politics of Rage* and *From George Wallace to Newt Gingrich: Race in the Conservative Counterrevolution*.

His interests lie in southern and twentieth-century U.S. history.

June Teufel Dreyer

June Teufel Dreyer received her Ph.D. from Harvard University. She is the chair of the Political Science Department at the University of Miami as well as director of the university's Honor's Program. She has served as chief Far East specialist for the Library of Congress, as the Asia advisor to the Chief of Naval Operations, and as commissioner of the United States–China Economic and Security Review Commission. She has authored several works, including *China's Forty Millions: Military Nationalities and National Integration in the People's Republic of China* and *China's Political System: Modernization and Tradition*.

Her research interests lie in the areas of Chinese military, cross-strait relations, Asian-Pacific regional relations, and ethnic minorities.

Betty Glad

Betty Glad received her Ph.D. from the University of Chicago. She is the chair of the Psycho-Politics Research Group of the International Political

Science Association, the former president of the International Society for Political Psychology (ISPP), former vice president and treasurer of the American Political Science Association (APSA), chair of the Presidency Research Group of the ASPA, and a professor of political science at University of South Carolina. She was awarded the 1997 ISPP Harold Lasswell Award for Distinguished Scientific Contribution to the Field of Political Psychology. She has authored several works, including *Jimmy Carter: In Search of the Great White House; Key Pittman: The Tragedy of a Senate Insider; Charles Evan Hughes and the Illusions of Innocence: A Study in American Diplomacy;* and *The Psychological Dimensions of War.*

Her research interests lie in the study of political leadership from a psychological perspective.

D. Sunshine Hillygus

Sunshine Hillygus received her Ph.D. from Stanford University. She is an assistant professor of government at Harvard University. She has served on the executive committee of the Center for American Political Studies and the 2003–04 Harvard University Graduate Admissions Council as well as serving as the 2000–01 president of the Political Science Graduate Student Association, and publication manager for *IT & Society*. Her works can be seen in *The Journal of Politics, American Journal of Political Science, IT & Society, The Internet and Everyday Life,* and *Making Good Citizens: Education and Civil Society.* Her honors include the Harvard University Milton Fund Grant, the 2002–2003 Heinz Eulau Political Behavior Fellowship, the 2002 Summer Political Methodology Meeting Best Graduate Student Poster Award, the 1997 Arkansas Political Science Association Best Student Paper Award, and the 1997–98 Sprint/National Conference of State Legislatures Graduate Fellowship.

Her research interests lie in American political behavior, campaigns and elections, political organizations, and information technology and society.

Darlene Clark Hine

Darlene Clark Hine received her Ph.D. from Kent State University. She is the former president of the Southern Historical Association, former president of the Organization of American Historians (OAH), former president of Southern Organization of Women Historians, and she is the Board of Trustees Professor of Afro-American Studies and History at Northwestern University.

She has authored several works, including *Black Victory: The Rise and Fall of the White Primary in Texas,* New Edition; *Speak Truth to Power: Black Professional Class in United States History; Hine Sight: Black Women and the Re-Construction of American History; Black Women in White: Racial Conflict and Cooperation in the Nursing Profession, 1890–1950; When the Truth Is Told: A History of Black Women's Culture and Community in Indiana, 1875–1950;* and *Black Victory: The Rise and Fall of the White Primary.* She also co-authored *African Americans: A Concise History,* Combined Volume; *The African American Odyssey,* Second Edition; and *A Shining Thread of Hope: The History of Black Women in America;* as well as editing *Black Women in the United States, 1619–1989; The State of Afro-American History, Past, Present, and Future;* and *Black Women in the Nursing Profession: An Anthology of Historical Sources.* She also has made contributions to *Journal of American History; The Negro Educational Review; Revisions; Peace and Change; Journal of Women's History; The Black Scholar; The Journal of Southern History; History News; Journal of Negro History; Southwest Review; The Southwestern Historical Quarterly; Negro History Bulletin; Teaching History, Souls: A Critical Journal of Black Politics, Culture, and Society; Signs; The History Teacher; Indiana Journal of Military History;* and *History News.*

Her research interests lie in African American history and black women in the nursing profession and in the Middle West.

Donald R. Kelley

Donald Kelley received his Ph.D. from Indiana University. He is the director of the Fulbright Institute of International Relations and a professor of comparative Politics at the University of Arkansas. He is the author of *Politics in Russia and the Successor States; Soviet Politics from Brezhnev to Gorbachev; The Politics of Developed Socialism: The Soviet Union as a Post-Industrial State;* and *The Solzhenistyn-Sakharov Dialogue: Politics, Society, and the Future.* He has also co-authored *The Economic Superpowers and the Environment: The United States, the Soviet Union, and Japan.* In addition, he has edited several works, including *A Decade of Post-Communism; After Communism: Perspectives on Democracy; Soviet Politics in the Brezhnev Era;* and *The Energy Crisis and the Environment: An International Perspective;* as well as co-editing *The Sons of Sergei: Khrushchev and Gorbachev as Reformers; Perestroika Era Politics: The New Soviet Era Legislature and Gorbachev's Political Reforms;* and *Old Myths and New Realities in United States-Soviet Relations.* He also has contributions appearing in *Journal of Politics,*

American Political Science Review, Polity, Soviet Studies, and *American Behavioral Scientist.*

His fields of interests lie in Russian politics and the former Soviet states.

Robert Levgold

Robert Levgold received his Ph.D. from the Fletcher School of Law and Diplomacy. He is an executive member and former director of the Harriman Institute of Columbia University (1986–1992), former director of Soviet Studies at the Council of Foreign Relations (1978–1984), and a professor of political science at Columbia University. He also serves as a trustee of the Carnegie Endowment for International Peace, a member of the National Bureau of Asian and Soviet Research, the Center for Defense and Disarmament Studies, the Committee on International Security Studies of the American Academy of Arts and Sciences, the International Forum of the U.S.-Russian Business Council, the Davis Center for Russian Studies at Harvard University, the Watson Institute for International Studies at Brown University, and the Foundation for International Peace and Democracy.

He has authored several works, including *Thinking Strategically: The Major Powers, Kazakhstan and the Central Asian Nexus,* as well as co-authoring *Swords and Sustenance: The Economics of National Security in Belarus and Ukraine; Belarus at the Crossroads; Russia and the West: The 21st Century Security Environment;* and *Russian Security and Euro-Atlantic Region.* He has also co-edited *After the Soviet Union: From Empire to Nations.* He has made contributions to such journals as *The National Interest, Foreign Affairs,* and the book *A Century's Journey.*

His research interests lie in the foreign policies of Russia, Ukraine, and the other new states of the former Soviet Union, U.S. relations with the post-Soviet states, and the impact of the post-Soviet region on international politics of Asia and Europe.

Randy W. Roberts

Randy Roberts received his Ph.D. from Louisiana State University. He is a professor of history at Purdue University. He authored numerous books including *Papa Jack: Jack Johnson and the Era of White Hopes; Jack Dempsey: The Manassa Mauler;* and *Pittsburgh Sports: Stories from the Steel City;* as well as co-authoring *My Lai: A Brief History of Documents; Charles A.*

Lindbergh: The Power and Peril of Celebrity; The Steelers Reader; A Line in the Sand: The Alamo in Blood and Memory; "But They Can't Beat Us:" Oscar Robertson and the Crispus Attucks Tigers; John Wayne America; Heavy Justice: The State of Indiana v. Michael G. Tyson; Where the Domino Fell: America in Vietnam, 1945–1990; Winning Is the Only Thing: Sports in America since 1945, and numerous texts and readers.

His research interests lie in the areas of U.S. history, U.S. sports history, and the history of popular culture.

Todd G. Shields

Todd Shields received his Ph.D. from the University of Kentucky. He is the director of the Diane D. Blair Center of Southern Politics and Society, assistant director of the Fulbright Institute of International Relations, chair of the Political Science Department, and associate professor of political science at the University of Arkansas. He has authored *Money Matters: Campaign Finance Reform and Congressional Elections,* as well as many contributions to scholarly journals, including *The Communications Review, Research in Social Science and Disability, American Politics Quarterly, Journal of Disability Policy Studies, Journal of Rehabilitation,* and *Publius.*

His fields of interest lie in political behavior, methodology, and political psychology.

Dorothy McBride Stetson

Dorothy McBride Stetson received her Ph.D. from Vanderbilt University. She is the co-convener if the Research Network on Gender Politics and the State (RNGS), director of the USA Team, director of the Abortion Issue Network, and a professor of political science at Florida Atlantic University and the founder of the university's women's studies program.

She has authored several works, including *A Woman's Issue: The Politics of Family Reform in England: Women's Rights in France, Women's Rights in the U.S.A.: Policy Conflict and Gender Roles; Comparative State Feminism: Abortion Politics: Public Policy in Cross National Perspective:* as well as editing *Abortion Politics: Women's Movements and the Democratic State: A Comparative Study of State Feminism.*

Her research interests lie in comparative studies of women and public policy.

Jeannie M. Whayne

Jeannie Whayne received her Ph.D. from the University of California-San Diego. She is the chair of the history department, professor of history at the University of Arkansas, director of the Arkansas Center for Oral and Visual History, and editor of *The Arkansas Historical Quarterly*. She has authored *A New Plantation South: Land, Labor, and Federal Favor in the Twentieth Century Arkansas;* as well as editing *Cultural Encounters in the Early South: Indians and Europeans in Arkansas* and *Shadows Over Sunnyside: Evolution of a Plantation Arkansas, 1830–1945* and co-editing *The Governors of Arkansas* and *The Arkansas Delta: Land of Paradox*. She co-authored *Arkansas: A Narrative History*. She has contributions appearing in *Agriculture History, Locus, Forest and Conservation History,* and *Mississippi Historical Quarterly*. Her honors include the 1995–96 Arkansiana Award for *New Plantation South,* the 2001-02 Arkansiana Award for *Arkansas: A Narrative History,* two Certificates of Commendation from the American Association of State and Local History, the 1993 Virginia C. Ledbetter Prize for Best Book in Arkansas Studies, and the 1996 Outstanding Mentor from the University of Arkansas.

Her areas of interest lie in the social and economic history of Arkansas and the South.

Randall B. Woods

Randall Woods received his Ph.D. from the University of Texas. He is a John A. Cooper Sr. Distinguished Professor of Diplomacy in the Fulbright Institute of International Relations at the University of Arkansas. He has authored several works, including *Fulbright: A Biography; The Dawning of the Cold War: America's Quest for Order, 1945–1950; A Changing of the Guard: Anglo-American Relations, 1941–1946;* and *A Black Odyssey: John Lewis Waller and the Promise of American Life*. His honors include receiving the 1994 University of Arkansas Alumni Distinguished Faculty Award for Teaching and Research, the 1996 Robert H. Ferrel Prize for Best Book on Foreign Relations, the 1996 Virginia Ledbetter Prize for Best Book in Arkansas Studies, and nominated for the Pulitzer Prize and National Book Award, all for *Fulbright: A Biography*.

His research interests lie in Afro-American history, United States diplomatic history, and the United States and Vietnam.

Notes

Introduction by Todd G. Shields, Jeannie M. Whayne, and Donald R. Kelley

    1. Arthur M. Schlesinger, "Historians Rate the U.S. Presidents," *Life*, November 1, 1948, 65, 68, 73; and Arthur M. Schlesinger, "Our Presidents: A Rating by 73 Historians," *The New York Times Magazine*, July 29, 1962, 12, 40, 43.

    2. Thomas A. Bailey, *Presidential Greatness* (New York: Appleton-Century, 1966); Clinton L. Rossiter, *The American Presidency* (New York: Harcourt Brace, 1956); Eric Sokolsky, *Our Seven Great Presidents* (New York: Exposition Press, 1964); and Gary M. Marranell, "The Evaluation of Presidents: An Extension of Schlesinger Polls," *The Journal of American History* 57, no. 1 (June 1970): 104.

    3. Dean Keith Simonton, *Why Presidents Succeed: A Political Psychology of Leadership* (New Haven: Yale University Press, 1987).

Chapter One: Bill Clinton: The Character Issue Revisited by Betty Glad

    1. Stephen Carter, *Integrity* (New York: Harper Collins Publishers, 1996), 8–12.

    2. Reinhold Niebuhr, *Moral Man and Immoral Society* (New York: Charles Scribner's Sons, 1932), xi–22.

    3. The week in which he emphasized temperance, for example, he would leave to "chance" his other failings. Displaying the chart for the week in which he emphasized temperance, showing no failings on that virtue, he marked a scattering of failures on five other items. We never see what he did with the virtue of chastity. Ben Franklin, *Writings* (New York: The Library of America, 1987), 1385–87.

    4. For Cleveland, see Rexford G. Tugwell, *Grover Cleveland* (London: Macmillan), 41–42; and Richard E. Welch, *The Presidencies of Grover Cleveland* (Lawrence, Kans.: University Press of Kansas), 39.

    5. For the correlation of Machiavellianism and legislative success see Dean Keith Simonton, "Presidential Personality: Biographical Use of the Gough Adjective Check List," *Journal of Personality and Social Psychology* 51, no. 1 (1986): 153.

6. For Washington, see John Alden, *George Washington* (Baton Rouge: Louisiana State University Press, 1984), 73–80; and John Ferling, *The First of Men* (Knoxville: University of Tennessee Press, 1988), 443. For Franklin, see Thomas Fleming, *The Man who Dared the Lightning* (New York: Morrow, 1971), 22, 405, 408 and Claude Ann Lopez and Eugenia W. Herbert, *The Private Franklin* (New York: Norton, 1975), 21, 84, 86. For Hamilton, see Marie B. Hecht, *Odd Destiny: The Life of Alexander Hamilton* (New York: Macmillan, 1982), 325–32, 340; and Jacob E. Cooke, *Alexander Hamilton* (New York: Charles Scribner's Sons, 1982), 177–83. For Jefferson see Elizabeth Marvick, "Jefferson's Personality and His Politics," *The Psychohistory Review* 25, no. 2 (Winter 1997): 127–63. For a careful weighing of Jefferson's purported affair with Sally Hemmings, a light-skinned slave on his plantation, see Annette Gordon-Reed, *Thomas Jefferson and Sally Hemmings, An American Controversy* (Charlottesville, Va.: University Press of Virginia, 1997).

7. David Herbert Donald, *Lincoln* (New York: Simon and Schuster, 1995), 373–80.

8. Donald, *Lincoln*, 380.

9. As the October 27 transcripts of an ExComm. meeting show, Kennedy was the one at that meeting who put himself in the shoes of the Soviet leader, Khrushchev. See James Blight, Joseph Nye, and D. A. Welch, "The Cuban Missile Crisis Revisited," *Foreign Affairs* 66, no. 1(Fall 1987): 170–188.

10. Betty Glad and Daniel J. Crabtree, "The National Security Advisor as Policy Maker: How Brzezinski Led the President and Outmaneuvered Others during Normalization of Relations with China," (paper at APSA Conference, Boston, 2002.)

11. For the Paine quote, see William A. Degregorio, *The Complete Book of U.S. Presidents* (Fort Lee, NJ: Barricade Books, Inc.,1993), 15. See also John Alden, *George Washington* (Baton Rouge: Louisiana State University Press, 1984), 73–80.

12. Elizabeth Marvick, "Jefferson's Personality and His Politics," *The Psychohistory Review* 25, no. 2 (Winter 1997): 127–63.

13. Donald, *Lincoln*, 15.

14. Betty Glad, *Jimmy Carter: In Search of the Great White House* (New York: Norton, 1980), 304–11.

15. Fred I. Greenstein, *The Hidden-Hand Presidency: Eisenhower as Leader* (New York: Basic Books, 1982).

16. Garry Wills, "The Clinton Principle," *The New York Times Magazine,* January 19, 1997, 31.

17. Interview of William Leuchtenburg, "What Makes or Breaks a President," *Charlotte Observer,* October 6, 1996.

18. See Paul Quirk and William Cunion, "Clinton's Domestic Policy: The Lessons of a New Democrat," in Colin Campbell and Bert A. Rockman eds., *The Clinton Legacy* (New York: Chatham House Publishers, 2000), 200-25.

19. The package included a five-year plan to reduce the deficit by over $700 billion. Clinton criticized the GOP's proposal of reducing the budget without increasing taxes, which he called "nothing but a shield to keep the wealthiest Americans from paying their fair share" and "a real disservice to this country." See *Facts on File,* July 1, 1993, 485.

20. *Facts on File,* February 4, 1993, 62.
21. Bob Woodward, *The Agenda: Inside the Clinton White House* (New York: Simon and Schuster, 1994).
22. Woodward, *Agenda,* 282–309.
23. Woodward, *Agenda,* 272–81. As Secretary of the Treasury Rubin said in the midst of the negotiation over the budget plan, "the well to do" are "running the economy and they make the decisions about the economy. And so, if you attack them, you wind up hurting the economy and wind up hurting the president." See 239.
24. The Democratic National Committee, which was supposed to coordinate a coalition of labor unions, consumer groups, and senior citizens never got its act together. (They even had to cancel a Nation Health Care Awareness Day scheduled for September 14 for lack of planning.)
25. Dana Priest and Michael Weisskopf, "Death From a Thousand Cuts," *Washington Post National Weekly Edition,* October 17–23, 1994.
26. Wills, "The Clinton Principle," 34.
27. Bill Nichols, "NAFTA Vote Casts a Long Political Shadow," *USA Today,* November 17, 1993.
28. Ann Devroy, "Clinton Administration to Step Up NAFTA Campaign Effort," *Washington Post,* October 2, 1993.
29. Jessica Lee, "Dem's Opposition Leaders Nursing 'Bumps and Bruises,'" *USA Today,* November 19, 1993.
30. Devroy, "Clinton Administration to Step Up." In a compromise with some Democrats led by Senator Max Baucus, Clinton said he would consider reinstating the "Super 301" section of U.S. trade law. This section lists "countries with the most serious barriers to U.S. trade and sets down a timetable for dealing with these barriers." See also Devroy and Peter Behr "Sugar Producing States Targeted by Clinton for NAFTA Votes," *Washington Post,* November 3, 1993.
31. Devroy, "Clinton Administration to Step Up."
32. Kenneth Cooper, "House Approves U.S.-Canada-Mexico Trade Pact on 234 to 200 Vote, Giving Clinton Big Victory," *Washington Post,* November 18, 1993.
33. Marjorie Connelly, "The 1994 Elections," *New York Times,* November 13, 1994.
34. Eric Pianin and John F. Harris, "Clinton, Congress Reach '96 Budget Agreement" *Washington Post,* April 25, 1996.
35. *Facts on File,* August 29, 1996, 622.
36. The bill would make available block grants to states, introduce nationwide work requirements for welfare recipients, and place time limits on eligibility for welfare assistance. To secure support, a few concessions were made to Clinton's concerns. In a major victory for the Clinton administration, the final bill would provide $14 billion over the next six years for childcare services to families on welfare. Also the administration succeeded in convincing House and Senate negotiators to include a provision that would guarantee all qualified poor people continued access to healthcare through the Medicaid program.

37. See *Facts on File*, August 29, 1996, 622. The welfare bill did not guarantee state-assisted workfare, which had provided a safety valve in his earlier proposal for welfare reform, providing backup for those who might be willing to work but be unable to find a job.

38. Dan Balz, "Clinton Wins by Wide Margin," *Washington Post*, November 6, 1996.

39. The Mexican national oil company would inform its buyers to deposit a certain portion of their payment into a Federal Reserve Bank fund as collateral for the loans. Wall Street lenders would be repaid on $30 million in short-term loans that would come due in the following year.

40. See Kevin Merida, "Hill Critics Assail Clinton Initiative to Bolster Mexico's Economy," *Washington Post*, February 2, 1995; and Ann Devroy and Clay Chandler, "Clinton Bypasses Congress, Provides Loans to Mexico," *Washington Post*, February 1, 1995.

41. Merida, "Hill Critics Assail Clinton."

42. It is true that one of his first moves—an order in June 1993 that missiles be fired on Iraqi intelligence headquarters—was supported by two-thirds of the American public. But that strike had been in retaliation for the Iraqis' involvement in a plot to assassinate former president George Bush.

43. Patrick Bogan, "Warlord's Forces Kill 12 US Soldiers in Somalia," *Herald* (Glasgow), October 5, 1993.

44. Prior to the skirmish the House had voted 406 to 26 to request that the president clarify and explicitly outline U.S. goals in the mission. See Clifford Krauss, "House Urges Clinton to Limit American Role in Somalia Conflict," *New York Times*, September 28, 1993.

45. Bob Dole tried to introduce an amendment putting conditions on the dispatch of troops to Haiti, and Sam Nunn warned that Haiti was not a "vital" American interest. See Taylor Branch, "Clinton without Apologies" *Esquire*, September 1996, 126.

46. Douglas Jehl, "Showdown with Haiti: Overview," *New York Times*, September 17, 1994.

47. See also Colin L. Powell and Joseph E. Persico, *My American Journey* (New York: Random House, 1995), 598–602.

48. George Stephanopoulos, *All Too Human* (Thorndike, Maine: Thorndike Press, 1999), pp.538–41.

49. Richard Morris, *Behind the Oval Office: Winning the Presidency in the 1990's* (New York: Random House, 1997), 21.

50. Helen Dewar and Kevin Merida, "Opposition to Invasion Appear Unswayed by Address," *Washington Post*, September 16, 1994. In July 1994 the UN Security Council signed a resolution that authorized the use of any necessary means (including force) to remove the military dictators from power and restore the democratically elected leader Aristide.

51. Branch, "Clinton without Apologies," 110.

52. Davis Rosenbaum, "Senate Praises Clinton on Haiti but Urges U.S. Withdrawal Soon," *New York Times*, September 22, 1994.

53. Robert Squier, quoted in R. W. Apple, "Clinton's Gain: The Big Stick Speaks," *New York Times*, October 12, 1994.

54. Morris, *Behind the Oval Office*, 20. Clinton promised to keep some U.S. troops in Haiti until sixteen months after Aristide's return (which would be until the inauguration of Aristide's successor). See Bradley Graham, "U.S. Pessimistic About Democracy in Haiti," *Washington Post*, October 9, 1994.

55. Norman Kempster, "Clinton Vetoes Removal of Bosnia Arms Embargoes," *Chicago-Sun Times*, August, 13, 1995.

56. Juan Walt, "Clinton Strikes at Terrorism," *USA Today*, January 25, 1995.

57. Gary Young and David Gough, "FBI Studies Video Footage as Blasts Toll Hits 186," *Guardian* (London), August 10, 1998.

58. Ann Devroy, "Clinton's Open House Quite Full: Thousands Accept Invitation," *Washington Post*, January 23, 1993.

59. Sara Fritz, "Deaths in Somalia Spark Flood of Opposition in the U.S." *Los Angeles Times*, October 17, 1993.

60. Rosenbaum, "Senate Praises Clinton."

61. Thomas Edsall and Dan Balz, "Lack of Invasion Allows Democrats a Bit of Relief," *Washington Post*, Sept. 20, 1994.

62. Rosenbaum, "Senate Praises Clinton."

63. James Risen, "Militant Leader Was a U.S. Target Since the Spring," *New York Times*, September 6, 1998.

64. Risen, "Militant Leader Was a U.S. Target."

65. Michael Grunwald, "Charges Filed Against bin Laden," *Washington Post*, November 5, 1998.

66. Grunwald, "Charges Filed Against bin Laden."

67. Morris, *Behind the Oval Office*, 25-27.

68. Interview of Joe Klein in James D. Retter, *Anatomy of a Scandal: An Investigation Into the Campaign to Undermine the Clinton Presidency* (Los Angeles: General Publishing Group, 1998), 264. Employing the Million Index of Personality Style and the NEO Personality Inventory checklist, the psychologist Aubrey Immelman gives a portrait of Bill Clinton that does not contradict this study. See "The Political Personalities of 1996: U.S. Presidential Candidates Bill Clinton and Bob Dole," *Leadership Quarterly*, forthcoming. Clinton, Immelman concludes is " more extroverted than Dole, less neurotic, more open to experience, more agreeable, and slightly less conscientious."

69. Robert B. Reich, *Locked in the Cabinet* (New York: Alfred A. Knopf, 1997), 83.

70. Devroy, "Clinton's Open House ."

71. See Evan Thomas and others, *Back from the Dead* (New York: Atlantic Monthly Press, 1997), 22.

72. Woodward, *The Agenda*, 223–24.

73. Woodward, *The Agenda*, 225, 328.

74. Woodward, *The Agenda*, 328–29. See also Reich, *Locked in the Cabinet*, 180.

75. For press critiques of the president's weak handling of the Whitewater documents see Martin Walker, *The President We Deserve* (New York: Crown, 1996), 207.

76. Retter, *Anatomy*, 251–252.

77. Tom Rosentiel, *The Beat Goes On: President Clinton's First Year with the*

Media, (New York: Twentieth Century Fund Press, 1994), 21; and Walker, *The President We Deserve,* 333.

78. Morris, *Behind the Oval Office,* 101, 164.

79. Morris, *Behind the Oval Office,* 111.

80. Evan Thomas et al., *Back From the Dead,* 91

81. Reich, *Locked in the Cabinet,* p.165

82. Michael Kelly, "Saint Hillary: Hillary Rodham Clinton and the Politics of Virtue" *The New York Times Magazine,* May 23, 1993. Still, the president's wife was an asset in many ways. She pushed the president to settle for a balanced budget in 1995 (see Morris, *Behind the Oval Office,* 163). Even David Brock argues that she is not the power-hungry opportunist he had expected to find, and her links to Whitewater and other scandals were not as strong as he had thought (David Brock, "Confessions of a Right-Wing Hit Man," *Esquire,* July 1997, 53–55, 106–7). Though the relationship between Bill and Hillary Clinton remains difficult to assess at this point, Robert Reich, secretary of labor under Clinton, writes that he "never sensed that their marriage was in trouble" and that he saw no evidence of the president's supposed womanizing. Reich, *Locked in the Cabinet,* 16.

83. Branch, *Clinton without Apologies.*

84. Richard Morris, *Partners in Power* (New York: Henry Holt and Company, 1996) and James Stewart, *Blood Sport: The President and His Adversaries* (New York: Simon and Schuster, 1996). The sources these authors used were the same ones consulted by David Brock for his story that first drew national attention to the sex scandals. See David Brock, "Living With the Clintons," *American Spectator* 17, January 1994, 18–30.

85. A. M. Rosenthal, "Where Was Character?" *New York Times,* October 8, 1996.

86. Maureen Dowd, "Bill Be Limbo." *New York Times,* October 10, 1996.

87. Stuart Taylor "Her Case Against Clinton," *The American Lawyer* (November 1996): 57. In the coverage of the Monica Lewinsky story, as Jules Witcover noted, "as often as not, reports were published or broadcast without a single source named or mentioned in an attribution so vague as to be worthless." After examining 1,565 statements made in the mainstream press in the first week of the Monica Lewinsky story, the Committee of Concerned Journalists, headed by Bill Kovach of the Harvard Nieman Foundation, came to a similar conclusion. Even when stories turned out to be demonstrably false, the retractions received less attention than the original charges. The infamous Clinton two-hundred-dollar haircut, which had purportedly held up traffic at an Los Angeles airport, had no such consequence. But major news centers such as the *Washington Post* and the *Los Angeles Times* buried the retractions and the *New York Times* had none at all.

88. John Kennedy, "Interview with Mike McCurry," *George,* March 1999, 78–79.

89. Joe Klein, *The Natural* (New York: Doubleday, 2002), 164. Journalist Todd Purdam tells of Clinton's visit with him while in the reporting pool on Air Force One. For two hours straight he talked about everything from the cruel possibilities of the Information Age to Chelsea leaving for college and the physical quirks of six world leaders. Todd S. Purdum, "Faces of Clinton," 36.

90. Meredith Oakley, *On the Make: The Rise of Bill Clinton* (Washington, D.C.: Regnery Publishing, Inc., 1994), 4.

91. Brummett, *High Wire: From the Backwoods to the Beltway—The Education of Bill Clinton* (New York: Hyperion, 1994), 269.

92. Quoted in Stanley Renshon, *High Hopes, The Clinton Presidency and the Politics of Ambition* (New York: The New York University Press, 1996), 151. Clinton also lacked the security that would have come from having a strong and caring father figure in his life. His birth father died before he was born and his stepfather was an alcoholic.

93. Stanley Rehnson sees Clinton's flexibility and willingness to compromise as proof that he has no inner core and no set of values and convictions. Thus Clinton's identification of himself as a New Democrat was a camouflage for his big government tendencies (131). The president's commitment "to end welfare as we know it," is simply assumed to contradict his proposal to make the government the employer of last resort (84). Clinton is lying when he states his desire to make abortions rare but then as president lifts the ban on abortion counseling at government-financed clinics (264). To be for free-trade agreements, on condition that it be accompanied by side agreements acceptable to labor and environmentalists is to embrace another contradiction (264). Clinton's suggestion that there is a healthcare crisis in the United States is belied by the fact that "everyone knows that the US has one of the finest medical services in the world" and Americans generally like their physicians (295). Clinton's failure to stand behind the appointments of Kimba Wood and Lani Guinier when they became political liabilities is proof that he has no loyalty to his friends (105). Indeed Renshon suggests that the president who Clinton most resembles is Nixon. Both men were characterized by high ambition, skills, and problems with integrity and authenticity in personal relations (117).

94. Some of the "best takes on Clinton" McCurry suggests were from the "older more curmudgeonly reporters like Helen Thomas." Kennedy, "Interview with Mike McCurry," 79.

95. All poll data in this article is taken from the web pages of the *Washington Post* (http://www.washingtonpost.com), the *Los Angeles Times* (http://www.latimes.com), and *Gallup* (http://www.gallup.com).

96. For Clinton's support among women voters, see Andrew Phillips, "The Clinton Paradox," *Maclean's*, February 19, 1998, 31. Many women seemed to be following the words of Susan B. Anthony: "If a man's public record be a clear one, if he has kept his pledges before the world, I do not inquire what his private life may have been."

97. Richard Morin and Claudia Deane, "Poll Shows More Citizens Satisfied with Government: Approval of Clinton Still High; Hill Support Grows." *Washington Post*, January 21, 1998.

98. Juliet Eilpenim, "Gingrich Awaits Starr Report," *Washington Post*, April 5, 1998.

99. For a critique of the political right and its campaign against Clinton see Joe Conason and Gene Lyons, *The Hunting of the President: The Ten-Year Campaign to Destroy Bill and Hillary Clinton* (New York: Thomas Dunne Books, 2000) and David Brock, *Blinded By the Right* (New York: Crown Publishers,

2002). For the Clinton Whitewater scandal, see Morris, *Partners in Power* (New York: Henry Holt and Company, 1996) and Stewart, *Blood Sport: The President and His Adversaries* (New York: Simon and Schuster, 1996).

100. Brummett, *High Wire*, 269.

101. As Branch notes, "Haiti alone refutes the entire brainless chorus about Bill Clinton's lack of conviction." See Branch, *Clinton Without Apologies*, 111, 170.

102. Kennedy, "Interview with Mike McCurry," 79.

103. The Starr report with all its unnecessary details was designed to humiliate the president and undermine the kind of respect for the president that is usually a condition of his ability to exercise authority.

104. For queries in the sex life of Clinton's critics see Gail Sheehy, "The Inner Quest of Newt Gingrich," *Vanity Fair*, September 1995,147–54, 217–22; Gail Sheehy, "Valley of the Doles," *Vanity Fair*, September 1996, 279–85, 338–46; Susan Paterno, "An Affair to Ignore," *American Journalism Review* 19, no. 1 (January/February, 1997): 31–33; and Herbert S. Parmet, *George Bush* (New York: Scribner, 1997), 179, 239–41, 355, 502. Roger Stone's charges on *Politically Incorrect* that Clinton had made advances to his wife at President Nixon's funeral were followed by a story in the *National Enquirer* on September 24 charging that Stone and his wife frequented a group-sex club. See Retter, *Anatomy of a Scandal*, 266–67. Also illuminating is Gennifer Flowers, *Passion and Betrayal* (Del Mar, Calif.: Emily Dalton Books, 1995).

105. For scrutiny of the Clinton accusers see Lars-Erik Nelson, "Whatever Happened to Whitewater?" *The New York Review of Books*, August 13, 1998, 4–6; Gene Lyons et al., *Fools for Scandal: How the Media Invented Whitewater* (New York: Franklin Square Press, 1996), 11–22, 84–87; and Retter, *Anatomy*, 16–109, 190–94, 197.

106. David Brock, "The Fire This Time," *Esquire*, April 1998, 144. For a summary of how, in retrospect, "a small financial mess in an incestuous Arkansas culture. . . surged out of control," see Walker, *The President We Deserve*, 253. Even an analysis of the details of a leader's religious life creates new opportunities for controversy and the fudging of commitments. If Washington, Jefferson, and Franklin, deists that they were, had to answer questions today about their particular religious perspectives, it is not at all clear they would survive the process. John Adams would have difficulties if he had tried to explain that he did not see Jesus as the literal son of God and that he did not believe in the Trinity. Indeed, when Jimmy Carter's religion became a major theme in his presidential primary campaign of 1976, he hedged on whether or not he believed in the literal interpretation of the Bible. Either choice could have lost him votes. Though Clinton had not highlighted his religion, some even purport to see into his heart, claiming that his long-term attendance at his local Baptist church is for political reasons, to make a display of his religiosity, rather than from any innate convictions. This despite that fact that he was a devoted churchgoer during his childhood and has been a regular one since 1980.

Chapter Two: Clinton and the Press by Ken Bode

1. These footnotes provide the references for most of the information in this chapter. A good bit of the research is based on my own reporting (which I have indicated as such in the text) or on events and statements that were widely reported and are a matter of public record.

2. Howard Fineman, "Gary Hart: A Candidate in Search of Himself," in Robert Shogan, ed., *Bad News: Where the Press Goes Wrong in the Making of the President* (Chicago: Ivan R. Dee, 2001), 133.

3. Betsey Wright's list information comes from author interviews, 1987; the story also is told in David Maraniss, *First in His Class: The Biography of Bill Clinton* (New York: Simon and Schuster, 1995), 439–41.

4. Betsey Wright, from the post-election round table discussion at Harvard's Institute of Politics; Charles T. Royer, ed., *Campaign for President: The Managers Look at '92* (Hollis, N.H.: Hollis Publishing Company, 1994), 188.

5. Royer, *Campaign for President,* 67.

6. Shogan, *Bad News,* 154.

7. Photos of Elizabeth Ward did appear in *Playboy* and her name appeared on the list in Larry Nichols's lawsuit. She initially denied, then later confirmed that she had been Clinton's lover.

8. Royer, *Campaign for President,* 62–4.

9. Larry J. Sabato and S. Robert Lichter, *When Should the Watchdogs Bark? Media Coverage of the Clinton Scandals* (Washington, D.C., Center for Media and Public Affairs, 1994), 58–62.

10. David S. Broder, *Behind the Front Page: A Candid Look at How the News Is Made* (New York: Simon and Schuster, 1987), 158.

11. Royer, *Campaign for President,* 183.

12. Royer, *Campaign for President,* 185.

13. Walter Kirn, "The End of the Affair," *The New York Times Magazine,* May 26, 2002, 11–12.

14. Jeffrey Birnbaum as quoted in David Shaw, "Bad News: Clinton and the Media," *Indianapolis Star,* October 17, 1993.

15. Shaw, "Bad News."

16. Devroy as quoted in Shaw, "Bad News."

17. Ruth Marcus, "The White House Isn't Telling Us the Truth," *Washington Post,* April 21, 1994.

18. Shaw, "Bad News."

19. Howard Kurtz, *Spin Cycle: Inside the Clinton Propaganda Machine* (New York: The Free Press, 1998), 25. Similar assessments of Clinton's minimal regard for reporters may also be found in Peter Goldman and others, *Quest for the Presidency 1992* (College Station: Texas A&M University Press, 1994), chapters 7 and 8.

20. Kurtz, *Spin Cycle,* 83, 280.

21. Ted Bogasian, *The Press Secretary,* PBS television documentary, VHS (2001).

22. Kirn, "The End of the Affair," 11.

23. Leonard Downie Jr. and Robert G. Kaiser, *The News About the News:*

American Journalism in Peril, (New York: Albert A. Knopf, 2002). See also Alicia C. Shepard, "White Noise," *The American Journalism Review* 21, no. 1 (January/February, 1999): 20–25; and "The Perils of Punditry," *Columbia Journalism Review* 37, no. 5 (January/February, 1999): 42–45.

24. Downie and Kaiser, *The News About the News,* 57.

25. The Institute of Politics, ed., *Campaign for President: The Managers Look at '96* (Hollis, N.H.: Hollis Publishing Company, 1997), 209–14. Also, see Downie and Kaiser, *The News About the News,* 56–62.

26. Kurtz, *Spin Cycle,* 296.

27. Kurtz, *Spin Cycle,* 300.

Chapter Three: Assessing the Clinton Presidency: The Political Constraints of Legislative Policy by David Brady and D. Sunshine Hillygus

1. Scholars of psychology have concluded that great presidents are characterized by "an open mind and taciturn manner." Historians, on the other hand, have rated past presidents on five criteria: leadership qualities, accomplishments/crisis management, political skills, appointments, and character/integrity.

2. R. Neustadt, *Presidential Power and the Modern Presidency: The Politics of Leadership from Roosevelt to Reagan* (New York: The Free Press, 1960); Thomas Cronin, *The State of the Presidency* (Boston: Little and Brown, 1980); and Clinton Rossiter, *The Supreme Court and the Commander-in-Chief* (Ithaca, N.Y.: Cornell University Press, 1951).

3. George C. Edwards, *At the Margins: Presidential Influence in Congress* (New Haven, Conn.: Yale University Press, 1989); Jon Bond and Richard Fleisher, *Polarized Politics* (Washington, D.C.: Congressional Quarterly Press, 2000); and Terry Moe and William G. Howell, "The Presidential Power of Unilateral Action," *Journal of Law, Economics, and Organization* 15 (1999): 132.

4. David Donald, *Lincoln* (New York: Simon and Schuster Books, 1995); Robert Dalleck, *Flawed Giant: Lyndon Johnson and His Times, 1961–1973* (Oxford: Oxford University Press, 1998); and Richard Reeves, *President Nixon: Alone in the White House* (New York: Simon and Schuster Books, 2001).

5. David McCullough, *John Adams* (New York: Simon and Schuster Books, 2001).

6. Moe and Howell, "The Presidential Power," 132.

7. Keith Krehbiel, *Pivotal Politics: A Theory of U.S. Lawmaking* (Chicago: University of Chicago Press, 1998); Keith Krehbiel, "Institutional and Partisan Sources of Gridlock: A Theory of Divided and Unified Government," *Journal of Theoretical Politics* 8 (1996): 7; David Brady and Craig Volden, *Revolving Gridlock* (Boulder, Co.: Westview Press, 1998).

8. If legislators are uncertain about the policy consequences of their actions, they are unlikely to change the status quo. Conversely, when there is demand for action—as in the early 1970s for environmental legislation—uncertainty might trigger a major policy change that never would have

passed if the outcome were known. Members also face uncertainty about how their constituents will react to their decisions. In fact, members of Congress spend quite a lot of time trying to figure out how their votes will be received back home.

9. The size of the gridlock region is determined by looking at the difference in preferences between the pivotal members on both edges. If the policies of the forty-first and sixty-seventh members are quite similar we would find a small gridlock region. However, given the polarization of preferences in recent Congresses, the gridlock region has been quite large.

10. Sam Kernell, *Going Public: New Strategies of Presidential Leadership* (Washington, D.C.: Congressional Quarterly Press, 1995).

11. Brandice Canes-Wrone, "The President's Legislative Influence from Public Appeals," *American Journal of Political Science* 45, no. 2 (2001): 313.

12. A classic example was Ronald Reagan's speech to the nation just before the vote on his 1981 tax cuts.

13. Brookings Institution, *Beyond Gridlock* (Washington, D.C.: Brookings Institution 1993).

14. Theda Skocpol, *Boomerang: Health Reform and the Turn Against Government*, paperback ed. (New York: W. W. Norton, 1997).

15. Brady and Volden, *Revolving Gridlock,* 103.

16. The most conservative and liberal senators are not a surprise—Helms (N.C.), Nicholas (Okla.), Gramm (Tex.), and Wallop (Wyo.) holding down the right and Kennedy (Mass.), Wellstone (Minn.), and Metzenbaum (Ohio) holding down the left. The critical legislators—those in roughly the thirty-eighth to fifty-second positions (so, the median and filibuster pivots)—consist of nine Democrats (seven from the South and border states, with one each from Nebraska and Arizona) and five Republicans (from Oregon [two], Maine, Pennsylvania, and Rhode Island). In sum, the pivots and median voters are conservative Southern Democrats or moderate Republicans.

17. The thirteen new members arrayed from left to right were two liberal Democrats (Boxer [Calif.] and Braun [Ill.]); two moderate-liberal Democrats (Murray [Wash.] and Dorgan [N. Dak.]); two moderates (Feinstein [Calif.] and Feingold [Wis.]) and a conservative who became a Republican (Ben Campbell [Colo.]). The six new Republicans ranged from moderates (Hutchinson [Tex.] and Gregg [N.H.]) to conservatives (Bennett [Utah], Kempthorne [Idaho], and Faircloth [N.C.]) with Cloverdale (Ga.) in between.

18. Brady and Volden, *Revolving Gridlock,* chapter 5.

19. Brady and Volden *Revolving Gridlock,* also provide a more detailed analysis of "switching voters" (voters who switch from first voting against the proposal and then voting for the proposal in a later vote) as an additional test on their model. This analysis provided a measure of Clinton's influence on legislators as he attempted to move them to support his proposals. Most importantly, it illustrates that the votes that Clinton was able to win came not just from Democrats but rather from legislators who held preferences close to the proposed legislation. In other words, they show that the vote switchers are often pivotal and near the median—Breaux (La.) or Boren (Okla.), rather than Kennedy (Mass.) or Wellstone (Minn.).

20. Nathan Littlefield, "Bradley: Substance Over Style 2000," *Yale Herald Online*, March 2, 2000, http://www.yaleherald.com/archive/xxix/2000.03.02/opinion/bradley.html.

21. ABC News Live, "The Clinton Years," *Nightline*, 2000, http://abcnews.go.com/onair/nightline/clintonyears/clinton/chapters/2.html, chapter 2.

22. The filibuster pivots were moderate Republicans such as Jeffords (Vt.), Cohen (Maine) and Specter (Pa.).

23. Brady and Volden, *Revolving Gridlock*, chapter 5.

24. Considering just the items in the contract, as of mid-December 1995 the Senate still had in committee House crime legislation including required restitution to victims (HR 665), modification of the exclusionary rule (HR 666), and block grants to give communities control over funds (HR 728). The national security legislation passed by the House (HR 7) had not been reported out by a committee. The parts of the contract covering civil law and product liability (HR 988) had not passed out of committee, and the Senate had not yet considered term limits (SJ Res. 21). On those contract items where the Senate had acted, they had passed or were about to pass legislation that differed from the House versions. As a result, legislation involving the line-item veto, welfare (HR 4 and HR 2491), tax credits, Social Security benefits, capital-gains cuts, and frivolous suits against companies were all in conference. The line-item veto passed both houses but was still in conference when the budget battle began. And both constitutional amendments—term limits and the balanced budget amendment—had failed to get the two-thirds vote necessary for passage. The reform perhaps most popular with the American public—campaign-finance reform—had not even been considered because it was clear that no bill acceptable to both Democrats and Republicans was possible.

25. *Congressional Quarterly Weekly Report*, 1995, 3712–13.

26. The basic steps in the reconciliation process are (1) passage through both houses of a budget resolution that contains the economic assumptions, the tax component of the budget (reduced as in 1981 or raised as in 1993), the cuts in expenditures (discretionary and entitlements), and the instructions to the relevant authorizing committees in regard to the amounts (though not in regard to how to meet the reconciliation targets); (2) passage through regular means of the tax bill and thirteen appropriations bills; and (3) after the House-Senate conferences, the passage of a final reconciliation package.

27. *Congressional Quarterly Weekly Report*, 1995, 3505.

28. *CBS Evening News*, November 15, 1995.

29. David McKay, "Presidential Strategy and the Veto Power: A Reappraisal," *Political Science Quarterly* 104, no. 3 (Autumn 1989): 447.

30. There was an ongoing debate over whether to use CBO estimates versus Office of Management and Budget (OMB) estimates.

31. This difference can be attributed to a combination of lower expenditures and slightly higher corporate-tax revenue (given a balanced budget).

32. Specifically, the Clinton balanced budget proposal projected savings of $102 billion in Medicare, $52 billion in Medicaid, $43 billion in welfare, $296

billion in discretionary spending including national defense, $60 billion from closing corporate loopholes, and $87 billion in tax cuts, for a total savings of $526 billion. This plan projected an increase of $97 billion in savings over Clinton's December proposal. The president's tax cut was over three years, with the possibility of renewing the cuts if the economy performed well. The cuts in discretionary spending, Medicare, and Medicaid were backloaded such that the brunt of the cuts would be felt in the last two years—2001 and 2002. For example, $185 billion of the $296 billion in discretionary cuts were scheduled for the last two years. The Republican plan cut $99 billion more in Medicare, $65 billion more in Medicaid, $88 billion more in discretionary spending, $37 billion more in welfare, and a whopping $154 billion more in taxes. In sum, there were major differences between the president's budget and the Republican Congress's budget.

33. This coalition seemed unlikely given the preferences of the median Republican in the House. The bipolar distribution of preferences was significantly shifted toward the conservative end of the spectrum by the 1994 congressional elections. The conservative pole greatly outnumbered the liberal pole with more than 120 Republicans having an a ADA score of 0; thus, the median voter in the House had an ADA score of about 20 while the veto pivot was a Democrat with an ADA of about 75. Obviously, those in the middle—from 25 to 70 in ADA scores—were not numerous. Given this distribution of preferences, finding middle ground would be hard, especially on the all-important budget. Moreover, the reconciliation bill that the House had passed was already viewed as a major compromise by many House Republicans, and much movement away from their bill and toward the president's budget would cause mass defections among Republicans especially in the House.

34. House median (ADA=40), Senate median (ADA=55), Left filibuster (ADA=70), Right filibuster (ADA=15).

35. Median ADA of 40.

36. Adam Clymer and Lizette Alivarez, "With Minimal Fanfare, Congress Calls it Quits," *New York Times,* December 17, 2000.

37. *New York Times,* "An Ineffectual Congress," November 1, 2000.

38. Examples include 21st Century Community Learning Centers, AmeriCorps, Community Development Block Grants, Federal Perkins Loans, housing opportunities for people with AIDS, adult education to name a few.

39. We recognize that these regressions are fraught with a number of assumptions and limitations. This analysis provides a quick and dirty look at the effect of Clinton's policy efforts.

40. Johnathan Rauch, *Government's End: Why Washington Stopped Working.* (Washington, DC: Public Affairs, 1999).

Chapter Four: African Americans and the Clinton Presidency: Reckoning with Race, 1992–2000 by Darlene Clark Hine

1. African American appointees to Clinton's cabinet: Jesse Brown, secretary of veterans affairs; Ronald H. Brown, secretary of commerce; Mike Espy, secretary of agriculture; Hazel O'Leary, secretary of energy; Togo West,

secretary of the army and secretary of veterans affairs; Alexis Herman, secretary of labor; Rodney Slater, secretary of transportation; and Lee P. Brown, director, Office of National Drug Control Policy.

2. Quoted in Robert L. Allen, *The Port Chicago Mutiny: The Story of the Largest Mass Mutiny Trial in U.S. Naval History* (New York: Warner Books, 1989), 174. Sociologist Allen posits that the men who engaged in the work stoppage after the explosion did so because their previous twin processes of accommodation to a dangerous situation—"discounting" and "balancing"—no longer worked. He defined "discounting" as a "process in which the enlisted men came to minimize, to discount, the apparent risks involved in loading munitions." He defined "balancing" as a "process by which the men balanced their grievances against the perceived benefits of Navy life" (162). I am persuaded that black Americans have deployed identical coping processes—balancing and discounting—throughout the modern history of their relations with the Democratic Party.

3. Derrick Bell, *Faces at the Bottom of the Well: The Permanence of Racism* (New York: Basic Books, 1992), 15, 23.

4. Farai Chideya, *The Color of Our Future: Race for the 21st Century* (New York: Quill, William Morrow, 1999), 77. Also see Tom W. Smith, *Ethnic Images* (Chicago: National Opinion Research Center, University of Chicago, 1990).

5. Russell Jacoby and Naomi Glauberman, eds., *The Bell Curve Debate: History, Documents, Opinions* (New York: Times Books, 1995).

6. Hanes Walton Jr. and Robert C. Smith, *American Politics and the African American Quest for Universal Freedom* (New York: Addison Wesley, Longman, 2000), 42–43.

7. Walton and Smith, *American Politics,* 207–8.

8. Ralph Ellison, "The Myth of the Flawed White Southerner," in *The Collected Essays of Ralph Ellison,* ed. John F. Callahan (New York: Modern Library, 1995), 552-62.

9. Ellison, "The Flawed White Southerner," 562; Robert S. Dallek, *Flawed Giant: Lyndon Johnson and His Times, 1961–1973* (New York: Oxford University Press, 1998).

10. Alex Poinsett, *Walking with Presidents: Louis Martin and the Rise of Black Political Power* (Lanham, Md.: Madison Books, 1997), 128–37. During the Johnson administration Martin pushed forward the appointment of Thurgood Marshall for the U.S. Supreme Court, Robert Weaver as secretary of housing and urban development, and Andrew Brimmer to the Federal Reserve Board. Martin later recalled, "By the time of the Marshall appointment, we had put several hundred blacks in various positions of importance" (137).

11. Martin proved to be especially adept at developing innovative ways to enlarge the black electorate. As his biographer Alex Poinsett noted, "With the help of the National Beauty Culturists League, the United Beauty School Owners and Teachers Associations, and a barbers' union in Chicago, he established a grassroots organization to distribute campaign literature through the members' shops. . . . Nearly every black person in America could be counted on to visit such an establishment at least once during the campaign" (146). Taking inspiration from Louis Martin, whom I had the pleasure of interview-

ing in 1991, I conducted an informal ethnographic survey of the owners, stylists, and their clients at five beauty salons and barber shops to gauge black popular reactions and opinions of Bill Clinton during his campaigns and presidency. Between 1992 and 2002, I spent hundreds of hours conversing with the patrons and stylists at five beauty-culture businesses: Carolyn Young's The Ultimate Touch on the south side of Chicago; Mark Anthony's in Lansing, Michigan; Paul Johnson's Professional Hair Design in Orangeburg, South Carolina; Ms. Edna's The Beauty Trap in Palo Alto, California (it no longer exists); and Jocelyn Merriweather of Patrick's Salon in Lansing, Michigan. Throughout this ten year period I never encountered an African American who disliked Bill Clinton. The most frequently voiced refrain was appreciation for the way he respected black humanity and supported their desires for equality of opportunity. A second often-heard comment was appreciation for the economic recovery and boom. People who thought they would never work again or own their own home credited Bill Clinton for the jobs secured during the 1990s. When asked about the sources that helped them form their political opinions they most often named *Jet, Ebony, Black Enterprise,* Tom Joyner's radio show, BET programs, their ministers, and some cited performers such as comedian Chris Rock. See also Darlene Clark Hine, "Booker T. Washington and Madam C. J. Walker," in *Speak Truth to Power: Black Professional Class in United States History,* ed. Darlene Clark Hine, (Brooklyn, N.Y.: Carlson Publishing, 1996), 95–104 for a discussion of the importance of the beauty-culture business in black economic history.

12. Hine, "Booker T. Washington and Madam C. J. Walker," 137.

13. It is useful to note, according to Poinsett, *Walking with Presidents,* "Out of Carter's thirty-seven appointments, nine were to appellate court judgeships (at that level Nixon and Ford had appointed none), including two who Martin had helped bring into the federal judiciary under Johnson: A. Leon Higginbotham and Damon Keith. The other seven were Theodore McMillian, Amalya Kearse, Joseph Hatchett, Jerome Farris, Nathaniel Jones, Cecil Poole, and Harry Edwards" (185). Carter's thirty-seven black appointments were the most striking feature of his presidency. Carter appointed nine black judges to the federal courts in the South. This symbolized a strong commitment to the enforcement of civil-rights laws. He also instructed all departments of the federal government to implement affirmative action programs.

14. Poinsett, *Walking with Presidents,* p.54.

15. Vernon E. Jordan, with Annette Gordon-Reed, *Vernon Can Read! A Memoir* (New York: Public Affairs Press, 2001), 328.

16. Paula Wilson, "Rise and Fall of the Surgeon General," *USA Today,* May 1997.

17. Lani Guinier, *The Tyranny of the Majority: Fundamental Fairness in Representative Democracy* (New York: The Free Press, 1994), vii. Also see Lani Guinier, *Becoming Gentlemen: Women, Law School, and Institutional Change* (Boston: Beacon Press, 1997); and *Lift Every Voice: Turning a Civil Rights Setback Into a New Vision of Social Justice* (New York: Simon and Schuster Adult Publishing Group, 1998).

18. Kenneth W. Warren, "'As White as Anybody': Race and the Politics of

Counting as Black," *New Literary History* 31 (2000): 709–26, 724; Toni
Morrison, "Talk of the Town," *The New Yorker,* October 5, 1998, 31–32; Phil
Gailey, "Baffled by Black America's Love Affair with Bill Clinton," *St.
Petersburg Times,* February 25, 2001; and DeWayne Wickham, *Bill Clinton and
Black America* (New York: Ballantine Books, 2002).

19. Randall Robinson, *Defending the Spirit: A Black Life in America* (New
York: Dutton, 1998), 194. In 1977 Randall Robinson founded TransAfrica to
lobby for black political prisoners in South Africa, chief among them Nelson
Mandela. In 1986 the Congressional Black Caucus persuaded its colleagues to
enact a U.S. trade embargo against South African and sustained it over
President Reagan's veto.

20. Robinson, *Defending the Spirit,* 207, 209, 213, 217,

21. Darlene Clark Hine, William C. Hine, and Stanley Harrold, *The African
American Odyssey* (Upper Saddle River, N.J.: Prentice Hall, 2003), 582–85.

22. President Bill Clinton, "On Affirmative Action," July 19, 1995, in , *Bill
Clinton and Black America,* ed. DeWayne Wickham, (New York: Ballantine
Books, 2002), 258–60.

23. Carl T. Rowan, *The Coming Race War in America: A Wake-up Call*
(Boston: Little, Brown and Company, 1996), 133. For a complete copy of the
text of Clinton's speech, "On Affirmative Action: National Archives,
Washington, D.C. July 19, 1995" see Wickham, *Bill Clinton and Black America,*
243–60. Clinton recounted a series of jarring statistics to prove his case that
affirmative action was still very much needed: "The unemployment rate for
African Americans remains about twice that of whites. . . . [I]n the nation's
largest companies only six-tenths of one percent of senior management positions are held by African Americans. . . . [T]he Chicago Federal Reserve Bank
reported that black home loan applications are more than twice as likely to be
denied credit as whites with the same qualifications." 251.

24. John Lewis, with Michael D'Orso, *Walking With the Wind: A Memoir of
the Movement* (New York: Simon and Schuster, 1998), 466.

25. Lewis, *Walking With the Wind,* 457.

26. Clyde Woods, *Development Arrested: Race, Power, and the Blues in the
Mississippi Delta* (London: Verso, 1998), 277. Woods declared that, "with the
stroke of a pen, Clinton has implemented . . . the destruction of the six-
decades-old national social compact and the creation of a new generation of
economically defenseless African American" 177.

27. Robin D. G. Kelley, *Yo'Mama's Disfunktional!: Fighting the Culture Wars
in Urban America* (Boston: Beacon Press, 1997), 82.

28. Quoted in Fred D. Gray, *The Tuskegee Syphilis Study: An Insider's Account
of the Shocking Medical Experiment Conducted by Government Doctors against
African American Men,* (Montgomery, Ala.: New South Books, 1998), 126; Also
see "President William J. Clinton's Remarks: Remarks by the President in
Apology for Study Done in Tuskegee," *Tuskegee Truths: Rethinking the Tuskegee
Syphilis Study,* ed. Susan M. Reverby, (Chapel Hill: University of North
Carolina, 2000), 574–77. The president announced a number of measures
among which was a promise "to build that lasting memorial at Tuskegee."

29. Satcher quoted in Gray, *The Tuskegee Syphilis Study,* 160–61.

30. Clinton quoted in Gray, *The Tuskegee Syphilis Study*, 114–15, and Reverby, *Tuskegee Truths*, 575.

31. Gray, *The Tuskegee Syphilis Study*, 164

32. Allen, *Port Chicago Mutiny*; Contra Costa County Office of Education, "The Port Chicago Disaster: A Resource for Students and Teachers" (Pleasant Hill, CA, 2000). http://intergate.cccoe.k12.ca.us/pc/; Thurgood Marshall had long concluded that the Port Chicago trial represented "one of the worst 'frameups' we have come across in a long time." Lou Potter, with William Miles and Nina Rosenblum, *Liberators: Fighting Two Fronts in World War II* (New York: Harcourt Brace Jovanovich, 1992), 132, 134.

33. Radio interview of the president on the Tom Joyner Morning Show, November 2, 1998. Copy in author's possession. Released by the White House, Office of the Press Secretary.

34. Martin Luther King, quoted in Tavis Smiley, *Hard Left: Straight Talks about the Wrongs of the Right* (New York: Anchor Books, 1996), 39.

Chapter Five: Clinton, Fulbright, and the Legacy of the Cold War by Randall B. Woods

1. Stephen M. Walt, "Two Cheers for Clinton's Foreign Policy," *Foreign Affairs* 79, no. 2 (March/April 2000): 63.

2. Walt, "Two Cheers," 78–79.

3. Sandy Berger, "A Foreign Policy for the Global Age, *Foreign Affairs* 79, no. 6 (November/December 2000) 22–23.

4. Randall Bennett Woods, *Fulbright: A Biography* (New York: Cambridge University Press, 1995) 543–44, 688.

5. Woods, *Fulbright*, 137–40.

6. Woods, *Fulbright*, 212–25.

7. Woods, *Fulbright*, 334–39.

8. Randall Bennett Woods, "The Rhetoric of Dissent: J. William Fulbright, Vietnam, and the Crisis of Liberal Internationalism," in *Critical Reflections on the Cold War: Linking Rhetoric and History*, eds. Martin J. Medhurst and H. W. Brands, 187–208 (College Station, Texas, 2000) .

9. Woods, "The Rhetoric of Dissent."

10. Walt, "Two Cheers," 65.

11. Walt, "Two Cheers," 65–66.

12. Berger, "A Foreign Policy," 23–24.

13. See Emily O. Goldman and Larry Berman, "Engaging the World: First Impressions of the Clinton Foreign Policy Legacy," in *The Clinton Legacy*, eds. Colin Campbell and Bert A. Rockman, (New York: Chatham House Publishers, 2000), 229.

14. James McGregor Burns and Georgia J. Sorenson, *Dead Center* (New York: Scribner, 1999) 26–28, 137–38.

15. Walt, "Two Cheers," 66–67; and Goldman and Berman, "Engaging the World," 232.

16. William G. Hyland, *Clinton's World: Remaking American Foreign Policy* (Westport, Conn.: Praeger, 1999) 141–42,148–49.

17. Berger, "A Foreign Policy," 25. See also Goldman and Berman, "Engaging the World," 241–42; and Burns and Sorenson, *Dead Center*, 295–96, 300–01.

18. Laura Neack, *The New Foreign Policy: U.S. and Comparative Foreign Policy in the 21st Century* (New York: Rowan and Littlefield, 2003) 3–11, and Hyland, 115–17.

19. Hyland, *Clinton's World*, 29–30.

20. Hyland, *Clinton's World*, 34–36; and Burns and Sorenson, *Dead Center*, 295–310, 322–24.

21. Burns and Sorenson, *Dead Center*, 173–75, 181–82.

22. Hyland, *Clinton's World*, 51–64; and Neack, *The New Foreign Policy*, 129–31.

23. Hyland, *Clinton's World*, 51–64.

24. See Goldman and Berman, "Engaging the World," 239–40; Hyland, *Clinton's World*, 59–54; and Burns and Sorenson, *Dead Center*, 137–38, 178–85.

25. See Goldman and Berman, "Engaging the World," 244–45; and Hyland, *Clinton's World*, 68–73.

26. Neack, *The New Foreign Policy*, 94; Hyland, *Clinton's World*, 162–66; and Burns and Sorenson, *Dead Center*, 320–23.

27. Hyland, *Clinton's World*, 163–81; and Burns and Sorenson, *Dead Center*, 68, 137, 176, 299.

28. Hyland, *Clinton's World*, 132–33; and Burns and Sorenson, *Dead Center*, 174–79, 181–82.

29. Hyland, *Clinton's World*, 194.

30. Hyland, *Clinton's World*, 44–45.

31. Burns and Sorenson, *Dead Center*, 311–13.

32. See Goldman and Berman, "Engaging the World," 246–48 and Burns and Sorensen, *Dead Center*, 311–13, 322–23.

33. See Goldman and Berman, "Engaging the World," 245.

Chapter Six: Rightward Currents: Bill Clinton and the Politics of the 1990s by Dan Carter

1. Michael Waldman, *POTUS Speaks: Finding the Words That Defined the Clinton Presidency* (New York: Simon and Schuster, 2000), 151.

2. E. J. Dionne, *Why Americans Hate Politics* (New York: Simon and Schuster, 1991), 330.

3. Dionne, *Why Americans Hate Politics*, 331.

4. On this point, Dionne acknowledged his debt to Harvard sociologist Theda Skocpol's widely read "Sustainable Social Policy: Fighting Poverty Without Poverty Programs," *The American Prospect* 2 (Summer 1990): 58–70.

5. Jon F. Hale, "The Making of the New Democrats," *Political Science Quarterly* 110 (Summer 1995): 22, 226.

6. Clinton and his running mate Al Gore outlined their lengthy agenda in *Putting America First: How We Can All Change America* (New York: Times Books, 1992) though the emphasis quickly shifted in the campaign to an overwhelming emphasis upon reviving the lagging American economy.

7. In my analysis of the struggle over healthcare, I have relied upon a number of works, notably Theda Skocpol's *Boomerang: Clinton's Health Security Effort and the Turn Against Government in U.S. Politics* (New York: W. W. Norton and Company, 1996) and Nicholas Laham's *A Lost Cause: Bill Clinton's Campaign for National Health Insurance* (Westport, Conn.: Praeger, 1996). Skocpol's study is particularly valuable because she had access to a number of key White House architects of the Clinton plan, including Hillary Clinton and Ira Magaziner.

8. For the rationale for much of the White House plan, see Paul Starr, *The Logic of Health Care Reform: Why and How the President's Plan Will Work* (New York: Whittle Books in association with Penguin Books, 1994)

9. Adam Clymer, "Clinton Asks Backing for Sweeping Change in the Health System," *New York Times*, September 23, 1993.

10. George C. Edwards III, "Frustration and Folly: Bill Clinton and the Public Presidency," in *The Clinton Presidency: First Appraisals*, eds. Colin Campbell and Bert A. Rockman, 225–52 (Chatham, New Jersey: Chatham House Publishers, 1996).

11. Edwards, "Frustration and Folly," 245.

12. "Kristol Ball: William Kristol Looks at the Future of the GOP," *Policy Review*, 67 (Winter, 1993), 15.

13. Two articles that capture the visceral opposition to the Clinton proposal are Ralph Kimmy Bennett "Your Risk Under Clinton's Health Plan," in the March 1994, *Reader's Digest* and Robert E. Moffit "Clinton's Frankenstein: The Gory Details of the President's Health Plan," which appeared in the Heritage Foundation's magazine, *Policy Review* 67 (Winter 1994): 4-17.

14. Skocpol, *Boomerang*, 17.

15. Although advocates of the Clinton healthcare program emphasized the cost-containment possibilities of their plan, no one believed that full health-care coverage could be achieved without additional expense.

16. Obviously, this is a simplification of the many differences that exist among those who have written on the subject. In reviewing this subject, the most useful (or influential) works were Michael Harrington *The Other America* (New York: McMillan, 1962); Frances Fox Piven and Richard Cloward, *Regulating the Poor: The Functions of Public Welfare* (New York: Pantheon, 1971); and Michael Katz, *The Undeserving Poor: From the War on Poverty to the War on Welfare* (New York: Pantheon Press, 1989).

17. William Julius Wilson, *The Truly Disadvantaged: The Inner City, the Underclass and Public Policy* (Chicago: University of Chicago Press, 1987). In a later work, *When Work Disappears: The World of the Urban Poor* (New York: Alfred A. Knopf, 1996), Wilson sought to formulate guidelines for policies that would take into consideration past racial discrimination as well as non-racial factors, emphasizing the creation of well-paying jobs. Needless to say, his call for government as an employer of last resort was not popular in the 1980s.

18. George Gilder, *Wealth and Poverty* (New York: Basic Books, 1981), 82–92, 103. As a number of critics have noted, Gilder was intent upon restoring the traditional patriarchal family.

19. Gilder, *Wealth and Poverty*, 227–28.

20. Charles Murray, *Losing Ground: American Social Policy, 1950–1980*, (San Francisco: Encounter Books, 2000).

21. Martin Gilens, *Why Americans Hate Welfare: Race, Media, and the Politics of Antipoverty Policy* (Chicago: University of Chicago Press, 1999), 68, 147. For a discussion of the connection between race and welfare from a liberal perspective see Gilens and Jill Quadangno, *The Color of Welfare: How Racism Undermined the War on Poverty* (New York: Oxford University Press, 1994). See also Herbert J. Gans, *The War Against the Poor: The Underclass and Antipoverty Policy* (New York: Basic Books, 1995) and Katz, *The Undeserving Poor*. Thomas and Mary Edsall described the political linkage between such racial issues and other social and economic issues in *Chain Reaction: The Impact of Race Rights, and Taxes on American Politics* (New York: W. W. Norton, 1991).

22. And Murray and his co-author Richard Herrnstein made the connection explicit on the eve of the great welfare-rights debate with the publication of their book, *The Bell Curve*. Murray and fellow author Richard Herrnstein argued that a large percentage of African Americans (and some whites to be sure) were so genetically inferior they were beyond the reach of any palliative measures (*The Bell Curve: Intelligence and Class Structure in American Life* [New York: Free Press, 1994], 360, 549).

23. Gilens, *Why Americans Hate Welfare*, 19.

24. Clinton and Gore, *Putting America First*, 164–168.

25. Quoted in Gertrude Schaffner Goldberg and Sheila D. Collins, *Washington's New Poor Law: Welfare "Reform" and the Roads Not Taken, 1935 to the Present* (New York: The Apex Press, 2001), 197. James McGregor Burns and Georgia J. Sorenson critically describe the politics surrounding the adoption of the measure in *Dead Center: Clinton-Gore and the Perils of Moderation* (New York: Scribner, 1999), 225–39.

26. Morris, who had become the president's closest political advisor, frantically warned of dire consequences if Clinton failed to approve the measure. "If he vetoes, he'll lose [the 1996 presidential election]," Morris told Clinton and his aides. George Stephanopoulos, *All Too Human: A Political Education* (Boston: Little, Brown and Company, 1999), 419–22.

27. Frederick Hayek, *The Road to Serfdom* (Chicago: University of Chicago Press, 1944). While any list would be somewhat arbitrary, most historians of American conservatism would probably add to Hayek's book Ayn Rand's best-selling novel *The Fountainhead* (Indianapolis: The Bobbs Merrill Company, 1943); Richard Weaver's *Ideas Have Consequences* (Chicago: University of Chicago Press, 1948); and Russell Kirk's *The Conservative Mind, from Burke to Santayana* (Chicago: H. Regnery Co., 1953). For an overview of the role played by these and other writers and intellectuals see George H. Nash, *The Conservative Intellectual Movement in America Since 1945* (New York: Basic Books, 1976).

28. Daniel Bell, ed., *The New American Right* (New York: Criterion Books, 1955); Arnold Forster and Benjamin Epstein, *Danger on the Right* (New York: Random House, 1964); and Richard Hofstadter, *The Paranoid Style in American Politics, and Other Essays* (New York: Alfred A. Knopf, 1965). Hofstadter's essay,

originally delivered as a lecture at Oxford University in the fall of 1963, was clearly triggered by the Goldwater movement.

29. Lisa McGirr, *Suburban Warriors: The Origins of the New American Right* (Princeton, N.J.: Princeton University Press, 2001).

30. George G. Kaufman and Kenneth T. Rosen, *The Property Tax Revolt: The Case of Proposition 13* (Cambridge, Mass.: Ballinger Publishing Company, 1981); Terry Schwadron, ed., *California and the American Tax Revolt* (Berkeley: University of California Press, 1984); David O. Sears and Jack Citrin, *Tax Revolt: Something for Nothing in California* (Cambridge: Harvard University Press, 1982).

31. Michael Lienesch describes the conservative emphasis of this religious thrust among evangelicals in *Redeeming America: Piety and Politics in the New Christian Right* (Chapel Hill: University of North Carolina Press, 1993). For statistics on religious growth in the post–World War II era, see Winthrop S. Hudson, *Religion in America* (New York: Charles Scribner's Sons, 1965), 396; Phillip E. Hammond, *Religion and Personal Autonomy: The Third Disestablishment in America* (Columbia, S.C.: University of South Carolina Press, 1992), 114; William L. O'Neill, *American High: The Years of Confidence, 1945–1960* (New York: Free Press, 1986), 214–215. Figures on the growth of the Catholic Church are from the annual *Official Catholic Directory for the Year of Our Lord . . .* beginning in 1941 and continuing through 1975. In *One Nation under God: Religion in Contemporary American Society* (New York: Harmony Books, 1993), Barry A. Kosmin and Seymore P. Lachman point out some of the flaws in the gathering of this religious data (4–7, 298–99), but their useful caveats do not alter the overall picture.

32. McGirr, *Suburban Warriors.*

33. Thomas J. Sugrue, "Crabgrass-Roots Politics: Race, Rights, and the Reaction against Liberalism in the Urban North, 1940–1964," *The Journal of American History* 82, no. 2 (September 1995): 551–78

34. See for example, William Buckley's defense of white southern segregationists in *The National Review* 4 no. 7 (August 24, 1957): 148. As late as the mid-1960s, *The National Review* was a forum for intellectuals like Ernest Van Den Haag who defended racial segregation on the grounds that blacks were intellectually inferior to whites. Van Den Haag, "Intelligence or Prejudice," *The National Review* 26, no. 48 (December 1, 1964): 1059–63. Thirty years later, conservative social scientists Richard Herrnstein and Charles Murray made explicit Van Den Haag's cautious racism in their book, *The Bell Curve: Intelligence and Class Structure in American Life.* While many conservatives were uncomfortable with the Herrnstein-Murray endorsement of irremediable black inferiority, the book received positive reviews from a number of conservative journals.

35. Dan T. Carter, *From George Wallace to Newt Gingrich: Race in the Conservative Counterrevolution, 1963–1994* (Baton Rouge: Louisiana State University Press, 1996) 19, 23, 35, 45; Kevin Philips, *The Emerging Republican Majority* (New Rochelle, N.Y.: Arlington House, 1969). Despite his political exploitation of white resentments, Nixon—unlike his more conservative Republican successors—was, in Leonard Garment's words "operationally

progressive." Dean J. Kotlowski, *Nixon's Civil Rights: Politics, Principle, and Policy* (Cambridge: Harvard University Press, 2001), 259. See also Kenneth O'Reilly, *Nixon's Piano: Presidents and Racial Politics from Washington to Clinton* (New York: The Free Press, 1995) 285–86.

36. Dan T. Carter, *The Politics of Rage: George Wallace, the Origins of the New Conservatism and the Transformation of American Politics,* (New York: Simon and Schuster, 1995), 375–77.

37. In a rare 1998 interview with a *Washington Post* reporter, the reclusive Scaife referred to dozens of individuals surrounding Clinton who had died "mysteriously," and he added: "Listen, he [Clinton] can order people done away with at his will." Robert G. Kaiser, "Scaife Denies Ties to 'Conspiracy,' Starr; Patron of Conservative Groups Criticizes Clinton Probe, Gingrich, Republican Party," *Washington Post,* December 17, 1998. Perhaps the best account of these efforts is found in Jeffrey Toobin's *A Vast Conspiracy* (New York: Random House, 2000).

38. Phil Kuntz, "Citizen Scaife," *Wall Street Journal,* October 12, 1995; Robert G. Kaiser and Ira Chinoy, "How Scafie's Money Empowered a Movement" from series "The Right's Funding Father: Fighting a War of Ideas," *Washington Post,* May 2-3, 1999; Haynes Johnson, *The Best of Times: America in the Clinton Years* (New York: Harcourt, Inc.), 260–64; Alan Crawford, *Thunder on the Right: The "New Right" and the Politics of Resentment* (New York: Pantheon Books, 1980), 3–41.

39. Key works on the rise of religious conservatism are Steve Bruce, *The Rise and Fall of the New Christian Right: Conservative Protestant Politics in America, 1978–1988* (Oxford: Clarendon Press 1988); Michael Lienesch, *Redeeming America: Piety and Politics in the New Christian Right* (Chapel Hill: University of North Carolina Press, 1992); Duane Murray Oldfield, *The Right and the Righteous: The Christian Right Confronts the Republican Party* (Lanham, Mass.: Rowan and Littlefield Publishers, 1996); and William Martin, *With God On Our Side: The Rise of the Religious Right in America* (New York: Broadway Books, 1996).

40. In the aftermath of the 2000 election Bush advisor Karl Rove fretted that the most unexpected shortfall in votes was "among self-identified white, evangelical Protestants, Pentecostals and fundamentalists. If you look at the electoral model, there should have been 19 million of them. Instead, there was [sic] 15 million." *Investor's Business Daily,* December 18, 2001. Rove's complaint is consistent with voting data which shows that—while evangelicals have made a dramatic shift in their allegiance from the Democratic to the Republican Party—their turnout at the polls did not significantly increase during the 1980s and 1990s. Warren E. Miller and J. Merrill Shanks, *The New American Voter* (Cambridge: Harvard University Press, 1996), 229–32.

41. Stanley B. Greenberg, *Middle Class Dreams: The Politics and Power of the New American Majority,* rev. ed. (New Haven: Yale University Press, 1996), 295–97; *New York Times,* November 13, 1994.

42. Harold W. Stanley summarized this debate in "Southern Partisan Changes: Dealignment, Realignment or Both?" *Journal of Politics* 50 (February 1988): 64–89. In the aftermath of the 1994 election, however, Walter

Burnham pointed to the increasing number of contested Democratic seats and a corresponding rise in uncontested Republican races and predicted decisive realignment. Burnham, "Realignment Lives: The 1994 Earthquake and its Implications," in Campbell and Rockman, *The Clinton Presidency,* 392n4.

43. Garry Wills, *Reagan's America: Innocents at Home* (Garden City, NJ: Doubleday, 1987).

44. Robert Reich, *Locked in the Cabinet,* (New York, Alfred A. Knopf, 1997), 157.

45. Greenberg, *Middle Class Dreams.*

46. See especially chapter 5, "Partisans or Independents," in Bruce Keith and others, *The Myth of the Independent Voter* (Berkeley: University of California Press, 1992).

47. Barbara Sinclair, "Trying to Govern Positively in a Negative Era: Clinton and the 103rd Congress," in Campbell and Rockman, *The Clinton Presidency,* 121.

48. Greenberg, *Middle Class Dreams,* 312.

49. Steven Rosenstone and John Mark Hansen, *Mobilization, Participation, and Democracy in America* (New York: Macmillan, 1993), 3. See also Raymond Wolfinger and Steven Rosenstone, *Who Votes* (New Haven: Yale University Press, 1980).

50. Miller and Shanks, *The New American Voter,* 65–67, 91. As the two authors conclude, the "post–New Deal turnout rate is twenty-five points lower than that of the New Deal," both among voters with no more than a grade school education and those with completed high school educations.

51. Table 8, "Reported Voting and Registration of Family Members, by Age and Family Income: November 2000," 2000 U.S. Census. The level of voting participation in fact seems to closely follow family income, moving steadily from 72 percent for the wealthiest American down to 28 percent for the poorest 20 percent.

52. See, for example, Reich, *Locked in the Cabinet,* 292.

53. Strom Thurmond, *The Faith We Have Not Kept* (San Diego: Viewpoint Publishers, 1968), 38; Thomas Sowell, *Washington Times,* October 27, 2002. In 1983, columnist George Will had gone even further in defending low voter turnout. Full participation in Weimar Germany, he noted ominously, had led to political instability and, ultimately, to the rise of Hitler. George Will, "In Defense of Nonvoting," *Newsweek,* October 10, 1983, 96.

54. Benjamin Highton and Ramond Wolfinger, "The Political Implications of Higher Turnout," *British Journal of Political Science* 31 (January 2001): 192.

55. Highton and Wolfinger, "The Political Implications," 184–85. Highton and Wolfinger place considerable emphasis upon the low turnout of younger voters, but they cite no evidence to suggest that these younger voters are more likely to vote for conservative and/or Republican candidates.

56. As Rosenstone and Hansen concluded, the evidence is clear that voters' confidence in their ability to act effectively in politics generally increases the level of participation. *Mobilization,* 3.

57. Michael Janofsky, "Housing for Poorer Neighbors Offends Vail's Rich," *New York Times,* September 5, 1999; see also Edward N. Wolff, *Top Heavy: A*

Study of the Increasing Inequality of Wealth in America (New York: Twentieth Century Fund Press, 1995); Frank Levy's *The New Dollars and Dreams: Americans Incomes and Economic Change* (New York: Russell Sage Foundation, 1999); and Kevin Phillips's more popular (and polemical) *Wealth and Democracy: A Political History of the American Rich* (New York: Broadway Books, 2002). The most recent work is by Thomas Piketty and Emmanuel Saez, "Income Inequality in the United States, 1913–1998" and it shows a continuing growth in inequality and a general stagnation in the earning levels of Americans below the top twenty percentile. See http://papers.nber.org/papers/W8467.

58. John C. Weicher, "The Inequality Myth: Getting Richer (At Different Rates)," June 14, 1995; Bruce Bartlett, "The Rich Get Richer, and That's All Right," July 10, 1995; and Michael Novack, "The Inequality Myth: What Wealth Gap?" *Wall Street Journal*, July 11, 1995.

59. Few issues are more subject to ideological disputation than the issue of income maldistribution. Conservatives argue that the calculations of "liberal" economists do not take into account indirect benefits (such as food stamps and Medicaid) while liberals counter that conservatives make a similar methodological failure, refusing to calculate the benefits to middle-class taxpayers such as the deductibility of home-mortgage interest payments. Using a conservative research approach that included indirect benefits for low-income Americans, the Census Bureau concluded that household income for the poorest 20 percent had stagnated through the 1980s, but increased 10 percent during the 1990s. In contrast, those in the top twentieth percentile saw an income increase of more than 65 percent during these same years with much of that going to the top 1 percent. U.S. Census Bureau, 2000, [Revised August 22, 2002], "Income Inequality, 1947–1998, especially Table 4, "Measures of Household Inequality, 1967–1998."

60. Herbert E. Alexander, "Spending in the 1996 Elections," in *Financing the 1996 Election*, ed. John C. Green (Armonk: M. E. Sharpe, 1999), 15. All figures have been converted to 2002 dollars to account for inflationary differences. During these two decades median household income in the United States increased less than ten percent.

61. Specific figures are from the Center for Responsive Politics. Of course liberal groups and labor unions engage in the same kind of issue advocacy ads, usually on behalf of mostly Democratic candidates, but their resources are far outweighed by the funds available to corporate and business interests.

62. Preliminary figures for 2002 are from the Federal Election Commission Reports as calculated by *PoliticalMoneyLine* at http://www.tray.com. There simply is no agreed on figure for political expenditures; the one thing on which observers agree is that the amount spent was increased dramatically. See Elizabeth Drew, *The Corruption of American Politics: What Went Wrong and Why* (New York: The Overlook Press, 2000).

63. Janet M. Grenske, "PACs and the Congressional Supermarket: The Currency is Complex," *American Journal of Political Science* 33, no. 1 (1989): 1–24. Richard Hall and Frank Wayman summarize this "money doesn't matter" literature in "Buying Time: Moneyed Interests and the Mobilization of

Bias in Congressional Committees," *The American Political Science Review,* 84 (September 1990): 798.

64. Quoted in Mark Green, "The Evil of Access," *The Nation,* December 30, 2002, 16. In the same article Green quotes current Georgia Democratic senator Zell Miller as describing his disgust at the end of a day in the fundraising cubicles in which he constantly reminded potential contributors of his membership on key senatorial committees: "I always left that room," said Miller, "feeling like a cheap prostitute who'd had a busy day."

65. David Firestone and Richard A. Oppel Jr. "Critics Say Security Bill Favors Special Interests," *New York Times,* November 19, 2002, A-28; Sheryl Gay Stolberg, "A Capitol Hill Mystery: Who Aided Drug Maker?," *New York Times,* November 29, 2002. In the mid-1990s, a number of political scientists began to raise questions about earlier, and more benign, interpretations of the role of campaign contributions and lobbying. David Austen-Smith and John R. Wright, "Counteractive Lobbying," *American Journal of Political Science* 38 (February 1994): 25–44; David Austen-Smith, "Campaign Contributions and Access," *The American Political Science Review* 89 (September 1995), 566–81; and Frank R. Baumgartner and Beth L. Leech, "The Multiple Ambiguities of Counteractive Lobbying," *American Journal of Political Science* 40 (May 1996): 521–42.

66. George Packer, *Blood of the Liberals* (New York: Farrar, Straus and Giroux, 2000), 388–89.

Chapter Seven: The Women's Movement Agenda and the Record of the Clinton Administration by Dorothy McBride Stetson

One of the thornier issues in the women's movement literature is the relation between women's movements and feminist movements. Some distinguish between them, arguing that feminism involves a specific ideology while others use the terms interchangeably. Because the U.S. women's movement has not had a strong non-feminist component, here the terms are used interchangeably. For comparative analysis, however, it is important to distinguish between non-feminist gender-conscious political activism and feminist gender-conscious political activism.

1. When the votes were counted, however, the gender gap was only 4 percent: 45 percent of women compared to 41 percent of men voted for Clinton. The gender gap reflects the preferences of all women voters; the women's movement reflects gender-conscious political activism. The latter were supporters of Clinton.

2. In 1996 a majority of women voters agreed with feminists by giving 54 percent of their votes to the president, representing a gender gap of 11 percent over men's support.

3. Jessie Allen, "Feminists and the Sex Scandal," *Dissent* 46, no. 1 (Winter 1999): 21–24; Tara Zahra, "The Feminism Gap," *American Prospect* 42 (January/February 1999): 20–22.

4. For IWY agenda, see Caroline Bird, ed., *What Women Want.* (New York: Simon and Schuster, 1979). For information on the movement in the 1990s,

see Sheila Tobias, *Faces of Feminism: An Activist's Reflections on the Women's Movement* (Boulder: Westview Press, 1997) and Nancy Whittier, *Feminist Generations: The Persistence of the Radical Women's Movement* (Philadelphia: Temple University Press, 1995).

5. Myra Marx Ferree and Beth B. Hess, *Controversy and Coalition: the New Feminist Movement Across Four/Three Decades of Change*, 3rd ed. (New York: Routledge, 2000); Myra Marx Ferree and Patricia Yancy Martin, eds., *Feminist Organizations: Harvest of the New Women's Movement* (Philadelphia: Temple University Press, 1996); Jennifer Leigh Disney and Joyce Gelb, "Feminist Organizational Success: the State of the U.S. Women's Movement in the 1990s," *Women and Politics* 21, no. 4 (2000): 39–76.

6. Women's support remained strong and carried over into the 2000 election with a 12 percent gender gap in favor of Al Gore: 54 percent of women and only 42 percent of men voted the Democratic ticket.

7. Allen, "Feminists," 23.

8. RNGS Project focuses on the impact of women's movement activism on state responses with special attention to the effectiveness of women's policy offices (state feminism). Forty-five scholars from Europe, North America, Australia, and Japan are studying policy debates in fourteen countries and the European Union. For initial findings in the project, see Dorothy McBride Stetson, ed., *Abortion Politics, Women's Movements and the Democratic State: A Comparative Study of State Feminism* (Oxford: Oxford University Press, 2001); Amy G. Mazur, *State Feminism, Women's Movements and Job Training: Making Democracies work in a Global Economy* (New York: Routledge, 2001). Initial research on issues of partial-birth abortion, welfare reform, and trafficking can be found in Dorothy McBride Stetson, "US Abortion Debates 1959–1998: the Women's Movement Holds On," 247–266; in Stetson, *Abortion Politics*; Dorothy McBride Stetson, "Welfare Reform: America's Hot Issue," working paper prepared for RNGS conference, University of Turin, November 7–9, 2001; Dorothy McBride Stetson, "The Invisible Issue: Prostitution and Trafficking of Women and Girls in the United States," in *Prostitution and State Feminism*, in Joyce Outshoorn. ed., forthcoming.

9. Dorothy McBride Stetson and Amy G. Mazur, "Defining Women's Movements Cross-Nationally and Over Time: Lessons from the Project of the Research Network on Gender, Politics and the State," prepared for presentation at the annual meeting of the Canadian Political Science Association, Toronto, May 29–31, 2001.

10. Jane Mansbridge, "What Is the Feminist Movement?" in *Feminist Organizations: Harvest of the New Women's Movement*, Myra Marx Ferree and Beth B. Hess, eds. (Philadelphia: Temple University Press, 1996) 27–33.

11. Barbara Ransby, "Black Feminism at Twenty-One: Reflections on the Evolution of a National Community," *Signs* 25 no. 4 (2000): 1214–21,1218.

12. Mary Fainsod Katzenstein, *Faithful and Fearless: Moving Feminist Protest Inside the Church and the Military* (Princeton: Princeton University Press, 1998).

13. William A. Gamson, *The Strategy of Social Protest*, (Homewood, Ill.: the Dorsey Press, 1975).

14. For the typology of representation that includes descriptive and sub-

stantive categories, see Hanna Fenichel Pitkin, *The Concept of Representation* (Berkeley: University of California Press, 1967). See Thomas R. Rochon and Daniel A. Mazmanian, "Social Movements and the policy Process," *Annals of the American Academy of Political and Social Science* 528 (July 1993): 75–87 for a full discussion of social movement effects on process change.

15. Karen Beckwith, "Beyond Compare? Women's Movements in Comparative Perspective," *European Journal of Political Research* 37 no. 4 (June 2000): 431–468, 436.

16. Seyla Benhabib, "From Identity Politics to Social Feminism," in *Politics at the Turn of the Century,* A.M. Melzer, J. Weinberger, and M.R. Zinman. eds. (Lanham, Md.: Rowman and Littlefield, 2000), 27–41.

17. The equality/difference debates date back at least to the post–Civil War period . A recent manifestation is the debate over identity politics versus equality politics. See Sandra F. VanBurkeleo *"Belonging to the World": Women's Rights and American Constitutional Culture, (*New York: Oxford University Press, 2001) and Benhabib, "From Identity Politics."

18. Women's Appointment Project. "Women's Appointment Statistics." National Women's Political Caucus and National Council of Women's Organizations. 2001. http://www.appointwomen.com.

19. Jennifer Segal, "Representative Decision Making on the Federal Bench: Clinton's District Court Appointees," *Political Research Quarterly* 53 (March 2000), 137–50.

20. By contrast, there has been little interest in such mechanisms in the George W. Bush administration. He established no office of women's outreach in the White House and proposed to eliminate the regional offices of the Women's Bureau. Conservative allies have also recommended the elimination of DACOWITS, an advisory committee to the Department of Defense to promote the status of women in the armed services.

21. The U.S. Supreme Court reviewed a Nebraska statute nearly identical to the congressional acts and declared it an undue burden on women's liberty and thus unconstitutional (Stenberg. v. Carhart [120 S.Ct. 2597.2000]). Nevertheless, President George W. Bush has indicated if the ban passes again he would sign it.

22. Felicia Kornbluh, "Feminists and the Welfare Debate: Too Little? Too Late? *Dollars and Sense,* November/December 1996, 24–5, 39–40.

23. Gwendolyn Mink, *Welfare's End,* (Ithaca: Cornell University Press, 1998).

24. Equality Now, Planned Parenthood Federation of America, International Women's Health Coalition, NOW, Women's Environment and Development Organization, Catholics for a Free Choice, Protection Project, Coalition Against Trafficking in Women, Sisterhood in Global Institute, National Black Women's Health Project, Feminist Majority, Gloria Steinem, Center for Women Policy Studies.

25. The feminist ideology that views sexual oppression as basic to all other forms of male dominance is sometimes called *dominance feminism.* The term *radical feminism* is a bit misleading these days since the argument that women need to be empowered to fight back against sexual exploitation is a mainstream

idea in the women's movement and is the motivation behind sexual harassment policy and rape law reforms.

26. Trafficking Victims Protection Act of 2000, Public Law 106-386.

27. United Nations, *Protocol to Prevent, Suppress and Punish Trafficking in Persons, Especially Women and Children, Supplementing the United Nations Convention Against Transnational Organized Crime*, (New York: United Nations, 2000).

Chapter Eight: Clinton's China Policy by June Teufel Dreyer

1. The Chinese government claims that no one was killed inside Tiananmen Square in putting down the demonstrations. Although some eyewitnesses disagree, the government has never said that no one died *outside* Tiananmen Square. Hence the terminology that is used here.

2. Holly Burkhalter, "Put The Squeeze On Beijing," *New York Times*, May 25, 1992.

3. Editorial, "Squandering Leverage on China," *New York Times* March 23, 1992.

4. David Lauter, "Clinton Blasts Bush's Foreign Policy Record," *Los Angeles Times*, August 14, 1992.

5. Nicholas D. Kristof, "China Worried by Clinton's Linking of Trade to Human Rights," *New York Times*, October 9, 1992.

6. Kristof, "China Worried."

7. Nicholas Kristof, "At Work Where the Cold War's Ice Still Lingers," *New York Times*, October 30, 1992.

8. Keith Bradsher, "Aides Meet Today on Dispute Over Sales to Iran and China," *New York Times*, January 5, 1993.

9. Keith Bradsher, "U.S. Export Panel is Said to Back Jet-Engine Sale to China Military," *New York Times*, January 6, 1993.

10. Thomas L. Friedman, "Clinton Says Bush Made China Gains," *New York Times*, November 20, 1992.

11. Elaine Sciolino, "Abuses by Serbs the Worst Since Nazi Era, Report Says," *New York Times*, January 20 1993.

12. Nicholas Kristof, "In a Nod to U.S., China Plans to Free 2 Dissidents," *New York Times*, February 2, 1993.

13. In the Bush meeting, the Dalai Lama was led into the White House through a side door. In the Clinton case, his entry was through the front door, but the meeting was formally scheduled with Vice President Al Gore. Clinton "dropped in" and talked briefly with the Dalai Lama. "Clinton Meets Dalai Lama; Discusses Rights in China," *New York Times*, April 28, 1993; Valerie Strauss, "'A Simple Buddhist Monk': Tibet's Exiled Dalai Lama Opening His Heart To His Enemies," *Washington Post*, April 30, 1993.

14. Reuters, "Human Rights Issues Prompt Levi Strauss Cuts in China," *New York Times*, May 5, 1993.

15. Calvin Sims, "China Steps up Spending to Keep US. Trade Status: June Deadline Looms for Extension of Privileges," *New York Times*. May 7, 1993.

16. Nicholas Kristof, "Some See Half-Empty Glasses in U.S. China Pacts," *New York Times*, May 10, 1993.

17. Editorial, "Favor Freedom in China," May 10, *New York Times*, 1993.

18. Nicholas Kristof, "Clinton Aide Ends China Trip with No Sign of Accord," *New York Times*, May 13, 1993.

19. See, for example, editorial, "U.S. Avoids Crisis With China," *Yomiuri* (Tokyo), May 31, 1993; and editorial, "A Deft Human-Rights Prod At China," *The Plain Dealer* (Cleveland), June 3, 1993.

20. Isabel Hilton, "Proof That Pressure Works on Peking: The West's Hand in Dealing with China Has Never Been Stronger," *The Independent* (London), June 1, 1993.

21. Leonard Spector, "China's Nuclear Factor," *Christian Science Monitor*, June 11, 1993.

22. *South China Morning Post* (Hong Kong), "Slick Willie Takes the Heat Off," May 31, 1933, 4.

23. *South China Morning Post* (Hong Kong), "A Weak Man in the White House," Sunday edition, May 30, 1993.

24. See, e.g., Irving Kristof, "China Says U.S. Harasses Ship Bound for the Mideast," *New York Times*, August 8, 1993; Nyan Chanda, "Drifting Apart," *Far Eastern Economic Review* (Hong Kong), August 26, 1993.

25. Author's conversation, July 18, 2000. Source is a retired government official who was involved in the matter.

26. Steve A. Holmes, "U.S. Determines China Violated Pact on Missiles," *New York Times*, August 25, 1993; Steven Greenhouse, "$1 Billion in Sales of High-Tech Items to China Blocked: Retaliation Over Missiles," *New York Times* August 26, 1993; Patrick E. Tyler, "China Calls American Trade Sanctions Unjustified," *New York Times* August 27, 1993; Patrick E. Tyler, "China Protests U.S. Trade Sanctions," *New York Times* August 28, 1993.

27. Cherian George, "West Wanted to Cut China Down to Size: Senior Minister Lee," *Straits Times* (Singapore), October 14, 1993.

28. Steven Greenhouse, "Aerospace Industry Seeks Weaker Sanctions on China," *New York Times*, August 28, 1993.

29. Michael R. Gordon, "Israel Selling China Military Technology, C.I.A. Chief Asserts," *New York Times*, October 12 1993; Michael R. Gordon, "Israel Sells Arms to China, U.S. Says," *New York Times*, October 13, 1993; Patrick E. Tyler, "Rabin Says Sales to China Didn't Break U.S. Law," *New York Times*, October 14, 1993; A.M. Rosenthal, "On My Mind: Here We Go Again," *New York Times*, October 15, 1993.

30. Chris Yeung, "Dissidents on Trial Day after China Lost Games," *South China Morning Post* (Hong Kong), October 18, 1993; *South China Morning Post* (Hong Kong), "China Stifles Dissent Again," October 20, 1993; Sheila Tefft, "China's Political Repression Persists After Olympic Loss," *Christian Science Monitor*, October 26, 1993.

31. Editorial, "Building Bridges to China," *Boston Globe*, October 21, 1993.

32. Elaine Sciolino, "Clinton Takes Political Risk in Talking to Chinese," *New York Times*, November 17, 1993.

33. Patrick E. Tyler, "U.S. And China Agree to Expand Defense Links," *New York Times,* November 2, 1993.

34. Daniel Williams and Jeffrey Smith, "U.S. Softens Military Line On Beijing," *Guardian* (London), November 3, 1993.

35. Sheila Tefft, "U.S. And China Agree To Pursue Rights Talks," *Christian Science Monitor,* October 13, 1993.

36. Patrick E. Tyler, "Haig Scorns U.S. for Its Tough China Policy" *New York Times,* October 28, 1993.

37. Elaine Sciolino, "U.S. Will Allow Computer Sale to Court China," *New York Times,* November 19, 1993.

38. *New York Times,* "China Stiffs the President," November 23, 1993.

39. Editorial, "U.S. Relations with China: Push But Don't Shove: Washington Must Calibrate National Interests Carefully, Not Emotionally," *Los Angeles Times,* November 23, 1993.

40. Jim Mann, "Tough Choices Ahead for the Administration," *Los Angeles Times,* March 20, 1994.

41. Charles Krauthammer, "Major Embarrassment in China," *Washington Post,* March 20, 1994.

42. Patrick E. Tyler, "Beijing Says It Could Live Well Even if U.S. Trade Was Cut Off," *New York Times,* March 21, 1994.

43. Edward Gargan, "Gauging Consequences Of Spurning China," *New York Times,* March 21, 1994.

44. Daniel Williams, "Christopher Cites Progress on Human Rights in China: Report Could Result in Lesser Trade Sanctions," *Washington Post,* May 24, 1994.

45. David S. Cloud, "Renewal of China's MFN Status Angers Some Lawmakers," *Congressional Quarterly,* May 28, 1994, 1372.

46. *Guardian* (London), "The China Wall Has Suddenly Crumbled," May 28, 1994.

47. David E. Rosenbaum, "China Trade Rift with U.S. Deepens," *New York Times,* January 29, 1995; Tony Walker, "A 'Maturing' Marks Copyright Deal— U.S. Officials Detect More Businesslike Beijing with Hopes for Future," *Financial Times* (London), February 28, 1995.

48. Lee Michael Katz, "China Sending Ambassador Back to Washington," *USA Today,* August 19, 1995.

49. Elaine Sciolino, "C.I.A. Report Says Chinese Sent Iran Arms Components," *New York Times,* June 22, 1995.

50. Editorial, "A Judicious Show of Resolve: Reacting to Chinese Threats, U. S. Moves Carriers Closer to Taiwan," *Los Angeles Times,* March 12, 1996. This article errs in saying that it was Republicans who proposed explicit military commitments to Taiwan. The support was bipartisan, and large. A former member of the Senate Foreign Relations Committee staff told the author that Clinton decided to dispatch the carrier battle groups only after Nancy Pelosi (D-Calif.) and Christopher Cox (R-Calif.) informed him that they had a veto-proof majority for such legislation. (private communication to author, July 1, 2002).

51. Seth Faison, "Tension In Taiwan: The Polemics: China Denounced U.S. 'Interference' in Dispute with Taiwan," *New York Times,* March 22, 1996.

52. Steven Erlanger, "U.S. Won't Punish China over Sale of Nuclear Gear," *New York Times*, May 11, 1996.

53. David E. Sanger, "China Arms Aides Are Sought by U.S. in Smuggling Plot," *New York Times*, May 23, 1996; Bruce Gilley and Nigel Holloway, "Guns and Money: Illicit Arms Trade Puts China on the Defensive," *Far Eastern Economic Review*, June 6, 1996.

54. Craig R. Whitney, "China Signs Deal with Airbus Jets for $ 1.5 Billion: Seen As Signal to U.S.—Beijing Shows It Might Turn to Europe if Clinton Links Trade to Human Rights," *New York Times*, April 11, 1996.

55. Robert D. Hershey Jr., "China Has Become Chief Contributor to U.S. Trade Gap," *New York Times*, August 21, 1996.

56. Debra J. Saunders, "America: The Pushover Country," *San Francisco Chronicle*, March 6, 1996.

57. Alan Tonelson, "Protecting Ourselves," *New York Times*, May 16, 1996.

58. Such was the judgment of columnist Thomas Friedman. See Thomas L. Friedman, "The New China Consensus," *New York Times*, May 20, 1996.

59. R. W. Apple, "Clinton Concedes China Policy Hasn't Helped Much on Rights," *New York Times* January 29, 1997.

60. David Johnston, "Classified Data in China Case Was [*sic*] Mishandled, Report Says," *New York Times*, July 16, 1999.

61. Lynn Sweet, "China's Ties to DNC Probed," *Chicago Sun-Times*, February 16, 1997; Robert A. Rosenblatt, "GOP Intensifies Donations Probe; Congress: Panel Subpoenas 20 More Witnesses Amid Allegations of Overseas Role in Fund-Raising Controversy," *Los Angeles Times*, February 17, 1997.

62. Reproduced in full in Edward Timperlake and William C. Triplett II, *Year Of The Rat* (Washington, D.C.: Regnery Publishers, 1998), 112–13. Timperlake and Triplett believe there is overwhelming evidence that there is a link between the PRC's campaign contributions and Clinton's China policy.

63. Thomas J. Duesterberg, "Clinton's Favoritism Imperils Free Trade," *Wall Street Journal*, February 25, 1997.

64. Author interview, Washington, D.C., April 6, 2002.

65. Author interview, 2002.

66. "Sino-U.S. Ties on an Upswing," *Straits Times* (Singapore), April 4, 1998.

67. *Report of the Senate Select Committee on U.S. National Security and Military/Commercial Concerns with the People's Republic of China* (Washington, D.C.: U.S. Government Printing Office, 1999). The document is popularly known as the Cox report, since Congressman Christopher Cox (R-Calif.) chaired the bipartisan committee.

68. Pan Rui, "Take a Further Look at the Dual Character of U.S. Policy Toward China," *Jiefang ribao* (Liberation daily), (Shanghai), May 22, 1999, translated in National Technical Information Service, Foreign Broadcast Information Service (Washington, D.C.), June 19, 1999.

69. Steven Lee Meyers, "Chinese Military to Resume Contacts with the Pentagon," *New York Times*, January 6, 2000.

70. Steven Mufson and John Lancaster, "State Department Human Rights Report Slams China, Others," *Washington Post*, February 26, 2000.

71. James Kynge and David Murphy, "UN Commissioner Attacks China's Rights Record," *Financial Times*, March 3, 2000.

72. Thomas Ricks, "Taiwan Seen as Vulnerable to Attack," *Washington Post,* March 31, 2000; Bill Gertz and Rowan Scarborough, "Inside the Ring: Taiwan Report Held," *Washington Times,* March 31, 2000.

73. "Moderation Urged on Taiwan," *New York Times,* April 10, 2000, quotes U.S. ambassador to Beijing Joseph Prueher as saying "viewing China as an enemy could become a self-fulfilling prophecy."

74. Samuel R. Berger and Gene Sperling, "Trade Will Hurt China's Hard-Liners," *New York Times,* May 18, 2000.

75. Mark Groombridge, "China's Entry to WTO Will Help Reforms," *Australian Financial Review,* May 29, 2000.

Chapter Nine: Clinton Foreign Policy and the Revolution in the East by Robert Legvold

1. The list grew rapidly, but the best early examples were Charles Krauthammer's two defining articles, "Universal Dominion: Toward a Unipolar World," *The National Interest* no. 18 (Winter 1989–90): 46–49 and "The Unipolar Moment," *Foreign Affairs* 70, no. 1 (America and the World 1990–91), 23–33.

2. See David Gergen, "America's Missed Opportunities," *Foreign Affairs* 71, no. 1 (America and the World 1991–92): 1–19.

3. The 1991 State of the Union Message, *New York Times* (January 30, 1991).

4. Christopher Layne and Benjamin Schwartz, "American Hegemony— Without an Enemy," *Foreign Policy* no. 92, (Fall 1993): 5–23.

5. Charles Krauthammer, "America Rules: Thank God; Who Else Should Call the Shots? China? Iran? The Russian Mafia?" *Time,* August 4, 1997.

6. Quoted in Layne and Schwartz, "American Hegemony—Without an Enemy," 9–10. The principal author was Paul Wolfowitz, then the under secretary of defense for policy. He would revive the idea ten years later, when as the deputy secretary of defense, he helped shape the 2002 national security strategy of George W. Bush's administration.

7. "The 1992 Campaign: Excerpts from a Speech by Clinton on U.S. Role," *New York Times,* October 2, 1992.

8. Robert Kagan, "The Benevolent Empire," *Foreign Policy* no. 111 (Summer 1998): 33.

9. The sharpest criticism came from Michael Mandelbaum, who was personally and politically sympathetic to the administration, indeed, one of its original foreign-policy advisors, but his argument was instantly embraced by the administration's partisan critics. (See his "Foreign Policy as Social Work, *Foreign Affairs* 75, no. 1 [January-February 1996]: 16–32.)

10. Arnold Wolfers, ed., "The Goals of Foreign Policy," *Discord and Collaboration* (Baltimore: Johns Hopkins University Press, 1962), 73–77.

11. Private communication from Strobe Talbott, December 1, 2002.

12. Stephen M. Walt makes all of these points when coming to the defense of the Clinton administration in "Two Cheers for Clinton's Foreign Policy," *Foreign Affairs* 78, no. 2 (March-April 2000): 63–79.

13. William J. Clinton, "Remarks by the President in Freedom House Speech," The Hyatt Regency, Washington, D.C. (October 6, 1995), The White House, Office of the Press Secretary.

14. As is clear from the following excerpt from Strobe Talbott's memoir of these years, Clinton's comment was not a throw-away line in one speech. "Clinton had been reading biographies of Roosevelt and Truman that convinced him that neither had grand strategies for how to exert American leadership against the global threats posed by Hitler and Stalin. Rather, they had "powerful instincts about what had to be done, and they just made it up and they went along." Strategic coherence, he said, was largely imposed after the fact by scholars, memoirists and the "the chattering classes." It was "a huge myth that we always knew what we were doing during the cold war," he said. (Strobe Talbott, *The Russia Hand: A Memoir of Presidential Diplomacy* [New York: Random House, 2002], 133).

15. Joseph S. Nye Jr., *The Paradox of American Power: Why the World's Only Superpower Can't Go It Alone* (New York: Oxford University Press, 2002).

16. Thomas L. Friedman, "Clinton Inherits Conflicts That Don't Follow Rules," *New York Times*, December 13, 1992.

17. Warren Christopher, "Securing U.S. Interests While Supporting Russian Reform," address before the Chicago Council on Foreign Relations, March 22, 1993.

18. Strobe Talbott, who read a draft of this chapter, reacted by writing, "As someone who ran that gamut himself, I assure you that the hopes at the beginning were tinged with plenty of apprehension and the weariness/misgivings at the end were made easier to bear by the recognition of [the] distance covered," from the many moments of "upheaval" and potentially "irreversible setback" in the early and middle years to the relative steadying of the relationship by the end (Private communication, December 1, 2002). Judged from the outside, however, in my view the contrast in broad outline is unmistakable.

19. Remarks by President Bush and President Yeltsin in Exchange of Toasts, The State Dining Room, The White House, Office of the Press Secretary, June 16, 1992, 1.

20. "A Charter for American-Russian Partnership and Friendship," The White House, Office of the Press Secretary, June 17, 1992.

21. "Remarks by President Bush and Russian President Boris Yeltsin in Joint Signing Ceremony," The White House, Office of the Press Secretary, June 17, 1992, 2.

22. "Remarks by President Bush and President Yeltsin, The Rose Garden," The White House, Office of the Press Secretary, June 16, 1992, 2.

23. "Remarks by the President in Address to U.S./Russian Business Summit," The White House Office of the Press Secretary, June 17, 1992, 2.

24. See James M. Goldgeier and Michael McFaul, *Power and Purpose: U.S. Policy toward Russia after the Cold War,* (Washington, D.C.: The Brookings Institution, 2003), 68–86.

25. Thomas L. Friedman, "Turning His Sights Overseas, Clinton Sees a Problem at 1600 Pennsylvania Avenue," *New York Times*, April 2, 1992.

26. Speech of the President to The American Society of Newspaper Editors, United States Naval Academy, Annapolis, Maryland, Office of the Press Secretary, April 1, 1993, 5.

27. "U.S. Support for Russian Reform: An Investment in America's Security," Address at the Hubert H. Humphrey Institute of Public Affairs at the University of Minnesota by Secretary Christopher, May 27, 1993, *Dispatch* 4, no. 22, U.S. Department of State Bureau of Public Affairs, 1.

28. "U.S. Support for Russian Reform," 2.

29. In Strobe Talbott's account, Clinton emerges repeatedly as the one pushing hardest in this direction, often over the reservations of his advisors, particularly, his domestic advisors. (Talbott, *The Russia Hand*.)

30. "A New Generation of Russian Democrats," Address by Secretary Christopher at the Academy of the National Economy, Moscow, October 23, 1993, *Dispatch* 4, no. 43, U.S. Department of State Bureau of Public Affairs, 1.

31. Talbott tells the story of how Yeltsin had told Clinton of the prospective firings during the summit, but refused to listen to the president's attempt to get him to reverse the decision (Talbott, *The Russia Hand,* 117–18).

32. "Forge Realistic, Pragmatic Relations with Russia," Remarks by William J. Perry at George Washington University, March 14, 1994, *Defense Issues* 9, no. 19 (1994): 1.

33. "Forge Realistic, Pragmatic Relations," 2.

34. Zbigniew Brzezinski, "The Premature Partnership," *Foreign Affairs* 73, no. 2 (March/April 1994), 67–82.

35. "Remarks by the President in Live Telecast to Russian People," The White House, Office of the Press Secretary, January 14, 1994.

36. The problem over the sale of nuclear technology to Iran, it should be noted, did not begin in this period. It traced back at least to 1993, and at no point had the Russians shown a readiness to accept the administration's argument.

37. In an October 1996 speech Talbott noted, "Quite a few Russians have made clear that they believe America's real strategy—indeed, this Administration's real strategy—is actually to weaken Russia, even to divide it. It does not much reassure them to hear us say we want to see Russia fulfill its 'greatness.' In their ears, that word has a mushy, disingenuous, even deceitful ring. It sounds as though we are talking about the cultural genius of Tolstoy and Tchaikovsky—not about the brawnier brilliance of Kutuzov and Zhukov." (From "America and Russia in a Changing World," Deputy Secretary Talbott, U.S. Department of State, *Dispatch* 7, no. 44, October 28, 1996.)

38. Talbott recounts Yeltsin and his advisors' desperate eagerness to have the summit take place as planned, but their passion was for fear that a cancellation would signal to international markets that the Clinton administration was giving up on Russia, not because of what they expected the summit to accomplish (Talbott, *The Russia Hand,* 279–83).

39. For the joint Yeltsin-Clinton Press conference, where Yeltsin mentioned the plan, see Associated Press, "Excerpts from Clinton and Yeltsin Remarks: 'Peace and Stability,'" the *New York Times,* September 3, 1998.

40. He developed these points with several audiences, including Yeltsin,

but most fully in a speech to the Moscow Institute on International Relations (MGIMO), September 1, 1998. (The White House, Office of the Press Secretary, Moscow, Russia, September 1, 1998.)

41. Secretary of State Madeleine K. Albright, Address to the U.S.-Russian Business Council, Chicago, Illinois, October 2, 1998. Office of the Spokesman, U.S. Department of State.

42. Deputy Secretary Strobe Talbott, "Gogol's Troika: The Case for Strategic Patience in a Time of Troubles," Address at Stanford University, November 6, 1998.

43. For representative samples see, Vladimir Kuznechevsky, "NATO's Plans—For Half the World," *Rossiskaya gazeta,* April 15, 1999 and E. Akhundova, "Will NATO Bomb Karabakh As Well?," *Obshchaya gazeta* April 15–21, 1999.

44. Talbott, *The Russia Hand,* 4.

45. In his first major foreign policy campaign speech at the Reagan Library, November 19, 1999. (For a summary, see R. W. Apple Jr., "Bush Questions Aid to Moscow in Policy Talk," *New York Times,* November 20, 1999.)

46. See the joint reports of the Carnegie Endowment for International Peace and the Center for Foreign and Defense Policy (Moscow), *U.S.-Russian Relations* (Washington: Carnegie Endowment, 2000) and Celeste Wallander "The Dynamics of U.S.-Russian Relations: A Critical Perspective," Policy Memo Series no. 111 (March 2000), Program on New Approaches to Russian Security, Davis Center for Russian Studies, Harvard University (http://www. fas.harvard.edu/~ponars).

47. The charge was most aggressively made and for transparently partisan purposes in the Cox "special advisory group" report mentioned earlier: *Russia's Road to Corruption: How the Clinton Administration Exported Government Instead of Free Enterprise and Failed the Russian People* (U.S. House of Representatives, September 2000), particularly Chapter 4.

48. For a report of the document still in draft, see R. Jeffrey Smith and Barton Gellman, *Washington Post,* August 5, 1993.

49. For a full review of the ill-fated initiative and the tangled developments bringing it down, see Steven Erlanger, "U.S. Peacekeeping Policy Debate Angers Russians," *New York Times,* August 29, 1993. The angry Russians were nationalists who seized on reports of the document to reinforce their already advanced anti-American preconceptions. At the time, the Yeltsin leadership, in contrast, still rather welcomed the thought of U.S. help in dealing with turmoil in neighboring regions.

50. Stephen Kinzer, "Summit in Turkey: The Caspian Accord; Caspian Lands Back a Pipeline Pushed by West," *New York Times,* November 18, 1999. In the article Kinzer wrote, "Construction of this pipeline, estimated at $2.4 billion, would give the United States and other Western countries access to an important new source of energy. But the main significance was that it would draw the new nations near the Caspian, which were part of the Soviet Union only a decade ago, away from Russia and give the United States greater influence in the region."

51. In 2002 Uzbekistan indicated that it was withdrawing from active

participation in GUUAM, but its subsequent vacillation left the picture murky.

52. In March 1999, Vafa Guluzade, then Aliev's national security advisor, asserted that Azerbaijan was ready to offer air bases to NATO. Soon thereafter, an experienced analyst of the region wrote, "Azerbaijan's attempt to involve U.S. military forces in the Caspian Sea region is seen as a terrible idea whose time has unfortunately come." (See Michael Lelyveld, "Caucasus: U.S. Military Presence In Caspian Appears Inevitable," *RFE/RL*, February 4, 1999.) Aliev would later say this was not official policy, but Gen. Tofik Agaguseinov and Defense Minister Safar Abiev made noises similar to Guluzade's during the same period.

Chapter Ten: The Clinton Show: Notes on a Postmodern President by Randy Roberts

1. Thomas C. Reeves, *A Question of Character: A Life of John F. Kennedy* (New York: Free Press, 1991), 234.

2. Inaugural Address of the United States President William J. Clinton, January 20, 1993.

3. Michael Waldman, *POTUS Speaks: Finding the Words That Defined the Clinton Presidency* (New York: Simon and Schuster, 2000),31–38.

4. David Riesman, with Nathan Glazer and Reuel Denney, *The Lonely Crowd: A Study of the Changing American Character* (New Haven: Yale University Press, 1960), 9–24.

5. Riesman, *The Lonely Crowd*, 22.

6. Neal Gabler, *Life the Movie: How Entertainment Conquered Reality* (New York: Knopf, 1999), 224.

7. Gabler, *Life the Movie*, 224–244. Gabler neatly reviews the debate over the nature of modern man.

8. For a fine critique of postmodern theory see David H. Hirsch, *The Deconstruction of Literature: Criticism after Auschwitz* (Providence, R.I.: Brown University Press, 1991).

9. Daniel J. Boorstin, *The Image: A Guide to Pseudo-Events in America* (New York: Harper and Row, 1961), 45–76.

10. David Maraniss, *First In His Class: A Biography of Bill Clinton* (New York: Simon and Schuster, 1995), 9.

11. Gabler, *Life the Movie*, 161.

12. Phil Stern, *Phil Stern's Hollywood: Photographs 1940–1979* (New York: Knopf, 1993), 97.

13. Gabler, *Life the Movie*, 148–49. Gabler summarized Stolley's views.

14. Dick Morris, *Behind the Oval Office: Winning the Presidency in the Nineties* (New York: Random House, 2nd ed., 1997), 50–55.

15. Bruce Miroff, "Courting the Public: Bill Clinton's Postmodern Education," in *The Postmodern Presidency: Bill Clinton's Legacy in U.S. Politics*, ed. Steven E. Schier, 106-123 (Pittsburgh: University of Pittsburgh Press, 2000), 113–114.

16. Todd S. Purdum, "Facets of Clinton," *New York Times Magazine*, May 19, 1996, 36–41, 62.

17. Miroff, "Courting the Public," 109.

18. Landon Y. Jones, "Road Warriors," *People*, July 20, 1992, 68–79; "Mail," *People*, August 10, 1992, 4.

19. "Hollywood Toes the Party Line," *People*, October 5, 1992, 53.

20. "High Infidelity," *People*, September 7, 1998, 52–59.

21. "Tress Test," *People*, December 12, 1993; Morris, *Behind the Oval Office*, 181–82.

22. Morris, *Behind the Oval Office*, 431–38; Jonathan Schell, "Master of All He Surveys," *The Nation*, June 21, 1999, 25–30.

23. William C. Berman, *From the Center to the Edge: The Politics and Policies of the Clinton Presidency* (Lanham, Mass.: Rowman and Littlefield Publishers, 2001), 62.

Conclusion: President Clinton: A Pragmatic and Defensive Player by Todd G. Shields, Jeannie M. Whayne, and Donald R. Kelley

1. Larry Bartels, "Partisanship and Voting Behavior: 1952–1996," *American Journal of Political Science* 44, no. 1 (January 2000): 35–51; Alan Abramowitz and Kyle Saunders "Ideological Realignment in the U.S. Electorate Reconsidered," *Journal of Politics* 60, no. 3 (August 1998): 634–53

2. Karen Kauffman and John Petrocik, "The Changing Policies of American Men: Understanding The Sources of the Gender Gap," *American Journal of Political Science* 43, no. 3 (July 1999): 864–87

3. Lawrence Dodd and Bruce Oppenheimer, eds., *Congress Reconsidered* (Washington, D.C.: Congressional Quarterly Press), 2000

4. Diane D. Blair, "The Big Three of Late Twentieth-Century Arkansas Politics: Dale Bumpers, Bill Clinton, and David Pryor," *The Arkansas Historical Quarterly* 54 (1995): 53.

5. Blair, "The Big Three;" Ernest Dumas, *The Clintons of Arkansas* (Fayetteville: University of Arkansas Press, 1993).

6. Blair, "The Big Three," 61.

7. Blair, "The Big Three," 61.

8. John Brummett, *High Wire: The Education of Bill Clinton* (New York: Hyperion, 1994), 239.

9. Ben F. Johnson, *Arkansas in Modern America* (Fayetteville: University of Arkansas Press, 2000), 230.

10. David Maraniss, *First in His Class: A Biography of Bill Clinton* (New York: Simon and Schuster, 1995), 377.

11. Johnson, *Arkansas in Modern America,* 239.

12. Maraniss, *First in His Class,* 399.

13. Brummett, *High Wire,* 23.

14. Johnson, *Arkansas in Modern America,* 232.

15. Brummett, *High Wire,* 24.

16. Paul Frymer, Thomas P. Kim, and Terri L. Bimes, "Party Elites,

Ideological Voters, and Divided Party Government," *Legislative Studies Quarterly* 11 (1997): 213.

17. Brummett, *High Wire*, 26.

18. Maraniss, *First in His Class*, 403.

19. Larry Sabato, *Feeding Frenzy: Attack Journalism and American Politics* (Baltimore, Md.: Lanham Publishers, 2000).

Index